# THE PRIEST
# AT PRAYER

# THE
# PRIEST AT PRAYER

*By*

E.  ESCRIBANO, C.M.

*Translated from the Spanish by*
B.  T.  BUCKLEY,  C.M.

NEWMAN   PRESS
WESTMINSTER
MARYLAND

*First published* 1954

SUPERIORUM PERMISSU

NIHIL OBSTAT : CAROLUS DAVIS, S.T.L.,
CENSOR DEPUTATUS
IMPRIMATUR : E. A. MORROGH BERNARD,
VIC. GEN. WESTMONASTERII,
DIE 2a FEBRUARII, 1954

MADE AND PRINTED IN THE
REPUBLIC OF IRELAND BY
CAHILL AND CO., LTD., FOR
CLONMORE AND REYNOLDS,LTD.

# CONTENTS

## FIRST PART

## THE PRIEST AND THE ETERNAL TRUTHS

5

## SECOND PART

## THE PRIESTLY MINISTRY

## THIRD PART

### VIRTUES AND VICES

FAITH :

9

# ACKNOWLEDGMENTS

Acknowledgments are due to His Eminence Cardinal Griffin, of Westminster, and to Burns Oates, Ltd., for their kind permission to make use of Mgr. Ronald Knox's version of the Old and New Testaments.

*The Scriptural quotations in inverted commas are from this version.*

Acknowledgments are also due to Sheed and Ward, London, for permission to quote from Mr. Sheed's translation of the *Confessions of Saint Augustine.*

To Joseph F. Wagner, publishers, New York, for permission to quote from the text of Canon Law as given in *The New Canon Law,* by the Rev. Stanislaus Woywod, O.F.M.

To Burns Oates, Ltd. for their permission to use the English translation of Prayers before and after Mass by the joint editors of *The Missal in Latin and English* (Burns Oates, Ltd., 1949), the Rev. J. O'Connell, M.A., and H.P.R. Finberg, M.A., F.R. Hist. S., and also for permission to use extracts from Bl. Pius X's letter to Catholic priests.

And, finally, a word of thanks to the Very Rev. Fr. J. O'Doherty, C.M., former Provincial of the Irish Province of the Vincentian Fathers, for his kind encouragement during the preparation of this translation; and to Miss Winnie Maher, Dublin, for considerable help in the typing of the manuscript.

# TRANSLATOR'S PREFACE

During the process of translating this first volume of
Fr. Eugene Escribano's *Meditaciones Sacerdotales* I
asked the author for a special preface to the English
edition. It was promised, but death overtook him before
that promise was fulfilled. He died in Madrid, June
22nd, 1951.

The second and third volumes of *Meditaciones
Sacerdotales*, based on readings from the Liturgy,
appeared only a short time before the author's death,
but the first volume, of which this is a translation,
appeared in 1928, and so far has gone through four
Spanish editions. From its first appearance it was most
enthusiastically received and praised, and several Spanish
Bishops recommended it officially to their clergy. It
stands apart from the other two volumes both in matter
and, it would seem, in intrinsic merits.

Many hundreds among the thousands of priests who
suffered martyrdom for their Faith, their priesthood, and
their country were, no doubt, indebted to this book as an
aid to devotion and a means of fostering a deep spirit
of prayer. Fr. Escribano himself was well known
throughout Spain, and was universally regarded as a
champion of priests and priestly ideals, exhibiting in his
own person and manifold works of zeal a living demonstration of those ideals.

With sentiments of veneration for Fr. Escribano and
the priest martyrs of the Spanish civil war, the translator offers this English version to all priests of the

English-speaking world in the hope that it may help to prepare them also, if needs be, for the supreme sacrifice and, at all events, for their day-to-day priestly life and activities.

Fr. Escribano was the perfect model of hard work and genuine piety. For over half a century he took up an amazing variety of works; after a few years tied down to a school desk, he launched out into popular missions in the Spanish countryside, living among the poor, hard-working country people of N.W. Spain, preaching to them, spending very long hours in the confessional, getting to know their economic and social problems. He also went into towns and studied the conditions of working people there, gave lectures to them, discussed the whole problem of intensifying the Christian life of the people. Wherever he went he kept his eyes and ears alert for traditional folklore and regional customs, artistic monuments and spiritual opportunities. He was a keen student of history and literature, a poet who, though little known, has been considered by outstanding critics one of the very best of the century in Spanish literature. But his passionate interest was for the Sacred Scriptures, the writings of the Fathers of the Church, the history and achievements of the Congregation to which he belonged, and the Liturgy. Thus he was admirably equipped for his principal work: the giving of retreats to diocesan priests. And thus is explained the wealth of Scriptural and patristic knowledge that we come across in the present book. We can see, by the manner of his quoting and making personal comments, how well he had assimilated these great sources.

The author has published something like thirty

volumes dealing with ascetical doctrine and practice, with materials for the guidance of the Vincentian mission and retreat preacher, with the lives of our Lord and His Blessed Mother, with the folklore and history of Spain, with episodes of heroism on the part of the Sisters of Charity and the Catholic laity during the Spanish civil war, with first-class lyrical and epic poetry, and with sociological problems of the day. A truly prodigious activity at the service of a great mind, a grandiloquent tongue, a heart afire with zeal, and a most charming manner. Priest, teacher, poet, preacher, retreat and mission director, journalist, editor, organizer of charitable and pious Associations; everything that could be marshalled behind the triple Vincentian banner of " clergy, people, and charity."

*The Priest at Prayer* is the first of Fr. Escribano's books to be translated into English. It is not a book providing meditations for every day of the year; and of set purpose, in order to leave priests free and anxious to delve into the Scriptures and the liturgical books for inspiration in prayer. The style of the book is very marked in the original Spanish: a most forceful, colourful, and variegated diction, classical purity, a blend of terseness and almost torrential eloquence, energy to the point of fierceness on occasions, tenderness that never degenerates into sentimentalism, soul-searching analysis always redeemed by an overwhelming sense of God's Mercy and Forgiveness.

N.B. An appendix containing excerpts from Bl. Pius X's " Letter to Catholic Priests " and Preparation before and Thanksgiving after Mass has been added to their English edition by the translator.

# MORNING PRAYERS

V/. In nomine Patris, et Filii, et Spiritus Sancti. Amen.

V/. Veni, Sancte Spiritus.

R/. Reple tuorum corda fidelium, et tui amoris in eis ignem accende.

V/. Emitte Spiritum tuum et creabuntur.

R/. Et renovabis faciem terrae.

## OREMUS:

Deus, qui corda fidelium Sancti Spiritus illustratione docuisti, da nobis in eodem Spiritu recta sapere, et de ejus semper consolatione gaudere. Per Christum Dominum nostrum. R/. Amen.

V/. Benedicta sit sancta Trinitas et indivisa Unitas.

R/. Confitebimur ei, qui fecit nobiscum misericordiam suam.

V/. *Let us place ourselves in the presence of God.*

We firmly believe, O God, that thou art here present, that thou beholdest us, hearest us, knowest all our thoughts and desires, and the most secret inclinations of our hearts, and that thou art always graciously willing to hear our prayers. R/. Amen.

V/. *Let us adore God and thank him for all his benefits.*

We adore thee, O God, and we acknowledge that

thou art our sovereign Lord and absolute Master, that we depend on thee for all things, that thou hast created us, redeemed us with the Blood of Jesus Christ, thy beloved Son, and made us children of thy Church by the grace of baptism. For so many and such precious favours we offer thee, O God, our most sincere and heartfelt thanksgiving. We give thee thanks for having preserved us during the past night; and in general for all the graces, spiritual and temporal, which we have received at thy hands from the moment of our birth until this hour. Through the same Jesus Christ our Lord. R/. Amen.

V/.   *Let us beg of God the grace to live holily this day, and let us offer him all our actions.*

O almighty and eternal God, who hast brought us to the beginning of this day, preserve us by thy power that we may not fall into sin, but that all our thoughts, words, and actions, being directed by thy holy grace, may tend only to the fulfilment of thy holy commandments.   R/. Amen.

V/.   We belong to thee, O God, we offer thee all our thoughts and desires, all our words and actions; vouchsafe to prompt them by thy holy inspirations, and to sanctify them by enabling us with thy grace to accomplish lovingly in all things thy holy will.   R/. Amen.

V/.   *Let us make acts of contrition, faith, hope, and charity.*

*An act of contrition.*

O my God, I am heartily sorry for all my sins, because by them I deserve thy just punishment here and hereafter, because I have been ungrateful to thee, my greatest Benefactor, and above all, because I have offended thee, the most perfect and most loving God, my Saviour, who died on the cross for my sins. I am firmly resolved to amend my life, never more to offend thee, and to avoid the occasions of sin. R/. Amen.

### An act of faith.

O my God, I firmly believe whatsoever the Holy, Roman, Catholic, and Apostolic Church believes and teaches. I believe these truths, O God, because thou, the infallible Truth, hast revealed them to her. In this faith I am resolved to live and die. R/. Amen.

### An act of hope.

O my God, relying on thy promises, I hope, through the infinite merits of Jesus Christ, that thou wilt grant me eternal life, and the graces necessary to obtain it. R/. Amen.

### An act of charity.

O my God, I love thee with my whole heart and above all things, because thou art infinitely good and perfect. Grant that I may love thee more and more, and for all eternity. I love my neighbour as myself for the love of thee. R/. Amen.

*Pater noster. Ave, Maria. Credo in Deum.*

V/. *Let us invoke the protection of the Blessed Virgin.*

*Omnes:* Sub tuum praesidium confugimus, sancta Dei Genitrix: nostras deprecationes ne despicias in necessitatibus nostris; sed a periculis cunctis libera nos semper, Virgo gloriosa et benedicta.

Per sanctam virginitatem et immaculatam conceptionem tuam, purissima Virgo, emunda cor et corpus meum. Amen.

*Ave Maria* (ter).

Angele Dei, qui custos es mei, me tibi comissum pietate superna, hodie illumina, custodi, rege, et guberna. Amen.

(100 *days. Plenary, once a month and on October 2 if said daily, morning and evening; and at the point of death if frequently said.*)

V/.    Divinum auxilium maneat semper nobiscum.
R/.    Amen.

*Then follows the reading of the meditation, after which:*

### LITANIAE SS. NOMINIS JESU.

(Seven years.   Plenary once a month.)

V/.    Kyrie eleison.          R/.    Christe eleison.
V/.    Kyrie eleison. Jesu,    R/.    Jesu, exaudi nos.
       audi nos.
V/.    Pater de caelis, Deus,
       Fili, Redemptor mundi, Deus,
       Spiritus Sancte, Deus,
       Sancta Trinitas, unus Deus,
       Jesu, Fili Dei vivi,
       Jesu, splendor Patris,
       Jesu, candor lucis aeternae,
       Jesu, rex gloriae,
       Jesu, sol justitiae,
       Jesu, fili Mariae Virginis,
       Jesu amabilis,

*Miserere nobis.*

Jesu admirabilis,
Jesu, Deus fortis,
Jesu, pater futuri saeculi,
Jesu, magni consilii angele,
Jesu potentissime,
Jesu patientissime,
Jesu obedientissime,
Jesu mitis et humilis corde,
Jesu, amator castitatis,
Jesu, amator noster,
Jesu, Deus pacis,
Jesu, auctor vitae,
Jesu, exemplar virtutum,
Jesu, zelator animarum,
Jesu, Deus noster,
Jesu, refugium nostrum,
Jesu, pater pauperum,
Jesu, thesaure fidelium,
Jesu, bone pastor,
Jesu, lux vera,
Jesu, sapientia aeterna,
Jesu, bonitas infinita,
Jesu, via et vita nostra,
Jesu, gaudium angelorum,
Jesu, rex patriarcharum,
Jesu, magister apostolorum,
Jesu, doctor evangelistarum,
Jesu, fortitudo martyrum,
Jesu, lumen confessorum,
Jesu, puritas virginum,
Jesu, corona sanctorum omnium,

*Miserere nobis.*

V/.  Propitius esto.      R/.  Parce nobis, Jesu.
V/.  Propitius esto.      R/.  Exaudi nos, Jesu

V/. Abo omni malo,        R/. Libera nos, Jesu.

Ab omni peccato,
Ab ira tua,
Ab insidiis diaboli,
A spiritu fornicationis,
A morte perpetua,
A neglectu inspirationum tuarum,
Per mysterium sanctae incarnationis tuae,
Per nativitatem tuam,
Per infantiam tuam,
Per divinissimam vitam tuam,
Per labores tuos,
Per agoniam et passionem tuam,
Per crucem et derelictionem tuam,
Per languores tuos,
Per mortem et sepulturam tuam,
Per resurrectionem tuam,
Per ascensionem tuam,
Per sanctissimae Eucharistiae
     institutionem tuam,
Per gaudia tua,
Per gloriam tuam,

*Libera nos, Jesu.*

Agnus Dei, qui tollis peccata mundi,
             R/. Parce nobis, Jesu.
Agnus Dei, qui tollis peccata mundi,
             R/. Exaudi nos, Jesu.
Agnus Dei, qui tollis peccata mundi,
             R/. Miserere nobis, Jesu.
Jesu, audi nos.    R/. Jesu, exaudi nos.

## OREMUS:

Domine Jesu Christe, qui dixisti: Petite, et accipietis;
quaerite, et invenietis; pulsate, et aperietur vobis:

quaesumus, da nobis petentibus divinissimi tui amoris affectum, ut te toto corde, ore, et opere diligamus, et a tua numquam laude cessemus.

Sancti nominis tui, Domine, timorem pariter et amorem fac nos habere perpetuum: quia numquam tua gubernatione destituis, quos in soliditate tuae dilectionis instituis: Qui vivis et regnas in saecula saeculorum. R/. Amen.

## ANGELUS.

V/.    Angelus Domini nuntiavit Mariae:

R/.    Et concepit de Spiritu Sancto.

Ave Maria.

V/.    Ecce ancilla Domini:

R/.    Fiat mihi secumdum verbum tuum.

Ave Maria.

V/.    Et Verbum caro factum est:

R/.    Et habitavit in nobis.

Ave Maria.

V/.    Ora pro nobis, sancta Dei Genitrix.

R/.    Ut digni efficiamur promissionibus Christi.

## OREMUS:

Gratiam tuam, quaesumus, Domine, mentibus nostris infunde: ut qui, angelo nuntiante, Christi Filii tui incarnationem cognivimus, per passionem ejus et crucem, ad resurrectionis gloriam perducamur. Per eundem Christum Dominum nostrum.

R/. Amen.

*(Ten years. Plenary once a month to all who say it thrice daily.)*

Gloria Patri, (ter).

## TEMPORE PASCHALI.

### REGINA CAELI.

Regina caeli, laetare, Alleluia,
Quia quem meruisti portare, Alleluia,
Resurrexit sicut dixit. Alleluia.
Ora pro nobis Deum. Alleluia.
V/.   Gaude et laetare, Virgo Maria; Alleluia.
R/.   Quia surrexit Dominus vere.   Alleluia.

### OREMUS:

Deus, qui per resurrectionem Filii tui Domini nostri
Jesu Christi mundum laetificare dignatus es; praesta,
quaesumus, ut per ejus Genitricem Virginem Mariam,
perpetuae capiamus gaudia vitae. Per eumdem Christum
Dominum nostrum.   R/. Amen.

Gloria Patri, (ter).

# EVENING PRAYERS

V/. In nomine Patris, etc., as on page 17.
V/. *Let us place ourselves in the presence of God,*
*and give him thanks for all his benefits, parti-*
*cularly those we have received from him this*
*day.*

We firmly believe, O God, that thou art here present,
that thou beholdest the most secret thoughts of our
hearts, and art graciously willing to hear our prayers.
Grant us grace to present to thee this night's tribute of
our homage, love, and petition, with such sentiments of
respect and fervour that we may deserve to obtain all its
blessed fruits. We shall commence it, O God, by offering thee the liveliest sentiments of our gratitude and
praise for the benefits, spiritual and temporal, which thou
hast vouchsafed to confer upon us, and especially for
those bestowed upon us this day. Give us, O God, a
deep sense of this thy great goodness, and the grace to
turn it to the account of thy glory and that of our own
sanctification.

> *Let us beg of God the grace to know and*
> *detest the sins which we have committed this*
> *day.*

O most merciful God, who willest not that the sinner
should perish, but rather that he should be converted:
illuminate the darkness of our understanding that we
may see the malice and deformity of sin. Grant us the
light we stand in need of to discover in particular the

faults into which we have fallen this day; but in making them known to us, grant us grace so sincerely to detest them that we may never again fall into any of them.

> *Let us consider what sins we have committed by thoughts, words, actions, or omissions, directing our attention particularly to those faults to which we are most inclined, as also to those failings to which we have yielded, contrary to the resolutions taken this morning at prayer.*

(Here a brief pause.)

> *Let us excite ourselves to sorrow for having offended God; and let us most humbly implore his pardon, resolving never more to offend him, by the help of his holy grace.*

O God, we are penetrated with the deepest sorrow for having offended thee, because thou art infinitely good and sovereignly worthy of love, and because sin is displeasing to thee. We humbly ask pardon through the merits of Jesus Christ, and we firmly resolve, with the assistance of thy grace, never more to offend thee, and to do penance for our sins.

> *Let us earnestly endeavour to put ourselves in the state in which we desire to be found at the hour of our death.*

What shall become of us, O God, if we be obliged to appear before the tribunal of thy justice? We have deserved hell; our whole life has been a continual series of ingratitude and sin. We fly to thy mercy as our only refuge; we implore it through the merits of Jesus Christ our Saviour; and, in the hope of obtaining it at the hands of thy infinite goodness, we bow down in adoring submission to thy sovereign will, and humbly declare our readiness to die at that moment and in the manner which thy providence has determined. Yes, O God, we sincerely offer thee the sacrifice of our lives; we wish to die in order to possess and love thee for all eternity. O divine Jesus, who didst die for us, be mindful of thy death at the moment of ours; grant us the grace to die in thy love, and receive our souls into thy hands.

Confiteor . . .

V/.   Misereatur nostri omnipotens Deus; et, dismissis peccatis nostris, perducat nos ad vitam aeternam.

R/.   Amen.

V/.   Indulgentiam, absolutionem, et remissionem peccatorum nostrorum tribuat nobis omnipotens et misericors Dominus.

R/.   Amen.

V/.   Dignare, Domine, nocte ista.

R/.   Sine peccato nos custodire.

V/.   Miserere nostri, Domine.

R/.   Miserere nostri.

V/.   Fiat misericordia tua, Domine, super nos.

R/.   Quemadmodum speravimus in te.

V/.   Domine, exaudi orationem meam.

R/.   Et clamor meus ad te veniat.

V/.   Dominus vobiscum.

R/.   EEt cum spiritu tuo.

## OREMEUS:

Visita, quaesumus, Domine, habitationem istam, et omnes insidias inimici ab ea longe repelle: angeli tui sancti habitent in ea, qui nos in pace custodiant; et benedictio tua sit super nos semper.

Respice, quaesumus, Domine, super hanc familiam

tuam, pro qua Dominus noster Jesus Christus non
dubitavit manibus tradi nocentium, et crucis subire
tormentum: Qui tecum vivit et regnat in saecula
saeculorum.

R/.  Amen.

### LITANIAE LAURETANAE B.M.V.

*(Seven years. Plenary once a month.)*

| | | | |
|---|---|---|---|
| V/. | Kyrie eleison. | R. | Christe, eleison. |
| V/. | Kyrie eleison. Christe, audi nos. | R. | Christe, exaudi nos. |
| | Pater de caelis, Deus, | R. | Miserere nobis. |
| | Fili, R e d e m p t o r mundi, Deus, | | ,,    ,, |
| | Spiritus Sancte, Deus, | | ,,    ,, |
| | Sancta Trinitas, unus Deus, | | ,,    ,, |

Sancta Maria,
Sancta Dei Genitrix,
Sancta Virgo virginum,
Mater Christi,
Mater divinae gratiae,
Mater purissima,
Mater castissima,
Mater inviolata,
Mater intemerata,
Mater amabilis,
Mater boni consilii,
Mater Creatoris,
Mater Salvatoris,
Virgo prudentissima,
Virgo veneranda,

*Ora pro nobis.*

Virgo praedicanda,
Virgo potens,
Virgo clemens,
Virgo fidelis,
Speculum justitiae,
Sedes sapientiate,
Causa nostrae laetitiae,
Vas spirituale,
Vas honorabile,
Vas insigne devotionis,
Rosa mystica,
Turris Davidica,
Turris eburnea,
Domus aurea,
Foederis arca,
Janua caeli,
Stella matutina,
Salus infirmorum,
Refugium peccatorum,
Consolatrix afflictorum,
Auxilium Christianorum,
Regina angelorum,
Regina patriarcharum,
Regina prophetarum,
Regina apostolorum,
Regina martyrum,
Regina confessorum,
Regina virginum,
Regina sanctorum omnium,
Regina sine labe originali concepta,
Regina in caelum assumpta,
Regina sacratissimi rosarii,
Regina pacis,

*Ora pro nobis.*

Agnus Dei, qui tollis  R/.  Parce nobis, Do-
  peccata mundi.                  mine.
Agnus Dei, qui tollis  R/.  Exaudi nos, Do-
  peccata mundi.                  mine.
Agnus Dei, qui tollis  R/.  Miserere nobis.
  peccata mundi.

V/.  Ora pro nobis, sancta Dei Genitrix.
R/.  Ut digni efficiamur promissionibus Christi.

### OREMUS:

Concede nos famulos tuos, quaesumus, Domine Deus,
perpetua mentis et corporis sanitate gaudere; et, gloriosa
beatae Mariae semper Virginis intercessione, a praesenti
liberari tristitia, et aeterna perfrui laetitia.

Sanctissimae Genitricis tuae sponsi, quaesumus,
Domine, meritis adjuvemur; ut quod possibilitas nostra
non obtinet, ejus nobis intercessione donetur.

Omnes angeli, omnes sancti et sanctae Dei, consolatio
pauperculae animae meae, et vos praesertim, patroni et
protectores mei, impetrate mihi gratiam non peccandi
de caetero, simul et sancte vivendi, ut tandem plenus
meritis vestro consortio aggregari merear. Per Christum
Dominum nostrum.   R/. Amen.

(Read the first point of the next morning's meditation.)

*All:* Per sanctam viginitatem et immaculatam conceptionem tuam, purissima Virgo, emunda cor et corpus
meum. Amen.

Ave Maria (ter).

Sub tuum praesidium confugimus, sancta Dei Genitrix: nostras deprecationes ne despicias in necessitatibus
nostris; sed a periculis cunctis libera nos semper, Virgo
gloriosa et benedicta.

# FIRST PART

# THE ETERNAL TRUTHS

## ESTEEM FOR THE PRIESTLY VOCATION

### FIRST MEDITATION

#### God's Choice of Me

### I

I have a vocation; that was the conviction which prompted me to become a priest, and allowed the door-keepers of the sanctuary to give me admission.

I have a vocation. God, the God who called each star in the vault of the sky by its own name, called me; He looked upon my lowliness; He made my inmost being ring with His irresistible Voice.

A vocation is "A disposition whereby Divine Providence, in accordance with His Own Good Pleasure, chooses and reserves certain men for the work of His ministry, and bestows upon them the requisite qualities and graces."

Christ can therefore say to me what He said to the Apostles:

> You have not chosen me; but I have chosen you.
> —(*John xv,* 16.)

Peace be to you.

As the Father hath sent me, I also send you.

—(*John xx,* 21.)

Blessed be Thou, Lord, whose secret word sowed in my soul the seeds of my entire priestly life. Let them not perish. Let them bring forth full fruit in due season.

## II

But, just for a moment, let us suppose that God did not really call me, that I stole my way into the sanctuary.

Whatever the facts, natural and human, or even sinful, that determined my submission to Holy Orders, I must agree that God alone can mark the centre of my soul with His indelible Seal; only a Hand like His can probe so deep; only God, the one true Giver of the Sacraments, imprinted upon me—because such was His Good Pleasure—the sacramental seal or Character that makes me His Priest for ever.

I have every right then to adapt St. Paul's utterance: " I am a priest of Jesus Christ, by the Will of God."

My God, I bow to Thy sovereign Ordinance.

I will gladly exhibit this Seal of Thine.

May heaven and earth acknowledge it and exclaim: " He is a priest of Christ!"

## III

God's choice fell on *me*! Why?

My qualities of mind and character gave me no advantage over other men of my own age, place and condition. In God's eyes I was nothing more than the least of them. So many others would have been found with more talent, more drive for high endeavour, more balance and practical wisdom!

And with regard to innocence of life and capacity for virtue, frankly, I must confess, after tearing away the mask of self-conceit, that, with so many misdemeanours and evil habits staining my soul at the time of my presentation for Holy Orders, I deserved to become a vessel of wrath rather than a vessel of election.

The only merits and aptitudes I see in myself, O God, are the hidden designs of Thine incomprehensible Mercy!

## IV

Samuel the Prophet said certain words to young Saul which conveyed a hint of the royal dignity God had chosen him for; and Saul, a comely and daring youth, falls back with genuine astonishment and exclaims:

"Me? a man of Benjamin, the smallest of Israel's tribe? sprung from a clan that is named last among the clans of Benjamin? What means this greeting thou hast given me?"—(*I Kings ix*, 21.)

And what shall *I* say, I who have been chosen by God Himself to be a friend and brother to my Lord Jesus Christ, dispenser of His Mysteries, voice of His doctrine and precepts, and almoner among men of His ineffable gifts?

### RESOLUTION

Humbly prostrate before the Divine Majesty, I shall often consider myself unworthy of His baffling choice of me. Well might the faithful say of me what was said of Saul by his fellow countrymen:

"Can such a man as this bring us victory?"
—(*I Kings x*, 27.)

B

# ESTEEM FOR THE PRIESTLY VOCATION

### Graces of Ordination

## I

Let us consider the scene in which St. John records one of the phases of the institution of the priesthood.

Appearing to His Apostles, the Risen Christ says to them:

> Peace be to you; as the Father hath sent me, I also send you.

And having said this, he breathed upon them, and said to them:

> Receive ye the Holy Ghost; whose sins you shall forgive, they are forgiven them; and whose sins you shall retain, they are retained.— (*John xx,* 21-22.)

The symbolical gesture of breathing upon the Apostles clearly recalls, and even imitates, the first creating of the human soul: *He breathed upon his face the breath of life.* But on this occasion the breath of life is the very Spirit of God infused into the Apostles and into all ordained priests, not so much for their own benefit as for them to transmit—as Adam transmitted physical life —to all those who were to become throughout the centuries children of God, children *born, not of blood, nor of the will of the flesh, nor of the will of man, but of God.*—(*John i,* 13.)

## II

Consider some of the graces which that Life-giving breath of Christ has imparted to you.

In the first place, by way of remote preparation for the priesthood, it gave you perhaps from early childhood a marked bent towards the clerical state; it gently and powerfully steered your will and all your propensities towards the priesthood.

Eventually, when the significance of your acts dawned upon you, you found your soul engraved by the Finger of God with your vocation's noblest aim—you wanted to work for the salvation of others, and your heart kept on saying perhaps with St. Paul:

> "For my own part, I will gladly spend and be spent on your souls' behalf, though you should love me too little for loving you too well."—(*II Cor. xii,* 15.)

Thus, without effort, almost without understanding the meaning of it, you found yourself enriched with the divine germ of those beautiful qualities and virtues that one day were to wreathe your glorious priestly diadem.

## III

Recount the graces you have received through the Sacrament of Holy Orders.

Besides Sanctifying grace there is the Sacramental grace: divine enlightenment and assistance forthcoming to you whenever there was a sacred ministerial duty imposing a difficulty upon you, or an obstacle to surmount for the right fulfilment of your manifold obligations.

Turn over and over in your mind, in particular, the sovereign powers wherewith you have been invested:

the divine commission to preach the word of God; your unfettered handling of the Body and Blood of Christ; the announcing and communicating to sinners of the grace of reconciliation. . . .

*Quid retribuam Domino pro omnibus quae retribuit mihi . . . ?*

## RESOLUTION

Dear Lord, I who am so profuse in my compliments and tokens of gratitude towards my neighbour for the smallest kindness, have I ever spent so much as a quarter of an hour pondering over and thanking Thee for the gift of my priesthood?

From now onwards not a day will pass without my doing this, at least in my morning and evening prayers.

## ESTEEM FOR THE PRIESTLY VOCATION

### THIRD MEDITATION

### *Reverence for my Priesthood*

### I

The world, Christ's enemy, has at all times devised ways and means of destroying faith in Christ, of spurning His precepts and ruining His Church. It has tried to do away with Christ and His work by persecution, heresy, immoral propaganda, scorn, etc.; but so far it has invented nothing more simple and effective than the dishonouring of the priest. Very simple indeed, and no need for any great display of learning or power: just the calumnies and facile irony of a facile literature; but so effective, that what subtle heresiarchs or implacable tyrants failed to achieve, namely, the uprooting of the Faith among the people, was within a very short time and over vast territories obtained by the simple expedient of burying the priest in the mire of contempt.

So needful to my divine vocation is appreciation and esteem, in order to give the work of God a firm footing!

## II

Great indeed would be my guilt if this contempt, so destructive for the Faith, were to begin from my own lack of self-esteem.

The loss of any priest has its roots perhaps in the priest's loss of esteem for his own state. He casts a covetous eye upon other walks of life, which appear to him worthier of honour, nobler, and happier; he begins to feel discontented with his lot; he gradually comes to think of his priesthood as a crushing burden. . . .

In such a frame of mind how can a priest fail to experience a loathing for his many ministerial duties? How will he contrive to conduct himself with the dignity and composure required of him?

If you do not respect yourself, *who* will respect you?

What reverence will you command if in your own esteem you rank so low?

It is possible that if a patient and thorough investigation were made in any country, town, or parish where the clergy are treated with disdain or positively ill-treated, we should discover that it all originated from the lack of appreciation and even contempt in which certain priests held their own priestly dignity. And once again would be literally fulfilled the words: *Perditio tua ex te!* " It is thy own undoing."—(*Osee xiii,* 9.)

### III

And how must I esteem myself?

1.   Higher than a king. Over the estates of my realm
the sun never sets, never a slanting ray touches them.
The limits of my kingdom are the height of heaven and
eternity, the depths of the gates of hell. A king can lose
his crown, not I my priestly character. A king will grant
to his loyal subjects estates, titles, and distinctions; I
can give entry into the Kingdom of Heaven.

How must I esteem myself?

2.   Mightier than an angel; who may inspire, direct,
reproach the soul God confided to his keeping, but his
action is only on the surface; while I, in forgiving sin,
heal the soul's deepest wounds; and in the other Sacraments I infuse the grace of God and refashion the soul
to God's image and likeness.

How should I esteem myself?

3.   Like unto God; for like Him I impart grace; like
Him I pardon. *Grace has been given through Jesus
Christ. Who can forgive sin but only God?*
I thank Thee, O Lord, for having given such dignity
and such power to men.

### RESOLUTIONS

1.   I shall always see that my conduct bears the
priestly stamp; I shall be a priest in private and in
public, in the street, and in the church; always and
everywhere. Shall I be like the actor who sometimes
plays the rôle of a king, but only on the stage? Shall
I be a priest only at the altar? No, I shall preserve the
dignity befitting my state always, wherever I may be.

2.   I shall hold all priests in affectionate and respect-

ful regard; and if I think their lives sometimes fall short of the mark, I shall, at least, esteem them all for the dignity of their calling.

3. I shall never withhold from them those tokens of reverence that so many good lay people never refuse to the priest; for example taking my hat off to them in the street.

# HOLINESS OF THE PRIESTHOOD

## *The Priest as the "Man of God"*

### I

How numerous the recommendations and precepts given to the priests of the Old Law for their sanctification!

> "They are men set apart for their God, and must never bring reproach on his name; they burn incense to the Lord, offer their God his consecrated loaves, and shall they not be holy?"
>
> —(*Lev. xxi*, 6.)

> "He that has any blemish shall not be allowed to offer his God the consecrated loaves, nor to come forward and do him service."—(*Lev. xxi*, 17, 18.)

What precautions God orders Moses to take lest the people should approach Mount Sinai, the throne of God's Majesty! How many purifications were imposed, interior and exterior, even to remain at the foot of the mountain!

If we stop to compare priesthood with priesthood, ministry with ministry, holiness with holiness: that of Sinai with that of our Altars; perhaps in our dread and amazement we shall cry out with Manue, Samson's father: *Morte moriemur, quia vidimus Dominum*— "This is certain death, we have seen the Lord." (*Judges xiii*, 22.)

## II

If the soul of any just man is God's throne, how much the more must I, a priest, be God's temple pure and undefiled!

The first place of worship in a parish is not the parish church but the parish priest; his heart and lips are the Ark where one must find the divine Law; his body is the Tabernacle where the Body and Blood of Christ is reserved each day; and his consecrated hands are the altar-stone on which is offered every morning the only Victim pleasing to God.

If so chaste and pure had to be the womb where the Son of God took our flesh and dwelt for nine months, how pure must be the body and soul where He takes up His abode every day? If so holy the breasts that suckled the Infant-God, what must be the lips purpled each day with the Blood of the Lamb of God?

*His sepulchre shall be glorious,* says Isaias, prophesying of the stone sepulchre that enclosed the dead Body of Christ for two days. What then shall be demanded of my body wherein the eternally glorified Christ so frequently makes His dwelling? Will cleanliness be required only of lifeless matter? or will there be shifts and changes in God's love for holiness?

Will it be a matter of indifference to God whether He dwell in a heart that is holy or in a heart that is impure, simply because I am a priest?

## III

The Crusades were the great enterprise of the Middle Ages.

For this purpose God raised up or awakened great souls: Peter the Hermit, Godfrey, the flower of the nobility, men of valour. From every nation they flocked, as to a banquet, and left their bones on the hills and deserts of Asia. What treasures were spent! What heroism! What generous blood! And for the sole purpose of rescuing the empty Tomb of Christ, and of making it a place of prayer for all the Christian nations.

The enterprise most worthy, most noble and glorious for me, a priest, will be a life-time struggle against all seductions both from within and from without; routing in my soul all the hosts of the evil spirit, preserving pure this heart of mine, which is not an empty tomb, but a shrine elected by my Lord Jesus Christ for Himself.

### RESOLUTION

I shall frequently repeat the *Domine, non sum dignus ut intres sub tectum meum;* and perhaps the continual sense of my unworthiness will be a fire purifying me from my faults and imperfections.

## HOLINESS OF THE PRIESTHOOD

### SECOND MEDITATION

*The Priest as the "Father of Souls"*

### I

" The purpose for which any high priest is chosen from among his fellow-men, and made representative of men in their dealings with God, is to offer gifts and sacrifices in expiation of their sins."

—(*Hebrews v*, 1.)

So my first obligation, as a priest, is to offer prayer and sacrifice for the salvation of souls.

As a father of souls, I must pray and weep before God for the sins of the world, with all the love of a father for his beloved children.

And what is the fragrant incense of prayer that appeases the Divine Wrath? What is the sacrifice that God has never disdained? *Cor contritum et humiliatum* —a heart that is contrite and humbled.

God will hardly listen to prayers for other men if the tongue that utters them He detests; if the heart whence they rise, far from being contrite, is hardened by pride and obdurate in wickedness; if my hands, when raised to Heaven, are steeped in sin.

## II

*" Keep yourselves unsullied, you that have the vessels of the Lord's worship in your charge."* (*Is. lii, 12.*)

I am the one set apart, the one consecrated by the Finger of God and by the anointing of His Holy Spirit, to carry the vessels of the Lord; not chalices of silver and gold, not artistic treasures, but rather, those most precious vessels for whose sanctification and redemption Christ, the Almighty and Eternal God, deigned to die on a cross; souls to whom it has been given to know the mystery of the Kingdom of God; souls made sanctuaries of the Holy Ghost, tabernacles of the Body of Christ.

It is my duty to make those vessels so clean that I leave them worthy to contain God. If the hands that wash are unwashed, will they not add to uncleanliness and minister to profanation?

Faith and devotion constrain me to show in my external demeanour towards the people the loftiest regard; similar to that which I have, for instance, in the celebration of Mass. God forbid that in my relations towards the faithful, the Mystical Body of Christ, I allow myself anything derogatory to the esteem that is their due as souls redeemed by the Blood of the Lamb without stain.

### III

An obligation I cannot escape is good example.
St. Peter's admonition to priests rings in my ears:

> " Be shepherds of the flock God has given you. Carry out your charge as God would have it done, cordially, not like drudges; generously, not in the hope of sordid gain; not tyrannizing, each in his own sphere; but setting an example, as best you may, to the flock."—(I *Peter v.* 2, 3.)

From a practical and even a theological point of view, the most unanswerable argument for our Faith and morals is a *Saint*. Give me a saint, that is, a constant imitator of Jesus Christ, and his life will provide an adequate solution to any specious problem raised by irreligion. A good priest is worth more than a dozen works of apologetics. Shall I be worth at least one? Or will my life be a book of apologetics for evil?

### RESOLUTION

My God, am I intimately and fully convinced of these truths? If slackness and foibles keep me far away from genuine holiness of life, do I at least believe that my calling, my God, and my neighbour are crying out for me to acquire it?

This conviction I shall take to heart and engrave on my mind, if only as the first step along the path of perfection.

# MORTAL SIN IN THE PRIEST

## The Nature of Sin

### I

Sin is an evil. Nobody desires evil as such, for evil and desirable are mutually-exclusive terms. Therefore our desire for evil is by reason of the good we think it includes, viz.: pleasure, utility, prestige. But sin, being an evil, carries with it the privation of some good, because evil is simply *privatio boni*.

When I yield then to sin, I show that, for me, there is a greater good to be found in what is sinful—for example, sensual pleasure, of a nature so low-grade and fleeting—than the good I forfeit by sinning: the eternal law of God which I trample underfoot, the grace I deprive myself of, the Divine Goodness from which I depart; in a word: God.

My God! Thou art the price I pay for the good I seek in sinning!

How often have I not purchased the shameful dalliance of lust, the shadowy pomp of pride, and the illusory gain of this world's goods, with Thee, Coin of Infinite value!

Was I not overcharged? Did I not, O Sovereign Good, hold Thee too cheap? Lord, I treated Thee like devalued currency!

## II

God can prefer the particular good of one creature to that of another; for instance, the good of man to that of an animal; and, in a certain sense, God can desire the particular evil of one creature in so far as it redounds to the good of another; for example, the destruction of an animal inasmuch as it benefits man. But His own Goodness God desires absolutely, in every instance, and above all other good, with an intensity and a love infinite and eternal; for the simple reason that God's Goodness is the one Essential Good, the inexhaustible Source of all good.

Consequently, God must necessarily, with a necessity intrinsic to His very Being, hate sin; for sin severs from His Goodness—*aversio a Deo*—and rates His Goodness lower than the glimpse of some fugitive and degrading good. The measure of this Divine Hatred—the only hatred harboured by the Divine Essence—is the Love of His own Goodness, which is infinite.

I, poor wretch, was steeped in the Almighty's infinite and necessary Hatred whenever I sinned grievously!

And yet I said in my cocksure foolhardiness: *I have sinned, and what harm hath befallen me?* (*Eclus. v*, 4.)

And the curse of God wrapped me about, sank like water into my inmost being, soaked, like oil, into the marrow of my bones! (*Cfr. Ps. cviii*, 18.)

## III

Who am I? I was born when God willed; die I must when and as God pleases; I depend upon Him for the least atom of my being—that is what it means to be a creature and to have a Creator!

Moreover, I am something very small, insignificant—

*tamquam nihilum ante Te*—and He is the Being *par excellence,* infinite, unchanging, boundless.

On irrational creatures God has imposed laws which they carry out blindly, inexorably; to me, God gave them engraven on my heart and mind, made them mine to reject or to abide by of my own free will.

God, the Eternal, with whose grandeur heaven and earth is charged, beckons to me as He beckoned to the stars, places me before His Sovereign Might, and resting His Eyes upon me, those Eyes of which the sunlight is but a faint reflection, He intimates to me at each moment through the voice of my conscience : " Do what I order thee; keep my commandments "; and I, the sinner, reply, *" I will not serve ";* and face to face I rebel against obedience due to Him, and tear myself away from His dominion. Is that not outrageous?

## RESOLUTION

I will often make acts of perfect contrition with all the earnestness of a soul truly contrite and humble; before going to bed, in case God may demand my soul that same night; on rising in the morning, in order to begin the day with a soul cleansed by tears of repentance; as often as I enter a church, so that this interior holy water of penance may purify me; but above all, as soon as I have had the immense misfortune to fall into serious sin—lest my last hour surprise me in such an unhappy state, and there should overtake me a sudden, hopeless doom.

# MORTAL SIN IN THE PRIEST

## Malice of Sin

### I

The soul of every human being living by God's grace is God's temple. What of the soul that has lost this grace by mortal sin?

It is still the temple of God: at least it still retains sufficient spaciousness and suitable structure to be the dwelling of Him whose throne is the highest Heaven and the whole earth His footstool.

The soul of the sinner is indeed a temple: it was created by God for that purpose; but now that the temple has been rendered unholy, profane, polluted, by the filth of sin, God, its rightful Dweller, has fled, and will not return until it be made clean by repentance.

The most beautiful cathedral, if seriously and publicly profaned, will have the Blessed Sacrament taken away from it until it be reconciled with due solemnity; because it has forfeited that decency and decorum which its Guest demands. For church styles will change with the varying tastes of the times: one epoch will choose the Gothic style, another the classic or Romanesque; but there will ever be a style and an ornamentation without which the most sumptuous architecture will be unworthy to house God. *"Holy is Thy house, and must needs be holy until the end of time."* (Ps. xcii.)

So too, a soul unadorned by the holiness of grace, though made to be God's temple, and still retaining the design and structure of such, is nevertheless held in abhorrence and is repudiated by its Lord; it is given up to ruin and ignominy, like a deserted and accursed house.

This was my soul when I grievously sinned; this it is now if in sin I still continue.

## II

There are terrible diseases—cancer, for example—that so entwine themselves around the deep, vital fibres of the organism as to become one with them. There are subtle poisons and malignant tumours that encrust upon, and soak into, the entrails, and there they remain unprobed until the grave, where at length they evaporate and perish among the ashes of the dead body.

A more penetrating cancer is sin, which all the strength of men and angels is powerless to extirpate from the substantial tissues and essence of our spirit.

Death, a corrosive that annihilates the germs of every physical disease, in the presence of the disease of mortal sin becomes a fixing bath. When death's icy breath passes over mortal sin in the soul, it fixes the sin there for ever; and with such force, so deeply, that neither the influx of eternity, nor oceans of tears, nor even the flames of Hell with all their penetrating and grappling of the soul's inmost being, will succeed in toning down a single shade or in effacing a single lineament. Is there any disease more intimate or more detestable?

Only the Blood of Jesus Christ takes out that stain; only the Fire of the Divine Spirit has power to burn so deeply and eradicate that dreadful cancer.

If thus thou art infected, my soul, let us go searching, even if it should mean spending all we possess; let us go searching until we find that health-giving and vivifying Spirit!

### III

But my dull intellect, notwithstanding its close attentiveness and anxious striving, does not seem fully persuaded nor manages to grasp how a human act, sometimes merely internal, other times as quick as a flash of lightning, and, in certain cases, as innocuous, it would seem, as the petal of a flower; how such an act can carry with it so much malice. After pondering all the reasons, metaphysical and theological, I must frankly confess perhaps that I do not understand; I do not see in sin such an abominable monstrosity to be shunned at all costs.

*I* don't see or understand, but God does; and His judgement is infinitely just!

These two divine, infallible facts bear witness:

1.   God, who is Equanimity, Goodness, and Justice Itself; Who is the Infinite Lover of man, being the Father that He is; by His very Justice is constrained to allow a single mortal sin unrepented of to find its meet punishment in the everlasting misery of Hell.

My God, Thine all-seeing Eyes must behold something incomprehensibly horrible and detestable in that act which we call sin, and which perhaps to my eyes seems a harmless piece of mischief or a childish prank. Lord, I believe in the clear-sightedness of Thine unclouded Vision rather than in the range of my limited mind!

2.   Jesus Christ, the all-innocent Lamb whose bleatings might turn the hardest heart into a fountain of mercy; Jesus Christ, the Eternal Word, the Co-Equal and Consubstantial Son of God in Whom the Father finds all His Delight; just because He clad Himself with the garment of our iniquities and went surety for the

transgressions of men, His brethren; just for that appearance of the mere shadow of sin which God finds in Him, He is allowed to be sacrificed so mercilessly that His torments have come down the centuries filling all generations with dread and sorrow.

This is the overwhelming lesson of the Cross. The red characters of His Blood portray the malice of sin. Only a sinister power like sin could possibly snatch away the human life of the Son of God! Now I see, dear Jesus, that my sins deserve one essential name: abomination.

## RESOLUTION

From now onwards, every day, I shall pluck from the Tree of the Cross the first and most visible fruit that is offered to every passer-by or to whosoever shelters in its shade: an immense detestation of sin and a clear knowledge of its malice.

Contemplating Jesus Christ crucified I can only cry out with David: *"Who knows his own frailties?"* Delicta, quis intelligit. . . ? (Ps. xviii, 13.)

Who cannot decipher the detestable thing that sin is from the Blood-written letters upon the mangled frame of Christ on the Cross?

# MORTAL SIN IN THE PRIEST

### THIRD MEDITATION

*Special Malice of Sin in the Priest*

## I

" Such a transgression, if it be committed by the high-priest then in office, brings guilt upon the whole people, and he must make amends for it by offering to the Lord a young bullock without blemish."—(*Lev. iv,* 3.)

" Or perhaps the whole people of Israel has been betrayed into a fault, transgressing the Lord's command unwittingly. If so, when they find out their error, they will bring a young bullock to the tabernacle door in amends."—(*Lev. iv,* 13.)

The thought-provoking thing about this divine ordinance in the Old Testament is, that God requires the same expiation for the transgression of one priest as for that of the whole people; in the divine Balance a priest's sin weighs as heavy as the sin of an entire nation. Such is the divine Assessment!

You may object that the above text refers to transgressions committed unwittingly, not to sins in the strict sense of the word. Quite so. But does not the argument gather far greater force when it comes to conscious and grievous faults on the part of the priest of the New Law? Is there a single sin in me that does not in some way or other " betray " my people into sin? Does not every sin either deprive me of grace, or at least render me less capable of co-operating worthily in the sanctification and salvation of souls?

## II

Why should my transgressions be tantamount to those of a whole people?

Because for the people—and people means the laity in general—every allowance must be made: the necessity of being in the midst of worldly affairs which by their very nature are full of pitfalls; ignorance, through lack of time for serious application to the study of the eternal truths; inadvertence to realities so distant and so different, it would appear, from the daily tenor of their lives; human weakness, reluctant to take the spiritual remedies Christ has established for its healing.

Can I adduce similar excuses for myself? My one business and occupation should be to save souls, my own soul and others as well; and should there be ignorance on my part, my guilt would be twice as great:

> labia sacerdotis custodient scientiam et legem requirent ex ore ejus.—(*Malachy ii, 7.*)

"No utterance like a priest's for learning; from no other lips men will expect true guidance."

True it is, I am naturally weak, like any other child of Adam, and perhaps weaker at times; but I am by my very office constrained to be in continual touch with the divine sources of all energy: prayer and the Sacraments. If I fail to find therein strength and victory, canst Thou not say to me, O Lord, in the lament of Thy prophet: *Quae utilitas in sanguine meo? (Ps. xxix,* 10.)

## III

*Whose sins you shall forgive, they are forgiven them.* (*John xx,* 23.) And shall I yield to sin? I to whom Christ has given His own tremendous power to forgive?

Shall I commit sin, I who have been raised from servant to steward and guardian of His House and Domain? The words of the loyal and chaste Joseph well befit my lips:

> "My Master entrusts everything to my cause, and keeps no count of His belongings; there is nothing of his but I, by his appointment, have the keeping of it."—(*Gen. xxxix,* 8, 9.)

What a treacherous abuse of confidence if I should

offend the Divine Prisoner who has put Himself in my hands, chained as He is by the Sacramental species!

I, who, in the last resort, am but another Christ—*alter Christus*—shall I make my sins appear as coming from Him? Shall I put Him to the blush for my own misdeeds?

> "Priests, that despise my law, violate my sanctuary . . . am I not defiled by their company?"
> —(*Ezech. xxii*, 26.)

Lord! Lord! . . . If from anybody Thou hadst a right to expect everlasting fidelity and love, it was surely from me; no, not guile, not villainous treason, not a bartering with Thy Person and Thy Law, after the manner of Judas . . . or for even less!

### RESOLUTION

With God's assistance and blessing I will never sin; I will flee from sin as from the fangs of a serpent; but if any day I should allow myself to be ensnared, by Thy grace, O God, do for me what Thy Apostle enjoins on those who gave vent to anger against their brethren: *Sol non occidat super iracundiam vestram!* (*Eph. iv*, 26.) The sunset must not find Thee still angry; Thou must forgive me in answer to repentance and confession before the day is ended!

## MORTAL SIN IN THE PRIEST

### FOURTH MEDITATION

*Effects of Mortal Sin in the Priest*

### I

When mortal sin has been committed, there opens up between God and myself an abyss that no created being can bridge. I scrapped the title-deed sealed with the Blood of Christ, a deed conferring not so much a title of friendship as that of a child of God; and I became God's enemy, the slave marked out for all the fulminations of His Justice. Yes, this remains my lot and portion instead of the inheritance of a son, instead of the eternally blissful Life of God, the patrimony of His children.

Lost in the total shipwreck of my fall are the treasures of merits and good works which I had been amassing patiently, hour after hour, in my painful endeavour to redeem my fallen nature, and bring it to its charted course. My past life has left me empty-handed; my present is tormented with remorse, and is exposed, like a rudderless boat, to the waves of passion that sin has roused and lashed to increasing fury; and in the future, there awaits me the penalty imposed by the divine Sanctions: eternal death, banishment from my Heavenly Father.

Before sinning, why not weigh up carefully in my mind whether the pleasure or advantages of sin outbalance such tremendous losses?

## II

From the tree of evil there is another fruit that only the hand of the priest plucks, a fruit reeking with poison, a poison more indigestible and destructive.

When a mortal sin has been committed—for example, dallying with a lustful thought or with a desire deliberately conceived by the mind and embraced by the will, be it ever so brief or denied fulfilment—how difficult it is, in practice, for the poor priest not to fall the same or the following day into the most dangerous of all sins, profanation of the Sacraments!

If you sinned during the afternoon or evening for instance, when the morning comes and the hour approaches to say Mass, are you sure to confess beforehand? How many hindrances will arise from laziness, bashfulness, or even the wiles of Satan, to make you fritter the time away hesitant, afraid to take the step, all the while adding to your own confusion of mind and smothering your weak will in a thousand excuses that end, in spite of the obligation *sub gravi* to make your confession if there is any reasonable opportunity of doing so, by driving you unconfessed to the sacristy, and from there, after vesting, to the Altar for an unworthy celebration of the Mass! And oh! if once you trample upon the Body and Blood of Christ by a sacrilegious Mass, what will your conscience not be capable of perpetrating!

## III

That same day, perhaps after the Holy Sacrifice you have just profaned, you may be required to sit in the tribunal of Penance or to administer Extreme Unction, and each one of those acts to which you are committed by reason of your ministry will be for you, unworthy minister, a dreadful profanation. And in the second round of your calamitous procedure the hour to say Mass will arrive again, and you will do so less reluctantly than in the first, and you will find it very much harder to seek out a confessor for the remedy; and as the days go by you will feel an increasing horror for the Sacrament of Penance; and if from some motive of human respect you eventually feel bound to make your confession, a false shame will grip your heart, will choke the words of sincerity in your throat, and you will continue sinning and profaning all that is most holy week after week, and perhaps month after month, and year after year. And then, who will assess the heavy load of crime that weighs on your soul? Who will reduce to figures the multitude of your iniquities?

Soon, very soon, the blackest soul in your parish, in the town, will be you!

## IV

And you will lose everything into the bargain: refinement of thought and feeling, leaving you impotent for an understanding and vital possession of the eternal truths; and your faith, gradually consuming, like a burning coal exposed to a strong wind, and driven further and further away from your conscious mind and buried beneath the grime and dust of sin, will not give forth light or warmth, and . . . God forbid—as happens often enough—that it should die out altogether and for ever! Yes, this is the path trodden by those of Christ's ministers who proved apostates and traitors to their God and His ministry.

Renegades, apostates, not so much by their errors defended with regrettable talent and propagated with cynical daring, as by those silent infidelities and apostasies whose only mouth-piece was the stench of their scandalous and abject lives. Ministers of Christ disbelieving in Christ! This infernal paradox is the abyss into which more than one priest has been hurtled by mortal sin!

## V

But let us suppose that, by the mercy and forbearance of God, you are not falling so low and you still keep undiminished your faith in the very Christ whom you subject to daily profanation. That faith of yours will be so lifeless and so reticent that the clamour and tumult of your passions and your drunken cravings to give them satisfaction will drown the shouts of a supernaturally enlightened conscience, and the habit of unheeding those shouts will harden your noblest faculties; the searing effect of each new fall unrepented of will form a crust of insensibility around your moral conscience (cfr. *I Tim. iv*); you will have departed from God so far, so far, that His powerful call to repentance will fall on deaf ears.

And your life will come to a close, and your last hour will hover around you, and in you will be fulfilled the terrible curse of the Eternal Wisdom:

> "Since my call is unheard, since my hand beckons in vain, since my counsel is despised and all my reproof goes for nothing it will be mine to laugh, to mock at your discomfiture, when perils close about you."—(*Prov. i*, 24-26.)

> You shall seek me and shall not find me and where I am you cannot come.—(*John vii*, 34.)

## RESOLUTIONS

1. Not to facilitate a lapse on the score of its being easily atoned for and pardoned; for I have just seen how sin inoculates with a poison that, by a process as swift as inexorable, can reduce me to the lowest degree of spiritual vitality, to final impenitence, and eternal death.

2. O Lord, I shall fear Thy hidden judgements which, for one single mortal sin, could leave me abandoned and permit me to fall into the dark abyss of impotency for good and of terrible power for evil.

# MORTAL SIN IN THE PRIEST

## FIFTH MEDITATION

### *Malice of Scandal in the Priest*

#### I

#### *Nature of scandal*

Another poisonous fruit of mortal sin in the priest is usually scandal.

Let us define scandal with theological accuracy: *Dictum vel factum minus rectum praebens alteri occasionem ruinae spiritualis*—Something said or done which falls short of moral rectitude and which provides for another the occasion of spiritual ruin.

It may be a case of simply providing the opportunity, that is: a certain facility, greater than the ordinary, for sinning, in response to the mere presence or knowledge of the thing said or done which bears the appearances of evil. Or a person may be in some way the cause of sin, for example: by praising, persuading, or coercing another with regard to evil.

Your scandal will be *indirect* if you reasonably foresee that another will be moved to sin because of your words or actions, even though you may not intend it; and *direct* if you intend another person to sin, either for the sake of satisfying your own passions or for the delight—the fiendish delight—of seeing your neighbour offend God and lose his soul.

## II

### Malice of scandal

Indirect scandal is a sin against charity, and even against justice, if the person giving scandal is bound *ex officio* to avoid it; for example, a parish priest or a prelate, whose office it is to edify, to "build up" the souls that God has entrusted to him.

Direct scandal, besides being against charity, offends against the virtue or commandment which the scandal induces to transgress; for instance, scandalising against holy purity will contract a twofold malice: one against charity for others, and the other against the sixth commandment.

The scandal will be more or less grave according to the greater or lesser spiritual ruin brought about, or to the more or less strong influence and effectiveness which we exercise for evil by our evil word or deed, or the more or less directly we foresee or seek the commission of sin by another.

Who but God will weigh and measure the evil propensities awakened in other hearts by the atmosphere of my life so unworthy of my priesthood? And for how many was this a decisive force for plunging them into the vortex of sin?

## III

### Malice of scandal from the priest

To scandalise is to kill the divine life of grace in

souls, a life more precious than all natural life, *quoniam melior est misericordia tua super vitas.* (Ps. lxii, 4.) It is to wrench them away from God their Father and to make them incur eternal loss. Do you know of anything more opposed to the idea we all have of what a priest of Christ should be?

A priest giving scandal! What a paradox! Salt that corrupts and rots, light that darkens, water that stains and bemires, shepherd who scatters and slaughters the flock, father of souls who murders them with his own hands and throws them like carrion into the cesspool of hell; Christ—*sacerdos alter Christus*—who re-sells for a trifle souls purchased with divine Blood and throws them back to the devouring jaws of Satan.

## RESOLUTION

With all the force and zest of my love for my priestly vocation and for Jesus Christ my Lord and God I shall detest scandal, the poisoned weapon of the spirit of darkness for overcoming the Redeemer of men and for annulling the supernatural action of the Catholic priesthood. With acts of heartfelt contrition at least, I shall wipe out the cursed trail of evil left by my transgressions real or apparent.

Henceforth, nobody shall find in my life a basis for delinquency; I do not want any Christian, when sinning, to be able to point to my sinful life and claim the slightest justification and excuse, repeating the verse from one of Seneca's tragedies: *Quid divos decuit, mihi turpe putem?* which we might translate: " What is good enough for the priest is good enough for me."

# MORTAL SIN IN THE PRIEST

*Harm done by the Scandalous Priest*

## I

### *Harm to individual souls*

Our passions seek a support—pretexts, excuses, at least some glimpse of good—and never have they found a more solid one than the life of the bad priest. If the person appointed to defend morality with his conduct, his words and his ministry; if he whose name and garb seem a living reproach to evil; if he who commands God's grace and God's strength to tame the unruly impulses of the heart and of fallen human nature; if *he* sets an example of sin, what will the other mortals do who are supposed to look up to him as their guide, their master, and their model?

The best defence, an impregnable defence, of evil living is the bad priest; he is the unwholesome yeast that leavens and corrupts the entire mass of the faithful who know him.

## II

### *Harm to the flock*

There are thousands of communities whose history is befittingly epitomised in St. Paul's cutting reproach: *Sine Deo in hoc mundo;* whole towns and villages that have in actual fact apostatised; that have fled from Holy Church for all time; without the Sacraments even at the hour of death; where all the efforts of the most skilful and zealous pastor to bring them back to God meet with failure; from which the very radical capacity for conversion seems to have been torn away by some accursed power.

Don't you know, or haven't you heard, of these pitiful apostasies? How many parishes there are even in countries of Catholic tradition more difficult to convert than the heathen or the followers of Mahoma! A priest will spend all the energies of a life-time of apostleship in a parish like this, and, when presented to the Divine Judge, he will be forced to say:

> Master, we have laboured all through the night and have caught nothing.

Look for the primary cause of that obstinacy, and you will nearly always come across a scandalous priest. So terrible is the power for evil of the bad priest!

## III

### Harm to the whole Church

Try to find a heretic, a calumniator, or any opponent of the Church, who in his attacks and diatribes does not base his hostility on crimes committed by the Church's ministers: you will not find one.

The heresies of our times—if from a doctrinal point of view they deserve the name and not that of sheer apostasy—those social and political systems that have de-christianised the masses and severed from Jesus Christ and from the bosom of His Church the nations united to Him for many centuries, what new dogmas, what great sophisms, have they brought to their own defence? Ordinarily, just one: the dishonouring of the clergy, covering them in the mire of calumny, the bringing to light of our personal shortcomings; and by that expedient alone they have succeeded in persuading thousands upon thousands of souls to renounce Christ and consider Him no longer their Saviour and their God.

Have there not been in my priestly life, dear Lord, evil deeds that in the hands of Thy enemies have become thorns to Thy brow, spittle to Thy face, a tattered cloak of derision upon Thy shoulders, presenting Thee thus disfigured to the eyes of the gullible masses with the sarcastic *Ecce Homo*?

### RESOLUTION

I shall make an impartial study of my life to see whether there is anything—any sinful practice, any habit of doubtful morality, any friendship open to suspicion —whereby I am a stumbling-block to my neighbour; or at least, any sin of omission: slackness in the fulfilment of my duties, want of circumspection in my speech, etc., etc. For I am convinced that it is not necessary to be a great sinner to be the cause of scandal. It could happen that the only basic reason for my condemnation before Christ would be my having caused the downfall of the weak by my thoughtlessness.

## MORTAL SIN IN THE PRIEST

### SEVENTH MEDITATION

*Punishment of the Scandalous Priest*

### I

A day of dread and horror, the day when Christ, the Prince of Pastors, the Great Shepherd, will come to judge His bad ministers, wolves in shepherd's clothing! His Wrath will be the equal of His overflowing love that made Him give life and blood to the task of redeeming souls and snatching them from the wolves of hell.

"The day will surely come, and is not far off, when the Shepherd of shepherds will reveal Himself to the whole world and will reveal the works of each one; and He who now chastises the sins of others through His priests will on that day Himself condemn the evil wrought by His priests, and condemn with unmatched rigour."—(*Hom.* 17 *on Luke—St. Gregory, Pope.*)

How Christ will say to the scandalous priest, with lips tremulous with indignation, what Moses said to Aaron:

"What grudge hadst thou against this people, that thou hast involved them in such guilt?" —(*Ex. xxxii,* 21.)

## II

*Woe to him . . . he that shall scandalise one of these little ones that believe in me, it were better . . .*— (*Matt. xviii,* 7.)

Note the similarity, almost the identity of this threat with that which Jesus pronounces against the traitor Apostle: *Woe to that man by whom the Son of Man shall be betrayed: it were better . . .*—(*Matt. xxvi,* 24); which implies that he who puts souls to the sword of bad example is as hateful to Christ as Judas who sold Him to the torments of the cross; as criminal and as deserving of punishment.

If such woe upon him who shall hurt the conscience of *one* single soul, what will be, in the sight of God, the

c

unworthy priest who by his perverse inspiration and example can root up morality and perhaps the faith of a whole parish, of a whole district, and for several generations? Such is our bad example's force of expansion!

### III

Describing the good shepherd as one *who giveth his life for his sheep,* our Divine Lord compares him with the hireling who

> seeth the wolf coming and leaveth the sheep and flieth . . . because he is a hireling, and he hath no care for the sheep; and because the shepherd flees, the wolf catcheth and scattereth the sheep.
>
> (*John x,* 11-13.)

Sheep without a shepherd are sheep without guardian and guide, lost and wandering, a flock dispersed, an easy prey to the ravening wolves. And all because the shepherd fled!

Now, what would happen if the shepherd did not flee, but actually turned into a ravening wolf and shut himself up within the fold? What sheep would escape from his clutches? Who would defend them? It is Pope St. Gregory who makes this sad reflection. (*Hom.* 17 *on Luke.*)

If Christ will so severely punish the hireling, what of the shepherd turned wolf?

### IV

What sort of punishments does the Good Shepherd allot to the scandalous priest?

The Gospels do not mention them by name, but how they underline the terrific severity of them!

It would be horrible torture to a priest to have a millstone tied round the neck and to be drowned in the depths of the sea; and yet, according to Jesus Christ, this would be kindness itself in comparison with the punishment in store. *It were better . . .*

And if we are not moved by the threats of the eternal punishment infallibly coming down upon our scandals, let us hear at least those other punishments mentioned by the prophet Malachias:

> " That path you have forsaken; through your ill-teaching, how many a foothold lost! . . . What wonder if I have made you a laughing-stock, a thing contemptible in all men's sight, priests that so ill kept my command. . . . —(*ii*, 8, 9.)

When we consider the utter contempt with which some people, even seemingly devout Catholics, treat their priests in certain countries, can we assign any other cause but that which God gives us in the foregoing text?

## RESOLUTION

I will atone until my last breath by an exemplary and fervent priestly life for the damage that my years of dissipation may have done in the Church of God. I will uproot the tares and sow wheat more plentifully.

# VENIAL SIN

## *The Nature of Venial Sin*

### I

The catechism speaks of venial sins as an offence which is lightly committed and easily pardoned, but prepares the way for mortal sin. Theologians define it as "a free act of the will adhering to something forbidden by the Law of God, but without breaking with God our Last End". It is an attachment to something which, while not severing us from Life's appointed destiny, is not conducive to it and cannot be squared with it.

There are two kinds of venial sin:

1. Venial by reason of an imperfect act, through lack of knowledge or consent in the person committing it; such as negligence in promptly rejecting a grave temptation to sensuality, or assent to an evil suggestion in a state of semi-consciousness.

2. Venial by reason of the object which in itself is of lesser moment and which therefore does not seriously impair one's love for God or for the neighbour; as, for example, the stealing of a small sum of money, or a jocose lie.

### II

Venial sin suffers slight comparison with mortal sin: it does not infringe the essence of the moral order, that is, the primary purpose intended by the Divine Lawgiver; it does not wreathe the creature's brow sacrilegiously with God's own incommunicable Attribute of being our Last End; it does not take the soul out of the path of salvation, although there is undue diversion and a slowing down of progress; it leaves the spirit intrinsically alive to grace and endowed with the beauty and splendour essential to a child of God; no, it does not extinguish the vital principle of the supernatural life, grace; and therefore venial sin is a wound in a living body, and, as such, is curable, amenable to the healing force of grace; it is, as the catechism says: easy to remedy and pardon—*veniabilis*. The aforementioned contrast should in the first place make us detest and flee from mortal sin.

### III

If the effects of *venial* sin, as outlined above, should persuade me that it is of slight importance, I have made a bad mistake; the only thing they prove is, that such is the enormity of mortal sin that all other evils hardly deserve the name; moreover, they provide me with a criterion for judging the terrible menace of venial sin, being as it is a disposition and road leading straight into the dark abyss of mortal sin. In the case of venial sin *ex imperfectione actus,* the conclusion is legitimate, because a will that defends itself from grave temptation remissly, or half consents to it, is not far from entire surrender, should the assault intensify. And as regards venial sin *ex parvitate materiae,* the momentum of its thrust will drive me to mortal sin, unless I re-establish the only barrier against it: complete submission of my will to the Will of God. But alas! I have got into a rebellious frame of mind concerning small things; my free-will has revelled in the furtive delight of by-passing the Laws. Will not a habit like this eventually drag me down to disobedience in things of greater moment?

"Little things despise, and little by little thou shalt come to ruin."—(*Eclus. xix,* 1.)

## RESOLUTION

I shall meditate on the dangers of my lesser defects which I deal with so indulgently. I shall reflect on the process of my past and all-too-frequent falls from God's grace, in order to understand with meridional clarity what without reflection I have already perceived in a dark manner; namely, that when I plunged into mortal sin I had for several days been slipping and sliding towards the abyss down the gentle slope of puny attachments and of petty illicit actions that were, after all, but a mask for my love of the forbidden fruit of deadly poison.

# VENIAL SIN

### SECOND MEDITATION

## *Effects of Venial Sin*

### I

Venial sin demands further reflection.

Although it does not gangrene and destroy the essential comeliness imparted by grace, venial sin at least contaminates the soul's supernatural beauty; it hinders the diffusion of exterior loveliness, it fetters those activities of the supernatural life which one may consider its radiance and splendour; like stains or burns marring a beautiful face.

When you sin venially you commit an act that is useless, because it cannot be directed to your Last End; you halt on the path that leads to union with the Supreme Good, like a thoughtless child sent on an errand playing by the road-side; and because the matter is linked up with the perfection of the moral order and concerns to some degree life's ultimate goal you incur a real transgression, you really and truly disobey your Lord and your God.

And will you have the audacity to consider negligible a thing that offends God's infinite Majesty, that is lacking in reverence towards His Greatness and gratitude for His benefits, that diminishes His Glory, and is unmindful and contemptuous of His Love? My soul, are not these deterrents enough?

## II

God, who has no hatred for anything He created, not even for suffering or for the most hideous freaks of nature, cannot but abhor, as long as He loves His own infinite Goodness, eternally and with unrelenting hatred, a single venial sin. And, in token of that detestation, He punishes it with such fearful torments in Purgatory that there is nothing in the world to equal them, neither the torments of the martyrs nor, perhaps, even those of Jesus Christ Himself in His passion and Death.

Further weight is added to this truth if we bear in mind that for no reason whatever and for nobody in this world or the next is it lawful to commit a venial sin: not even to deliver the world from all its pangs and sorrows; not even to bring about all imaginable good; nor to convert all heathens and sinners, nor to open the gates of heaven to the whole race of Adam, nor even to quench the flames of hell and reduce them to cold ashes; for God would hate it, detest it everlastingly.

And yet, O Lord, I commit it for any futile pretext, with the greatest ease; sometimes for no reason at all, just for the pleasure of doing something! Have pity on my unmindfulness; open my eyes that I may see, and tremble.

### III

Reflect on another great harm of venial sin. When it forms a habit, the soul drifts into the deplorable state of spiritual lukewarmness attended by all the risks so vividly described by Our Lord in the Apocalypse when reproaching the Angel of the Church of Laodicea:

" A message to thee from the Truth,
the faithful and unerring witness,
the Source from which God's creating began:

I know of thy doings,
and find thee neither cold nor hot;
cold or hot, I would thou wert one or the other.
Being what thou art, lukewarm, neither cold nor hot,
thou wilt make me vomit thee out of my mouth.

I am rich, thou sayest, I have come into my own;
nothing, now, is wanting to me.

And all the while, if thou didst know it,
it is thou who art wretched,
thou who art to be pitied.
Thou art a beggar, blind and naked."

(*Apoc. iii*, 14-18.)

Dear Lord, can it be that I am turning into something so repugnant to Thee, so sickening and nauseating, that Thou art ready to spew me out? Am I going to be something vomited and unclean? And how wouldst Thou take me again to Thy fatherly bosom? Only of a dog it is said: *"Canis versus ad vomitum"* . . . And I have no fears? And I even boast of my merits and virtues? Oh, *"I am rich . . . nothing, now, is wanting to me!"* Presumption, luckless child of tepidity!

## IV

I shall avoid at all costs any venial sin fully deliberate. It may be a relatively small thing, but to harbour it so unconcernedly is no small proof of the low esteem my Heavenly Father inspires me with, seeing that I so easily and continually offend and slight Him, even though my transgressions be not of the calibre of those that sufficed to crucify Him. Is there a child, with but an average sense of dutifulness, who would behave like this towards his earthly father? Lord, Thou couldst befittingly reproach me after each venial sin with the words of the prophet: *If then I be a father, where is my honour?* —(Mal. i, 6.)

### RESOLUTIONS

Whenever there is no mortal sin to confess, I shall aim at freeing myself during the following week or so, that is, until my next confession, of some definite venial sin; for instance: not to give way to carping criticism or to deliberate distractions during my spiritual exercises, etc.; and to achieve this I shall avail myself of the following means:

1. Resolute determination.

2. Sincere repentance as soon as I have fallen into the specified fault, together with a purpose of amendment.

3. To take this as the so-called " virtue of practice " for the interval before my next confession, bringing all my examinations of conscience to bear on it, both the particular examinations before meals and the general before going to bed.

4. When preparing for my next confession, I shall start by examining my conscience on that particular fault, and I shall not fail to sum up its exact nature and the number of times I have committed it since my last confession; and in my accusation, this will be the first item; for example: " I accuse myself of giving way to anger seven times."

# THE CREATION

## *My Creaturely Dignity and Duties*

### I

God brought all creatures out of nothing by His impersonal command: *Let there be light, let there be a firmament, let the earth bring forth, etc.*

But when creating man, He begins with *Let us make,* not *let there be;* and, with Himself as Model,—*to our image and likeness.* But man is not yet, not even after that ample phrase so full of power and majesty. God bends His heavenly Might, no, not to touch the summits of lofty mountains, but down to the depths where, *from the slime of the earth,* He fashions the body of Adam. So that man alone among all visible creatures can say to God with the psalmist: *Tu formasti me et posuisti super me manum tuam:* "It is Thou that hast fashioned me, Thy hand that has been laid upon me."—(*Ps. cxxxviii,* 5.)

That goes for Adam, you'll say, what about me? In a certain sense, I am more to be wondered at than my first parent. What an immense power God must have given to Adam for him to be the source of all the blood and vital energy to thousands of generations! *Omnia ossa mea dicent: Domine, quis similis tibi? Cor meum et caro mea exultaverunt in Deum vivum.* "The Living God! at His Name my heart, my whole being thrills with joy."—(*Ps. xxxiv,* 10; *Ps. lxxxiii,* 3.)

### II

Will not that have been sufficient for the fashioning of man? No. That indeed was something beautiful, but lifeless. God contemplated the work of His hands with delight, and, bending over it *He breathed into his face the breath of life, and man became a living soul.*—(*Gen. ii, 7.*)

My spirit is not, like the heavens, the work of God's Fingers—*opera digitorum tuorum;*—my soul cannot say to its Maker, like the body: *Manus tuae plasmaverunt me:* my spirit God breathed into me from the depths of His own Being, like a breath that I exhale from the recesses of my lungs; that is what my soul is: *spiritus, spiraculum,* the Breath of God. Has anything more mysterious, more profound and beautiful ever been said about the nature of my soul? Is it possible to go further without touching pantheism?

If this is testimony from God, what must my soul be but God's own image, cast and moulded in His Heart, bearing the marks of God's attributes, and, in a sense, divine?

Recognise, my soul, thy dignity; regret having trailed thy mantle of glory through earthly mire.

### III

To the foregoing proofs of ineffable love on the part of God, there is another, tenderer still.

More than a hundred years ago, more than a thousand, a million, a thousand million . . . how will my imagination encompass the thought, the magnificent reality? . . .

From all eternity . . . God thinks of me . . . Before the first break of the first dawn; before the coverlet of the skies was spread, God thought of me!

What is the choicest favour we ask of a friend? "Keep me in your thoughts." And throughout the ever-lasting years, Thou, O Lord, dost keep me in Thy thoughts; not for a moment do I slip from Thy remembrance. But Thou dost not think of me as the savant thinks of the object of his learning and investigations; Thou thinkest of me, dear Lord, from the dawning of Thy eternal Day as the lover thinks of and keeps in perpetual remembrance the beloved of his heart:

> With unchanging love I love thee, and in mercy I have drawn thee to Myself.—(*Jer. xxxi*, 3.)

God loves me, loves me from all eternity! And so often have I complained with bitterness of soul that nobody cares a damn for me! And all the time God was loving me with an unchanging, everlasting love!

O divine Lover, eternal Lover, what wonder that Thou ask for my cold and fleeting love?

The thing that defies all explanation is the niggardliness with which I have been refusing it to Thee throughout my whole existence, to squander it, instead, among a host of puny creatures, fetishes of the hour that show me neither gratitude nor reward except to lacerate my heart and hand when I try to clutch them.

## RESOLUTION

I have learnt that Thou, my God and my Father, though in need of nought that is mine—*quia bonorum meorum non eges (Ps. xv, 2)*—hast nevertheless a longing for something which only I can give, just one small thing: my love, my heart; and Thou dost long for this with such intensity as to stoop down and beg it of me, like a lover of his beloved, like a mother of her only son: *Son, give Me thy heart.*—(*Prov. xxiii, 26.*)

Lord, sever with the sword of Thy Power the bonds that have bound my heart and enslaved it to lower, tyrannical creatures; I wish, at long last, to surrender my heart into Thy hands, that it may become a censer exhaling the immortal fragrances of holy love to Thee who didst create and fashion my whole being with individual care: *qui finxit sigillatim corda eorum.*— (*Ps. xxxii,* 15.)

# SALVATION

*Importance of my Salvation*

## I

God created me! There is real delight in relishing this lofty truth.

God created me; I am His handiwork; to Him belongs my body with its intricate structure; His are the delicate organisms that serve the soul's spiritual faculties; a world more wonderful and of wider span than the sensible world of sky, land, and sea. His, in sum, is all this being which I call my own, and which He placed as the keystone of the arch of creation.

It is obvious then, that God did not make me for the sake of merely entertaining Himself, in order, shall we say, to while His time away or kill the boredom of an empty eternity, to amuse Himself like a child making mud pies or blowing bubbles!

Even more admirable than the constitution of my being is my purpose and destiny: my elevation to the dignity of a child of God, the infusion into me of the Spirit of His Only-begotten Son, His Eternal Word; the share He has allotted me in the inheritance of my Heavenly Father; in a word, my salvation. *Hereditas mea praeclara est mihi!* "No fairer lot could be mine; no nobler inheritance could I win!"—(*Ps. xv*, 6.)

## II

As a pledge of this destiny, God engraved our souls with the yearning for salvation.

Good or bad, we all wish to save our souls; and

although the desire for selfish enjoyment here below may lie deep in our hearts, as perhaps the mainspring of our lives, we nevertheless want to save our souls. Probe the dark recesses, and, more or less deep down, more or less alive, that desire of salvation will be discovered; a desire that in the dizziest moods and excesses is never wholly extinguished. If any sinner were to be asked while in the very act of plunging into the miry and turbulent waters of sin, "Do you wish to save your soul?" he would instantly reply: "Of course I do!"

A pity that this unquenchable longing for salvation, which seems akin to something instinctive, is not more often coupled with a serious consideration of St. Augustine's famous dictum: "Qui creavit te sine te, non salvabit te sine te."

### III

In order to kindle our desire of salvation, let us feed the flames by meditating on the following two questions put to us by our Divine Lord:

> What doth it profit a man, if he gain the whole world and suffer the loss of his own soul?
>
> Or what exchange shall a man give for his soul?—(*Matt. xvi*, 26.)

The Son of Man will one day come in the glory of His Father, escorted by angels, to give to each one according to his works. If on that day your evil works entail the eternal loss of your soul, if Christ the Judge condemns you, what will you have gained by hoarding up money, by adding possession to possession, pleasure to pleasure, honour to honour, benefice to benefice? What will it avail to have been a priest, a bishop, a pope, and to show forth the ineffaceable character of the priesthood for all eternity? *What doth it profit? What doth it profit? . . .*

Nobody, reflects St. Bernard, would accept a month's enjoyment at the price of forty years of misery. And shall I, a man in my sane mind, accept an hour of pleasure at the cost of endless suffering?

## IV

*What exchange shall a man give for his soul?*

In the event of your losing your soul before the scrutiny and Judgement-Seat of God, do you hold anything in reserve? Any assets wherewith to bribe the Judge and elicit a withdrawal of the sentence? Money? Influence? Persuasive oratory? Useless, every bit of it! He will give, not according to one's words or dignities or friendships or wealth, but according to one's works. (*Matt. xvi,* 27.)

Only one kind of currency passes there: good works; and not those that you might do then but those done during this life. Mark it well; your eternal salvation is to be the fruit of the life you are living now.

Is my life such, so well-ordered, so in keeping with the Will of God, that it can yield fruit of life everlasting?

### RESOLUTIONS

1. To bring practice into line with profession. Do I profess to save my soul? Then I shall regulate my life by the demands of success in this enterprise, and with the Psalmist I shall often say: *Vide si via iniquitatis in me est, et deduc me in via aeterna.*—(*Ps. cxxxviii,* 24.)

2. To engrave on my soul, as the heraldic expression of my entire existence, the motto from the Gospel: *What doth it profit a man if he gain the whole world and suffer the loss of his own soul?*

# THE REDEMPTION

## The Tremendous Lover

### I

" We have learned to recognise the love God has
in our regard, to recognise it, and to make it our
belief."—(I *John iv*, 16.)

I know and I believe in God's love for me; I hold it
with the same firm conviction as any other article of
belief. I believe in God's loving choice of me, His high
esteem. And yielding to the spell of this belief, I am
going to throw myself at the feet of Christ crucified and
there repeat with St. Paul the glorious Hymn of the
redeemed :

> The Son of God, who loved me, and gave Him-
> self for me!—(*Gal. ii*, 20.)

Christ, the God-Man, the Divine Will poured into a
Human Heart; Christ, of His own most free will, loved
me, me personally with all the obscurity and wretchedness attaching to my life's story; and to convince me of
His love He gave Himself up to death for my sake.
Well-tested indeed is the love whose declaration is signed
and sealed by the lover's own life and blood; no proof
of love more profound and true!

> Greater love than this no man hath, that a man
> lay down his life for his friends.—(*John xv*, 13.)

Rather than doubt Thy love for me, O Lord, I must
doubt and deny every other love : the love of my father,
whose life of toil and privations is written large and

fruitfully over the welfare of his son; or the love of my mother, wrought of tears and sorrows. . . .

Dear Lord, I know and believe, and on bended knees I confess, the charity Thou hast for me.

## II

"Thanks be to God for His unutterable bounty to us."—(II *Cor. ix*, 15.)

But shall I be asked for nothing in return?

If Thou art going to ask something of me, Lord, I am afraid; Thou hast a right to *so* much!

Yes, I am determined to make a request from my Cross.

Speak, Lord.

That thou love me. . . . *Thou shalt love the Lord thy God with thy whole soul and with thy whole mind.* (*Matt. xxii,* 37.) *He that loveth father or mother more than me is not worthy of me.* (*Matt. x,* 37.)

O heart I made, a Heart beats here!
Face, My hands fashioned, see it in Myself!
Thou hast no power, nor mayst conceive of Mine,
But love I gave thee, with Myself to love,
And thou must love Me, Who have died for thee!
(BROWNING.)

Is that all Thou askest? to love Thee? . . . What less could I do? . . . I ask my dog to love me, for the bone and dry crust I throw to it, and Thou hast given me all Thy Blood. Hast Thou anything else to ask?

Yes. *If you love me, keep my commandments.*—(*John xiv,* 15.)

Lord, my heart was sore afraid lest Thou mightest

require me to shed at least half of my blood for Thee, or to undergo some fearful martyrdom; and that would not have exceeded Thy rights, seeing that Thou hast suffered all for me. But no, I am required to keep Thy commandments. And what does that requirement amount to? To acting reasonably in everything Thou commandest me, to act in keeping with the lawful aspirations of the rational being that I am; and therefore, to follow the only course that brings me to the shores of the land of eternal happiness. *If thou wilt enter into life, keep the commandments.* (*Matt. xix,* 17.)

Just think of it! Jesus Christ appears before my eyes amid the tortures and ignominy of His Cross, mangled, torn, steeped in streams of Blood, pleading with anguish from each gaping wound; and He says to me: " My son, if thou intendest to make some return for all the pain thou hast cost me, thou hast only to follow, out of love for me, the one road that leads to thy own true happiness."

My Jesus, I know not when Thou art the more sublime: when dying for me on the shameful gibbet, or when pleading with me, like a beggar, not to refuse Thee the pleasure Thou derivest from seeing me obey the law of my own supreme welfare!

### III

Lord, what has been my response? Do I love Thee? Dare I say so, having offended Thee hundreds of times for a few crumbs of vile satisfaction? Do I love Thee when I make any puny creature my preference and run after it so recklessly?

And do I keep Thy commandments? Thou knowest

I do not; this is abundantly clear, even to me. Ah, many, many a time I have broken my covenant with Thee, thrown off Thy yoke, sundered Thy healthful bonds, and said "*I will not serve.*" (*Jer. ii*, 20). Try as I may, I shall never number the offences I have committed against Thee who hast loved me to the death upon the Cross, to the shedding of Thy Blood.

In Lucifer's rebellion there is at least an element of the sublime, that sublimity portrayed by Milton so vividly, and, before Milton, by the greater poetry of the Sacred Scriptures. An angelic creature, limited in his being, limited in duration—because he had a beginning—with the audacity to hurl defiance into the face of the Infinite Whose sovereign Attributes he well recognises, into the face of the Almighty who had just brought millions of worlds into being out of nothing by dint of a mere act of the Will. Yes, in that rebellion, criminal as it was, I can glimpse some trace of mysterious and fascinating grandeur.

But, my crucified Jesus, in my offences and continued rebellion against a God-made-Man nailed to a gibbet and streaming with Blood, can I or anyone else discover the slightest hint of captivating arrogance or of sublime strength? Is it sublime to pour vinegar into the wounds, or make mockery, of One who is nailed and agonising?

So, besides being ungrateful and criminal in offending Thee, O Lord, I have just been despicably mean and vile.

## IV

Even supposing that during my life as a priest I have refrained from sinning grievously, and have always sworn to serve Thee; Thou, on Thy part, hast loved me with all the strength of Thy Being; Thou hast loved me, so to speak, with Divine Passion, with a sort of incomprehensible precipitancy, with impatient longing to die for me:

> I have a baptism wherewith I am to be baptised, and how I am straitened until it be accomplished!
> —(*Lk. xii, 50.*)

*How straitened!* How impatient! Lord, it is as though Thy breast were all too small, as though Thy Heart, under the stress of such vehement desire, would leap its bounds.

I am enlisted in Thy service; Thy lover and servitor is the name I prize. But do I serve Thee? Well, perhaps I do. But how? Against the grain, as it were. If I do not offend Thee more, if I do not wrench myself away from Thee entirely, is it not because there is still a remnant of fear restraining me? Or rather, it is because Thy infinite mercy has encompassed me about with granite-rock ramparts to keep me within the citadel of my duty; because Thou hast walled me in, lest I flee or stray. Thou pursuest me, and at my side Thou art constraining me, oh! so gently, so lovingly, and yet almost irresistibly, with Thy grace, with Thy subtle inspirations, with Thy Shepherd's gentle call, lest I hold back. And with all this, how hard I find it to forge ahead!

Thou, dear Lord, so ardent in Thy love for me; I, so tepid and remiss in requiting Thee!

Am I above Thee? Do I excel Thee in gifts and graces?

## RESOLUTION

I propose to re-enact in my heart every day, however briefly—for instance, in my thanksgiving after Mass—

the pathetic scene of the Adoration of the Cross on Good Friday.

Christ crucified, newly unveiled by the priest, is shown to the people, while priest and people intone the *Ecce lignum Crucis in quo salus mundi pependit!* And then the crucifix is laid on the ground for all to contemplate in silence for a while. Afterwards, the suspense is broken by the doleful tones of the choir singing:

> Popule meus, quid feci tibi
> aut in quo contristavi te;
> responde mihi,

during which the weeping faithful prostrate themselves three times as they approach to kiss the Cross; and in answer to the remonstrations voiced by the choir, they can only babble:

> Sanctus Deus,
> Sanctus Fortis,
> Sanctus Immortalis:
> Miserere nobis!

I shall re-enact this scene in my heart between Christ and my sinful soul every day, either before the altar or before the crucifix in my bedroom when retiring for my night's rest.

# DEATH

## FIRST MEDITATION

### *Its Certainties*

#### I

A day will arrive—who will dare to doubt it?—when I myself shall be the one who is seriously ill, the one past recovery, the one dying, with people around me beginning to worry about preparations for my burial: the laying out, the coffin, the funeral, obituary cards. . . .

Do you think these details are somewhat ludicrous, unworthy of the seriousness of a meditation? Apply them to yourself, and perhaps they will have the effect of plunging you into deep thought.

If the thought of death does not impress me or deter me from evil, as the Scriptures promise it will, it is because I think of someone else's death, not my own.

My God, frankly, I have never really given a thought to my own death, I have hardly believed in it, despite the fact that I see the face of death so near in my daily ministrations and almost feel its icy breath.

#### II

When my time comes everything and everywhere around me will echo that " responsum mortis " of which St. Paul speaks. God forbid that I should be the only one deaf to its challenge!

Let us picture the scene. The priest comes to hear your last confession; the tinkling bell heralds your Viaticum; then follow the Last Anointings, the prayers for the recommendation of the soul, and the low mumblings, drawn faces, and silent tears of relatives and friends standing round your bed—if indeed there is anyone at all to weep your departure! Your whole body is in a cold sweat, there is a gradual stiffening of your features, a twitching of your rigid fingers as if trying to clutch at something, the cold impression of the crucifix on your livid half-open lips; and the shadows of death crowd upon you thicker and thicker, and your eyes acquire that fixed look as if pursuing sights that vanish from you. . . .

My Lord and Saviour Jesus Christ, who for love of me didst submit to the anguish of dying, do not fail me Thou when everything and everyone else forsakes me!

## III

At long last your soul will quit the body, leaving it a repulsive heap of lifeless matter.

The bells you so often heard toll or had tolled for others will now toll for you. The funeral service that you so often chanted for others is now to be chanted for you. And there will be a burial, your very own; and the officiating priest, while your body sinks into the earth, will seal your disappearance from this world with a last supplication wherein you will lose even your name:

> *Anima ejus et animae omnium fidelium defunc-torum,*
>
> *per misericordiam Dei requiescant in pace. Amen.*

And then, what will this world have to offer you?

What will become of those material goods that you seemed to have fused with your inmost soul, so deeply had you buried them within your heart's affections? Your name will be struck off all the lists of the living; your benefice, office, money, titles, every one of them will be handed over to another; and people will be quite indifferent and oblivious; they are used to these irrevocable resignations!

If you think the consideration of these incidents is of some avail to you for the prudent steering of your life and spirit, turn them over in your mind frequently; if you consider them useless, throw them overboard, bury them fathoms deep: century after century has stood witness to men whose one code is:

> Let us eat and drink and be merry for to-morrow we shall die.—(*Is. xxii*, 13.)

## RESOLUTION

I shall often take as subject of my daily meditation my own death, a future but inescapable fact; and I shall run through, one by one, all the probable circumstances that are apt to impress me the most.

Now I see why the remembrance of the Last Things, of death in particular, has been of such little value to me, in spite of the well-known text:

> Remember thy last end and thou shalt never sin.

It is because I have thought of death in the abstract or as applied to someone else. So from now I shall come to grips with the thought of my own death, and I shall take this bitter thought as a leash to my unbridled passions.

# DEATH

## SECOND MEDITATION

### *Its Uncertainties*

#### I

What thoughts have you at the back of your mind
concerning your death? If you voiced them honestly
perhaps you would say something like this:

"Yes, of course, I'll die one day, but I'm no less
convinced that I have many a long and happy year
before me yet. A ripe old age already? I'll get riper
still. All aches and pains? Oh, I'll get better or at
least some relief; if not, I'll jog along somehow.
Other men younger and healthier than myself may
die soon and perhaps go off in a flash? Now, why
should that bother me and rob me of my sleep?
I feel so sure of myself that I might even say with
the rich hoarder of the Gospel: *Soul, thou hast
much goods laid up for many years. Take thy
rest: eat, drink, make good cheer. (Luke xii, 19.)*
Moreover, when at long last my hour does come I
shall have time enough and to spare for preparing
myself; I shall sight death approaching from afar;
its coming will be that of a placid summer evening,
not like a squall. Yes, I shall have ample time to
get myself ready to die the death of the just."

Honestly, now, could you swear that your imagination never plays this trick on you? Doesn't it amount
to a firm conviction? Or, at least, don't you lead a life
that argues this conviction?

## II

We base our convictions on reasons, and the solider the reasons the firmer the conviction. So let us see the reasons for this intimate conviction as to the manner of your death.

Experience? Stretch your imagination, muster around you all those acquaintances of yours who have died: parents, brothers and sisters, relations, classmates. . . . How many came by that distant and tranquil fading out of their earthly existence which you allot yourself so convincingly?

Call to mind your fellow-priests who have given to Christ an account of their stewardship. How many arrived at that long-delayed and peaceful death which you seem to be so sure of?

Or will you have the exclusive privilege of saying with the evil-doers quoted by Isaias the prophet:

> We have entered into a league with death, and we have made a covenant with hell?—(*Is. xxviii,* 15.)

## III

Is the Faith your pledge and security? The Faith! Through the mouth of the same prophet God answers you:

> And your league with death shall be abolished, and your covenant with hell shall not stand.— (*id.* 18.)

The Faith! Read the Gospels. In two long chapters —the 24th and 25th according to St. Matthew—our Saviour's final preaching is devoted to teaching us by facts, by parables, by concise and shattering phrases, the truth contained in the following words:

Ye know not at what hour your Lord will come. At what hour ye know not the Son of Man will come.

And speaking in particular about His evil ministers who say in their hearts: *my Lord is long a coming,* and begin to show themselves unmerciful towards their neighbour, and indulge in lustful pleasure, Christ swears by all that He is, on His word of a God, that

The Lord of that servant shall come in a day he hopeth not, and at an hour that he knoweth not.

Neither the day nor even the hour!

Therefore, your convictions are diametrically opposed to the lessons of experience and—what is still more tragic—the solemn warning of Christ. Who is right?

O my Jesus, how clearly I see that the root and origin of my unpriestly life was that stupid confidence of the wicked servant! *My Lord is long a coming.*

## RESOLUTIONS

1. I shall struggle with myself until I destroy that false sense of security, that conviction of living many a long year and of dying the death of a saint, which has no other support than the tenacious instinct of self-preservation.

2. I shall often meditate upon the fatal uncertainties surrounding my last hour, and I shall implore my Lord Jesus Christ to grant me an intimate conviction of the truth of His teachings on this point. Lord, let my mind and my very heart voice the certitude underlying Thy words: *Heaven and earth shall pass away, but my Words shall not pass away!* (Matt. xxiv, 25.)

3. Convinced that Thou canst come any day, at any moment, I shall always be on the alert, my lamp

trimmed, lest the Bridegroom of souls should close on me the door of His everlasting dwellings.

*Vigilate! Et vos estote parati!*

# DEATH

### THIRD MEDITATION

## *Preparing for Death*

### I

Of all beings that live and die only man is capable of looking death in the face and of preparing to receive it long before it comes. He thinks of it; he knows for a certainty that it will come; he expects it, although usually as an unwelcome guest; he passes in review, perhaps, each of the painful impressions which its cold grip will imprint on his spirit and his flesh; he can even foretaste and relish it, with the deliberateness and courage of a long-suffering invalid relishing a bitter medicinal draught.

Has God given us this faculty of foresight merely to torment us and embitter our existence? By no means. Then let us receive it as a useful gift from God, as a stimulant to keep us ever on the watch, ready to accord our Judge a fitting welcome.

### II

In the exercise of your ministry take note; you will observe that the general rule is for people to die as they have lived. There is a terrifying exactitude in the phrase attributed to St. Jerome: " Qualis vita, finis ita." In other words: few equip themselves for the final hour by a special and immediate preparation.

There are some who die a sudden death: the bait is swallowed when least feared; and, according to the daily witness of experience, it is not the priestly category that contributes the smallest of quotas to these sad statistics. Others, the majority, die unexpectedly, because no one warns them of the danger, or rather, because people are all for hiding the danger from them: a diabolical conspiracy hatched round the dying to cast them defenceless and prematurely at the feet of Divine Justice. And there are souls with such an iron grasp on the things of earth that even if the Prophet Isaias were to come himself and warn them in the Lord's Name— *thou shalt die and shalt not live (Is. xxxviii, 1)*—they would disbelieve him and continue to stake their all on the slenderest hope of a fictitious recovery.

Lord, everything indeed conspires to underline the truth of Thy words:

At what hour you know not, the Son of Man will come.

To which of these three classes of people do I belong? Which is my preference? My God, I prefer to take orders from Thee: *Be ready.*

### III

Listen to St. Paul:

" The Son who sanctifies and the sons who are sanctified have a common origin, all of them; He is not ashamed, then, to own them as His brethren. . . .

And since these children have a common inheritance of flesh and blood, He, too, shared that inheritance with them.

By His death He would depose the prince of death, that is, the devil; He would deliver those multitudes who lived all the while as slaves, made over to the fear of death."—(*Hebrews ii, 11-15.*)

The devil was the prince of death, because by sin and death mankind had fallen under his dominion and into his possession; until Christ, by the merits of His own death, destroyed the devil's title of dominion and possession, and brought deliverance.

Before the death of Christ, to die was seemingly to fall into nothingness, or, at least, to lose the body for ever, the spirit to grope its way through shadows of the unknown. Christ expelled those shadows with His light, and because good Christians now belong to Christ, not to the devil, they are Christ's *to live and to die with Him;* and therefore, death opens up to them on their departure from this life prospects of unalloyed happiness.

Lord, let me not live like the heathen, a slave to death. Allow me to pluck from the Tree of Thy Cross this luscious fruit: joyful confidence and constant readiness in preparation for my death.


## RESOLUTION

I am going to apply to myself the fruits of the Redemption continually, by faith, love, and flight from sin; and should I fall at any time, I shall rise immediately with an act of contrition and the reception of the Sacrament of Penance. Thus, through Christ's death, I shall live, live all my days not a slave to the fear of ending them badly, but free and assured of my eternal salvation.

# THE PRIEST'S PARTICULAR JUDGEMENT

## FIRST MEDITATION

### *The Stark Reality*

### I

The fruit of all bad government, and even its efficient cause, is impunity: allowing the delinquent to go unpunished.

We have seen it these days in several countries: systematic robbery, assassinations, criminal gangs stalking through the busy thoroughfares of big cities in broad daylight.

Why? The governing authority was afraid of the criminal, who had become lord and master of judges and tribunals; the executive power was intimidated, its sanctions were inadequate or were not put into force.

Now, if God really exists; if it is true, according to the Book of Wisdom, that " Thy Providence, O Father, governeth " (*xiv*, 3); if God wields effective dominion over His free-willed creatures; then He cannot consent to impunity without being a bad ruler.

So I must make no mistake about it: in God there is Justice; in His Judgements there is righteousness; and one day He will call every one of us to account.

### II

A lively faith in the Divine Judgement is an absolute necessity for persevering in good or for rising up from evil. To doubt God's Judgement or to deny its existence

97

is a *carte-blanche* for every misdemeanour and disorder.

Early in the path of his straying the sinner stumbles against the temptation, against a kind of psychological need, to deny roundly or to call in question or to ignore the Divine Judgement.

How frequent and significant the texts of Holy Scripture recording this temptation!

> And they said: How doth God know? And is there knowledge in the Most High?—(*Ps. lxxii*, 11.)

> And thou sayest: What doth God know? And He judgeth as it were through a mist. The clouds are His covert, and He doth not consider our things; and He walketh about the poles of heaven. —(*Job xxii*, 13-14.)

> And they have said: The Lord shall not see: neither shall the God of Jacob understand.— (*Ps. xciii*, 7.)

And these cries of a bad conscience have resounded in the hearts of unbelievers throughout the ages. Have they ever been heard in mine?

### III

Is a temptation of this nature unlikely in a priest? If he should surrender to the tyranny of concupiscence he would feel it sooner than anyone else, for the simple reason that he has to struggle against a better-enlightened conscience and against a more continual reminder of God's Judgement; therefore, either the fear of God will win him over to the bridling of his passions, or, if he continues to sin, he will end up by silencing all fear of the Judgement, smothering it or denying its very existence.

And they perverted their own mind and turned away their eyes that they might not look unto heaven nor remember just judgements.—(*Dan. xiii, 9.*)

Do not these words apply to the bad priest?

On the other hand, a lively faith in this great truth would leave in us the same impression that was left in St. Augustine, who tells us:

"Nothing called me back from the deep abyss of carnal pleasures except the fear of death and of Thy Judgements, which never wholly departed from my breast."—(*Confessions vi, 16.*)

## RESOLUTIONS

1. I shall dread sin, especially sins of the flesh which, according to St. Thomas, cause faith to grow cold or to be lost.

2. I shall repeat acts of faith in the dogma of the Judgements to come, particularly when I fall into grievous sin.

3. I shall meditate frequently and deeply on this Last Thing, keeping in mind the fact that it is coming to me: *instat dies Domini.*

# THE PRIEST'S PARTICULAR JUDGEMENT

## SECOND MEDITATION

### *Preliminaries*

#### I

"All of us have a scrutiny to undergo before Christ's judgement-seat, for each to reap what his mortal life has earned, good or ill, according to his deeds."—(II *Cor. v*, 10.)

Not even St. Paul, who ventured to say "we shall sit in judgement on angels" (I *Cor. vi*, 3), considered himself exempt from this all-embracing assessment of his life's free acts.

The very Mother of God herself was not exempt! Free from all stain of sin, original and actual, free from the loss of maidenhood even when she became a Mother, but not free from being weighed in the Divine Balance. Shall I be more privileged?

Lord, I believe that one day, perhaps quite soon, Thou wilt come to judge my life; so I shall take to heart the words of The Preacher:

> Fear God, and keep his commandments: for this is all man:
>
> And all things that are done, God will bring into judgement for every error, whether it be good or evil.—(*Ecclesiastes xii*, 13-14.)

## II

My soul will leave the body; all its immense energies, dispersed until then among an endless number of creatures and over the boundless realm of its dreams and illusions, drained through each bodily sense and organ, will be gathered together and concentrated within itself, within their fountainhead and reservoir. Like flocks of birds overtaken by the night, they will home to the roost. These scattered energies will blend into one great yearning: to see God, to possess Him, to enjoy Him, the last remaining Good, the One Source where the soul can quench its burning thirst for eternal happiness.

And thus my soul, alone—"*tacita per umbras*"—silent through the shadows, with no companion but that unquenchable yearning, with no possessions but its good or evil deeds, will start journeying through the regions of its immortality. It will hardly have taken the first steps when it beholds the dreaded Judge face to face, who will say: "I am Jesus, and I come to ask thee for an account of thy stewardship, for thou canst be steward no longer."

## III

*Ego sum Jesus.* How shall we transcribe this first confronting of the Redeemer with the soul of the unworthy priest?

"I am Jesus: no longer the Crucified Jesus whom people, including His own ministers, were free to discuss, to insult, or disdainfully to ignore like a god of straw; no more the Jesus of the Tabernacle, silent, reserved, hidden beneath the meagre appearances of bread. Year in and year out thou didst bandy Me hither and thither, treating Me with discourtesy and irreverence and thoughtlessness such as no equal of thine would have tolerated, treating Me with every kind of profanation and sacrilege. And from My hiding beneath the Sacramental Species I said nothing, not a murmur of complaint, not a sob or sigh came from My lips; nor even on My cheeks didst thou surmise the flush of shame; nor didst thou feel the quick beating of My sorrowing heart, as Judas did in the Garden.

"Such great forbearance belongs to the past; for

I have rent My Sacramental vesture, wrenched the nails from My hands and feet. See here! The crown of thorns is become the Crown of the Lord and Eternal King, the purple of My Blood is My mantle of infinite Majesty; the Cross is transformed into My throne of Power and Glory; the long-drawn-out silence of My Patience has changed to overwhelming Indignation; and I come to thee, not to suffer thee, not to have compassion, not to forgive: I come to judge thee. *I am Jesus!*"

## RESOLUTION

I shall think more often of Christ, Judge of living and dead, surrounded with pomp and splendour, as He is portrayed in the ancient prophecies and the Gospels, so that my love for Him may blend with a healthy and chastening fear as well as with confidence. I need this fear as a breakwater to my tidal waves of passion.

Oh if only I could strike the rock of my heart until there sprang instinctively to my lips these cries of the *Dies irae*!

> Quid sum miser tunc dicturus?
> Quem patronum rogaturus,
> Cum vix justus sit securus?

# THE PRIEST'S PARTICULAR JUDGEMENT

### THIRD MEDITATION

### *The Process*

### I

Jesus comes to render to me according to my works. There He is on the Judgement-seat to pronounce irrevocable sentence, to declare my eternal destiny. The Books are opened: the Book of my own conscience and the Book of God's Providence. The Lamb of God breaks the seals of my conscience, seals which my pride and fear had kept tightly bound. The mists of my mortality which had obscured the reading of my conscience—if indeed I ever took the trouble to read it —are swept away by the Light of His Divine Countenance. And the Book of God's Providence reveals every movement of my free-will; for every letter in the Book was written down and stereotyped at the moment of each of my decisions.

I am going to know myself, at last. And with what confusion! No self-deception, no allowances, no false colours. I shall have to look into myself and judge myself more mercilessly than would my bitterest enemy. I shall see fulfilled in me the request voiced by St. Augustine: *Domine, noverim me!* Lord, may I know myself!

Jesus, the thought of that moment fills me with dread.

## II

The account-books of my stewardship are opened before my eyes, and my *Debits, Credits,* and *Deficit* are shown to me.

*Debits.* God's benefits to me: my sublime priestly dignity, so purely a gift, so little appreciated; the ocean of graces in which the Lord immersed my existence and my ministry. Yes, Christ could also weep for me and say:

> If thou hadst also known and that in this, thy day, the things that are to thy peace.—(*Luke xix,* 42.)

*Credits.* My niggardly returns: my good works—if I

had any—so worm-eaten with defects, so hollow and devoid of right intention; my abuse of holy things, my profanation of the Sacraments, my dissipated life, my deeds perhaps infamous and sacrilegious, the hidden dregs of my sensual complacencies and lewd desires My God! If in the sight of my fellow men Thou were to draw aside the veil and expose all this, I should die of shame; what shall I do or say in Thy august Presence? *Quid sum miser tunc dicturus?*

*Deficit:* ineffable benefits corresponded to with monstrous disloyalty and rebellion; the ten thousand talents of the insolvent servant. . . . If only I could throw myself at Christ's feet and soothe His Anger with the plea: *Have patience with me . . . !*

### III

If *there* my accounts are not in order, I shall have only one possible escape: to cast myself away from Christ for ever, into the regions of eternal malediction. *Depart from me, ye cursed.*

> Dilexit maledictionem et veniet ei,
> et induit eum sicut vestimentum,
> et intravit sicut aqua in interiora ejus,
> et sicut oleum in ossibus ejus..—(*Ps. cviii*, 18.)

" Cursing shall wrap him about, sink like water into his inmost being, soak, like oil, into the marrow of his bones."

I shall balance my accounts with my eternal damnation; I, a priest appointed to bless others, even Christ Himself, shall be for all eternity . . . a *curse!*

> Unto whomsoever much is given, of him much shall be required.—(*Luke xii*, 48.)

A most severe judgement shall be for them that bear rule.—(*Wisdom vi*, 6.)

And if over souls, and over Christ Himself, I bear rule, how do I bear it? At my own whim and fancy, perhaps, in imitation of Pilate's arrogance towards Christ:

> Knowest thou not that I have power to do with thee what I will?

Have I not the power to make Christ descend upon the altar, to ill-treat Him, to imprison Him, to cast Him out? . . .

A most severe judgement shall be for them that bear rule.

## RESOLUTION

Now is the time to soften the Judge's Heart, to make Him merciful towards me.

I shall be an inexorable judge of my own cause: I shall sound the depths of my soul, bringing my iniquities to the light of my conscious mind, acknowledging them for what they are, lamenting them as they deserve; I shall stir my heart to repentance, and accuse myself to God's minister, whose power is solely to forgive.

I shall do this at least once a week, making my confession with the proper dispositions.

Grant me, O Jesus, the strength of will to carry out this resolution.

# HELL

## FIRST MEDITATION

### *Hell really does Exist*

### I

Reason can lead us to the threshold of this terrible mystery. The human soul, being of its nature immortal, is capable of everlasting reward or punishment. Having left the body, it is no longer "in via", and the good or evil accruing from past deeds changes from act or habit to a state of permanency. Death is a kind of photographic "fixing bath" of the soul; grace or guilt are engraved upon the conscience ineffaceably; and the soul would more easily be smashed to atoms than forfeit the imprint of virtue or vice with which it left this mortal life. Having lost its former flexibility for good or evil, the soul harbours within its deepest depths and throughout its being those supernatural or perverse qualities of which it was found possessed at the hour of death. Beyond this life souls do not change their moral status; the eternal renders them unchangeable.

My soul, wouldst thou be for ever and ever what thou art to-day?

### II

But human reason has eyes too weak for the contemplation and scrutiny of the eternal, so let the Faith, let God, speak.

Wouldn't it be an absurdity, a scandal, sheer madness,

for Christ to have died merely to obtain for us temporal goods, or to deliver us from transitory evils?

A human life united personally, substantially, to the Divine Word, and therefore, the Life of a God; a life more precious than all creation; a life prized at the infinite value of the Godhead; such a life could reasonably be spent only to avert an evil that is, in some sense, also infinite; it could be given in ransom only to purchase a glory that is boundless and unending.

O Lord! Thy Divine Blood, so cheaply spilt along the path of the sinful children of Adam, trampled underfoot " sicut stercus in via " by every passer-by; O Lord! Thy Body shattered and nailed to the wood of the Cross, like a captured bird of prey to the lintel of a farmhouse door; O Lord! Thy holy Cross is for my reason and even for my finer sensibilities the unanswerable argument, that for the obstinate sinner there await eternal torments . . .

### III

Not for a moment throughout the long life of the Church will you find this dogma of Hell unaccepted or unwitnessed to by the Church and all her children: Oecumenical Councils and local Synods, the Fathers, ecclesiastical writers, the Symbols of the Faith, the arts and letters; they all bear witness to belief in Hell, with a steadfast, unswerving conviction, notwithstanding the dread and terror this belief inspires. It is in every age a leash on which the Church keeps her children subject to the fear of God, even in the midst of soft, corrupt, and hostile civilisations. Shall I deny that unchallengeable fact?

My God, it is only by wrenching myself away from

this Holy Mother's loving bosom where, as in a downy nest, Thou didst lay me almost as soon as I came into the world, that I could possibly deny or even call in question the existence of that appallingly mysterious "Second Death", the name given to eternal damnation by the Beloved Disciple. I believe it, Lord, and I confess it; *aid Thou my unbelief.*

## IV

But, . . . is there any dogma of our Faith recorded in the New Testament more fully and in terms more peremptory than that of Hell?

St. John, in the Apocalypse, makes frequent mention of *the pool of fire, which is the second death,* where the enemies of God and of the Lamb will finally be cast. In accents of ancient prophecy St. Jude speaks to us, in his Canonical Epistle, of sinners who are like "*fierce waves of the sea, with shame for their crests; wandering stars, with eternal darkness and storm awaiting them*".— (*Jude,* 13.) And St. Paul assures the Thessalonians that Christ will avenge Himself on evil-doers by condemning them to eternal punishment. (*cfr. II Thess. i.*)

How God longs for me to meditate upon His eternal chastisements! For He knows my heart so well! Like the sea: calm and beautiful at caress of dawn, rippled by the gentle breeze, held in check by the sandy shore; but in the evening, how it swells and hurls its billows with thunderous roar against the strand! What havoc, if uncontained by strong resisting jetties and breakwaters!

## V

It would take many a sheet merely to copy out from the New Testament what Christ, our Lord and God, has told us of Hell's torments and of their endless duration. Over fifteen times He deals with Hell either explicitly or by implication: He speaks of "*eternal torment*", "*everlasting fire*", "*the worm that dies not*", "*the great gulf fixed between*", "*weeping and gnashing of teeth*" . . .

So I must choose: either confess that there is indeed an endless punishment which I can incur, and incur soon if I offend God grievously; or, if I deny its existence, I must jettison all my faith as so much useless ballast, disbelieve in Christ, and even account Him a common quack or a victim to delusion. Shall I dare to choose the latter?

Jesus: until I come across another Master better qualified to teach than Thou, of longer standing, of greater power in word and deed, whose life is more admirable in virtue, whose wisdom shines more resplendently; I abide, dear Lord, by Thy divine teachings. And when I look into the lives and teachings of those who deny this great truth I find them, Lord, so manifestly inferior to Thine in every way, that they merely serve to clinch the argument in favour of following Thee alone.

## Resolution

Since fight I must—*militia est vita hominis*—instead of squandering my energies trying to swim against the tide of eternal Truth, I shall struggle with the buffeting waves of my own passions, which, however strong, are more easily overcome than the infallible word of God: *Verbum Domini manet in aeternum*. (*Is. xl*, 8.)

I shall fight particularly against lust, nearly always the seat of unbelief and apostasy.

# HELL

## A Priest can be Damned

### I

The Church has always believed that Her priests, from the highest members of the Hierarchy to the lowest, can incur eternal damnation. That explains why in Her literature and in the pictorial and sculptural arts She has always allowed Her ministers to be portrayed within the dwellings of everlasting woe. Go through Her cathedrals and most sumptuous churches, examine retables and tapestries, and the miniatures and illuminations in the old liturgical books; turn over the pages of the most famous literary works of Christendom in bygone centuries; perhaps it will scandalise you to see the boldness and frequency with which artists and writers develop, with a realism now obsolete, the theme of the priest, of the religious, of the prelate or pope, plunged into the eternal abyss. And the Church not only keeps silent, not merely refrains from strictures and censure; She arrays Herself in these works of art as in rich attire, and She exposes them to the eyes of the faithful and of the whole world.

Would She conduct Herself thus were She not infallibly certain that Her own ministers can also die the " second death "?

What support could I find for persuading myself of the contrary?

## II

Unprotestingly She has allowed the greatest boldness of speech from those very champions whom She honours with the title of Fathers of the Church, and Saints.

What priest has not winced under the well-known text from St. John Chrysostom?—

> "I speak not with rashness, but what I feel and mean: among priests, I reckon that not many will be saved, but many more perish, not so much on account of their own sins as for the sins of others, which they have not put a remedy to."

We may not be all aware that such a hair-raising statement was written for Prelates; as will be obvious to anyone reading the third Homily "In Actibus Apostolorum", in particular the paragraph headed in every edition of Migne's Patrology by the title: *Episcopi Officium*. (Migne. St. John Chrysostom, vols. viii-ix, p. 59.)

Still more daring is the opinion voiced by St. Vincent Ferrer:

> "There are nine heavens through which the nine Choirs of Angels are distributed, and with them the elect, according to their merits and their calling in life. The sixth heaven is that of the Dominations. It is the place for those who wield human authority: emperors, kings, rulers, and the governors of states; Authorities that ruled justly and whose rule rested on legitimate claims. . . .

> "The same applies to Prelates who entered in by the door, and, when inside, first mastered themselves properly . . . and were more solicitous about souls than about their emoluments. When such as

these come to die they are placed in this sixth order, to the accompaniment of great honours. When they pass through the different Choirs of Angels, Archangels, etc., in each one there is a great festivity. The Angels say: 'Let us make a great feast, because it is so many years since any one of these came through here' . . ." (*Sermo iii, De Omnibus Sanctis.*)

What security shall I find in my priesthood if, according to these Saints, those in high places run such risks?

The conclusion is obvious: God will not save me for being a priest, but for being a good one.

### III

Fear of the eternal torments makes St. Paul exclaim:

"I do not fight my battle like a man who wastes his blows on the air.

"I buffet my own body, and make it my slave; or I, who have preached to others, may myself be rejected as worthless."—(*I Cor. ix*, 26-27.)

In the bitter struggles of flesh against spirit, the spirit trying to subdue and master the flesh, in that glorious but costly achievement, the Apostle of the Gentiles recognises the fear of eternal reprobation as his main driving-force. And he applies to himself the warning he gives to others:

"You must work to earn your salvation, in anxious fear."—(*Philip ii*, 12.)

That was St. Paul, the man rapt to the third heaven; the man who swears there is no power in heaven, on earth, or under the earth, that can prevail to wrench him away from the love of Christ!

No wonder: it was the Divine Master Himself who gave that lesson to all the Apostles:

> And I say to you, my friends (*a friendly warning*)
> Be not afraid of them who kill the body, and after
> have no more power that they can do.

He tells them to fear neither the sword that sunders the flesh, nor the wild beast that can crush their bones, nor the fire that can bite into the entrails and devour them; because none of this can reach the sanctuary of the soul.

> But I will show you whom you shall fear; fear
> ye him who, after he hath killed, hath power to cast
> into hell. Yea, I say to you: fear him—(*Luke xii,
> 4-5.*)

And those Apostles: Peter, the Prince of the Apostles, John the beloved disciple, etc., so loving, so enamoured of their Master, so docile to every one of His teachings, especially to those given them in confidence, as friends; throughout their lives they feared and trembled for their eternal salvation; they feared those everlasting pains so graphically described by Jesus Christ.

O Jesus, wilt Thou care more for me, as a priest, than for Peter and Paul and John? Is my dignity greater than theirs? Have I laboured and suffered for Thee more than they? Am I better and holier? Then why do I not fear to damn my soul, as they so feared? Could not my scant fear betoken reprobation?

## IV

That I, a priest, can lose my soul, Thou hast no need, Lord, to warn me: this bitter reminder I read in the depths of my being every day and many times a day; so evident it is.

In peril of condemnation is he who lives in danger of committing sin, and between sin and myself there is, to borrow David's expression, only the faintest line of separation; we are but a hair's breadth apart: *uno gradu dividimur.*

I trust that at present I am in the grace of God, but within a short while perhaps my passions, roused suddenly, will drive me to the edge of the precipice, or hurl me to the bottom of the abyss, of grievous sin, and leave me there naked to the lightnings of the Divine Wrath.

And how appallingly easy it is to contract a vicious habit! Three or four sinful acts, done with the gathering strength of passion's grip on the forbidden fruit, will suffice. And with the habit formed, with lapse after lapse, ah! I know only too well what happens: conversion seems impossible (nothing is impossible for God's grace!): neither my own reflections nor the warning from another's downfall nor the Sacrament of Penance nor even a spiritual retreat will avail to draw from my soul the poisoned shafts of vice. And when my last hour is come, my iniquities will be sealed by final impenitence. And eternally guilty, eternally I shall be punished.

## RESOLUTION

If I have contracted any vicious habit, to fight against it with all my strength and with all God's strength until I have rooted it out. If, by God's Mercy, I am free from so terrible a spiritual disease, to avoid every grievous sin. And in both cases, besides fleeing from the occasions of sin, to make frequent use of Confession preceded by a careful preparation.

This may put me to some inconvenience, but never to anything comparable to the pains of hell from which I thus escape. No pain too great if it spare me the pains that endure for ever!

# HELL

### THIRD MEDITATION

## *The Priest in Hell*

### I

How sad must be the ceremony of Degradation of a delinquent priest, when the rubrics of the Roman Pontifical are carried out with full solemnity!

The Bishop sits outside the church on a raised platform where he can be easily seen by all. He gathers round him his Church ministers, and also the secular Judge to whom the degraded priest is to be handed over. And the culprit is there, vested in the ornaments of his particular rank and status: bishop, priest, etc., but when the sentence of Degradation has been read the officiating Prelate strips him of the ornaments one by one:

"I take this mitre from thy head because thou hast profaned it, presiding unworthily."

"I pluck this ring from thee, the pledge of fidelity, because thou hast violated the Church, God's Spouse."

"We scrape and wipe the consecration from thy hands . . ."

And the culprit is handed over to the State to be dealt with like any ordinary criminal.

If I were a bad priest, what shame for me when Christ will strip my soul of all my priestly prerogatives and hand me over denuded of all good and love of God to the executioner of Hell, there to be tormented like any sinner, like the apostate, murderer . . .!

## II

It would not be so terrible if Christ, in degrading and condemning me, were to obliterate every trace of my priesthood, and I became in Hell just one among the many. But no, not even in Hell shall I lose my indelible Character of a priest; on the contrary, my priesthood will mark me out for recognition by the other damned, by the torturing demons, and by the very flames of Hell. Oh, the eternal hissing of all Hell on the hypocrisy and hideous crimes that dragged me down to that place of torment and abjection, down to that " sewer of the human race " (St. Thomas); crimes that in life I tried to cloak in priestly garb, in mumbled recitations, in a paraded semblance of virtue!

Not even among the infernal flames shall I be denied my pride of place, my coveted rights and privileges! I, a priest, higher and nobler in rank than any earthly monarch, shall stand pre-eminent in torment and ignominy, the bait of the biting tongues of all the damned.

The mighty shall be mightily tormented.— (*Wisdom vi, 7.*)

## III

Besides the pains common to all the eternally dis-inherited of the Heavenly Father : the pain of everlasting separation from God, the soul's supreme and only Good; the fire that is never quenched; the gnawing worm of conscience, deathless like the soul itself, ever fretting and consuming; the endless gnashing of teeth in blank despair; the weeping that continues unabated; besides these general pains there awaits the priest his own personal torture: the shame of being the butt of scorn to all Hell.

If the evil cunning of sinners remains rooted in them by death; if the lost soul so identifies itself with sin that it becomes, as it were, sin-made-man; if even here on earth the enemies of God and of His Church are so scathing in their epigrams of scorn and contempt hurled against the Catholic priest; what will they not invent, for all eternity, by way of insults with which to revenge themselves in some measure upon Almighty God in the person of His one-time minister?

Were we to gather the whole sweep of shameless calumnies and denigrating affronts that twenty centuries have heaped upon the head of the priest, what a library they would form!

All that, and more, and for all eternity, the condemned priest will have to bear from the infernal mouths of those confirmed in evil, like him, and embittered by their endless life of woe.

## IV

To allow the thought of this torment to sink still deeper, let us take a few verses from chapter xiv of the prophecy of Isaias, and let us apply them to the condemned priest in Hell. The passage we quote speaks primarily of the death of the King of Babylon, and it constitutes one of the sublimest passages written by the great Prophet:

> "The shadow world beneath is astir with preparation for thy coming; wakes up its giants to greet thee.

> "The great ones of the world, that ruled the nations, rise up from the thrones where they sit, hailing thee with a single voice:

> "'Thou too, in the same case as we, thou, too, like us!

> "'All thy pride sunk down into the world beneath. . . .

> "'What, fallen from heaven, thou Lucifer, that once didst herald the dawn?

> "'Who sees thee there, but will peer down at thee and read thy story . . .?'"—(*Is. xiv.*)

Is this the man who, with his preaching on the eternal truths, made us wince with fear? he who troubled and disquieted us in our sins, threatening with eternal punishment from God? he whose very garb was a reproach to us? he who was accounted holy, the undisputed representative of virtue? And now, his pride is sunk down to Hell; now, the mask that hid his face is torn away, and he is seen as criminal as the rest of us: "*he, too, like us!*"

If in this world my self-love can barely suffer the

slightest indication of a sneer, and feels the greatest
reluctance to confessing my sins to a fellow priest, what
will my feelings be in Hell? What shall I have to say
*then*?

I, who am so avid and eager for human happiness,
even for a few drops of forbidden sweetness and contra-
band pleasure; I, so addicted to the fugitive and secret
gratifications arising from sin; I shall have, in Hell, not
just a few moments, as on earth, but all eternity—the
Scriptural *aeternum et ultra*—in which to relish con-
tinuously my supreme unhappiness, my ever-enduring
infamy, the ceaseless gall and wormwood of remorse.

Is the pleasure which such-and-such a passion
procures me, and whose slave I am, so great, of such
sterling worth, that it should be bought at such a cost?
St. Bernard pertinently asks:

> "If you could enjoy for a month all the good
> things and pleasures of this world on condition that
> when they came to an end you would have your
> eyes gouged out, you would be plunged into a
> dark, infectious dungeon, and you would live there
> for forty years, steeped in all kinds of miseries;
> would you choose the enjoyment?"

Dear God, no, I do not wish to purchase a moment-
ary pleasure at the cost of eternal suffering.

## RESOLUTION

I shall often meditate on the pains in store for me if I
end up in Hell, especially when I am assaulted by the
tumult of the flesh. The thought of the eternal flames
will serve to cool down the ardours of lust. But also
when I am in affliction I shall console myself thinking

how often I have deserved to be cast into the *pool of fire*. Great beyond all measure is God's Mercy in commuting to me the penalty of endless torment for the brief pangs of this life; sharp and prolonged as these may appear, they will finally pass away.

# PURGATORY

*Existence and Nature of Purgatory*

## I

*Existence.*—" If anyone shall assert that every sinner who has received the grace of justification has his guilt forgiven and the debt of eternal punishment cancelled in such a manner that there remains no debt of temporal punishment to be paid either in this world or in Purgatory in the next, before he can enter the Kingdom of Heaven, let him be anathema."—(*Council of Trent, Session vi, canon* 30.)

I have sinned and sinned again. God, I trust, has deleted the stains from my soul through the Sacrament of Penance, and has condoned me the eternal punishment. But do I qualify for the ranks of those penitents whose sorrow for sin was so deep and intense that it cancelled all debt towards God, down to the last farthing? Does not the very facility with which I have relapsed testify to the contrary? Every grave sin of mine, therefore, has deposited a sediment which only suffering will wash away. And if to forgiven mortal sins I add my routine venial faults, surely there must needs await me, either in this life or in the next, a full flood of cleansing grief.

And yet, dear Lord, no sooner did real or imaginary suffering begin to afflict me than I asked in my own mind whether God was not lacking in justice, or excessive in chastising.

## II

*Duration.*—If I enter Purgatory I shall not leave it until all scores have been paid off, down to the last farthing; until Purgatory's fires and torments have cleansed me from every stain of rust adhering to the chains of my mortality, and effaced the ignoble imprint of creatures, which undue attachment left upon me.

How long will that total purification take? Surely very long indeed, if I consider, on the one hand, God's astounding readiness in forgiving me my innumerable and detestable sins; and, on the other hand, the meagre penance I have done and my trivial sorrow for having sinned.

The fact is that the Church holds Requiems for souls departed from this world centuries ago, and admits Foundation Masses in perpetuity. She therefore believes it possible that there are souls submerged within those expiatory flames for a duration that we on earth might measure in terms of hundreds of years.

Just try to think of it! After this life of sorrows there may be a still longer one in store for me—twenty, fifty, a hundred or more years of intense suffering! The mere possibility should fill me with dread. And during all this time I shall be prevented from reaching eternal bliss by the fetters of past forgiven but unatoned-for sin, because of my indolence, or on account of those venial short-comings which I now make so light of or even brazenly despise.

## III

*Pain of Loss.*—If the pain of loss is Hell's direst affliction, much more is it Purgatory's.

In Purgatory God will be my sole attraction. Lit up

already by rays of the Divine Love, I shall know, with
a clarity surpassing any previous realisation I had in this
vale of cloud and mirage, how immense, how ineffable
the happiness is which awaits me, and which is already
mine by right of conquest—*the crown of justice which
the Lord the just Judge will render to me.*

Happiness, eternal happiness, glorious goal of all my
endeavours, of all my yearnings; ever-flowing fountain,
City of God, enriched with flowing waters—*fluminis
impetus qui laetificat civitatem Dei* (Ps. xlv, 5)—where
my thirst for happiness will be slaked; ah! but the Hand
of Divine Justice will keep those waters from reaching
my lips for twenty, fifty, or more years! What a terrible
torture! Tantalus is child's play, in comparison. I see
the beckoning shores, the long-desired harbour, of the
Fatherland; I almost touch them; but the boat, dressed
and triumphant from the storms of earthly life, is held
at anchor: the child is withheld from its Father's and
Mother's fond embrace; the invalid, infected and
unclean, is kept in isolation until the immortal vesture
of the spirit is rid of every stain and germ of disease by
the consuming flames.

What agony, to spend years and years with eternal
bliss in sight, with an ever-burning thirst for it, and
yet to be hindered from its possession!

## IV

*Pains of sense.*—What are they? What names shall
we give them? Will there be fire? With all our discus-
sions, there is nothing we know for a certainty. Of
course the body will not go to Purgatory, because, as
St. Thomas points out, its supreme expiation consists
in its falling a prey to corruption and returning to its

parent dust. But the disembodied soul has its faculties very wide awake in the next life, and is therefore capable of intense agony and frustration.

If the reason for these mysterious penalties is to be found in my undue attachment to creatures: taking them as the final purpose of my striving, when I sinned mortally; stopping on my flight to God to relish their sweetness, when I sinned venially; have I not every motive to fear they will be long and terrible, knowing as I do the drunken fury and delight with which I have sought after sense-gratification, as though I were afraid lest the opportunity of pleasure might never return, or imagining, like the crafty woman in the Book of Proverbs, that *"stolen waters are the sweetest"*? (*Prov. ix*, 17.)

## RESOLUTIONS

1.　To bear in a spirit of penance the pains of life I cannot avoid, welcoming them from the merciful Hand of God who thereby, perhaps, wishes to lessen my Purgatory.

2.　To steer clear of venial faults, that could well be piling up for me in the next life a Purgatory of exceeding duration.

3.　To be devoted to the Holy Souls, going to their rescue with suffrages; if only so that one day I myself may not be left without assistance.

4.　By my preaching, Masses, and funeral services, to foster the well-rooted devotion of my people towards the souls in Purgatory, and even to avail myself of this particular devotion in order to bring strayed sheep back to God. It is often one of the last resources.

# ETERNAL LIFE

## FIRST MEDITATION

### *The Goal of all Priestly Aspirations*

#### I

*Quomodo cantabimus canticum Domini in terra aliena?*

"How shall we sing the song of the Lord in a strange land?"

The priest who does not aspire to heaven is for ever singing the Lord's songs in a strange land. For, every prayer I say, from the Mass to the final words of the Divine Office; all the Sacraments I receive and administer, the matter I preach and teach, my very name "priest": everything about me speaks of eternal life. And this *eternal life* is my social justification, the only thing I represent in this world.

If it is not also my first aspiration; if I cannot honestly call it *principium laetitiae meae,* the source and well-spring of my rejoicing; if I neither think nor interest myself about it; shall I not deserve the epithet of hypocrite?

#### II

Shall I, a priest, or anyone else for that matter, ever find happiness on earth, that happiness which leads us all a dance like moths fluttering round a light? Is true happiness to be found in the enjoyment of any of the pleasures of body and mind which this world can give?

Pleasure has been attached by God to the exercise of certain natural functions necessary or useful to life, but it is not an end in itself; it is a stimulant lest these activities should be neglected, with consequent danger to our individual lives or to that of the human race. It is a condiment ensuring that we eat, etc. Earthly pleasure, then, not being the final purpose of any living being, cannot be ours either, nor our final destiny. All the more so since these pleasures are doomed to extinction together with our terrestrial existence, whereas the soul takes with it to eternity all its thirst for happiness and perfection.

What will my soul do when it has had its fill of empty vanities here below and is left hungering, but fly to God, its only Good, in search of real sustenance?

### III

Our Divine Lord never spoke to us in terms of temporal satisfactions, nor did He offer to us what by word of mouth and, still more, by deed and a life of toil, He so utterly disdained.

> In the world you shall have distress.—(*John xvi*, 33.)

> If any man will come after me, let him deny himself and take up his cross and follow me.—(*Matt. xvi*, 24.)

In the " Our Father ", where He teaches us to ask for the truly good things of life, with regard to temporal goods He wishes us to ask only for our daily bread: our bodily nourishment reduced to its minimum expression; and He bestows a ninefold blessing upon those who despise all things terrestrial: Blessed are the poor, the meek and humble of heart, those that weep, those that suffer persecution and calumny . . . for theirs is the Kingdom of Heaven. (*Matt. vi.*)

Do not expect to hear of any other reward from Christ's lips; if you do, you have not properly understood the spirit of the Gospel; you make the Redemption meaningless, and Christ the Redeemer will say to you: *after all these things do the heathens seek.* (*Matt. vi. 32.*)

## IV

We save up for the future, all of us put something by. Is there a priest who, in his activities, emoluments, office and dealings with society, does not dream of making provision for a quiet old age free from worry and unhappiness? For this purpose, one will cultivate useful friendships, another will seek a lucrative position, a third will economise. It would seem something connatural to the human heart, and He who made us priests has not made us less human.

But would it not be more logical, and also a safer investment, to provide gradually for a happy eternity—which for many of us will arrive before old age? Eternal life is not so far away, in time or space; and even if it were, the means of transport to it are surprisingly rapid!

Lord, persuade me of the sheer practical wisdom of Thy exhortation:

Lay up to yourselves treasures in Heaven

because, if I follow it, I shall find that

Where thy treasure is, there also is thy heart.
—(*Matt. vi.*)

## RESOLUTIONS

1.  To meditate very frequently on the nothingness of this world's pleasures, until I am convinced that no real happiness has ever been mine in the past nor will be mine in the future if I rely on the world for it; and therefore, not to expect or put faith in any other substantial happiness outside that of eternal life.

2.  To fight against my delusions on this point, to shatter them, and to make my life's supreme aspiration consist in reaching the goal of life: eternal bliss.

Can I set myself a higher target in life? Does anything better satisfy my thirst for perfect happiness?

# ETERNAL LIFE

### SECOND MEDITATION

## *Meaning of Eternal Life*

### I

What our Lord usually calls *Eternal Life* is, according to St. Paul: "*A share in Christ's Kingdom, God's Kingdom.*" (*Eph. v,* 5); it is an inheritance we shall possess by full right of ownership.

If my name is written in the Book of Life, if God has included me in His glorious statistics, numbered me among His children and heirs, happy am I, indeed! I can then exclaim, with David:

> *Funes ceciderunt mihi in praeclaris, etenim haereditas mea praeclara est mihi.*—(*Ps. xv,* 6.)

"No fairer lot could be mine; no nobler inheritance could I win." There is no fate comparable to mine, neither of millionaire's first-born nor of heir-presumptive to an earthly throne.

My God, may Thy grace enable me to fulfil the precept of Thy Apostle:

> "Bestir yourselves then, brethren, ever more eagerly, to ratify God's calling and choice of you by a life well lived."—(*II Peter i,* 10.)

## II

What is contained in the treasures I am to inherit? We know that they are simply *ineffable,* they cannot be expressed in terms of earthly speech; nevertheless Holy Scripture has some lovely things to say, and we shall do well to consider a few of them.

> "He will wipe every tear from their eyes, and there will be no more death, or mourning, or cries of distress; no more sorrow: these old things have passed away."—(*Apoc. xxi,* 4.)

It will certainly be a novelty for us children of Eve to find ourselves, when our pilgrimage through this vale of tears is ended, ever without a pain or a sigh. This alone, judging by worldly standards and ambitions, would suffice and abound to make eternal life the goal of all our strivings after happiness. What more could one ask of God in payment of such paltry services?

## III

And yet this is hardly more than what we might call the negative side of heaven; the positive and principal part, which the human heart, even the most exacting, could little suspect, is symbolised in the following words:

E

" Here is God's Tabernacle pitched among men;
He will dwell among them, and they will be His
own people, and He will be among them, their
own God."—(*Apoc. xxi,* 3.)

" I will be His God, and He shall be my son."
—(*Id. xxi,* 7.)

" God's throne (which is the Lamb's throne)
will be there, with His servants to worship Him,
and to see His face, His name written on their
foreheads."—(*Id. xxii,* 3, 4.)

Heaven is the " pitched tent," the hearth and home,
where God will live with men, where He will be their
Father, and they His children; where God will make
all His children partakers of His divine joy, His riches,
and His perfections; just as in this world the children
see, possess, and enjoy their father's presence and love
and all his amassed wealth.

One day, everything belonging to God, and God
Himself, will be mine! So truly mine that I shall be
able to say with the Divine Word:

All things are delivered to me by my Father.—
(*Matt. xi,* 27.)

Father . . . all my things are thine, and thine are
mine.—(*John xvii,* 10.)

Lord, nothing written or thought of has such power
as this to move me and make me long for Heaven!


IV

Let us reflect on a few more passages of Holy Writ
so that we may come to a better understanding of what
is meant by heaven. St. Paul says:

> "At present, we are looking at a confused reflection in a mirror."—(*I Cor. xiii,* 12.)

We see God's Attributes in a dark manner, obscurely, like the reflections in those ancient mirrors which were merely burnished metallic surfaces. But, he continues:

> "Then, we shall see face to face; now, I have only glimpses of knowledge; then, I shall recongise God as he has recognised me."

When that happens, the words of Christ will be finally accomplished:

> "Eternal life is knowing thee, who art the only true God, and Jesus Christ, whom thou hast sent."
> —(*John xvii,* 3.)

To possess God in Person, with that same absolute and inalienable right of possession with which I possess a thought of my own mind; to possess Him with infinitely greater security than any temporal goods or even my own body; to make God completely mine, with everything that God is and has, with everything that God can do: *that* is eternal life!

O God, is there any possession on earth preferable to Thee?

## RESOLUTIONS

1. Serve your masters, the poor, for the love of Jesus Christ; for theirs is the Kingdom of Heaven, and it is they who will open the gates of Heaven to you.

2. Deposit your human acts, the whole product of your free will, in that Eternal Bank that knows no bankruptcy; and the result will be, here and now, that your heart will be where your treasure is.

# ETERNAL LIFE

## THIRD MEDITATION

### *Further Glimpses into Eternal Life*

I

Let us listen once again to the Beloved Disciple, who drank deeply from the Wisdom of the Father the mysteries of *eternal life*.

"See how God has shown his love towards us; that we should be counted as his sons, should be his sons. . .

"Beloved, we are sons of God even now, and what we shall be hereafter has not been made known as yet.

"But we know that when he comes we shall be like him; we shall see him, then, as he is."
—(*I John, iii*, 1-3.)

Our final destiny will be a surprise beyond the reach of human words; we shall become like God, like God in happiness and bliss and perfection, and like God the Source of happiness; because we shall see Him intuitively, without the veil of intellective "species", without the shadows of analogy, without mental processes, without creaturely intermediaries "who cannot tell me what I long to hear" (*St. John of the Cross*), and without the obscurities of faith. We shall live eternally in God's embrace, His Fatherly Eye the

Splendour of our eyes: *in lumine tuo videbimus lumen* (*Ps. xxxv*, 10); and that glorious gaze will transform us into the image of His Brightness, into His other self.

These eyes of mine, so avid to see and still so unsatisfied with all they have seen until now; eyes that drink in every honeyed drop of created beauty and are still athirst for more—*non saturatur oculus visu* (*Eccles. i*, 8); O Lord, keep them pure and worthy for the radiant and eternal Vision of Thee!

## II

While extolling God's Providence, King David, in psalm 35, seems to have caught a glimpse of the bliss of heaven:

Filii autem hominum, in tegmine alarum tuarum sperabunt. "Under the shelter of those wings the frail children of earth will find confidence"—all the elect will be gathered under the wings of Divine Love, under God's motherly protection, no longer a prey to the miseries of a world that has passed away.

Inebriabuntur ab ubertate Domus tuae, et torrente voluptatis tuae potabis eos;

"With rich store thou wilt nourish them, bid them drink deep at thy fountain of contentment"—perpetual hunger of a heart ever filled at the Banquet; perpetual thirst of a mind ever quenched at the Fountainhead of all delight;

Quoniam apud te est fons vitae, et in lumine tuo videbimus lumen.

"for in thee is the Source of all Life, and thy brightness will break on our eyes like dawn." In that Light, O God, where Thou dwellest—Light I could never approach were I not lifted up by Thy Mercy, like a tiny child snatched up into its mother's arms—I shall drink in light through every pore of my being.

Blessed are they, Lord, who dwell in Thy House; they shall praise Thee unendingly.

### III

Why continue? Even the Divine Revelations, when confined within the narrow limits of human utterance, are little more than the babblings of a child!

Think, ponder, contemplate, imagine, dream; multiply your longings a hundredfold; let all your visions of happiness crystallise into naked reality; harness all the inventive genius of the human race; what is the summit of all our anxious striving in comparison with what God has prepared for those that belong to Him? Little more than a " hop, skip, and jump " of childish play; a mere shadow of the triumphant reality.

The truest ever spoken about Eternal Life is contained in the words of St. Paul, which again are but a quotation from Isaias:

The eye hath not seen, nor ear heard : neither hath it entered into the heart of man, what things God hath prepared for them that love him.— (*I Cor. ii*, 9.)

Not in the whole ken of human vision, nor in the vast range of human hearing, nor in the almost fathomless depths of the human heart—in the heart that has never yet pronounced the word " satisfied "—can be compassed, even mentally, the good things God has in store for those that love and fear Him. Happy the soul created for such glory and such a kingdom!

## RESOLUTION

When my heart is seized with a thirst for pleasure that incites me to drink from muddy streams, I shall be patient; I shall remember that these " stolen waters " never quenched nor even mitigated my thirst, but rather rekindled it; I shall remain calm, keeping in mind that soon, very soon, I shall come to the well-spring of eternal Life, and plunge into the floods and torrents of God's delights. This will be my treasured hope, and a bridle to my passions.

# THE MERCY OF CHRIST

## FIRST MEDITATION

### *God's Mercy and Justice*

#### I

Now, what if I, a priest of the Most High God, have also been a sinner? What if I have trampled upon my supreme dignity, repeatedly profaned the Sacraments, and in particular the Sacrament of the Body and Blood of my Lord and Saviour Jesus Christ; or if, like the lewd elders of the Book of Daniel:

> "I dethroned my reason and turned my eyes away from the sight of heaven, forgetting the just awards ". . . ?

And if, like another prodigal child, debased, famished, ragged, and conscious of my own wretchedness, I make up my mind to go back to Thee; O Lord, how wilt Thou receive me? What dost Thou harbour in Thy Heart for me? What wilt Thou speak to me? Galling reproach? Sweetest compassion? Lord, leave me not in suspense; tell me clearly. What is Thy attitude towards Thy priests who perhaps for many a year by their misdeeds have administered to Thee gall and vinegar?

#### II

If I wish to know Christ's attitude and mind I must never forget that He is God

> "with whom there can be no change, no swerving from his course "

not a shadow of alteration (*James i,* 17).

I am decided to return to Him, but with what intention? Shall I use His Goodness as a shield to cover my continuance in sin? If that is my intention, I should heed the warning:

> Say not: the mercy of the Lord is great; he will have mercy on the multitude of my sins.
>
> For mercy and wrath quickly come from him: and his wrath looketh upon sinners.—(*Ecclus. v, 6-7.*)

And the Psalmist also gives warning:

> Oculi Domini super justos et aures ejus in preces eorum; Vultus autem Domini super facientes mala, ut perdat de terra memoriam eorum.—(*Ps. xxxiii, 16-17.*)

" On the upright the Lord's eye ever looks favourable; His ears are open to their pleading; perilous is His frown for the wrong-doers; He will soon make their name vanish from the earth."

This, then, is the welcome awaiting me from Jesus, the meek and mild, if I obstinately cling to evil, and if I am not determined to walk the ways of His adorable Will.

### III

Yes, Christ is indeed *meek and humble of heart* (*Matt. xi, 29*) but I must not deceive myself. From those meek eyes, from that humble Heart, there came at times the blazing wrath of Ancient Jehovah. And if I read the Gospel attentively I shall hear a true echo of the Psalmist's " Perilous is His frown for the wrong-doers."

> Jesus . . . groaned in the spirit and troubled

himself. . . . Jesus therefore again groaning in Himself. . . .—(*John xi, 33, 38.*)

And looking round about on them with anger,
being grieved for the blindness of their hearts. . . .
(*Mark iii, 5.*)

Our Divine Redeemer, long-suffering and forbearing
as He was towards our human weaknesses, found something repulsive and sickening to His Heart, something
so loathsome as to make Him almost appear to lose His
divine Serenity. What was it? The obstinate attempt to
deny, or the refusal to recognise, one's own sins, for the
purpose of continuing in sin. How terrible the threats
and curses of the Son of God upon such perversity!
(*Cfr. Matt. xxiii, 13 and foll.*)

## RESOLUTION

Sin is an evil thing, but it is immeasurably worse
to enlist the Mercy of God as an additional motive or
cause of my sinning; for that would be an outrage
against God's most wonderful Attribute.

No, dear Lord, I am not trying to return to Thee in
order to find in Thy magnanimous Heart a support for
sinning; I am not going to try to make Thee an accomplice of my sinful life; I wish to come to Thee repentant
and ready for anything rather than offend Thee again.

I recognise my faults, I declare myself alone responsible for them in the sight of Thy Justice; I regret above
all things my having offended Thee; with all sincerity
I promise, by Thy grace, to rectify and atone for the
past.

Lord, Thou who seest through to the depths of my
heart, art witness that I come to Thee without deceit
or guile.

# THE MERCY OF CHRIST

## SECOND MEDITATION

### *The All-Merciful Christ*

#### I

How will our Divine Lord welcome a heart returning to Him contrite for past disorders and humbled at the prospects of His Justice? With a Compassion befitting the great and merciful God that He is.

When the Son of God came down to earth—*tamquam Sponsus procedens de thalamo suo*—from the brightness of His Glory to the obscurity of the Virgin's womb, His Divine Immensity " dwindled to human infancy," He seems to be in a hurry to divest Himself before our eyes of the mantle of His sovereign Majesty; He speeds to earth, not with thunder and lightnings, not to open the sluices of the ocean—for Sinai and the Deluge were not so effective!—He comes to earth in search, not of the pure and noble remnants of our race, not to a hidden Noe or a persecuted Elias; He comes in search of sinners:

> I came not to call the just, but sinners, to repentance.—(*Luke v,* 32.)
> Christ Jesus came into the world to save sinners. —(*I Tim. i,* 15.)

John the Baptist, the last prophet of the Old Covenant, was a second Elias filled with the idea that the Messiah was to come to avenge, One whose axe was put to the root of the tree, whose winnowing-fan was ready

139

to purge the threshing-floor clean in order to gather the wheat and consume the chaff in unquenchable fire; but no sooner does he set eyes on Jesus than his mind seems to undergo an abrupt change. Who would have imagined that those very lips which had been preaching punishment and austere penance would suddenly break out into an expression of the utmost tenderness?

> Behold the Lamb of God! Behold him who taketh away the sin of the world!—(*John i, 29.*)

From the rock flowed honey.

## II

The idea launched by the Precursor was well confirmed by Jesus, in His actions, His sayings, and His parables.

*In Jesus's actions.* Why not search for them by reading the Gospel? What repentant sinner ever went to Him and was not welcomed with a thrill of fatherly emotion?

Now it is a woman caught in the act of adultery whom His mercy shields from the shower of stones prescribed by the implacable Law, and on whom He imposes no other penalty than to allow her penitential future to be steeped in the ineffable sweetness of His parting words:

> Neither will I condemn thee; go, and now sin no more.—(*John viii, 11.*)

Now it is the woman notorious for her light conduct, who in anxious fear takes refuge under the shadow of His compassion, and finds herself rehabilitated and defended from her accusers by the irresistible eloquence of the Divine Word. Now it is the publican, a public swindler, whom Jesus goes out of His way to meet and welcome an invitation from; the man who receives Jesus with the fragrant kiss of fourfold restitution for any ill-gotten gains. Now it is the good thief, who with three words from a cross next to Thine, O Jesus, steals away Thy very Heart, Thy forgiveness, and Thy Father's Kingdom closed until then even to the just! Prodigious Mercy Thine, that would be accompanied on Thy entry into the Kingdom by a criminal executed on the public gallows, as if he were Thy knight-companion!

Thou didst implore pardon even for those who sought it not, did not desire it. And lifted up on the cross of ignominy, it would seem as if Thy first and most urgent need was for Thee to pour all Thy strength into that sublime appeal:

> *Father, forgive them!*

Even those who were crucifying Thee and heaping insults upon Thy wounds. . . . *Father, forgive them.*

## III

*In Jesus's doctrine.* The Name He chose for Himself is redolent of Mercy, and distils the virgin honey of His Divine Compassion:

> Thou shalt call his name Jesus, for he shall save his people from their sins.—(*Matt. i,* 12.)

Only the life of Jesus, all steeped in loving-kindness and pity for sinners, enables us to grasp the exact meaning of the text:

> Go then and learn what this meaneth: "I will have mercy and not sacrifice."—(*Matt. ix,* 13.)

Those ritualistic Jews, O Jesus, did not believe in Thee; they knew more about their vain sacrifices and empty rites than about Thy ineffable Pity towards the delinquent children of Adam!

It is not those who are in health that have need of the physician, it is those who are sick; therefore, Jesus, the Physician of souls, comes to heal the worst and most rebellious of diseases. And, in order to feel for us, He, the Sinless One, wished to suffer the consequences of sin:

abandonment by God:

Deus, Deus, meus, ut quid dereliquisti me? (*Matt. xxvii*, 46):

shame and confusion:
and he began to fear and to be heavy . . . (*Mark xiv*, 33),

and remorse:

to grow sorrowful and sad. (*Matt. xxvi*, 37),

and every pain that a human being is capable of in body and soul. All because He became a Victim for our sins:

" Christ never knew sin, and God made Him into sin for us."—(*II Cor, v*, 21.)

And He stooped so close to the human heart in its greatest wretchedness that the Apostle could write:

" And so He needs must become altogether like His brethren; He would be a High Priest Who could feel for us and be our true representative before God."—(*Heb. ii*, 17.)

Abundant clarity is now shed, O Lord, on the lesson Thou gavest to Peter:

Thou shalt forgive thy brother, not seven times, but seventy times seven.

Thou, my Model of forgiveness, art therefore ready to forgive me four hundred and ninety times, which means, always, whenever I return to Thee contrite and humble.

## IV

Should these actions and sayings not suffice, I still have the loveliest of parables that came from the lips of the Master of the parable. St. Luke records them in his fifteenth chapter—"the sinner's chapter"—which we, who have so often sinned and in our bitterness of soul are ready to sin many times more, would do well to read and take into our blood.

Lord, those three parables in that chapter are Thy own Self-defence; Thou didst invent them to ward off the accusation which rankled most in the minds of Thy adversaries:

> "This man converses with sinners and eats with them";

and they explain Thy conduct, a conduct that to them seemed outrageous. Because Thou art the "Good Shepherd," Thou runnest after the lost sheep; because Thou art a "Father," Thou knowest how it pains to lose a child whose rearing cost so much pain and toil and love; because Thou art even the "Woman in love" who cherishes the ten golden coins given her by the bridegroom on their wedding day, Thou art all eagerness to find them when lost.

In order to show me what kind of a Heart Thou hast for sinners, it was not enough, O Lord, to compare Thyself to a simple shepherd, who possesses no treasure beyond his little flock; it was not enough to compare

Thyself to a tender-hearted father; no, Thou must needs delve into the heart of a woman, of a woman in love, and compare with hers Thy anxious solicitude while rummaging for the lost treasure: my soul lost among the refuse of my sinfulness; my soul, a drachma of little intrinsic worth, but treasured for the love Thou Thyself hast deposited therein.

### V

I say to you that even so there shall be joy in heaven upon one sinner that doth penance.—(*Luke xv, 7.*)

The sweetness of these words could melt a heart of stone. They are, dear Lord, the refrain closing those three magnificent stanzas of chapter fifteen, wherein, O Sovereign Troubadour of Heaven, Thou hast sung the praises of Thy eternal Pity. How could I so much as dream that my poor soul's return to Thee had power to move Thee so deeply, to produce in Thee such intense delight, as to rally all Heaven together to join with Thee in festive thrill and cheer? How shall I, who have given Thee so much displeasure throughout my long sinful life, refuse Thee at last this moment of delight? My sincere conversion will be a festive occasion not only for Thee, but for all Thy angels and saints as well!

Have words ever sprung from Christ's lips so revealing of His love for us? Do I not grasp their meaning? Or do I fail to understand what it is to love?

### RESOLUTION

I shall very frequently take the whole of chapter fifteen of the Gospel according to St. Luke for the subject of meditation, especially when I am aware of having fallen into grievous sin. That chapter has been the Divine Fisherman's net that has caught many a soul in its meshes.

# THE MERCY OF CHRIST

### THIRD MEDITATION

## Christ's Mercy Towards the Delinquent Priest

### I

But what if I, a priest, am fallen into grievous sin? Will Jesus Christ receive me back as readily as other sinners?

He will receive you with even greater love and delight than other sinners.

His Mercy, portrayed in the woman's careful search for the lost coin and in her enthusiastic joy at finding it, is Divine Love seeking to recover the lost image and likeness of Himself in every soul; but when He recovers the soul of a priest His Joy knows no bounds, for therein He sees also the likeness and participation of His Eternal Priesthood, His own priestly Character and Seal.

It is told of a certain ambassador, that he used a banknote of considerable value to take a light from a fire and light up a dark corner where he had lost a coin of his native country. "Not because it was of any intrinsic worth," he explained, "but because it bore the image of my King, and I could allow no one to trample it underfoot." The symbolical gesture was appreciated and applauded. What wonder, then, that Jesus should, even at the cost of shedding His Blood, go in search of the soul of the delinquent priest who, in spite of sin, still bears the living likeness of God's Attributes?

Lord, stoop down to the miry depths where sin has dragged me. Stoop down and bring me to Thy Light again. And may my divine priestly Character shine forth in all its former splendour.

## II

Indeed, the Good Shepherd is used to seeing His priests flee from Him, and He is never tired of searching for them and receiving them back without rebuff into the arms of His tender Mercy.

Two very touching instances have fortunately been left on record for us in the Gospel. Yes, two instances of delinquent priests, during the very lifetime on earth of the Eternal High Priest, being welcomed by His Mercy; though one of them refused It.

Take the case of Peter. He had just been made High Priest of the New Covenant in this world on the eve of Christ's Passion and Death. The consecrating hands were those of Christ; the ceremony, the sublimest ever witnessed by the ages, came after the Last Supper, which began with the washing of feet. The hands of a God beneath the grubby feet of a wretched fisherman! Surely that could have set the iciest heart ablaze with flames of eternal gratitude! That uncouth fisherman, plucked from the lowest stratum of society, was raised to the High Priesthood, raised without interstices, without merits, and made King of the new Race, dispenser and well-nigh owner of the infinite treasures of the Redemption!

But scarcely have three or four hours elapsed, when that "Rock," laid by the Supreme Architect as the corner-stone of His Church, crumbles like brittle clay at the questioning of a mere wench; he denies his Lord and Master. And how emphatically!

Woman, I know him not.—(*Luke xxii*, 57.)

Jesus, Thou hast lost everything: Thy first Apostle denies Thee, and despoils Thee even of Thy Name: *Hominem! Illum!*

He swears by all that is holy, by the Lord God, by the temple, that he knows no such man:

And again he denied with an oath: I know not the man.—(*Matt. xxvi*, 72.)

He deems it so important, Lord, not to know Thee that he thinks he is justified in calling upon Jehovah as unimpeachable Witness.

And, seeing that with all his pains he cannot convince the obstinate maid-servant, he curses himself, he fumes and frets and calls down upon his head all manner of malediction and punishment. Sure enough, the old fisherman from the coasts of Tiberias has not forgotten his formidable seaman's vocabulary!

He began to curse and to swear that he knew not the man.—(*Matt. xxvi*, 74.)

At all costs he must create the impression that Thou art an absolute stranger. And this he does but a few hours after having shared with Thee in the first Mass.

Dear Lord, my wickedness never went to such an extreme: the day of my first Mass I shall always hold as the holiest of my life; the fragrance of my priestly anointing continued in my soul for longer than twenty-four hours!

### III

And how did Christ deal with His delinquent High Priest? Surpassing all past tenderness and pity. Peter's terrible denials had scarcely faded from his lips when Christ, bandied by His executioners, struck, spat upon, was constrained to pass in front of the cowardly and disloyal disciple; and those divine eyes of Christ turned towards Peter, assailed him with such an impact of love and tender melancholy that the stunned fisherman broke into a torrent of tears.

And who is the first man to whom the Risen Christ appears? Peter. What would He say to him? Words of reproach? Words of forgiveness?—Oh why, sacred evangelists, did you not tell us in detail what happened at that first interview? Silence was preferable . . . it can so easily be guessed . . . the very sight of *that Man,* robed in glorious and immortal life, would be rebuke and pardon enough. . . .

O Lord, blessed be that infinite Mercy wherewith Thou receivest back Thy priests who have strayed and who return to Thee impelled by Thy sovereign graciousness!

### IV

After such execrable denials on the part of Peter, and such great-hearted forgiveness on the part of Christ, how clearly and deeply the Apostle would understand his Master's teaching:

> Lord, how often shall my brother offend against me, and I forgive him? Till seven times? . . .

> I say not to thee, till seven times, but till seventy times seven times.—(*Matt. xviii,* 21-22.)

How keen to pardon and reconcile sinners, he who was so graciously pardoned and reconciled!

## RESOLUTION

The lesson I shall learn is, not only to throw myself at the feet of my Saviour when I have sinned, but also, with divinelike compassion, to go in search of sinners, and never to demur when called to the confessional; on the contrary, to urge them to come, not allowing a single bad-tempered word to escape my lips against any repentant and sincere soul who entrusts to my pardoning power his iniquities, no matter how enormous these may be.

# THE MERCY OF CHRIST

### FOURTH MEDITATION

*Christ's Mercy towards the most sinful Priest*

### I

There is something even more impressive: the way Christ dealt with Judas.

The hardness of that heart, which not even the Good Shepherd could soften with all His tender loving-kindness, remains an appalling mystery.

What delicate tokens of predilection He lavishes upon him! Would that self-centred mind fail to notice them? Hardly. Because right from the first, Jesus drops veiled hints, but hints that were surely clear enough to the would-be traitor:

> Have I not chosen all twelve of you? And one of you is a devil.—*(John vi, 71.)*

Christ knows whom He is speaking to; He probes the dark recesses of that scuttled conscience; and yet, within a short while He gives him proof of the highest esteem by making him the administrator of the Apostolic College funds. (John xii, 6.) And would not Judas, while thieving from the common purse, take as addressed to himself the Master's frequent references to the unjust steward and the Lord's constant readiness to forgive?

How many hearts Thy doctrine would have softened, O Jesus, if they had heard it, like Judas, from those lips of Thine flowing with the milk and honey of Thy compassion!

## II

It would seem that everything was arranged by Christ on the night of the Last Supper with the express intention of bringing the treacherous Apostle to repentance. How many preferences! What loving appeals! . . .

Christ begins by informing Judas once again that He sees through his underhand designs, and follows every step:

> Amen I say to you, one of you that eateth with me shall betray me.—(*Matt. xiv,* 18.)

He resorts to terrifying threats, but threats still wrapped up in divinest compassion:

> Woe to that man by whom the Son of Man shall be betrayed; it were better for him if that man had not been born.—(*Matt. xxvi,* 24.)

When allotting places at the farewell banquet for each of His Apostles, it seems that He put Judas next to Him, so near as to have to eat from the same dish, their hands and eyes meeting:

He that dippeth his hand with me in the dish . . .
(*Matt. xxvi, 23.*)

And He honours Judas with a courtesy not shown to
the rest:

> And when he had dipped the bread, he gave it
> to Judas Iscariot.—(*John xiii, 26.*)

He deals with him so graciously, so affably, in so free
and friendly a manner that not one of the other
Apostles, not even the most alert among them, John or
Peter, detects Judas's duplicity or the slightest trace of
that limitless loathing and repulsion which the Divine
Master must have felt in His pure soul at being so close
to Satan's abject slave and viperous brood.

### III

Consider that amazing act of Self-abasement when
Jesus washed the feet of His Apostles.

> Knowing that the Father had given him all things
> into his hands, and that he came from God and
> goeth to God,
> he riseth from supper and layeth aside his
> garments, and, having taken a towel, girded him-
> self. . . . (*John xiii, 3-4.*)

Here is logic that the human mind will never compass.
*Because* the Father had given all things into His hands,
those same hands now perform the menial task of a
slave! Hands that hold all things in being, Hands that
possess the Godhead Itself, now take a basin of water
and wash the feet of uncouth and unkempt fishermen!

By whom did Jesus begin? Many of the Fathers say
He began by Judas. The Innocent Lamb of God on His
knees, His hands under the traitor's feet, leaving them

washed and kissed, with a kiss from the purest of lips!

We may well believe that, before rising, Jesus shot a glance of abysmal pity into the darkened depths of Judas's eyes. And would not Judas tremble all over? Would he not feel impelled to cast himself at the feet of the Master and yell out a confession of criminal intrigue?

O the mystery of iniquity in that wretched human heart! O the unfathomable depths of Mercy in the Heart of the Saviour!

### IV

Judas goes ahead as leader of the cruel villains charged with arresting and binding Jesus. In an endeavour to conceal his hypocrisy until the very last moment, he approaches his Victim with fiendish smile and sanctimonious demeanour, puts his arms round Him, reaches his lips to Jesus's peaceful brow, and imprints on it a kiss. . . . The fruit of deadliest poison ever presented to God by human depravity. What were all the buffetings, spittle, and coarse insults from Thy executioners, Lord, compared with that kiss? They were sweetest honey.

And Christ, who afterwards with a single word sent the arresting soldiery reeling to the ground, now looks intently upon Judas and makes a last appeal, the last and the tenderest:

> Friend, whereto art thou come?
> —(*Matt. xxvi,* 50.)

> Judas, dost thou betray the Son of Man with a kiss?—(*Luke xxii,* 48.)

When did Christ speak so affectionately to those who loved Him well? Friend! Judas! . . . O Lord, why dost

Thou pronounce that name which is to be until the end of time the most degrading stigma on the brow of fallen humanity?

*Judas, wouldst thou betray the Son of Man with a kiss?* . . . Lord, how it pained Thee! . . . Had it been a stab with a knife . . . but a kiss! . . .

## V

The consequences of his treachery perhaps went far beyond the traitor's calculations. This he realised when he saw Christ hanging from the Cross: the final outcome of his kiss. He was overwhelmed with remorse; with eyes enlightened by the flames of hell he saw into the depths of his own degradation; and, stung by shame and self-hatred, bent on self-obliteration, he hanged himself.

Let us imagine a scene like the following.

Judas, reeling like a drunkard, with a rope coiled round his arm, comes across Peter in *Haceldama,* the Field of Blood.

" Whither goest?"

" To hang myself."

" Poor Cain. But why?"

" So great is my crime that I deserve not pardon."

" Oh, but I too was a traitor, and He whom thou didst deliver for money I denied for nothing, as many as three times. In sorrow and tears I pleaded with Him, and He forgave me. Come with me; let us both go up to the Cross where He is hanging: the Blood that is being shed for the whole world's sins will wash out thine. . . ."

Let us also suppose that Judas takes Peter's advice, and, following the Bloodstains on the road, reaches Calvary just as the Holy Victim has been lifted up.

Making his way through the executioners he reaches the Cross, prostrates himself, and with forehead pinned to the bleeding feet of Christ he breaks out into an agonising cry that is heard above the sundering of the rocks: "My God, it was I who nailed Thee here; I who drained Thy Blood from Thee and trampled on Thee like a worm. I do not deserve Thy forgiveness; let the rocks cleave asunder and swallow me; command the lightning to strike me; give my name to the scorn of all the nations; but, merciful Lord, do not die, close not Thine eyes without a glance of pity upon me; let not death seal Thy lips before they have spoken Thy pardon; call me once again, as in the garden: friend!"

Had this actually happened—and a thousand pities it did not—what would Jesus have answered? There would have been an eighth word from the Cross, the most precious, the most divine in the whole Gospel . . .

Who knows? Who knows? Perhaps that eighth word, unspoken, hovering over His lips, Christ keeps for me, poor delinquent priest; to imprint it on my soul like a burning kiss as soon as I throw myself at His feet, repentant and determined to make good.

Shall I refuse Him the divine joy of whispering into my soul that word of pardon? Shall I be Judas to the very end?

## RESOLUTION

No, dear Lord, no; I will not seal Thy lips with my cold insensibility; I will not gag Thee with my stubborn continuation in sin. Speak to me. Speak to me. I repent more sincerely than Judas, having, like him, betrayed and trampled upon Thee. No more transgressions from now onwards; the chains are broken. I will not rise up from Thy feet until Thou hast forgiven me.

# SECOND PART

# THE PRIESTLY MINISTRY

## THE MINISTRY IN GENERAL

### FIRST MEDITATION

### *The Priest's Chief Occupation*

I

St. Paul writes to Timothy:

> "So much I tell thee by letter. . . . that thou mayest be in no doubt over the conduct that is expected of thee in God's household. By that I mean the Church of the living God. . . .—(*I Tim. iii*, 15.)

The Church is God's Household, a House built by Him, arranged by Him, with a wisdom immeasurably superior to the wisdom which Solomon revealed in the construction and furnishing of his royal palaces, and which so amazed and overwhelmed the Queen of Sheba.

But can you conceive of a house well ordered and wisely ruled where there is a large redundant staff of servants and stewards who have nothing to do but to kill time and vegetate in idleness under the shade of their master's protection?

So it stands to reason, Lord, that I, as steward and

Minister of Thy Household, have a task allotted to me, and if I do not carry it out I am a disgrace to Thy holy dwellings. Thou couldst repeat for my benefit the words of reproach Thou didst speak through the lips of the Prophet to Sobna, the prefect of the Temple: *What dost thou here, or as if thou wert somebody here? . . . the shame of the house of thy Lord.*—(*Is. xxii*, 15-18.)

## II

At our ordination we received the four Minor Orders and the three Major Orders, and each Order was instituted and conferred upon us for a specific purpose; each is but the Divine Power communicated to us for the exercise of a spiritual ministerial duty. This presupposes an office, an obligation, and a life-long one as far as our strength allows, because the " Character " of the Sacrament of Holy Orders is indelible. We are in priestly harness for life.

Thus the great Apostle exhorted his chosen pupil Timothy:

"A special grace has been entrusted to thee; prophecy awarded it, and the imposition of the presbyters' hands went with it; do not let it suffer from neglect."—(*I Tim. iv*, 14.)

Woe to the unfaithful servant who, having received the talent to trade with and multiply, through indolence or cowardice buries it underground! It was not precisely the wicked servant but the unprofitable one that the order was given to cast out into exterior darkness where there would be weeping and gnashing of teeth. (*Cfr. Matt. xxv*, 30.)

Is it possible, O Lord, that I am that unprofitable

servant who has wasted and squandered Thy riches and lawful gains?

## III

We became priests in answer to a calling. Which of us will swear that when he mounted the altar steps he had no vocation, and that instead of entering the sanctuary by the proper door he sneaked in from the back? Who among us would patiently bear to be called a "sneak" by the manner of our entry into the priesthood, or a "gate-crasher" into the sanctuary?

No, dear Jesus, I was really convinced that I heard Thy call, and those who numbered me among Thy Household staff were also convinced, and the Prelate who laid his hands on me was convinced; otherwise they would all have rejected me as an intruder.

I had a vocation. And what is a vocation? A special calling from God to consecrate myself to the priesthood. But would God have called me to a life of idleness, to the mere enjoyment of honour and benefice? Or did Jesus Christ institute a sort of honorary priesthood? Did He allow His Heart to be pierced by a lance on Calvary that there might issue forth a Sacrament destined to confirm me in sloth? That certainly is not His idea:

> You have not chosen me, but I have chosen you and appointed you, that you should go and bring forth fruit, and your fruit should remain.—(*John xv*, 16.)

### RESOLUTION

To live more contented each day with my state, and to esteem its occupations higher than those of any other walk of life, as being more useful to the neighbour, holier for myself, nobler in themselves and more ennobling to those who exercise them. These priestly occupations shall therefore take pride of place in my life, in my preferences, in my appreciations, in the intensity and time I give to them. Any other occupation, however congenial to me, I shall subordinate to those of my priesthood, and, if they prove a handicap, I shall forgo them entirely. Can I affirm, hand on heart, that, so far, I have lived up to this wise maxim?

My ministry is loftier and worthier than the exercise of any art or craft or profession, and yet so many people sacrifice to these their pleasure, time and very life. Shame on me if I account as little less than wasted the time I have to spend on my priestly duties!

## THE MINISTRY IN GENERAL

### SECOND MEDITATION

#### *Exercise of the Ministry*

### I

What are my ministerial duties? Those deriving from the Orders I have received and from my appointment.

Each tree, each being, is expected to give its own specific fruit: the olive-tree, olives; the vine, grapes; and of the doctor is required healing; of the lawyer, the defence of justice in lawsuits; and of the priest, the offering of the Great Sacrifice, the administration of the Sacraments, the announcing of the word of God, and prayer, voiced in the name of the Church. This is what we are priests for; for this we were ordained; this is what is imperiously demanded of us by God, by souls, by society, and by our priestly attire.

Have these been the fruits I have yielded up to now? If fruits of another species, no matter how exquisite they may seem, I shall be but a freak of a tree that fails to fulfil the Creator's precept that each fruit tree yield fruit after its kind. I should be like a vine-stock bearing, let us say, lemons. And if I bore no fruit at all, that would be worse still. I should be cursed with sterility, and eventually *Every tree that doth not yield good fruit shall be cut down and cast into the fire.*—(Matt. iii, 10.)

## II

It is not enough for just a few of the branches to bear fruit: they must all do so, otherwise they will be pruned as useless and harmful to the vitality of the others that do give fruit. In like manner, I must not content myself with exercising one or two of my ministerial duties, no more, and despise or dodge the rest, or exercise them only once in a while.

And how many pious and zealous priests easily get the idea that they have striven sufficiently in days gone by for the Glory of God, and brought to a successful issue an adequate number of tasks; so now, in the evening of their lives, it is only right they should enjoy a well-earned rest and gloat inactively over past endeavours!

These were not the sentiments of the Apostle of the Gentiles:

"May you live as befits his servants, waiting continually on his pleasure; may the closer knowledge of God bring you fruitfulness and growth in all good."—(*Cor. i,* 10.)

"And in its service I suffer hardship like a criminal, yes, even imprisonment; but there is no imprisoning the word of God."—(*II Tim. ii,* 9.)

Our Lord Himself expressed His Mind also on this point:

I must work the works of Him that sent me, whilst it is day; the night cometh, when no man can work.—(*John ix,* 4.)

Does my sloth and laziness try to hasten the night of my life, and turn my noon into darkness, against God's Will? Fruit trees are not always bearing fruit, you'll say perhaps, they have only one autumn in the year. Yes, but in our lives there was also a winter and a spring: those long years in which slowly, step by step, we prepared for Holy Orders; but once ordained, our autumn has begun, and God comes to us every day looking for fruit.

And will the priest be the only man without his years of rest and retirement? Will he never be pensioned off? Is there no superannuation for him? No, definitely; never. You may be forced to retire from active work because of waning physical strength or old age or bad health, but even then there still remains something to accomplish; for instance, the duty of reading the Office.

For the genuine minister of Christ the time for resting is not to be found in this life; to him more than to anyone else apply the words of the Apocalypse:

"Blessed are the dead who die in the Lord. Yes, for ever henceforward, the Spirit says, they are to have rest from their labours."—(*Apoc. xiv,* 13.)

## Resolutions

In future, this is how I am going to exercise the ministry:

1. With real affection, proving therein my love for my Lord and Saviour Jesus Christ. I shall begin my various duties by trying to picture the Redeemer saying to me, as He said to the Prince of the Apostles: *Dost thou love me more than these? Feed my lambs. . . . feed my sheep.*—(John xxi, 15.)

2. With promptness and zest. I do not wish to hear one day before the Divine Tribunal what was said to Capharnaum: *It shall be more tolerable for the land of Sodom and Gomorrha in the day of Judgement.*—(Matt. x, 15.) I do not wish to see myself judged and confounded by the doctor who rushes out to patients at all hours of the night, or by the soldier who keeps the country's flag flying amid the storm and stress of battle, amid wounds and death.

3. Disinterestedly. It may be all right for a stone mason, a road mender, or a miner, to work merely for the wages; but a curse on the priest who in everything he does will not fix his gaze first and foremost on the eternal reward!

# THE FIRST MINISTERIAL DUTY: PRAYER

## FIRST MEDITATION

### *The Nature of Prayer*

#### I

What is prayer? "Elevatio mentis in Deum," says St. Augustine: a raising up of the mind to God. It is the lifting up of the deepest and most spiritual part of our being, the mind, until God and the soul are linked together in intimate communication. It is the mind's loftiest and most generous soaring.

According to St. Chrysostom prayer is the act whereby mortal and transitory beings are taken up to the immortal Life of God through dealings with Him the most intimate and familiar.

If we listen to St. Bernard, it is a private audience we are given with the Eternal King seated on His starry throne attended by an immense retinue of blessed spirits, the soul being like a dirty little toad—" ranuncula vilis " —emerged from its infested pool and allowed to scale the heights of the royal palace where God reigns in the splendours of sanctity amid the angels and the just.

Or as St. Teresa gracefully puts it: " Prayer is nothing but a simple friendly affair, it seems to me; a conversing frequently and alone with the One who we know loves us. And if you don't love Him—because for love to be real and for friendship to be lasting certain conditions must be fulfilled—then, it (prayer) means that, realising how much it concerns you to have His friendship and

how much He loves you, you undergo the ordeal of
being often with One who is so different from you."
(*Life of St. Teresa, chap. viii.*)

## II

What is prayer? It is the most powerful weapon the
Creator has placed into the hands of man. Even between
man and man there is no power more irresistible than
the humble request.

Israel and Amalec were fighting: while Moses with
hands raised to heaven prayed, Israel won, but as soon as
Moses lowered his hands and ceased to pray, Israel
suffered defeat.

Another time, when the holy prophet besought the
angered Jehovah to forgive the people their crimes, the
answer was: *Leave me alone, that my wrath may be
kindled against them, and that I may destroy them.*
(Exod. xxxii, 10.) "Leave me alone"—as though the
agonising plea of the great leader were mightier than the
Almighty Himself: And Josue, by prayer, holds back
the restless chariot of the sun; and Elias for three years
suspends the rain, "lays a ban on heaven itself".
(*Ecclus. xlviii,* 3.)

Should the Old Testament not suffice, let us hear
Christ's promise:

> Therefore I say unto you, all things whatsoever
> you ask when ye pray, believe that you shall
> receive, and they shall come unto you.—(*Mark xi,*
> 24.)

Happy our lot, once we win over our distrustful
hearts to the truth of this divine promise!

### III

The practice of prayer, so excellent and powerful, is the priest's first ministerial duty.

How often the Lord commanded in the Old Testament: *let the priest pray!*

In the New Dispensation it is our daily duty: to pray in the Mass, to pray in the Canonical Hours, to pray in the administration of the Sacraments, to pray in every liturgical function. The framework, the pith and substance, of the entire Catholic liturgy and of Catholic worship is prayer; and this is the spirit that has animated the Church from her origins.

The Apostles voice their conviction through the voice of Peter that they have a greater obligation to pray than to distribute alms among the poor: "*It is too much that we should have to forgo preaching God's word, and bestow our care upon tables.*"—(Acts vi, 2.)

And is it not too much that I should forgo preaching God's word and praying, no, not for the sake of feeding the hungry, but rather for the sake of idling my time away, of running after my sports and pastimes, or, at least, after worldly interests?

### IV

On earth I am God's angel, like the angel of the Apocalypse who

> "came and took his stand at the altar, with a censer of gold; and incense was given him in plenty, so that he could make an offering on the golden altar before the throne of God, out of the prayers said by all the Saints."—(*Apoc. viii,* 3.)

Will it be the right thing for me to have that censer,

from which the pleadings of mankind rise up to God, extinguished and thrown into a corner?

### RESOLUTION

I resolve to turn my heart into a censer of continually burning prayer which with its fragrance may appease the divine Justice and incline Him to love and mercy.

When could I so much as dream that my poor heart was to render such noble service?

## THE FIRST MINISTERIAL DUTY: PRAYER

#### SECOND MEDITATION

### *The Priest must be a Man of Prayer*

#### I

The Archangel called Daniel "a man of desires". Isaias called Christ "a Man of sorrows". Why not call Him equally "a Man of prayer"?

Christ's first act on entering into the world was, St. Paul assures us (*Heb.* x, 5), to pray to His Heavenly Father. His last before dying was that tremendous cry: *Father, into Thy Hands I commend my spirit.*— (*Luke* xxiii, 46.)

During His Public Life He spends whole nights in prayer (*Luke vi,* 12), and at daybreak He returns to the temple to repeat His supplications (*John viii,* 2). While discoursing He raises His eyes to heaven and prays; He frequently teaches His disciples how to pray, and for the sake of engraving it on their memory He often repeats that supreme formula of prayer, the *Our Father*.

Our Lord, by example, teaching and recurrent exhortation, is the first Master of prayer.

O High Priest and Essential Mediator between God and man: Thou who hast not disdained to give me a special share in Thy Priesthood, see that there be accomplished in me one day the promise of Zacharias the prophet: "*I will pour out upon you a gracious spirit of prayer.*"—(Zach. xii, 10.)

## II

Where shall I turn to ask for help but to Thee, O Lord?

The enemy is manifold and strong and, unfortunately for me, quite used to getting the upper hand; what with the fascinating allurement of the objects that surround me, the weakness and miseries teeming within me, the peremptory and most serious nature of my obligations, the need to tame and shackle the well-nigh invincible concupiscence of the flesh, the life of angels that I must live, so near to my God and Saviour in ideals, in aspirations, in loves, in my very bodily demeanour. There is no nature, however well-endowed one may imagine it, with the fund of energies that I require.

To nobody more than me canst Thou say, Lord:

As the branch cannot bear fruit of itself, unless it abide in the vine; so neither can you, unless you abide with me . . . for without me you can do nothing.—(*John* xv, 4, 5.)

May I live continually in Thee, by Thy grace; and to Thee may I have recourse unceasingly in mind and heart!

## III

The Apostle calls the priest a man of God. The faithful would never have coined such a graphic turn of phrase by themselves, but their Christian instinct imparts to them what St. Paul received from the Holy Spirit: hence the faithful reward and respect in the priest one thing: the man of God.

Nothing is achieved by presenting ourselves to souls as men of books, or as geniuses steeped in profound lucubrations, or as orators of the well-rounded phrase and sparkling thought tinted with the magic splendour of a lively imagination; none of that invests us with the power over souls which characterises the Catholic priest.

The faithful demand that we descend to them, like Moses, from the pure unclouded summits of intimate communication with God, in order to speak to consciences in the Name of their Creator and their Saviour: that is, we must be men of prayer in the likeness of the Eternal Priest.

Are not our apostolic endeavours stricken with failure simply because we do not communicate intimately with God? The rays that radiated from Moses when he came down from the mountain do not radiate from us. The spirit of prayer does not shine in our countenances.

### RESOLUTION

To turn more frequently to God; not to begin any work of my ministry without praying first, and to pray as my Lord Jesus Christ would have me pray.

> If you ask anything of the Father in my name, He will give it you.

*If you ask*—so I will persevere untiringly until I am answered; *anything*—like a child entirely dependent upon, and expecting all from, his father; *of the Father*—with confidence, because no title like that of " Father " can so inspire me; *in my name*—the Saviour's name, and therefore I must ask only for those things that are a help, or at least not a hindrance, to the salvation He came on earth to bring me; *He will give it you*—a guarantee that if I pray under these conditions I shall most certainly obtain everything from my heavenly Father.

So my one and universal asset is prayer.


## THE FIRST MINISTERIAL DUTY: PRAYER

### THIRD MEDITATION

*Mental Prayer*

### I

If in my soul, illuminated by faith, there remains the tiniest spark of affection for supernatural good, or of hatred for sin and sin's necessary consequences, the love behind this affection or hatred will from time to time evoke an idea or a sentiment pertaining to its object. Meditation, therefore, in the sense of frequent and affectionate remembrance or reflection, is the *obbligato* accompaniment to the melody of love. Hence the Psalmist:

> Concupivi salutare tuum, Domine, et lex tua meditatio mea est.

> Meditabar in mandatis tuis, quae dilexi.

Quomodo dilexi legem tuam, Domine; tota die
meditatio mea est.

—(*Ps. cxviii.*)

" Weary it is, Lord, waiting for deliverance, but thy
law is my comfort. Fain would I have all my study in
the law I love. My delight is in thy bidding; ever my
thoughts return to it."

The only way to recapture this love, if we should
have the immense misfortune to be without it, would
be to meditate assiduously and systematically on God's
Goodness and promises. In the light of this Goodness
the supernatural treasures will stand revealed, they do
not shun the light of day. And why do we not passion-
ately desire them? Simply because we have not relished
the knowledge of them, an experimental knowledge that
only affectionate and sustained reflection will yield.

Grant me, O Lord, to bring my parched and thirsting
soul to those pure abundant waters where the seraphim
slake their thirst, and where legions of saintly souls have
drunk deep.

## II

It is not enough to believe; it is not good enough to
keep the soul-stirring divine truths stored away like
books of no practical use on the most recondite shelves
of the mind; these truths will be energy, impulse, and
fire, to the will and the other working faculties only
when they shed their light upon the intellect, arouse the
memory with their sublime evocations, inflame the will
with longing or inspire with dread; only when we
transform these truths by meditation into the daily
sustenance of our spiritual organism,

Why do I remain stone-cold in the presence of the truths of our holy Faith? Is it not, radically, because of my aloofness from the exercise of meditation?

Moreover, the priestly virtues, so delicate as they are, in vessels so brittle, amid the inclemencies of that harsh climate called the world, will germinate and reach maturity only if they are kept in their native warmth, like hothouse plants, in the grace of God and in an atmosphere of supernatural motivation. Such an environment is the product of chaste representations in the imagination, of pious reminiscences in the memory, of reasoning about holy things in the mind, and of spiritual yearnings in the will; that is to say, *meditation*.

And yet we wonder why our passions never seem to bend to control, why our virtues are lifeless or grow up so weak and rickety. Can't we see that the icy wind of a worldly and dissipated life is enough to nip them in the bud? Is there in my soul, open to all the gales of unruly desire, even the smallest plot of land sheltered by the warmth of piety where those virtues can germinate as in a nursery and come to maturity?

### III

In the confessional, in the pulpit, in our everyday dealings, we are obliged to speak a thousand times about the truths of our Faith and about Christian morals, in order to teach, convert, and consolidate the good begun.

If we try to impart all this to the faithful without having first made it part and parcel of our inmost being, both affectively and intellectually, by means of assiduous meditation, we shall closely resemble a man describing scenes only from hearsay, with the same inexactitude, conventionalism, and lack of feeling.

Let us bestow loving attention day in and day out upon what we have to expound to the faithful, and then, how different our speech will be! It will flow with the convincing and captivating tones of one who has contemplated a beautiful landscape and been wholly captivated by it.

There must be no mistake about it: only from frequent meditation shall we extract, by the grace of God, that overwhelming power of persuasion inherent in divine Truth, that evangelical unction, which is the soul of all fruitful apostolate.

## RESOLUTION

I frankly confess before God that I have flippantly underestimated the practice of mental prayer, notwithstanding the high esteem in which the Church has always held it. I see now, as clear as daylight, that this underrating has been the source of not a few of my spiritual misfortunes and of the fruitlessness of my ministry. By my undevout life, estranged from the atmosphere of the spirit of faith, I have been what St. Jude would call

> "a cloud with no water, driven before the winds;
> an autumn tree that bears no fruit, given over anew
> to death, plucked up by the roots."—(*Jude*, 12.)

Grant me, O God, steadfastness in carrying out for the remainder of my days this salutary resolution which in Thy Presence I now engrave on my heart; namely, never to omit for a single day the exercise of meditation; if it cannot be done in the morning, I shall make it in the evening or at any other hour. I am resolved to keep the law laid down in Canon Law:

" All clerics shall devote some time to mental prayer every day."—(*Can.* 125, *ii.*)

## THE FIRST MINISTERIAL DUTY: PRAYER

### FOURTH MEDITATION

*The Priest's Practice of Mental Prayer*

#### I

How long should my daily meditation last?

We all know St. Teresa's advice—if it is hers—to meditate for at least one quarter of an hour each day.

" If a soul perseveres in mental prayer, however many sins, temptations, and lapses the devil may bring about in a thousand different ways, I hold it a certainty that the Lord will finally see her safe in the harbour of salvation."—(*Life, chap. viii.*)

We should profit greatly if we read again and again this chapter eight of the life of that wonderful " Mater spiritualium." On this all-important theme it contains lapidary expressions, such as the following:

" Although we are always in God's Presence, it seems to me that those who take up prayer seriously are present to God in a different way, because they see that God is looking at them."

If I could only feel God's gaze on me for fifteen minutes each day! At the trifling expense of one quarter of an hour's " seeing that God is looking at me," this is the bargain I get: freedom from mortal sin, at least.

What excuse shall I make to Thee, Lord, on the Day

of Reckoning if even this I refuse Thee, and thus remain in sin?

## II

Where shall I meditate?

In the last resort, wherever God is, and He tells us:

> "Do I not fill heaven and earth?"—(*Jerem. xxiii*, 24.)

But, if you can manage it, choose a place of retirement:

> "When thou art praying, go into thy inner room and shut the door upon thyself."—(*Matt. vi*, 6.)

It would be preferable, perhaps, in your own bedroom, after dressing and saying your morning prayers, before you go out and get busy with other affairs; because if in the early morning your mental prayer was neglected or impeded, it is not easy to make it later in the day. And happy you if you can spend this quarter of an hour before the Blessed Sacrament, where it will be so much easier to place yourself in God's Presence, where everything is conducive to recollection, and where our Lord's promise finds literal fulfilment: *I am there in the midst of them.*

And what posture should I adopt?

Let it be devout, becoming, and naturally indicative of God's Presence. Christ, however, prayed prostrate upon the ground: the posture more of a slave and humbler than any other known to man—and Christ was the Only-Begotten of the Father! We, poor wretches, what shall we do? We may stand, sit, or kneel, as we please; as long as our demeanour reflects the highest respect for the Majesty of the One in Whose Presence we pray.

### III

At what time of the day?

At daybreak, after the example of the Psalmist:

> Praevenerunt oculi mei ad te diluculo ut medi-
> tarer eloquia tua.—(*Ps. cxviii*, 147.)

"Twilight comes, and I awake to plead with Thee."
And after the example of our Lord Himself:

> "Then, at very early dawn, he left them, and
> went away to a lonely place, and began praying
> there."—(*Mark i*, 35.)

Your early morning prayer will please God immensely,
because you will be starting the day with a gift of time
otherwise given to resting.

At no other time will your spirit be so free to mount
the calm regions of the divine Mysteries. Every hour
that slips by during the day leaves on one's conscious
mind a trail of worry, regret, or some deep sensorial
impression, like so much birdlime fettering the flight of
the mind from the things of earth.

Moreover, your early rising, if I may say so, will cut
at the roots of those serious dangers which a refined
sense of chastity encounters in over-sleeping, in the soft
and sensuous indulgence of drowsy semi-consciousness
when the weak human will is the only one asleep, while
the rabid instincts of the flesh emerge from their kennel
and begin to whine for their food.

The priest who does not rise early and who yields
with dilly-dallying complacency to the pleasure of morning dozing will not make his meditation; he will not
be devout, perhaps not even upright and honest; nor
will his parishioners be good Christians if their shepherd
is still sleeping when they have to be already at work

in fields, factories, and offices, having had to pass by a mute belfry, by the bolted and barred doors of a silent church, as though it were a shop that had gone out of business or a haunted house.

O Jesus, alone and forgotten in those churches that do not open until mid-morning, deliver Thy Church from the shame of seeing Her homes of prayer the last to open and the first to close, like so many redundant showrooms.

Give to Thy flock watchful and thoughtful shepherds who will rise at break of day to gather for themselves and for their sheep the manna of divine blessings.

## IV

What method of prayer shall I use?

Several authors have given their own: SS. Ignatius of Loyola, Peter of Alcántara, Francis de Sales, and among the masters of the spiritual life, Fr. Granada. They all agree as to the need for establishing some sort of orderly use of the mental faculties; so we might sum up in the words of Astete's popular Spanish catechism:

> "What is mental prayer?—That which is done by exercising the powers of the soul: remembering something good and holy with the memory; thinking about it and reasoning it out with the intellect; and with the will, making various acts, such as sorrow for sin, or various resolutions, such as to go to confession or to lead a better life."

But when all is said and done, perhaps the most suitable method for everyone, with few exceptions, will be that very simple procedure adopted by St. Teresa during those eighteen years of difficulty and dryness when she found herself unable to dispense with aids to meditation, and until God raised her to lofty supernatural contemplation. These are her words:

> " Now I seem to understand why the Lord provided that I should find no one to teach me (methods of discursive prayer), because it would have seemed an impossibility to persevere those eighteen years which I spent in such difficulty and such great aridity through not knowing, as I say, how to use my reasoning power in prayer. During all those years, except perhaps just after receiving Holy Communion, I never dared to settle down to prayer without a book; I was scared to be without it; I felt like going out defenceless to an armed mob. With this remedy—the book—which was like a bodyguard or a shield warding off the assaults of many distracting thoughts, I went along consoled. Not that aridity was the ordinary thing, but it came upon me whenever I was without a book, and my soul was immediately routed; but with the book my soul began to gather its thoughts together and to hold them caressingly. And often it was enough merely to have the book beside me. Sometimes I read a little, sometimes a lot, according to the favour the Lord dispensed me. And so it seemed to me at the beginning that as long as I had a book and could find solitude there was no danger which could deprive me of such great good."

What the great Mistress of the spiritual life so graphically depicts is rather like the usual comportment of our fickle and restless imagination than an extraordinary path of trial, don't you think so? Then, after the Saint's example, keep it on a leash during meditation, by the deliberate and well-pondered reading of a spiritual book.

## RESOLUTION

From to-morrow I shall rise early. Five o'clock? . . . Six? . . . It depends on the season of the year.

And I shall take all necessary measures to overcome my laziness. I shall not leave my bedroom without first having gone through my quarter or half-hour's meditation leisurely, unless I can easily do it in the church. This resolution will be part of my examination of conscience before going to Confession; and if I have failed, I shall accuse myself clearly and bluntly.

" *Perish the skill of my right hand* " (Ps. cxxxvi, 5) if I overlook this resolution!

# THE BREVIARY

FIRST MEDITATION

*An Obligation and a Treasure*

## I

As a mental focusing before the recitation of the daily Office, and now as a preamble to this meditation, let us heed the majestic voice of the Church echoing the rallying call of the royal Prophet:

> Venite, exultemus Domino, jubilemus Deo, Salutari nostro!

"Come, friends, rejoice in the Lord's honour; cry we out merrily to God, our strength and deliverer!" (*Ps. xciv*, 1.)

Throughout her whole history the Church has enjoined upon her priests the canonical Hours, composed chiefly of the psalms. Vestiges of this ruling are to be found in the *Apostolic Constitutions* of Pope St. Clement, in Tertullian, and even in Philo Judaeus' book on the *Therapeutae*.

The precept of the Lateran Council should be familiar to all priests: " Districte praecipientes, in virtute sanctae obedientiae, ut Divinum Officium nocturnum, pariter atque diurnum, studiose celebrent atque devote." A strict command, in virtue of holy obedience, that all priests perform the Divine Office, the night Office and the day Office, both diligently and devoutly.

Canon 135 of the new Code runs as follows:

" Clerics in Major Orders are under obligation

to recite daily all the canonical hours according to their proper and approved liturgical books."— (*Trans. Woywood.*)

It is therefore a grave, inescapable duty which I freely took upon myself at ordination. Have I, in actual practice, always considered it as such? Haven't I often claimed, under futile pretexts, to be released from this obligation?

## II

We should not undermine the force of this obligation imagining it to be merely ecclesiastical, something human. Even if it were, it would none the less be seriously binding in conscience. The Church, as the perfect Society that She is, has received from her Divine Founder the power to legislate, the power most essential to any self-contained human society properly constituted.

In reality, however, it is something more. The Divine Office is radically and substantially of Divine Law; it is of the pith and marrow of our priesthood, of priesthood in general; for, as the Epistle to the Hebrews expresses it:

"The purpose for which any high priest is chosen from among his fellow-men, and made a representative of men in their dealings with God, is to offer gifts and sacrifices in expiation of their sins." —(*Heb. v, 1.*)

Hence the Apostles thought themselves bound primarily to prayer, in preference to corporal works of mercy: *It is not reason that we should leave the word of God and serve tables . . . we will give ourselves continually to prayer and to the ministry of the word.* (Acts vi, 2 and 4.)

We are the lawful representatives before God, appointed by the Church; Her ambassadors at the Divine Court; and the ambassadorial petitions we are asked to present before God are not left to our private initiative, they are given us and even formulated for us word for word: the prayers of the breviary and other liturgical books. Mother Church knows only too well—for She understands her children as only a mother can—that left to our own devices we should make a hash of this petitioning, if we did it at all.

The Office, therefore, is of Divine Law as regards its essence, and of Ecclesiastical Law in the concrete form of its expression. Thus the priest who is physically debarred from reciting the breviary is dispensed by the Church, but not entirely; it is commuted to him for other prayers.

O God, I believe that it is Thou personally who hast laid upon me a strict obligation to pray more frequently than any other soul. I realise that at ordination I assumed the most honourable task of representing the great Kingdom of Thy Church before Thy lofty Throne.

I am the mouthpiece of over four hundred million Catholics, of countless sincere non-Catholics, and even of all mankind, of the entire creation: I speak for them before the Throne of the Most High.

What a sublime function! Who am I to deserve it?

## III

Justice—commutative justice very often, and always equity—bids me say my Office. If the Church imposes on me the obligation of prayer and sacrifice, it is quite right that I should find attached thereto the means of a livelihood; and vice-versa, if I accept the livelihood I also incur the corresponding obligations. This is the idea, implicit at least, in the minds of the faithful who have bequeathed their possessions to the clergy, demanding of them in return the divine praises. In the old foundations this was often laid down explicitly.

If the faithful provide me with a livelihood, if I am kept in food and clothes, and even live in the lap of luxury, at the expense of the faithful, so that I may fulfil my priestly obligations, what if I neglect my duty? Do I not hold myself up to scorn? I could well appropriate to myself the caustic comment which the humble, hard-working St. Vincent de Paul used to think applied to him: "Wretch! you're not even earning your daily bread!"

## IV

Apart from the foregoing motives and that of the common good, what spiritual treasures would be mine if I said the Divine Office properly! Treasures of the mind, treasures of the heart, imperishable treasures of the soul.

I should be making the holiest use of part of my day by the fulfilment of Christ's great precept: "*To pray continually, and never be discouraged*"; a precept reaffirmed afterwards by St. Paul: "*Never cease praying.*" (Luke xviii, 1; I Thess. v, 17.)

I should be steeping my spirit in the ever-fresh aroma of those old prayers of the Church, the only prayers worthy of God; of those psalms wherein the Divine Spirit pleads with unutterable groans and longings through the voice of all creatures visible and invisible, a pleading that runs through the whole scale of human love, feeling, and mysterious yearning.

And perhaps I shall also begin to be curious and delve

into the hidden treasures amassed in the liturgical books, in the Missal, Ritual, Breviary, etc.; books where one can learn the language that is pleasing to God, books abounding in sovereign beauty, enough to enrich many a literature; books that in sheer grace of style, depth of feeling, boldness and sublimity of thought, surpass the greatest literatures, either popular or classical.

Let us hang our heads in shame. To our confusion, it has taken strangers, lay-people, sometimes even atheists and enemies of Christ's Church, to penetrate our cathedrals and churches and bring to light their innumerable artistic treasures. We were like a stupid child who needed the assistance of a neighbour to point out to him the value of the furniture and jewels bequeathed him by his father. Learned men, even men with no religion, had to come from outside and explain to us the power and grandeur radiating from those liturgical prayers and canticles which we maul and mumble so listlessly day after day.

## Resolutions

1.  I shall never forget the practical issue: that the obligation to say the Office is *sub gravi,* and that therefore I commit a mortal sin the day I omit it entirely, or a notable part of it equivalent to one of the small Hours, unless I am excused for some good and solid reason of charity or justice or I am handicapped by some physical or moral impossibility; and if I hold a benefice, in the strict sense of the word, any unwarranted omission of the Office obliges me to make restitution.

2.  In my spare moments—and who hasn't them?— I propose to study the breviary: the psalter and the

prayers added by the Church. Could I honestly say that I ever spent so much as half an hour in such profitable study? Am I quite sure I don't consider the breviary something unrelated to practical life, futile, scarcely intelligible; in fine, something to be read just because it *has* to, because it's the law, and that's that? To persuade myself of the shallowness of this judgement, this very day I'm going to study slowly all the prayers of Prime and Compline in order to grasp their meaning thoroughly.

Jesus, grant me the grace to end my life with the recitation of Compline; I would take it as a sign of my predestination.

## THE BREVIARY

### SECOND MEDITATION

*The Way to Recite it*

#### I

After lively controversies the moralists have made the happy discovery that it is sufficient to recite the Divine Office with "virtual" intention and "external" attention in order to fulfil the precept of the Church. I have at least virtual intention of praising God by the mere opening of the breviary to recite it as usual. And external attention merely demands that while reading the breviary I should not distract myself with anything destined of its nature to preclude the application of my mind to what I am reciting. When these two requirements are met, and they are within everyone's reach, I shall have avoided grievous sin.

So there we are! We have argued with God about His rights and our duties, and now the matter is cleared up, the boundaries are drawn!

But surely, in God's service there is something more than refraining from insulting and offending Him grievously! If we cannot rise above this level, can we call ourselves children of God?

God requires of me, at least *sub levi*, internal intention also, and this internal intention is quite easy and can take a number of different forms, should my fickle mind soon tire of one. It is achieved by any of the four following means:

1.    Attending to the proper articulation of the words. This is called "material" attention, and it is sufficient.

2.    Fixing the mind on the ideas expressed—and beautiful, fervent and varied ideas they are!

3.    Considering with a simple act of the mind the Presence of God, of Jesus Christ in the Eucharist, our Blessed Lady, etc.

4.    Keeping in mind some particular intention I desire to obtain through the recitation of the Office; for example, the conversion of a sinner, the overcoming of an evil suggestion, etc.

Dear Lord, why should I consider it well-nigh impossible to live intimately united to Thee for one hour each day, and that one hour split up? Lord, strengthen my weakness.

II

We are asked to recite the Office "digne"—becomingly, worthily, which means we should pronounce the words properly, articulating every syllable—initial, middle and final—of every word, pausing at commas and full-stops, not rushing over asterisks; and yet, of course, without that excessive dragging which would be abnormal in ordinary human speech; but with that calm dignity that one would use in presenting an important matter to a person of note. God is satisfied if we speak to Him after the manner of our intercourse with people who inspire us with respect by reason of rank or lineage; He wants no ridiculous exaggerations unworthy of divine worship. Is that asking too much?

I am the Church's ambassador to God, ambassador in affairs of paramount importance. Who would ever think of entrusting an embassy to a scatter-brain or a stammerer?

Is the salvation of souls, which I have to negotiate with God through the Divine Office, of minor importance?

### III

A third help towards the worthy fulfilment of this duty is, to recite the Hours at their proper times: Matins and Lauds before Mass, Small Hours during the morning, Vespers and Compline in the afternoon or evening; and better still, never to retire for the night's rest without anticipating the Matins and Lauds of the following day. The Office, divided and said at the proper times, is not a burden; whereas, if allowed to pile up at the end of the day or night, it becomes intolerable. Better to advance the recitation within reasonable bounds than leave it to accumulate, especially if obstacles loom ahead.

And finally, to read the Office in a place conducive to recollection: in one's private study, in a field, alone.

etc., etc., and to give to each Hour the time and space it demands.

I wonder, Lord, whether it is not through considering this high ministerial appointment of mine a mere nuisance and a kind of gauntlet that I have to run at all costs as hurriedly as possible, that I have made no choice of place and have seized any odd scrap of time which, but for this obligation, I would have simply wasted!

## Resolutions

1. I shall consider the Canonical Hours my most important occupation, the primary purpose for which God grants me the day (after the offering of the august Sacrifice), the most worthy of me, the most meritorious. And the day I have not satisfied this obligation I shall account myself an unworthy priest and a dishonest man.

2. I shall not even be satisfied with being able to say "I've finished that anyway!" Certain it is that the signature of a notary, although in unreadable and in-elegant scribble, lends legal force to a public document . . . but have I no concern for the respect due to God and to my own ministry?

So, when purifying my intention at the beginning of the Divine Office, I shall always exclude, as injurious to God and to myself, the base idea of rushing through it as quickly as possible, as if to get rid of a crushing burden.

# THE SECOND PRIESTLY DUTY: THE HOLY EUCHARIST

## *Grandeur of the Mass*

### I

Hoc est corpus meum, hic est sanguis meus.
Hoc facite in meam commemorationem.

O the grandeur and simplicity of the Divine Power!
With words so brief and so unostentatious our Lord
gave fulfilment to one of the solemnest of prophecies:

> From the rising of the sun even to the going
> down, my name is great among the Gentiles: and
> in every place there is sacrifice and there is offered
> to my name a clean oblation. For my name is great
> among the Gentiles.—(*Malach. i,* 11.)

The glory of God's Name and knowledge of It spread
throughout the world: these are fruits of the Holy
Sacrifice of the New Covenant. It is the divine bestowal
in answer to the first petition of the Our Father:
*Hallowed be Thy Name.*

How often, my Jesus, I have felt ashamed of the
fruitlessness of my priesthood! I made a sad mistake.
With just the daily celebration of the Mass I co-operate
to bring about the greatest good of God and of
creatures: the furtherance of the glory of the Lord.

### II

There is no religion without sacrifice. Sacrifice has
always been considered the primary act of worship.

Hence, in the Old Testament, the greater and better portion of the liturgical practices were merely sacrifice in its various shapes and forms. But since that sacrifice was no more than shadow and symbol incapable in itself, for all its variety, of purifying and sanctifying souls, our Divine Redeemer, Eternal Priest, abolished it entirely, substituting in its place His own Oblation of infinite value on the Cross.

And with the intention of leaving His visible Church a sacrifice also visible, the Sacrifice of the New Pasch or Passover betokening His departure from this world to His Father; and that not only the authority but even the exercise of His Eternal Priesthood according to the Order of Melchisedech might not cease to exist on earth, He instituted the unbloody Sacrifice of our altars in remembrance and as a substantial perpetuation of His bloody Holocaust upon the Cross. Thus His infinitely precious Blood, shed once for all on Calvary, would be continually applied to us for the remission of our daily transgressions.

I thank Thee, Jesus, for that sovereign device of Thy love; and I thank Thee still more for wishing Thy Body and Blood to be offered to the Divine Majesty through these sinful hands of mine. *Yea, Father, for so hath it seemed good in Thy sight.*—(*Matt. xi,* 26.)


### III

To consecrate the Body and Blood of Christ is the Church's mightiest exercise of power.

To approach with imperiousness, with three words, the Right Hand of God, the Bosom of the Father, and there to lay hold, in a certain sense, on the Only-Begotten Son and bring Him down to earth; to renew each day, each hour, each moment, over the face of the earth, the most glorious, the most meritorious feat of the Word of God, His Sacrifice; to earn, to seek and find, for all her countless children their daily Bread, and to feed them with It, almost force It upon them, lest they hunger, faint and die; to bring Christ into the world, into this vale of tears, to the side of every banished child of Eve: Jesus Christ, comfort in every sorrow, aid and relief in all our miseries;—O Lord! for this alone Thy Church is worthy to be named mankind's chief Benefactress; and this our priestly dignity, the greatest and holiest power for good on earth.

How beautiful and true the words of St. Francis of Assisi to his friars: "Let us respect priests; their hands give us the Body of Jesus Christ."

## IV

Sacrifice, in the liturgical sense, is the outward offering by a lawfully appointed minister of something visible to God in order to acknowledge God's supreme dominion over us and our total submission to Him. Sacrifice for sin carries with it immolation of the victim offered: by the death of the victim, the shedding of its blood, the pouring out of the blood over the altar, the burning of it, or by any other means that indicate our acknowledgement of God's supremacy and our entire submission.

In the Mass the Victim whose Immolation is expressed and "signified" (in the profound sense of this word) by the dual Consecration of bread and wine is no other than Jesus Christ Himself, God and Man. He is the divinely-appointed Minister or Priest— *Sacerdos in æternum*—in His own right, whereas my priesthood here, as in the other Sacraments, derives from His: I am His vicar and dispenser. Thus He makes me a partaker of His Eternal Priesthood and bestows upon me the power which He exclusively owns of ratifying in His Name and Blood the New Covenant, just as the Old Covenant was ratified with the blood of animals.

The Holy Mass, besides being the chief act of adoration and submission to God, and therefore the primary expression of worship, is the most effectual of supplications. It has been the Church's tactics in every age to put before the eyes of God the Name of His own Son; She has never dared to pray without this recommendation: *per Dominum nostrum Jesum Christum Filium tuum.* How much greater, then, will her appeal be in the sight of the Father when She presents to Him not merely the name and remembrance of His Son but the very Son in Person, real and consubstantial with Him, seated on His Right Hand and likewise offering Himself on Calvary! It was impossible to devise a prayer more pleasing to God; and no wonder, for it was devised by the Son Himself who knows so well His Father's good-pleasure: *Neither doth anyone know the Father, but the Son.*—(Matt. xi, 27.) It is, moreover, a prayer that embraces the power and purpose of every other prayer: worship, thanksgiving, atonement, supplication, etc.

Then why has my inconstancy hindered me from lingering long and lovingly over these surpassing realities?

Why should my fickle mind treat the Holy Mass, the august Sacrifice of the Body and Blood of Christ, as if it were just something to be done because it can't remain undone, a formality, a burden to be disposed of?

## V

Such is the grandeur of the august Sacrifice of our Altars that God has brought the downfall of every other religious sacrifice in Its trail. Polytheistic religions fell, and with them their sacrifices, human sacrifices very often; as in ancient America. The new religions appearing after Christ, even heterodox Christian cults, are without sacrifice and sacrificer. But in Thy Church, O Lord, Thou hast wished to perpetuate the Offering of the pure and only victim, the Lamb of God that taketh away the sins of the world.

Another great quality of this holy Sacrifice is the essentially spiritual worship that it inspires. Never do we adore the Father in spirit and in truth so much as we do here; because neither the senses nor even the intellect are offered an object commensurate with their capacities; only the lowliest appearances of bread and wine; and therefore only a mind enlightened by faith, unsupported by any other natural light or guide, explains our adoration of this sublime Mystery, the adoration that enlists our entire personality.

## RESOLUTIONS

1. Gratitude to God for this great Gift shall be the outstanding feature of my life, in imitation of Blessed John de Rivera, the Patriarch of the Eucharist, who on his coat-of-arms embossed beneath the Sacred Host this motto: *Tibi post haec, fili mi, ultra quid faciam?* My son, what more can I do for thee after this?

2. I will value the act of celebrating the Holy Mass

as the highest of my spiritual life and the most pleasing to God my Father; and I shall ever be convinced, in theory and in practice, that Thou bearest with me, O Lord, on earth, in spite of my wretchedness, for the primary purpose of offering Thee every day, as long as my hands can lift up to heaven, the Body and Blood of the spotless Lamb.

## THE HOLY EUCHARIST

### SECOND MEDITATION

*Respect for the Mass and for Myself as Celebrant*

### I

Pope St. Gregory says: "Who will doubt that at the moment of Immolation the heavens open? Or that the angelic choirs are in attendance at this Mystery of Jesus Christ? and that the highest and the lowest, the visible and invisible, become one thing? *Et summa et ima sociare unumque ex invisibilibus et visibilibus fieri?*

SS. Chrysostom, Augustine, and other Fathers expound the same ideas. According to them, during the Holy Sacrifice the altar is surrounded by legions of glorious spirits.

What wonder that angels should attend, and attend with infinite self-abasement, where the very Lord of the heavenly choirs stoops to such depths of infinite condescension!

I quite believe it. What I find difficult to believe is

that a worm of the earth like me should be invested with such an awe-inspiring dignity, and that in my hands should become incarnate, as it were, the "full of grace and of truth," the Only-Begotten of the womb of the Virgin-Mother.

## II

Let us consider the tremendous respect with which the Church in her liturgy surrounds the celebrant. He can be the humblest of priests, an unknown chaplain or curate, one lacking in virtue and learning and without social standing; but scarcely has he reached the altar to say Mass when he is given all the honours and preferences. Would Jesus Christ Himself be given better treatment were He to appear in Person as Sacrificer, robed in the sacred vestments? All the faithful, without exception: kings, princes, bishops and even the Roman Pontiff, if present, will remain on bended knees while the celebrant stands; and in reciting the *Confiteor,* the Pope himself will bow towards him and say: *et tibi. Pater . . . et te, Pater,* and will prostrate to receive his blessings.

How clearly the rubrics and ceremonies give to understand that during the most holy Sacrifice only two persons demand attention and supreme respect: Jesus Christ, under the Sacramental species, and the priest, whose voice is instrumental of Christ's Presence!

While I celebrated, was I not perhaps the only person to forget this, and forget it dozens of times? Was I not the only person wanting in respect towards myself?

G

### III

The Mass is the very Immolation of Calvary, and therefore, the goal of Christ's coming to the world and living in mortal flesh. And in the Mass, the same as on Golgotha, there can intervene, or at least attend, a great variety of people in a variety of rôles.

What is the rôle of the priest when celebrating? Will he be one of Christ's executioners? one of the soldiers offering the Victim gall and vinegar? one of those cruel adversaries who mock at His sorrows and blaspheme? one of the crowd of the merely inquisitive who get a thrill from the tragic details of an execution? Or will he be found among those good souls who believe in Christ and accompany Him in His prayer and agony? Will he stand between the Mother and the beloved Disciple? No. My place and rôle, when saying Mass, is pre-eminent: I have identified myself with the Divine Victim and Sacrificer, with the Lamb of God and the Eternal Priest who immolates It; through my lips speak the lips, the omnipotence and the Heart of Christ: *Hoc est Corpus meum; hic est Sanguis meus.*

Have I ever esteemed myself, at least in those sublime moments, for what I am and represent?

### RESOLUTIONS

1. I promise my Lord, the infinitely self-abased Victim for love of me, and I promise myself, in my great representative capacity at the Altar, at least a profound interior respect. And exteriorly, I shall see to it that wherever the Mass is concerned there shall be absolute conformity with the prescriptions of the Liturgy, especi-

ally in connection with the cleanliness of vestments, sacred vessels, altar cloths, corporals, purificators, etc.; and also in the tidy appearance of the church and its altars. I shall bear out the truth of my daily declaration: *Domine, dilexi decorem domus tuae*: Lord, I have loved the beauty of Thy house.—(*Ps. xxi,* 8.)

2. And since the veneration which the Mass inspires the faithful depends, in no small measure, upon the priest's pious observance of the rubrics, I propose to revise the ceremonies of the Missal, so that in all earnestness, and as soon as possible, I may examine my conscience on how I abide by them.

I desire, for the Saviour's sake, to win the compliment paid to St. Vincent de Paul: " There indeed you have a priest who says Mass well! "

## THE HOLY EUCHARIST

### THIRD MEDITATION

### *The Sacrilegious Mass: its Malice*

### I

By a sacrilegious Mass is meant a Mass celebrated without the necessary dispositions. It would be sacrilegious to celebrate non-fasting, except in cases allowed by the law; with a grievously sinful intention; with a conscience branded with mortal sin unforgiven by the Sacrament of Penance or by a perfect act of contrition in a case where the priest is obliged to celebrate because otherwise some grave injury would befall either himself or the neighbour, and he has considerable difficulty in finding a confessor.

I should never lose sight of canon 807:

> "The priest who should find himself in mortal sin shall not dare to say Holy Mass without previous sacramental Confession, no matter how contrite he may be over his sins. If he has no chance to go to Confession and urgent need obliges him to celebrate, he shall make an act of perfect contrition before saying Holy Mass, and shall be obliged to confess as soon as possible."

Have I ever had the audacity to mount the altar steps without any one of those dispositions which the Church demands of me in the Name of God? If I have, I have celebrated sacrilegiously. That Mass, so holy in Itself, became for me an outrageous profanation, just as on Calvary Christ's torture, of infinite merit, became for the executioners who crucified Him their greatest crime.

## II

A sacrilegious Mass is a piece of the most refined and perverse hypocrisy.

Our Divine Lord's greatest loathing during His earthly career in the midst of a degraded society—as swollen with pious appearances as drained of all true spirit of religion—was for hypocrisy; and yet, He found nothing to equal the hypocrisy of His own unworthy celebrants, except perhaps in two of the saddest episodes of His Passion: Judas's kiss of treachery in the Garden, and the pitiless, mocking scene of the crowning with thorns. If I have ever said Mass sacrilegiously I ought to meditate on these two episodes and compare my conduct with that of Christ's tormentors. The striking similarity between the profanations of the Passion and mine will serve to convince me and force me to confess that my lips, when kissing the altar and paten and touching the sacred Species during a sacrilegious Mass, were the lips of a traitorous Judas, kissing before bartering away, flattering before tearing to pieces, rendering service before profaning. My knees were bent, my head bowed, as if to adore Jesus Christ; but, in actual fact, to smite Him with cynical daring, to spit upon Him, and crown Him with the sharp thorns of disloyalty: the disloyalty of a minister of Christ, chosen from among thousands.

On that day I joined the ranks of Pilate's pretorian bodyguard; like them, and with signal success, I played the part of mock-worshipper before that outraged and silent King.

I stood revealed as a hypocrite, a whited sepulchre . . .

## III

The sacrilegious Mass is the vilest profanation of the Son of God, of the Eternal Word.

However clean my hands, the Church obliges me to wash them before going up to the altar, and while at the altar I have to purify once again my fingers that are to touch the sacramental species. To handle the Blessed Sacrament with dirty hands would shock any Christian with the tiniest spark of faith left in him. And if a criminal were to throw the Sacred Species on a dung heap or even on the ground, we should tremble with horror.

Will it not be a far greater crime to enclose the Body of Christ and shed His Blood within a breast befouled by mortal sin?

> " Quantum flagitium in spurcissimam corporis tui cloacam sacratum Christi Sanguinem profundere!"
> —(*St. Thomas of Villanova.*)

What a detestable crime it is to pour the Precious Blood into a heart that erupts in sensual desires or breeds the worms of lascivious actions; to pour It as though It were body waste or kitchen slops!

## IV

If sin is such, essentially, because it is an offence against God, and if the more directly we offend God the more grievously we sin; let us see whether we shall find an act personally more injurious to God and Christ than the sacrilegious Mass. There is certainly little or no harm done to another human being, God's image, or to his belongings; it is a crime that goes directly against God, not merely against a precept sprung from God's lips, not merely a profanation of the Holy Name of God, like blasphemy; it is a crime that would sully, if that were possible, the very God Himself; a personal affront to God present as God and Man in our hands, in our lips, in our breast, when we consecrate and receive Him sacrilegiously.

Is there a vestige of faith left in the dark recesses of the sacrilegious priest's soul? Does he believe what Holy Mother Church believes, that what he holds in his hands is the true Body and Blood of our Lord Jesus Christ? He will answer, *yes, I do believe,* with the same firm adherence as when the same question is put to him at Holy Viaticum. . . . and yet he profanes It?

No, St. Peter Damian does not exaggerate when he declares that no one is ever found guilty of sinning more grievously than the priest who in celebrating unworthily befouls, so far as in him lies, the mysteries of the Saving Victim.

And St. Thomas, speaking with his customary theological precision and as a man of cold reasoning, says:

> "Nemo deterius peccat quam sacerdos qui indigne sacrificat."

No one sins worse than the priest who sacrifices unworthily.

Have I ever committed such a crime? If so, I became the worst type of sinner—nemo deterius peccat.

O God! What if I have had the misfortune to commit this crime each day for a whole month, a year, three, ten years . . . where will God, the Searcher of hearts, find a sinner more abominable?

# THE HOLY EUCHARIST

## FOURTH MEDITATION

### The Sacrilegious Mass: The Celebrant's Guilt

## I

Cursed be he that taketh gifts to slay an innocent person. And all the people shall say: Amen.

—(*Deut. xxvii, 25.*)

All Christian people, the whole human race, down through the ages have kept on repeating these words of Deuteronomy in their thundering denunciation of the traitor-disciple who delivered the blood of the Just One for a handful of silver: *a curse on him! Amen!*

Judas! . . . But why should he be considered the greatest of villains? It is true he sold his Master for a few coins, and it is certain that there was not even the semblance of a motive for doing so; but how quickly and with what terrible anguish he repented! Such anguish of mind, that Judas was driven with the violence of a hurricane to retract before his accomplices in the treacherous deal; he went so far as to call them unjust and murderers, like himself: *I have sinned in betraying innocent blood.* An admirable confession worthy of the most sincere penitent: concise, swift: a few words of burning lava; a lapidary inscription, as it were, engraved on the conscience and the brow of the new Cain by the Hand of God! *I have sinned!* I acknowledge the infamous deed, I have no excuse! *I have sinned!* Like David, like the prodigal son. With cunning and treachery I have betrayed the Blood, the life, of the Innocent One, the Just One who has a better right to live than anyone else, whose life is more precious than all other lives together!

Not satisfied with such a sincere avowal, Judas returns the money, which was the chief if not the only motive of his crime. He throws it at them when they decline to accept it, because it seared his hands and his inmost soul. And that was Judas, the miser, the thief. *He was a thief and, having the purse, carried the things that were put therein.*—(*John xii,* 6.) In fine, his fearful remorse drives him to undergo a penalty that to the poor wretch seems but the adequate punishment of his crime, the penalty of suicide. A criminal penance indeed, but also a hard one!

A greater crime than Judas's, perhaps there is none; but is there none still more repugnant? Who knows! Let us consider that of the sacrilegious priest.

## II

Take the case of a priest—would to God no such thing were possible!—who every day for a whole month, a whole year or more, barters away our Divine Lord by celebrating unworthily, perhaps for the sake of the five or ten shilling stipend, or perhaps for no special reason at all, just because he cares not what he does. He delivers His Master up to Satan, the master of his own corrupt heart; he does it hundreds and thousands of times; but does he ever entertain the idea of putting a halter round his neck and putting an end to his ignominious existence? Far from throwing away his ill-gotten gains, the price of his sacrilege and treachery—*pretium sanguinis*—perhaps he never feels even the slightest tremor of horror, not even the faintest chill or stirrings of remorse.

On the Day of Judgement, on the Day of the great Reckoning, Tyre and Sidon, the Supreme Judge tells us, will confront Bethsaida and Corozain; Sodom and Gomorrha will stand in accusation against Capharnaum, the chosen but ungrateful city; and may we not add that Judas will confront the sacrilegious priest, his disciple? Fixing his hellish, vulture gaze on the dark conscience of the profaner of the Holy Victim, probing the inmost depths of the priest's perversity, he may well spit into his face and snarl with contempt: You were a greater villain than myself!

### III

And already on the threshold of eternity, if the priest in meeting with Christ should ask: "Who art Thou, Lord?" Jesus may reply, not in the words He spoke to Saul, but with a look which could be transcribed: "For thee, I am a nobody; even my Name thou tookest from me; for while my Bride, the Church, kept on repeating every day from the first words of her liturgy to the last, kept on repeating through thy lips, with ecstatic self-abasement: 'My Lord and my God!' thou, with the voice of thy lewd concupiscences over-mastering thy heart and memory and imagination and every atom of thy foul being, didst declare: 'Impossible! How could I behave like this towards a real God? No, God is not here: this is nothing but a parody, a means of livelihood; the most I am doing is pretending; I'm a good actor on the stage.' And therefore, to thee I have been a nobody, whereas thou, at my profaned altars from the first word to the last that came out of thy infamous mouth, thou in all thy movements and at every step wast a cynical hypocrite, a poisonous viper." "The hour is come now to tear away every mask, to light up every dark corner, and to restore to each one his proper name."

### RESOLUTION

If avarice blinded Judas, perhaps the one thing that will blind me, to the point of profaning the Sacrifice of our Altars, is lust.

Out of every hundred sacrilegious Masses will not lust account for over ninety?

O Jesus! Thou who didst choose a Virgin to be Thy Mother, grant me absolute purity of body and soul, even though miracles be needed to curb my sensual cravings. I promise Thee that, by Thy grace, I shall always keep winning that noble battle fought by hearts that are pure, through the wielding of those weapons human and divine which have always been in the hands of the glorious self-conquerors who put their trust in Thee.

## THE HOLY EUCHARIST

### FIFTH MEDITATION

*The Sacrilegious Mass: A Punishment*

#### I

And the sacrifice shall fail: and there shall be in the temple the abomination of desolation.

—(*Dan. ix*, 27.)

This was the final signal given by Daniel the Prophet, and afterwards by Christ Himself, of God's impending Wrath upon His Chosen People of Israel: the sign of God's abandoning them totally and irrevocably to the severest of punishments.

Far more abominable than the discontinuance of the Jewish sacrifices and the setting up by the Romans of the statue of Venus in the *Sancta Sanctorum*—which many commentators think constituted the " abomination of desolation "—is the profanation of the New Sacrifice.

Incomparably greater is the iniquity of setting up the Holy of Holies in Person, the God-Man Christ who hallows all things, in a breast made unclean by grievous sin.

In olden times the Tabernacle of the Blessed Sacrament was often the breast of our Lady's statues. Shall Venus take our Lady's place?

Wilt Thou not abhor, O Lord, far more than the cessation of Sacrifice the offering up of this Sacrifice on a cesspool for an altar? What else is a sacrilegious Mass?

## II

Whip in hand, bursting with anger, the Divine Saviour drove from the outer court of the Temple those who were profaning it by buying and selling, as in a market-place, the requisites for the temple offerings ordained by the Law. *Zelus domus tuae comedit me, et opprobria exprobrantium tibi ceciderunt super me.—* (*Ps. lxviii, 10.*)

> "Was it not jealousy for the honour of thy house that consumed me; was it not uttered against thee, the reproach I bore?"

But, Lord, what if Thou hadst found them in the Holy of Holies? And what wilt Thou not do to those who day after day, year after year perhaps, instead of honouring Thee, as they are in duty bound, fling Thy *clean Oblation* into their impure hearts like sweepings into a refuse bin—that *clean Oblation* in which as in a spotless mirror Thou beheldest Thy Glory countless ages before the Offering was accomplished on earth?

Thou art patient; yes, but in a case like this Thy

patience would be our undoing. Having waited for so long, as though Thou hadst no eyes to see, as though the spate of our iniquities did not touch Thee personally, with what fury will the pent-up cataract of Thy Wrath descend when it finally leaps or breaks through the flood-gates!

### III

The most heroic act of self-denial in order to reach God, the greatest effort of the will under the impulse of grace in order to entrench themselves in good, was for certain Saints, it is said, their fleeing from home over the prostrate bodies of their children, over the breast of the adored wife or venerated mother, in fulfilment of St. Jerome's *per calcatum perge patrem;* such was their moral courage and constancy.

The priest who says Mass in mortal sin, because his feet are set in the way of evil, proceeds still further: he rides rough-shed over everything, he tramples everything underfoot, even the Body, Blood, Soul and Divinity of the Son of God: *per calcatum perge patrem! . . .*

It is this which explains the most appalling outcome of sacrilegious Masses: the hardening of the heart, impenitence.

The Blood of Christ is become the cementing force in the structure of our iniquities! The sacrilegious Sacrifice has put the last nail in the coffin of a soul dead and buried in its own wickedness! The profaning of the Most Holy has been the daily sledge-hammer blow on the anvil of a reprobate heart!

## RESOLUTION

I shall not allow a single month to go by without devoting one or more meditations to this frightful theme: " The sacrilegious Mass," so that it may soak deep enough to make me tremble at the very mention of it.

Lord, nail my fickle mind to the cross of Thy chastening fear, and let this thought be one of the nails!

# THE HOLY EUCHARIST

### SIXTH MEDITATION

## *The Sacrilegious Mass : A Criminal Parody*

### I

Perhaps the most effective deterrent from celebrating unworthily would be from time to time, with greater or lesser frequency according as unruly passion and the risk of falling into grave sin intensify, to open the Missal and to reflect on the outrageous paradox that every word and rite of the Holy Sacrifice becomes when pronounced by a priest estranged from the Redeemer and dispossessed of that most sacred and indispensable of ornaments, divine grace.

I should try to make these reflections; the sight of a priest profaning the Divine Victim will appear each time more tragic and diabolical; the horror of it will put me in mind of something akin to the " Black Mass " of magic lore in the Middle Ages.

Let me take a few samples for practice.

## II

With mortal sin on my soul I enter the sacristy and say while washing my hands: *Da, Domine, virtutem manibus meis ad abstergendum omnem maculam, ut sine pollutione mentis et corporis valeam tibi servire.* Give virtue to my hands, O Lord, to cleanse away every stain, so that I may be worthy to serve Thee free from stain of mind and body.—A cynical lie! Pilate was less of a hypocrite when he washed his.

*Dealba me, Domine, . . . ut in sanguine Agni dealbatus, gaudiis perfruar sempiternis.* Make me white, O Lord, . . . so that being made white in the Blood of the Lamb, I may deserve an eternal reward.—My heart belies my lips. Was it not my evil passions that tore to tatters the snow-white garment of grace and flung it at the feet of Satan, like a filthy rag?

*Praecinge me, Domine, cingulum puritatis. . . . ut maneat in me virtus continentiae et castitatis.* Gird me, O Lord, with the cincture of purity . . . so that the virtue of continence and chastity may always abide in me.—Hoots of derision from the demon of lust who keeps my heart bound with Venus's iron cincture!

*Domine, qui dixisti : Jugum suave est. . . . fac ut istud portare sic valeam, quod consequar tuam gratiam.* Lord, who hast said: My yoke is sweet . . . grant that I may so carry it as to merit Thy grace.—Well may the Lord, whom my deceitful lips have invoked as many as seven times before mounting the altar steps, answer me with pent-up rage: *A saeculo confregisti jugum!* Thou hast thrown off my yoke and broken asunder every bond, and said: "I will not serve!"

### III

I reach the altar, and, after the prescribed reverential gestures, I begin: *In nomine Patris, et Filii, et Spiritus Sancti. Amen. Introibo ad altare Dei.*

What a mockery! Not even the executioners on Calvary ever thought of such a thing. To begin the blackest crime of my life in the Name of the Father, and of the Son, and of the Holy Ghost! When Christ said: *The hour cometh, that whosoever killeth you will think that he doth a service to God (John xvi, 2)*, must I include Christ Himself among the victims? And when the catechism taught me to begin good works with the Sign of the Cross, surely it did not mean a sacrilegious Mass!

*Judica me, Deus, et discerne causam meam. . . .*— Did anyone ever curse himself more savagely? *Judica me, Deus!* Judge me, O God! . . . Lord, close Thine ears; listen not to this madman who in the presence of the whole Church beseeches Thee to condemn him and cast him into the unquenchable fire.

*Munda cor meum ac labia mea, Omnipotens Deus . . . Dominus sit in corde meo et in labiis meis . . .*

What do these words mean in my mouth? To ask God to dwell in a heart enslaved by evil:

> " Never yet did Wisdom find her way into the schemer's heart, never yet made her home in a life mortgaged to sin."—*(Wisdom i, 4.)*

### IV

Lavabo inter innocentes manus meas . . .
Domine, dilexi decorem domus tuae. . . .
Ne perdas cum impiis animam meam . . .

"With the pure in heart I will wash my hands clean. . . .
How well, Lord, I love thy house in its beauty . . .
Lord, never count this soul for lost with the wicked." . . .

How many detestable lies in such brief words! From
the first word of the psalm to the last I am spitting out
poison.

*Orate, fratres, ut meum ac vestrum sacrificium
acceptabile fiat* . . . Pray, brethren, that my sacrifice and
yours be acceptable to God. Yes, in itself the Sacrifice
is most acceptable, but in my sinful hands, abominable.

*Sursum corda. Habemus ad Dominum.* My heart
lifted up to the Lord? No, He is captive of my own
lusts that master and enslave me.

*Cum angelis et archangelis hymnum gloriae tuae
canimus.* What a discord, what disharmony my sinful
life introduces into the music of visible and invisible
creation! Far better to hold my tongue.

*Hoc est enim corpus meum. Hic est enim calix
sanguinis mei . . . in remissionem peccatorum.* But of my
sins a seal and confirmation.

*Corpus Domini nostri Jesu Christi custodiat animam
meam in vitam aeternam. Amen.* The Body of Christ my
soul's safeguard unto everylasting life? Why, I have just
been guilty of the Body and Blood of Christ; I have
eaten and drunk my own condemnation.

*Sanguis quem potavi adhaereat visceribus meis . . .*
Thy Blood which I have just drunk cleave to my inmost
being . . .

The Chosen Race, deicide and accursed, never made
such a request. *His Blood be upon us!* they said, but I,
in pouring It sacrilegiously into my stomach, pray for
It to become one thing with my inmost soul and body;

I ask It to share my own moral corruption; I pray that its healing power be annulled. . . .

Thus, every word spells a horrible blasphemy, compared with which a trooper's profanity sounds more like a maiden's prayer.

So what am I to do? What am I to say? Can I change the liturgical prayers and substitute others of my own more in keeping with my dreadful state of soul? Of course not. What I can do, what I must do, until I get out of mortal sin, is not to approach the altar to say Mass, to deprive myself of It because I am unworthy; unless I wish to be caught up in a tornado of Divine Anger at every rubric and liturgical phrase, which were certainly not meant for sullied lips and putrid hearts.

## RESOLUTION

Once a month, at least, I shall meditate on each phrase and rite and ceremony of the Mass in this manner, until I am absolutely convinced of the diabolical paradox incurred by the priest who celebrates in mortal sin. A meditation of this sort will deter me most effectively from ever saying Mass without the essential dispositions; otherwise I may consider I have lost my faith in the Presence of the Son of God upon the Altar; and then, not only my Mass but all my other ministerial duties, my clerical garb, and the very name of priest, will be no other than a parody, a clownish farce unbecoming any right-minded man; and I should be doing far less harm if I looked around for some other occupation in life: anything at all would tally better with fundamental decency.

# THE HOLY EUCHARIST

## SEVENTH MEDITATION

### *Belief in the Real Presence*

#### I

To-day I am going to give myself a reasoned answer to the question: how is it that this Mystery of the Holy Eucharist, one of the most baffling, one to which the human mind offers toughest resistance when left to its natural weakness, is nevertheless become for me one of the easiest and most soul-satisfying to believe?

I believe in the Real Presence of Jesus Christ, God and Man, in the most Blessed Sacrament; present in every Catholic Church where a priest, no matter how obscure he may be, has pronounced the formula of Consecration; present here beside me in the lowly tabernacle of my church.

Why do I believe it? Because Christ has guaranteed it to me—witness the four Gospels and one of St. Paul's Epistles—in terse and peremptory sentences that slam the door on all subterfuge or merely symbolical interpretation.

*This is my body.*
*This is my blood.*

These words, of themselves and in their context, admit of no other than the proper and natural meaning which the Church has ever given them from the very beginning, in Her inspired Scriptures, Her various liturgies, Her Oecumenical Councils; in the exegetical homilies of the Fathers, and in the robust faith of Catholic peoples.

I believe, Lord, with a firm and gratifying faith that even when these words of Consecration may have sprung from my unworthy lips, like lilies from the mire, in obedience to them Thou wert really and substantially present beneath the forms and appearances of bread and wine. I believe it because Thou, the Absolute Truth; Thou, the Essential and Unfailing Light; didst never deceive, art not one to deceive, much less the immense flock of little ones who adore Thee, seek Thee and receive Thee as being truly present; because Thou hast said it. Lord, I believe in Thy creative word.

## II

Why do I believe? Because Christ, the sole Author of the Sacraments, is all-powerful.

He summons the bodies of the dead, and they return to life from the corruption of the grave. He utters a word of command to the most rebellious diseases, either in the sick person's presence or several miles away, and those diseases leave not a trace behind. He reproves the boisterous winds and waves, and they sing down calm and silent, like a class of prankish school-boys at the shout of a feared master. He treads the sea, and it sustains Him with rocklike solidity. Over a few loaves and fishes He bestows a single word of blessing, and they multiply indefinitely.

Not once did Christ give a command—and He gave many—to any element of the material world, that He was not obeyed without the slightest resistance or hesitation. In other words, He ever showed Himself absolute —we might even say tyrannical—Master over matter, doing with it and in it whatever He willed; for the simple reason that it was He who had brought it into existence out of nothing, endowing it with the capacities He pleased. Will He not, therefore, be able to do with it more, infinitely more, than anything my blunt mind can possibly cope with?

Lord, I believe. For Thou canst annihilate the whole world, if it should please Thee; Thou canst transform it to Thy liking; Thou canst change the substance of bread and wine into Thy own Body and Blood, and thus multiply Thy Presence beyond all human scope and measure.

What was possible for Thee became an actual fact, for Thou didst say but the word, and never was it necessary for Thee to voice Thy commands to inert matter twice over.

*Ipse dixit, et facta sunt.*—(Ps. xxxii, 9.)

### III

Again, why do I believe? Because the whole Church believes. No, I am not alone; I share this belief with millions and millions of human beings from every nation, race, and climate; with all the centuries of Christian history, with people of every age and condition and temperament; with souls joyful and sorrowful, with souls raised aloft in the auroral splendours of grace, or sunk in the night of sin; with the little children who seal the first dawning of reason with an act of faith in Christ's Eucharistic Presence and their first Holy Communion, as with a morning star; with all who close their length of days with the heavenly clasp of Holy Viaticum.

I believe with the Church, whose faith in the Eucharist is Her very life. Wrench from Her this belief, and you will have destroyed Her entire liturgy, demolished Her cathedrals and churches, killed Her priesthood, effaced from Her history the most brilliant and holy pages written with Her blood and tears. It was for Thee, O Jesus in the Blessed Sacrament, that She allowed Herself to be persecuted and bled, and remnants of Her vesture and entrails to cleave to the claws of tyrants!

To-day, the same as in the catacombs, the same as in the Middle Ages, and in the century that witnessed the institution of the Feast of Corpus Christi; to-day, as truly as then, and perhaps even more so, this belief in the Eucharist urges the faithful on to the sublimest acts of adoration ever recorded in history. We have seen the Eucharistic Congress of Madrid, Rome, Chicago, Dublin, Buenos Aires, etc.; vast throngs of men, women, and children from every nation and class and walk of life kneeling and singing round the small white Host in the sumptuous boulevards and thoroughfares of our modern cities.

No, I am not alone. I believe, Lord, as all of these believe; and from the depths of my nothingness I adore Thee, my God, Whom love for me has brought to such depths of condescension!

## IV

Finally, why do I believe? Because this dogma harmonises so perfectly with the nature of God and the nature of man.

God, Who must needs be intimately and perpetually united to the least atom of His creation by the same

Love that moved Him to give it existence; God, present everywhere in every creature, became Man: the Man humanising, so to speak, the Attributes of the Godhead; the God " divinising," as it were, all the qualities of manhood; Flesh wherein God took up abode; God to Whom our flesh adhered . . . what wonder if this God-Man, feeling in the flesh the tendencies of His Divine Immensity, should decide to render effectual, even as Man, the Divine Attribute of being all in all and present in every part of the ransomed world!

Even this puny human heart of ours feels the urge to be at one and the same time in every place where there is something to see, something to hear, something to admire and love! The colossal strides of modern science, inventions already perfected and those still in the realm of dreams, what do they all seek to express? They but express those secret forces of matter and spirit which man is gradually mastering and harnessing and enlisting in the service of that restless human longing to multiply his presence and action simultaneously: to see everything and hear everything at the same time; hence, our railways, steamers, motor-cars, aeroplanes, telephones, radio and television sets. Man yearns to multiply his being indefinitely in time and space; he strives to imitate the Immensity of God Himself, of the God Who made man to His own image and likeness.

## V

Christ, with His God-Man's love and His Omnipotence, solved the problem—a problem which has always been a blind-spot keeping the human race in continual restlessness—in three short sentences:

*This is my body.*

*This is my blood.*

*Do this in remembrance of me.*

Words of greater power than the first *Fiat* of creation!

With those three short sentences, pronounced by Jesus in the Upper Room at Jerusalem, all obstacles of time and place vanish. His love throws off all fetters. He will be with us until the end of time, at any point of our planet where there is a priest and a soul yearning for Christ. Fulfilment will be given even literally to the promise with which He closed the cycle of His teachings:

> Behold I am with you all days, even to the consummation of the world.—(*Matt. xxviii,* 20.)

Praise to Thee, O Lord, Who, because Thou art true God, dost reach the remotest confines with Thy Wisdom and Strength; because Thou art true Man, art inflamed with the human longing to embrace and unite Thyself to all Thy redeemed; for Thou in Thy skill supreme hast effected with three short sentences what we mortals have been dreaming of and toiling for since the world began!

### RESOLUTIONS

1. I will make more frequent acts of faith in the Real Presence of Jesus Christ upon our altars. I shall try to drink in and saturate my mind with this most true, divinely-infallible, and divinely-human idea: that throughout the whole world there is nothing more adorable than a Consecrated Host. Oh, if only that radiant

hought would one day become the very life of my mind
nd the fire of my will!

2. And this I will also teach the faithful time and
ime again, until they of their own accord go eagerly in
quest of Christ in the Blessed Sacrament, loving Him
nd adoring Him in this Sacrament before everything
and everyone else, preferring His Presence to every
picture or statue or shrine, however devotional or miraculous; giving Him precedence over every popular Saint,
over the most Holy Mother of God Herself, over His
most cherished and venerated images.

## THE HOLY EUCHARIST

### EIGHTH MEDITATION

#### *Why the Mass was Instituted*

### I

Why do I believe? In considering the purposes our
Lord had in mind when instituting this wonderful
Sacramental Sacrifice I shall discover a further motive
of credibility, and not the least of them.

First purpose: To convert every square foot of earth
and sea into a Calvary purpled with the steaming Blood
of the Lamb. O Lover of this our earthly dwelling, it
did not satisfy Thee to shed Thy Blood on one Golgotha, it was Thy desire to turn the whole earth into
a Golgotha and an altar of Thy Sacrifice.

The very words of the institution of the Holy
Eucharist, in their original Greek recording, *This is my
body which is being delivered unto you*, would seem

to indicate an actual mystical Immolation there and
then. From that day onwards the Sacrifice of the Cross
was to be made a living and actual reality among us
every hour of the day and night, in every nation, in
every spot on earth; so that we can say of this globe of
ours: but a microscopic point lost in the unfathomable
abyss of the heavens, and yet Christ has turned it into
His most sacred Altar; because everywhere, even in the
most hidden and distant corners, the earth is at some
time or another being bathed in the Blood of the Victim
sacrificed for our sins.

## II

Second purpose: To establish the New Covenant:
*Novum Testamentum.*

> Drink ye all of this, for this is my blood of the
> new testament, which shall be shed for many unto
> the remission of sins.—(*Matt. xxvi,* 28.)

In these words of the consecration of the chalice it
is evident that Christ alludes to the rites with which
Moses ratified the Old Covenant:

> And he took the blood and sprinkled it upon
> the people, and he said: this is the blood of the
> covenant which the Lord hath made with you con-
> cerning all these words.—(*Exodus xxiv,* 8.)

The Old Covenant was made for the observance of
the Law—*which the Lord hath made with you concerning all these words;*—the New Covenant was made for
the sake of pardoning sins, in virtue of the Redeeming
Blood: *in remissionem peccatorum.*

Moses shed half of the victims' blood upon the

ground, and with the other half he sprinkled the heads of the Hebrews. Christ, not satisfied with shedding all His Blood on Mount Calvary, wishes to seal with It every soul that enters into His Fold by Baptism.

Every Communion, dear Jesus, is a seal, a hall-mark, an additional witness before heaven and earth, that I am Thine. After so many Communions, what atom remains of my person, body and soul, that does not exhibit Thy mark, that does not evoke the covenant I made with Thee?

### III

Third purpose: To erect a monument to the greatest of all achievements: Christ's Passion and Death, the divine work of the Redemption: *Hoc facite in meam commemorationem.*

> For as often as you shall eat this bread and drink the chalice, you shall shew the death of the Lord, until he come.—(*I Cor. xi, 26.*)

A monument that will last as long as the human race.

It is so natural for the human heart to want to erect lasting monuments! What are those monoliths, menhirs, mausoleums, pyramids, obelisks, and statues in materials like granite, marble, and iron, erected in every age to kings, travellers pioneers, and inventors, but the unquenchable human longing to eternalise an achievement, to perpetuate a name?

And what monument will the King of Kings erect to His enterprise, the world's Redemption? What materials will He choose? Marble of Paros? Bronze from the old Colossi? Stones from the eternal wonders of Egypt? . . . No, Christ's monument will be unique: His porphyry, His diamonds, His bronze, will be but a tiny consecrated Host—the meagre appearances of bread and wine.

And the pyramids will crumble, and the colossi will be thrown to the ground, and the marble statues will turn into dust, and the monoliths will be buried by the sands of the centuries; and even if cataclysms should fail to consume them, there will be the implacable beat of the weather eroding and pulverising them all. But the Monument to the Death of Christ, with all its fragile appearances, remains; with the passing of the years and after every hour It becomes still more gigantic; each Consecration and Communion is a new ashlar that nothing will move.

## IV

Fourth purpose: To infuse into my being the germ of a New Life, the life of grace, eternal life, the Spirit of Christ, the Spirit of God, the Holy Ghost—scriptural terms for divine grace.

A divine Germ that is immersed not only in the depths of the soul, sanctifying it and making it a child of God, but also in the flesh, which it saturates, depositing in every molecule of its corruptible nature the seed of immortality and glory. In fact, Christ attributes precisely to this Sacrament the resurrection of our bodies:

> He that eateth my flesh and drinketh my blood
> . . . hath everlasting life: and I will raise him
> up in the last day.—(*John vi,* 55.)

The Father gave to the Son to have Life in Himself and to communicate this Life to us through our contact with His Flesh glorified by Its union with the Word.

## RESOLUTIONS.

1. I shall consider Holy Communion the most vital of all my actions, and therefore, I shall keep my soul and body every day of my existence in the holy dispositions required for receiving worthily the Life-giving God.

2. I shall ask Christ's forgiveness for the meanness, due to my indolence and lack of faith, with which I have distributed to the faithful the Bread of the children of God—as though the Tabernacle keys were entrusted to me to keep that Bread in cold storage, as it were, instead of giving It out lavishly to all God's good children who ask for It and need It.

Jesus, I promise Thee I shall exhort everyone, in season and out of season, to receive Holy Communion frequently, just as I myself receive It daily; and each day I shall be less inclined to judge myself a worthier child of God than the rest of the faithful.

# THE HOLY EUCHARIST

### NINTH MEDITATION

*St. John, the Priest's Model in his Dealings with the Holy Eucharist*

## I

Let us read St. John's Gospel and his other writings. So steeped was he in the profound mysteries of his Divine Master's Heart that, when he takes up the pen to relate the Life-story of Christ, the very first thing that comes to his mind is Christ's Divinity: *In the beginning was the Word, and the Word was with God, and the Word was God. (John i, 1.)*

" *With God* "—from the Latin *apud Deum*—seems to have lost the force of the original Greek, where the preposition *pròs* before " *Theón,*" means not only "with God" but also "in God," "within God," "towards God."

When St. John deals with the Eucharist, instead of relating Its institution in detail, as the three Synoptists and St. Paul do, he tells us, in Christ's own words, only the chief fruits of this Sacrament:

> If any man eat of this bread, he shall live for ever;
>    . . . abideth in me and I in him.
>    . . . and I will raise him up in the last day.
> —(*John vi.*)

Blessed are the clean of heart, for they shall see God! How truly this is fulfilled in the beloved Disciple!

## II

We should learn from St. John how to deal with Jesus Christ hidden under the Sacramental Species.

The essential purpose of the priest is to offer sacrifice. There is no priesthood without sacrifice. So the more perfectly we perform this essential duty the better priests we are, and the better priests we are the nearer our approach to the Holiness and Greatness of the Victim we offer and of the Father to Whom It is offered. For the victims and oblations of old have vanished like shadows before the Light of the New Covenant, which, in abrogating them, substituted in their place the one Clean Oblation prophesied by Malachias (*i*, 11), Christ

ur God, the Holy One born of the Virgin Mary, the
Divine Victim of our altars.

To offer this Divine Victim is the essential reason for
my priesthood, my first ministerial duty, my sublimest
occupation, and, I may well add, the primary purpose of
my existence on earth.

Is my life adjusted to the requirements of this my
lofty destiny?

## III

Why not examine to-day, at this moment, quite
leisurely, the daily treatment which my Lord Jesus
Christ, Victim and Sacrament, receives at my hands? Is
there nothing on my conscience that puts me to
shame? . . .

What was the secret of that poignant sorrow in the
Heart of the Saviour at the Last Supper? What dis-
turbed Him most? He trembled, perhaps, not so much
at the vision of the agony of His impending Passion
and death with all the scourgings, crown of thorns, and
nailing to a cross, as because He saw, with infinite
dread, that from that hour, having instituted for all
ages the Sacrament of His love, He had given Himself
into the hands of His priests. From the gentle hands
of His Mother, which had fondled Him in infancy
and boyhood; from the hands of His Apostles and
Disciples, who with all their uncouthness were funda-
mentally good and loved Him sincerely; from those
hands He passed into the hands of so many, many
priests, some of whom were to imitate the traitor Judas.
And alas! He saw Himself surrendered to my hands,
these hands of mine, perhaps soiled, maybe even
cynical!

Not the least of Thy torments, dear Lord, to which Thy love constrained Thee!

## RESOLUTION

Solicitous and loving concern for everything that relates to Jesus in the Blessed Sacrament, especially within the church, will henceforth be classed as one of my chief acts of piety, and will receive the same measure of careful attention which I expect from those who look after my personal and priestly belongings.

If I do this, I shall have every right to proclaim before the assembled congregation, when purifying my fingers at the Offertory, the boast of the psalmist: *Domine dilexi decorem domus tuae, et locum habitationis gloriae tuae* (*Ps. xxv*, 8): Lord, how well I love thy house in its beauty, the place where thy own glory dwells!

Let the faithful learn from my example that the very first act of Christian piety looks towards Jesus in the Blessed Sacrament.

# THE PRIEST'S KNOWLEDGE OF CHRIST

### St. John the Evangelist as Model

## I

St. John stands out among the other Gospel writers for his profounder exposition of the Mysteries of the Word Incarnate. He is the Eagle that lives and writes with eyes fixed on the dazzling sun; his pen-strokes are lightning flashes. What other sacred writer has imparted profounder and more luminous ideas of Christ's Divinity? How one feels, when studying his Gospel, the truth of Christ's words: *He that seeth me seeth the Father also!*

No stereoscope ever brought out into such bold relief the profile and contours of a photographed object as the pages of the beloved Disciple, pages throbbing with life and love, plastically portray the nature and character of God hidden beneath the ephemeral forms of our humanity. And if, after his Gospel, we read St. John's letters and Apocalypse, we shall seem to hear but the Gospel's most wonderful echoes.

Taking stock of the few facts and features of his life as handed down to us by tradition, we can see that by sheer pondering over and living the Redeemer's " New Commandment," the aged Apostle—virgin, evangelist, divine, prophet and martyr—has condensed all his preaching and ideas in that trembling and tender-hearted and continually-repeated admonition: " Little children, love one another: for that is the Lord's command, and this alone, if done, is enough."

## II

Every occupation, trade and profession has its own particular principles and practices which are indispensable to its very existence; for example, medicine is built on a perfect grasp of the human organism, its ailments and their remedies; agriculture presupposes an understanding of the soil, seeds, etc.

Will my priesthood demand no specialised knowledge? And what will this knowledge be? Canon Law? Theology? No. A thousand times, no!

My special priestly sphere of knowledge and practice is nothing else than a deep and loving understanding of my Lord Jesus Christ. This is the need, the clamorous need, of my soul, simply because my whole priestly life and work has to reproduce the likeness of my one great Model: the Eternal Priest, according to the Order of Melchisedech, and the faithful themselves demand this of me, for they expect from me no other doctrine than that of Jesus Christ, and Christ *crucified*.

## III

Am I convinced of what I have just meditated upon? Do I put into practice the words of the *Imitation*: Let our highest endeavour be to meditate on the life of Jesus Christ? Or did I think that I had enough and even more than enough with moral and dogmatic theology?

I need this theology, certainly; and woe betide me if I do not know it! But in what theological disquisitions have I ever learnt knowledge through love, or love through knowledge, of my Divine Redeemer? This sacred discipline is learnt properly only through a continual, reflective and affectionate reading of the New Testament.

I am a poor sort of a minister of the Gospel if I have only a nodding acquaintance with the Gospel; if I scarcely read but the few short fragments of the Missal, and these so hurriedly, so inattentively, that I could not give an account of them after a hundred such readings!

Unfortunate, indeed, are the faithful who perhaps year after year sit listening to my preachments devoid of all unction and even of all mention of the Gospel!

## RESOLUTIONS

1.  To meditate on the fifty chapters of his writings by way of an offering to the Beloved Disciple. When I have steeped my heart in them I shall be able to appropriate to myself the well-known words: *De ipso Dominici pectoris fonte potavi*—I have drunk from the fountain of the Lord's own breast.

2.  To choose Mary for my Mother, and thus be able to apply to myself also the words: *the disciple took her to his own. (John xix, 27.)*

What a home St. John's was, governed and sanctified by such a good, sweet Mother!

Lady! Come and reign in the homes of all priests, putting dangerous occasions to flight, establishing therein the law and holy fear of God!

3.  To unite myself with Christ when I suffer; and though the boisterous rabble of my passions mock and jeer, to climb the road to Calvary until the Blood of the Crucified Redeemer touches me. Had St. John not stood at the foot of the Cross; had he remained afar off like the other disciples, would the Lord have said

to him: *Behold thy mother*? No, he would not have received such a Mother on that afternoon; She might possibly have been committed to the care of the converted Centurion.

4. To brave for Christ's sake the privations and struggles entailed by priestly chastity, and to be, like John, a virgin disciple of a Virgin Master, and a virgin adopted son of a Virgin Mother.

If I possess these virtues, Christ will find me worthy, like St. John, to enter into the sanctuary of His life and Heart; and Mary will keep me enshrined in her motherly care.

# ADMINISTRATION OF THE SACRAMENTS

### FIRST MEDITATION

### *Esteem for the Sacraments*

## I

We are shepherds of souls. To each one of us, in due measure, the Lord repeats what He said to the Prince of the Apostles: *Feed my lambs. Feed my sheep. (John xxi, 16-17.)*

The two kinds of pastures which I, as shepherd of souls, am obliged to provide for them are: the divine word, by my preaching of the Gospel; and the Sacraments, a nourishment still more sustaining than my preaching, because I thereby confer upon souls the spirit of God, grace.

Lord, I fear I may have slaughtered many sheep of Thy Flock, like a wolf; or, like a hireling, I may have allowed them to starve, keeping them away through my indolence, and even driving them away, from the sources of life. I fear Thou mayest have to say to me: *The little ones have asked for bread, and there was none to break it unto them. (Lament. iv, 4.)*

## II

The Sacraments! . . . Divine Signs that infuse into those who receive them worthily divine sonship. Only those who have received them in a holy manner, *in re*

229

*vel in voto,* are, in the full sense of the word, children of God.

The Sacraments! . . . The sole means of eradicating guilt from the soul and communicating the first grace, of keeping it there, of confirming or restoring its possession. All this is done by the priest when he administers the Sacraments.

I am empowered by Heaven to bring forth children of God, *who are born, not of blood, nor of the will of the flesh, nor of the will of man, but of God (John i, 13);* I am commissioned to nourish them, restore them to life, and lead them to the possession of the divine paternal inheritance. What do I do with this power which Christ has entrusted to my feeble hands? Have I received it, do I hold it, with a thankfulness befitting the Almighty's greatest gift to mortal man? Or do I often consider it an encroachment on my repose and on the enjoyment of a soft, leisurely existence?

### III

The lovely words of prophecy are fulfilled whenever the Sacraments are received: *You shall draw waters with joy out of the Saviour's fountains (Is. xii, 3);* and those of Christ Himself: *The water that I will give him shall become in him a fountain of water, springing up into life everlasting. (John iv, 14.)*

Through the power of the Sacraments the priest's hand possesses the art of healing souls: subtly he can penetrate to the deepest centre of the human spirit and cleanse the leprosy of sin, and bring back the life of grace where death had entered; he can cicatrize wounds and ulcers, strengthen the soul in good against its inborn weaknesses, and secure for it the possession of its Heavenly Father's Home.

There is no medical skill capable of doing for the organisms of the body what the priest does for souls through the instrumentality of the Sacraments.

Have I held this tremendous gift of healing in due esteem? Have I not frequently ignored the fact that this power was given to me, not to keep it chained, not to store it away, as in a museum or a safe, but to give it free scope?

## RESOLUTION

To remember the Apostle's instruction to Timothy: " *A special grace has been entrusted to thee . . . do not let it suffer from neglect* " (I *Tim. iv*, 14); and also our divine Lord's: *Freely have you received; freely give.* (*Matt. x*, 8.) To remember this every day, and also to bear in mind that in the Court of Divine Justice our Lord will rightly say to me, if I am negligent, what St. Basil said to the ungenerous rich: " Si non pavisti, occidisti "—if you failed to feed them, you slaughtered them; therefore give Me an account of the souls that perished because you denied them nourishment, the nourishment which was Mine, not your own, and which entrusted to you for its distribution; for you were but steward placed over My household for this very purpose.

*I will require his blood at thy hand!* (*Ezech. iii*, 18.) —I will demand an account for every soul you allowed to perish!

# ADMINISTRATION OF THE SACRAMENTS

## Reasons for Administering them Worthily

### I

*The Sacraments themselves demand it.*—Things of their nature so sublime and worthy, and in their fruit so divine and salutary, must needs be handled with corresponding devotion and piety.

> "That is how we ought to be regarded, as Christ's servants, and stewards of God's mysteries. And this is what we look for in choosing a steward, we must find one who is trustworthy."—(I *Cor* iv, 1-2.)

For a child to be admitted to Holy Communion the Church requires, as an indispensable condition, that he should at least know how to distinguish the Eucharistic from ordinary bread. Will it be asking too much of a priest that he should know how to distinguish between ordinary human actions and the most holy action that regenerates and sanctifies souls?

O Lord! We Thy priests can distinguish indeed, and discern; but how often, in administering Thy Sacraments and divine mysteries, we act with less respect, with more irreverence, with considerably less seriousness, than when talking to a beggar on the street . . . or playing a game of cards! . . .

## II

*The faithful demand it.*—We are obliged, according to the Council of Trent, to instruct the faithful in the nature and holiness of the Sacraments and even in the rites and ceremonies with which the Church surrounds their administration. But seeing that the frequent observance of this rule is very often either impracticable or, through our negligence, is allowed to become a dead letter, let us at least give the faithful an object lesson by the exact, devout and respectful manner of our administering the Sacraments, so that they may grasp the holy and divine reality beneath the outward symbols.

Could we swear, with hand on heart and mind uplifted to the God Who is to judge us, that the indifference, bordering so often on impiety, with which the faithful look around and talk and either receive or stray away from the Sacraments, is not a pallid reflection and rough copy of the rush, untidiness, frivolousness and lack of inward spirit which they are so used to observing in our manner of conferring them?

## III

*Our own self-respect demands it.*—The administering of the Sacraments, whether out of charity or of justice, always turns out to be in some sense a work of obligation, a duty of office; therefore it is a work that pleases God more than any other of supererogation.

It is also a real act of piety, at least as much so as saying the Rosary, making a meditation, visiting the sick or reading a spiritual book. I say, *at least;* in actual fact it is much more a work of religion and holiness than all the aforementioned exercises, which can be performed and be good in themselves without sanctifying grace, whereas woe betide me if I dare to give any of the Sacraments without being in God's grace!

Is it not a fact that I have not always, or perhaps never, considered things in this light? Do I not rather look upon this administering of the Sacraments as something I am formally engaged to do, and something always untimely, troublesome, and completely without personal profit, except for the stipend that sometimes goes with it? . . .

## RESOLUTIONS

1.  Never, never to approach the administration of the Sacraments unless I am in the grace of God, and, if necessary, to make a most sincere act of contrition together with a real determination to go to confession that same day or before saying Mass on the following day. But the surest and most practical way will be to go to confession beforehand, if I am in mortal sin.

2.  To administer them readily, as often as the faithful ask for them within the limits of reason and law and order; and to do so disinterestedly, decorously, piously.

3.  Henceforth to consider their administration as my chief pious exercise, the most profitable to myself, apart from the good they may do to others. Is there any meditation more soul-satisfying and effectual than, for example, to give the Holy Viaticum and at the same time to consider attentively and religiously the words I say and the actions I perform?

# THE ADMINISTRATION OF PENANCE

*Motives for hearing Confessions readily*

## I

*Gratitude.*—What would have become of me had I never confessed my own sins? All the grave sins committed since Baptism would be still infesting my soul; they would be branded on my conscience almost indelibly, and made blacker still by the muddy stream of sinful habit which without this Sacrament would have flowed on unchecked, staining with a deeper dye. What countless shameful falls this Sacrament has saved me from! What fearful remorse, what mental briars and thorns, it has plucked from my soul!

I might almost modify a text from St. Paul and exclaim: "By the Grace of God, through the Sacrament of Penance, I am what I am!"

Such incomparable benefits demand some form of gratitude; and I am quite sure that, in my case, the token most pleasing to God is, not to begrudge other souls the benefits which my confessors have made available to me.

## II

*Personal gain.*—The administration of this Sacrament carries with it incalculable advantages for the minister, the advantages of heavy, hard toil not at all pleasing to nature. So, in general, the first to do penance on this occasion is the priest administering it.

Now, if the penitential spirit is something essential to the Christian spirit:

> except you do penance, you shall all likewise perish—(*Luke xiii, 5*);

if our Divine Master's first sermon, as though He had taken it straight from the lips of His Precursor, was: *Do penance;* if my many slights and offences against the Creator bind me for life, and perhaps beyond this life, to a compensation wrought of the rigours of this virtue of penance; then, Lord, I thank Thee for giving me so near at hand this great opportunity of expiation through hard work, through a work as self-denying to me as it is helpful to others: the hearing of confessions.

There is another gain. Certain ministerial tasks are easily vitiated by vanity; for example, preaching and other public duties. How often the cankerworm of conceit gets into the holiest of endeavours, and gnaws and consumes them! But what a fool I should be if I were to swell with pride for having spent a few hours hearing confessions, giving bits of advice for the amendment of my penitents, when, according to St. Francis de Sales, the first qualification to be a good confessor is usually to know how to listen and let the penitents have their say.

### III

*The greatest work of mercy.*—The priest, deprived of the goods of this world,—and how desperately poor a priest can be!—will not make a headline by his substantial money contributions; many a layman can afford to outdo him in this respect; but are not the spiritual works of mercy far more meritorious in God's sight than the corporal? And if the Catechism does not enumerate the hearing of confessions among the spiritual works of mercy it is for the simple reason that this work belongs exclusively to the priest, or rather, because, while it includes them, it also eclipses every one of them. What work of mercy ever reaches the depths of the soul to bring God's pardon, like the work of the confessor?

I might well apply the words of St. Peter, when he healed the man born lame, and apply them with deeper significance:

> "Turn towards me: silver and gold are not mine to give, I give thee what I can."—(*Acts iii, 6.*)

> "In the Name of the Lord Jesus Christ thy sins are forgiven thee." "I absolve thee from thy sins."

## IV

*The Church commands you, implores you on bended knees.*—It is the Church's desire, formulated by the Council of Trent, that all who assist at Mass should, if duly disposed, share Holy Communion with the priest; and this anxiety is re-affirmed in canon 863 of the present Code:

> The faithful should be admonished, according to the decree of the Holy See, to receive the Eucharistic Bread frequently, and even daily; and that those who assist at Holy Mass should not only communicate spiritually, but be prepared to receive in reality our Lord in the Holy Eucharist.

The greatest good in any parish or public church is the number and frequency of good Communions. So I shall be deceiving myself if I imagine, and perhaps boast, that I am an excellent worker in the Lord's vineyard, unless I have promoted and succeeded in obtaining a frequent and proper approach to the Holy Table by all the souls confided in one way or another to my care. Yes, I may hear a number of slighting remarks or specious objections against the practice of frequent Communion, but I should clearly understand that I am an ignorant priest, unequipped with the practical science of salvation, if I fail to grasp this great and impregnable truth: the more Communions there are, the more crowded the churches are, the purer the morals, the more deep-rooted the Faith. In the divine Balance, all other works of zeal, without this, will hardly weigh more than a few grains of sand.

But how will the faithful communicate frequently if they do not confess frequently, that is, if I do not sit down frequently to hear them, if many hours of my priestly existence are not spent in the confessional, if I do not offer them every facility to approach? . . . Oh, let me be honest with myself! Cannot all my spoken, unspoken, and subconscious objections to frequent and daily Communion boil down to this: my reluctance to spend long hours in the confessional?

## RESOLUTIONS

1. Since Baptism is the first Sacrament of forgiveness and the gateway to the Sacrament of Penance, I shall not be put to the shame of seeing a single parishioner of mine unbaptised, if I can possibly avoid it. Nor shall I console myself thinking that the unbaptised will receive the Sacrament when they grow up,

for I realise the hindrances besetting them later in life. I shall remind neglectful parents of their grave obligation in this matter.

2. Sincerely acknowledging before God that hitherto I have shown no small reluctance to hear confessions, and have tried to shirk this ministerial duty under many a futile pretext; from to-day and until my dying day I shall submit to this task most willingly, a task so often the least esteemed and yet the most profitable to souls. I may not be much good at preaching, I may not be qualified for high ecclesiastical offices; but I do wish, dear Jesus, to become a good and constant confessor.

# THE ADMINISTRATION OF PENANCE

## SECOND MEDITATION

### Qualities of a Good Confessor

#### I

*Purity of intention and of soul.*—Clean must be the hand that cleanses; clean the soul of the confessor about to enter the depths of souls stained with human miseries in order to pardon their sins. What risks he runs, if he is not very pure, of adding stain to stain in himself and even in his penitents, and of profaning the Sacrament!

But purity of conscience in the sacred tribunal is not enough; because here, more than in any other ministerial duty, there is need of a pure and upright intention. It is here more than elsewhere, perhaps, that we do the work of Christ, for it is God's prerogative to probe the heart and to forgive sin; therefore, I must be worthy of Christ, I must respect Christ in myself, I must behave like Christ. And I must also keep in mind those grave words spoken by St. Paul:

> "No more Jew or Gentile, no more slave and freeman, no more male and female; you are all one person in Jesus Christ."—(*Gal. iii*, 28.)

They are simply souls, souls redeemed by Christ, souls approaching the Sacrament in order to purify and wash themselves clean in the Blood of the Lamb.

Can I honestly declare . . . shall I declare on the Day of Judgement, that in the confessional my one concern has been for souls, the remission of their sins, and their eternal salvation?

## II

*Kindness and meekness.*—To sinners, more than to anyone else, is addressed that tender appeal of our Lord's: *Come to me, all you that labour and are burdened : and I will refresh you . . . because I am meek, and humble of heart.*—(*Matt. xi*, 28-29.)

Gentlest Physician of stricken souls, never didst Thou prescribe for sinners a medicine that was not steeped in the sweetness of Thy immense compassion and tenderness!

No wonder! . . . Physicians of the body never chide their patient, they listen to him, ask him questions, pamper him; they suffer with a smile his impertinences and his pitiful self-centredness, they bear with his childish fears: all for the sake of curing him—if he does cure!—or of prolonging the existence of this mortal body, built to crumble into dust.

And I, a physician of souls, why do I not possess at least a grain or two of that same kindly disposition in order to heal immortal souls, for whom my Lord and God shed lavishly not only His ineffable sweetness but also the torrents of His Blood?

Or do I think that my ministry of healing souls yields a paltry remuneration as compared with the medical profession's? *I am thy reward exceeding great.* (*Gen. xv, 1.*) Yes, Lord, but all the same, I find it hard to convince myself.

> But if thou warn the just man, that the just may not sin, and he doth not sin: living he shall live because thou hast warned him, and thou hast delivered thy soul.—(*Ezech. iii, 21.*)

How much the more if by pardoning the sinner I make him a just man!

### III

*Readiness.—Come ye after me, and I will make you to be fishers of men.—(Matt. iv, 19.)*

So I am a fisherman of souls, and therefore I must go in search of them, wherever they may be. A fisherman who contented himself with arranging and spreading out his tackle and gear before the door of his house, waiting for the fish to come to him, would be held up to ridicule. It is not the fish that go in search of the fisherman. And it is I who should invent ways and means of getting people to crowd the church; I am the one who should possess the art and secret of drawing souls into the confessional.

What wouldst Thou think of me, dear Lord, if through my harshness, my indolence, and my dread of hard work, I drove them away? What, if, after approaching me already half converted or decided to flee from evil and desirous of peace and pardon, I threw them out, or received them so badly that I plunged them back into sin, and moreover, made Thy tribunal of Mercy hateful to them? Thou couldst with righteous anger say to me: *I will require his blood at thy hand.*—(Ezech. iii, 18.) And I should be Thy enemy, opposed to Thee, because I should be doing what Thou never didst do: break the bruised reed, and quench the smoking flax, with the chill blast of my sullen moods.

### RESOLUTIONS

1. Not only shall I sit down to hear confessions at the slightest indication from any penitent, without waiting to be called, I shall remain in the confessional at the most convenient times for the faithful; and if no one comes, I shall stay on reciting the breviary, reading some spiritual book, meditating, or performing my devotional exercises. Has it not been my own personal experience that the ordeal of searching for a confessor is greater than the actual confessing of my sins?

2. I shall welcome and bear with all my penitents with the utmost kindness, with the same affability that I expect to receive from my own confessor. How often would I go back to a spiritual father who received or treated me with malhumour? I shall let them speak, without interrupting them, except to encourage them, and without showing any evidence of surprise, however enormous their sins. Have I not perhaps committed the same sins myself? Am I not quite capable of committing sins even more abominable?

3. I shall not make the slightest discrimination with

regard to sex, social standing, or other inequalities. What a number of souls have been given offence! What seeds of mistrust and disesteem for the Sacrament of Penance have been sown by those vile discriminations! If there is to be any preference at all, let it be for the old rather than the young, for the poor rather than the rich, and, above all, for the men rather than the women. The well-to-do and the devout members of the fair sex will never have far to go to find a confessor, even if, because of the poor and the men crowding round my box, I myself am not immediately at their disposal.

4. I shall go to confession very frequently myself, as a sure sign of my love for this divine Sacrament. And if I am conscious of being in mortal sin, I shall go to confession before hearing others. Moreover, although not conscious of mortal sin, I shall make an immediate preparation for the hearing of confessions by an act of contrition, and ask God to purify me more and more.

## THE ADMINISTRATION OF PENANCE

### THIRD MEDITATION

#### Spiritual Direction

### I

In the Presence of Jesus Christ, God and Judge of living and dead, let us consider and make an impartial study of this particular subject, which, owing to misunderstandings, has given rise to lamentable abuses. We shall take the new code of Canon Law as our guide in everything pertaining to spiritual direction.

*Canon 588 :* During the entire course of studies the religious shall be under the special care of a prefect or master, who shall lead them on in religious life by timely admonition and instruction.

Canon 562 applies the same ruling to the Master of novices. Both these canons clearly give no right to the spiritual director to require of his religious subordinates any kind of manifestation of conscience, not even the right to hear their confessions, unless they go to him entirely of their own free will. Canon 1,358 rules that in each seminary there should be, besides the ordinary confessors, a spiritual director with the same attributions.

As regards the other faithful, nothing is laid down. Hence, their own parochial clergy and their confessors are sufficient to guide them along the way of salvation.

Only canon 530 speaks of the " manifestatio conscientiae ", in the following terms :—

1.   Religious Superiors are strictly forbidden to induce their subjects in any way to manifest their state of conscience to them.

2.   The subjects, however, are not forbidden to manifest of their own free will and choice their consciences to the superiors; on the contrary, it is proper that they should approach their superiors with filial confidence, and if they are priests, to reveal to them any doubts and anxieties of their consciences.

According to this Church law, every Superior is absolutely forbidden to constrain his subjects in any way, directly or indirectly, to manifest their consciences to him; although it is recognised as useful and con-

venient for the subject "ultro et libere", spontaneously
without any coercion or moral obligation, to declare his
doubts and moral anxieties to the afore-mentioned
Superior, if the latter is a priest.

It is useless to look for a single other allusion to
spiritual direction in the present Code; it would seem
as though the Church knew nothing more about this
matter—the Church that speaks and legislates so
copiously for confessors and confessed.

The conclusion should not be wider than the
premisses; therefore, a person can be a good Christian,
and even a great saint, either in the world or in religion,
without that continual and absolute subjection to a
spiritual director, and even without a director at all;
though, of course, one cannot deny that a director may
well be an asset and a guide when there is need for one.

## II

If we inquire about the exact scope of spiritual direction we have the answer, fortunately, in texts of the
highest authority.

First of all, the above-quoted canon 530, according
to which spiritual direction consists in revealing to a
priest, with filial confidence, doubts and anxieties
troubling one's conscience. And note that this direction
is something entirely different from confession, because
the Superior is severely forbidden to hear his subjects'
confessions, unless they " of their own free will ask to
be heard; but without grave reason this should not be
done habitually ". " Superiors must beware—says canon
516—of inducing, either personally or through others,
any of their subjects by force or fear or by importunate

urging, or in any other way, to come to them for confession."

It stands to reason, then, that in spiritual direction the person directed has no need to utter a single word indicative of sins past or present, seeing that sin alone is sacramental "matter" of confession.

It also follows, that to impose a narration of past sins, under the pretext that a person's spiritual background must be known before sound advice can be given to him, is a requirement exceeding the bounds of justice, and always a cruel and harsh one. How much of illusion or mere curiosity there is contained, perhaps, in investigations like these! How much more thankful souls would be to me if over their sad lapses, already pardoned, I mercifully drew the veil of oblivion! How much more I should be like God Himself!

> I am, I am he that blots out thy iniquities for my own sake: and I will not remember thy sins.
> —(*Is. xliii,* 25.)

And if they are yet to be forgiven, why demand their declaration, since in confession they are to be repeated?

In a word: everything will go well if I content myself with the two offices of judge and physician of souls which canon 888 assigns me towards penitents; and if I exercise these offices only in order to absolve and heal the wounds of mortal sins which must of necessity be brought to the tribunal, or of venial sins that penitents may choose to confess, or in order to answer to the best of my knowledge and ability the questions they ask me concerning matters of conscience, such as difficulties, anxieties, doubts, etc.

### III

Another text, whose testimony is of equally high authority, is contained in Leo XIII's decree *Quemadmodum* addressed to religious women on December 17th, 1890:—

> "Male fuit inducta intima conscientiae scrutatio quae unice Sacramento Paenitentiae reservata est."

"There was no right to introduce that close scrutiny of conscience which is reserved only to the Sacrament of Penance." And the great Pontiff cancels, and orders the erasure of, any rules that obliged religious women to make such an intimate declaration of conscience:

> "Irritat, abrogat eas in eo quod cordis intimam manifestationem quovis modo ac nomine respiciunt."

The same decree continues:—

> "Valeant ultro et libere aperire suum animum Superioribus ad effectum ab illorum prudentia in dubiis et anxietatibus consilium et directionem obtinendi pro virtutum adquisitione ac perfectionis progressu."

"They may spontaneously and freely open their minds to their Superiors in order to obtain prudent counsel and direction in their doubts and worries, for the purpose of acquiring virtue and progressing in perfection."

It tallies with the teaching of canon 530. It reminds me that when people spontaneously come to me for direction it is only to clear away worries and doubts which may prove an obstacle to the acquisition of virtue and to progress in perfection.

In doubts and worries about temporal goods I go to

a lawyer for help, but I go only when these doubts and worries torment me; when I have no worry at all, why should I go? And month after month may elapse without my being afflicted by any worry or doubt.

Dear God, like Thee, I wish to respect human consciences, above all, the consciences of the weak, of women and children. Our conscience is a coffer locked by God with two God-made keys: one, He keeps for Himself—*scrutans corda et renes*—so let us live in peace; God will not surrender that key to anyone, not even to the wisest of cherubim, who will not delve into my heart unless I open it to them.

The other key of my conscience, God gave it to me, and will never take it from me, and will oblige me to use it only for a single declaration, attended by all the divine precautions of the Sacramental Seal, of my sins to a confessor; and woe betide this confessor if he does not bury them in everlasting silence!

O God, in my dealings with souls I wish to be like Thee:

> For thy power is the beginning of justice: . . . because thou art Lord of all, thou makest thyself gracious to all. . . . being master of power, thou judgest with tranquillity; and with great favour disposest of us. . . .—(*Wisdom, cf. xii.*)

### IV

With a view to shedding further light on the nature of spiritual direction, let us take a paragraph from that wise and holy man, Fr. Granada, from a famous sermon he preached on the occasion of a scandal produced by one of his penitents:—

"Not even to confessors should the penitent give an account of the virtues or favours he has received from our Lord, if there is no particular need to do so. The rendering of a certain kind of obedience to spiritual Fathers is very dangerous, because it gives rise to familiar friendship between penitent and spiritual Father which the devil changes into carnal friendship. In matters of greater moment that may occur, it is sufficient to take counsel with a spiritual Father, when the latter is the proper person to give it."

So, neither virtues nor supernatural favours, and much less, sins, are the subject of ordinary spiritual direction.

Direction, according to this immortal writer, Fr. Granada, is: to take counsel with a spiritual Father when there arises a matter of greater moment, and when the Father is a person qualified to deal with it.

By what right—not to say, by what supreme injustice!—do I constrain anyone to live tied down to my sole direction, under pain of my displeasure and all the lightnings of my anger if I come to suspect the penitent of daring to stray from my confessional in order to confide his or her troubles and doubts to another?

If cloistered nuns are free, according to Canon Law, to call on three or four different confessors, who has authorised me to exercise a tyrannical monopoly over souls that enjoy absolute freedom, as children of God, to make their confession with a different confessor each time, so long as the confessor has the requisite faculties and the penitents approach with a right intention and the proper dispositions? Don't I make my own confession to whomsoever I please? Haven't I changed confessors whenever I wanted to? What would I answer if I were asked the impertinent question: "Who is your spiritual director?"

## RESOLUTIONS

1. Never to enjoin upon any penitent the declaration of his conscience outside confession, and, in confession, not to go beyond the limits required for the forgiveness of sin; and to explain to him the ruling of the Church on this point.

2. Often to remind penitents, men and women, that they are absolutely free to make their confession with another, if they please; and to tell them not to mind in the least whether I am offended thereby or no. Moreover, as a general rule, let them be ready to quit any confessor who shows particular inclination to have them go to him.

3. In my dealings with women penitents, to adjust my conduct to the following standards and orders given by the supreme Sacred Congregation of the Holy Office, 30th July, 1920:—

    i—Not to speak to them in terms of speech that can imply over-familiarity and intimacy;

    ii—Not to visit them or receive visits from them;

    iii—Not to indulge in long-winded conversations with them in the sacristy, guest-house, and parlour, under the pretext of spiritual direction;

    iv—Not to maintain written correspondence with them without real need.

# THE ADMINISTRATION OF PENANCE

FOURTH MEDITATION

## Respect for Penitents

### I

The Church, whom the Holy Ghost calls a "meek dove", and whom we all call "Holy Mother", appears to forget her meekness when it is a question of defending the purity and the respect due to the tribunal of Penance. Strange as it may seem, an unworthy priest can profane the most holy Body of Christ and the august Sacrifice a thousand times by celebrating sacrilegiously, and She, the Bride of the immolated Lamb, keeps silent, and holds no canonical penalty in reserve for the profaner; but if that same priest should sully his confessional ministry once only, through any lack of circumspection and respect towards even the lowliest of penitents: a poor old woman or a child, the Church forgets Her gentleness, throws off Her meekness of a dove and a Mother, and becomes an eagle swooping down to the attack, a lioness defending her offspring with her claws and deafening roar. So much so that the *latae sententiae* penalties which still remain in full force, without ready absolution, are mainly those which the confessor would incur if he failed to respect his ministry.

### II

What explanation is there for the transformation? It is one proof more that the Church is of Jesus Christ, and the only one that lives by His Spirit. For Her as for Her Bridegroom,—the Good Shepherd going in search of the lost sheep, and, when found, putting it on His shoulders with infinite compassion; the Father of the prodigal son all the more beloved for his wretchedness; —for Her, as for Jesus, there is no one worthier of pity and love than the soul who ran away perhaps, dragged hither and thither by unbridled fancy; than the soul who plunged with infernal delight into the miry depths of the flesh, holding God in less esteem than any base pleasure or pastime; yes, did all this, but finally, goaded by grace, begins to make an effort to come into the Light of God and to reach, if not the arms, the Feet of the Heavenly Father. And to think that the confessor, the very minister delegated by the pardoning Christ to regenerate that poor soul, should be the one to thrust it back again into the mire! . . . The Church, Mother of little ones and of all who suffer; the Church, with a heart formed and fashioned in the Mercy of Christ; the Church will sooner bear with the sight of the Most Blessed Sacrament Itself trampled upon or Her Divine Spouse nailed to the Cross.

O Blessed Mother of the weak and fallen! whose defence so melts Thee with compassion, enkindles Thy heart to wrath, and girds Thy arms with strength!

## RESOLUTIONS

1.   I shall very frequently study the terrible censures inflicted on *solicitantes, absolventes vel intendentes absolvere complicem,* and on *sigillum infringentes;* and both within the confessional and outside it I shall, by God's grace and favour, bridle my heart, my tongue, and

my whole being, with reins of steel rather than be found wanting in respect and reverence towards the Sacrament where the Lord's Blood is applied *unto the remission of sins.*

2. If ever or at any time I have reasonable grounds to fear a breaking or a loosening of the *sigillum,* I shall as often flee from the confessional rather than incur dishonour.

For God sees me; and the Church, all eyes, armed with the lightnings of divine Wrath, stands watch over me, always on the alert to safeguard that imposing and austere tribunal which the Judge of living and dead established *unto the remission of sins.*

# VISITATION AND CARE OF THE SICK

## *Importance of Attending the Sick*

### I

The heart of man is never in greater need than at the hour of death. While everything signifying love and pleasure on earth takes to flight away from the heap of repulsive bodily ruins, the soul, alone, abandoned to its own weakness, sees before it two relentless enemies: its own conscience, whose false lights begin to fade with the approach of Absolute and Eternal Truth; and the glimpse of God's supreme Judgement, against which there is no appeal.

And I, a priest, have the immense fortune to be granted by Christ and His Church the right to approach the dying person with the power to appease those enemies of his peace in that painful and inevitable last hour. Have I had any esteem at all for this divine power so exclusively mine? Have I been happy to wield this power assiduously?

### II

Of all our ministerial duties there is none which affords us more favourable opportunities of saving souls, both the soul of the sick person for whom the hour is come or is fast approaching to make a final decision, and the souls of his household and other people who surround his bed of death. If the sick person is in the state of grace at the final hour he will be irrevocably entitled to eternal life—momentum a quo pendet aeternitas; and as regards the bystanders, they will be vividly impressed by the Last Sacraments and pious rites administered, and by the touching prayers of the recommendation of the soul; and even more so, perhaps, by the burning faith, the priestly earnestness, and disinterested charity of the Lord's faithful servant who at that supreme hour acquits himself well, in spite of natural repugnances.

Have I had sufficient zeal and love for my neighbour not to miss those opportunities that come round in the life of families once in a while, and which leave such a deep mark on their faith and manner of life, on a faith perhaps not altogether fervent, and a manner of life not entirely Christian?

### III

This ministerial duty will be among the more pleasing to the divine Lover of the poor, who will say one day: *Come, ye blessed of my Father. . . . for I was hungry, and you gave me to eat . . . I was sick, and you comforted me.*—(*Matt. xx,* 34); especially dear to Him if He can add: " For I was in agony, and you accompanied me and came to My aid."

St. Teresa considers it very pleasing to our Redeemer to meditate on His Agony in the Garden in order to keep Him company, as it were, in His bitter loneliness. How much more thankful He will be to us if we really do Him this favour in the person of one of His little ones in death's agony!

When He expired on the Cross amid the contempt and derision of His whole nation, two lips there were that spoke out for Him and consoled Him. And how handsomely Christ rewarded that act of mercy! *This day thou shalt be with me in paradise.*—(*Luke xxiii, 43.*)

What a blessing if I am able to repeat that same act of mercy thousands of times during my life to my Lord Jesus Christ, who is suffering in all who suffer, agonising in those who are in death's agony! *Whatsoever you did unto the least of my brethren, you did it unto me.*

## RESOLUTION

As material for my morning meditation and for careful study, I shall read, one section at a time, chapter four of Titulus IV of the Roman Ritual: *De Communione Infirmorum,* and the whole of Titulus V: *De extrema Unctione, De Visitatione et Cura infirmorum, and De recommendatione animae.* A beautiful chapter of Pastoral Theology, which no priest can in conscience fail to know.

If I do this I shall learn to have greater appreciation of the Ritual, one of the really priestly books, but one with which, be it said to my shame, I am not very familiar. In this way I shall also learn how to assist the dying, and how the visitation of the sick, though they may not be actually dying, is to be earmarked as the most charitable and most personal of my ministerial duties.

# VISITATION AND CARE OF THE SICK

### SECOND MEDITATION

*Evils that arise from neglecting the Sick*

### I

One of the most pernicious sins committed by many Christian families is to allow a dying person to remain in ignorance of his real condition, and actually to prevent him from realising it by using every effort and device at their command. They would see him pass into eternity without his suspecting it, until the rays of Divine Justice are focused on him and the Supreme Judge Himself imparts the first definite news.

What an immense calamity it would be for the priest to become an accomplice to, and, in a certain sense, a perpetrator of, this crime! That the priest, the dispenser of Divine Clemency, should turn into a minister of God's Wrath: that Wrath most terrible, eternally implacable, solely hostile, which brings down upon a sinful soul the scourge of a sudden, unpremeditated and unprovided death, and with death, final impenitence and the irrevocable sentence of damnation! I, a priest, aiding and abetting the death of the sinner, the direst of misfortunes! This infernal power is not conferred by any of the Sacred Orders! Shall we have to suspect that Satan too has his Orders and has conferred one of them on certain neglecful priests in order to propagate the unchristian and irreligious death: death without the Sacraments, without the priest, without God? A more terrible plague than the non-denominational school, civil-registry marriage, or the unhallowed grave; because it means the death of the devil's own children in the hands of their father.

II

And that this sort of death exists even among Catholics, more widespread than schools without catechism, than cemeteries without the crucifix, than homes without the Sacrament of Matrimony or any other Sacrament, is the conviction of not a few priests, who are ready to give information to anyone willing to listen to them. They will prove to you, with sorrow, that in such and such a parish or city there are neighbourhoods where from fifty to ninety per cent. of those baptised in the Church die without the priest, without the crucifix, without so much as hearing the Name of Jesus; just like their own domestic animals. And yet those same families often appear to be Christian, they may even frequent the Sacraments, they seem to live in perfect tranquillity of conscience, and perhaps are zealous for and actively promoting pious and social works for souls; but when questioned, they will show the most callous unconcern about the prevailing tragedy. And we priests, distracted as we are by a thousand other incidents of the struggle against evil and error and spiritual dangers, are liable to dismiss the whole problem with almost the same criminal indifference.*

For a soul that has lived far away from the Sacraments and the commandments of God, and even for a pious soul, can you imagine a greater danger to salvation than to die without the last rites, without any notion of dying, without a thought about God? Is there any problem, therefore, more serious and acute and more pregnant with disaster?

### III

If my indolence as a priest served to aggravate the problem, have I not every reason to fear a like punishment when my hour comes?

Lord, when are Thy threats going to be fulfilled?

---

* This, unfortunately, applies to Catholic countries in Europe; but what about our own " lapsed " in English-speaking countries ? And what about non-Catholics ? (*Trans.*)

With what measure you mete, it shall be measured to you again.—(*Matt. vii*, 2.)

Judgement without mercy to him that hath not done mercy.—(*James ii*, 13.)

I don't know how far it is true, but I've heard it said that many priests die without the Sacraments. A certain diocesan legal authority of my acquaintance drew up statistics of priests who died without the Sacraments, and he found them in the majority. No one has entered into the Mind of God; no one can probe Its workings; but may we not surmise that more than one priest among those who ended their days in this manner were thereby made to suffer for their neglect of duty towards the sick?

## IV

Now let me see, by way of a practical conclusion to the foregoing considerations, what the Roman Ritual says in the tenth paragraph prefacing Chapter IV of the Titulus V:

When danger is imminent, the parish priest will advise the sick person not to allow himself in any way to be deceived by the cunning of the devils or the false promises of physicians or the flattery of relatives, which might hinder him from procuring in good time those things pertaining to the soul's salvation; but religiously to receive the holy Sacraments while his mind is still clear and his senses are unimpaired, and to receive them with becoming devotion and promptness, guarding against that fallacious and pernicious procrastination which in the past has thrust a great many into the eternal torments, and which, by the devil's persuasion, continues to thrust them day by day.

And canon 468 says:

The parish priest should assist with constant care and manifest loving-kindness the sick of his parish, especially at the approach of death, by fortifying them with the Sacraments solicitously and recommending their souls to God.

And in order to understand that as long as there is breath in the body the soul is not entirely out of my hands, and can still be equipped for the journey, the same canon continues:

The parish priest, or any other priest attending the sick, has the faculty to bestow the apostolic blessing with a plenary Indulgence for the moment of death; a blessing he should not omit to give.

So it is the Church's wish that I should not abandon the dying person until I have left him at the Judgement-Seat of God.

Such is my longing request for myself; won't others have the same desire and the same right?

## Resolutions

1. I shall hold this all-important ministerial task in higher esteem. I shall perform it with full accuracy. No one shall die, if I can help it, without God's Kiss upon his soul.

2. Although I may not be appointed to it, for the love of God and of souls I shall not refuse this work; on the contrary, I shall give full vent to my zeal, either by giving a helping hand to those who are in charge, or

by finding out who are sick among those living in my street or neighbourhood, or by visiting the hospitals, after the example of so many good priests.

O agonising Jesus! I wish to appear before Thy Judgement-Seat gloriously arrayed as a minister of the happy death—if only to benefit by the same mercy.

3. I shall place on the list of my customary pious practices the beautiful work of mercy of visiting the sick, even though the latter may not be near to death. Who knows but that the restoration of this practice among priests may serve to abolish or diminish those prejudices which often confront us at a sick person's bedside or keep the door slammed against our entry!

# PREACHING

## FIRST MEDITATION

### *Aim and Scope of Preaching*

#### I

The excellence of this ministerial duty is shown by the fact that the Apostles renounced corporal works of mercy when these became a hindrance to their task of evangelisation:

> "It is too much that we should have to forgo preaching God's word, and bestow our care upon tables."—(*Acts vi*, 2.)

And the sacred Council of Trent considers preaching the chief office of bishops: praecipuum Episcoporum munus (*Sess. V. de Reformat., c.* 2).

The Church deems it so essential to the priesthood that, in Christ's Name, She says to the newly-ordained: "Receive the Holy Ghost. Teach all nations. A priest must needs preach."

Do I possess an abiding conviction of the greatness of this mission? And do I consider it an essential and a very personal one?

#### II

What truths have I to announce to the world? *Verbum Dei*—the eternal and august teaching of the Word of God; the treasures of the Divine Mind hidden since the world began—*a constitutione mundi*—so profoundly enshrined within the Divine Essence, so beyond

the reach of any created intelligence, that the very
Hierarchies of Heaven had to learn them from the
Church to whose loyal breast her Bridegroom entrusted
them:

> "The principalities and powers of heaven are to
> see, now, made manifest in the Church, the
> subtlety of God's wisdom."—(*Eph. iii, 10.*)

Like the Angels to the shepherds of Bethlehem, we
are the divinely-commissioned messengers whose task
it is to scatter over the fact of the earth and to instil
into every ear and heart the sole Good News, the Gospel
of great joy.

> Behold, I bring you good tidings of great joy.
> —(*Luke ii, 10.*)

A messenger of good news has a right to a reward;—
what reward might we not expect to receive from mankind to whom we are "Angels" sent by God on the
ambassadorship of eternal joy?

## III

What should be the purpose of our preaching? The
mere enlightening of the intellect or the burdening of
the memory? The infiltrating of culture down to the
lowest social stratum? No; the guiding of souls to their
eternal destiny, the Sovereign Good.

> "Rid yourselves of all defilement, of all ill-will
> that remains in you; be patient, and cherish the
> word implanted in you which can bring salvation
> to your souls.
> Only you must be honest with yourselves; you

are to live by the word, not content merely to listen to it."—(*James i,* 21-22.)

The God of all Wisdom and Power was pleased to harness the eternal salvation of redeemed mankind to our priestly teaching:

> " and now God would use a foolish thing, our preaching, to save those who will believe in it." —(I *Cor. i,* 21.)

Creator and Saviour of souls! To think that Thou hast staked their everlasting happiness and the infinite price of their ransom on sounds articulated by my lips, on the fleeting words of man—and a man like me!

### Resolutions

1.  I shall greatly esteem this power which God has placed in my poor words: the power to penetrate consciences, to illumine and move them towards good, and to keep them on the road to heaven; for this is the loftiest use of human speech. Never is the tongue of man put to higher service: neither when it arouses whole nations to give their blood in the service of home and country, nor when it enters into subtle disquisitions about the essence and deepest causes of things and their mutual relationships, nor when it inebriates the senses with torrential harmonies. God was pleased to use a foolish thing, our preaching, to save those who are willing to believe in it.

2.  This shall be my first thought when preparing to preach, even the most rudimentary exhortation to little children.

What unction and gravity this simple idea would communicate to my priestly word!

# PREACHING

## SECOND MEDITATION

### Practical Points on Preaching

#### I

*Who has to preach?*—Out of justice, according to
canon 1327, the obligation rests with bishops, unless
they are legitimately impeded; and it is also their duty
to enlist the services of suitable preachers, besides parish
priests, to help them to perform this ministry of the
Word in their dioceses in a becoming manner.

Parish priests, administrators and others of similar
standing are also bound to preach, *ratione beneficii,* and
they will offend God grievously and jeopardise their
eternal salvation if they omit to preach for what grave
authors consider a notable length of time.

O Sovereign Judge of the living and the dead! How
many priests hast Thou rejected for ever from Thy
eternal dwellings for the crime of having refused Thy
children the bread of the divine Word which was theirs
by right of justice? How many villages, towns and
counties have lost the Faith or have grown lukewarm
and forgotten the fear of God, because they never heard
the voice of their shepherds!

But though you may not be strictly bound to this
task, if you have the canonical faculties, and if God
has not entirely withheld from you the gift of persuasion, offer yourself, within the limits of your ability

and your position, as an angel of the good tidings, keeping in mind the great reward:

> They that instruct many to justice shall shine as stars for all eternity.—(*Dan. xii*, 3.)
>
> He that shall do and teach, he shall be called great in the kingdom of heaven.—(*Matt. v*, 19.)

## II

*What should be preached?*—O Jesus, Model and Exemplar of the Gospel preacher, enlighten me; do not allow me to tarnish the chair of Truth—the only Truth that saves—with futile discourses of pretentious knowledge, whether human, profane, or frivolous, or perhaps even mundane and diabolical! Lord, Thou dost never deprive me of enlightenment, unless I wish otherwise, because the guiding lights shine in the Church's commands:

> *Canon* 1344, 1: "... it is the duty of the parish priest to preach to the people the Word of God in the customary homily."
>
> *Canon* 1345: "It is to be desired that in all churches and public oratories where people assist at Holy Mass on Sundays and Holy Days of Obligation a short explanation of the holy Gospel, or on any other point of Christian doctrine, be given to the people."
>
> *Canon* 1349: "The Ordinaries should insist that the parish priests have a mission given to their parishioners at least once in ten years. The parish priests, not excluding those of Religious Orders, are held to obey the Ordinary's regulations concerning these missions."

*Canon* 1347: "In sacred sermons there should be explained above all else the things the faithful must believe and practice in order to save their souls. Preachers of the Word of God should abstain from profane arguments . . . not preaching themselves, but Christ crucified."

As if this were not enough, the Council of Trent will help us out with more detailed explanations:

". . . teaching the things that all must know for salvation, and announcing to them with brevity and simplicity of speech the vices they must turn away from and the virtues they must pursue, in order to escape eternal punishment and be able to obtain heavenly glory."

—(*Sess. V. de Reformat., c. ii.*)

"During the celebration of Mass let them expound something of what is read therein, and declare, among other things, some of the mysteries of this most holy Sacrifice."

—(*Sess. xii de Sacrif. Miss., c. viii.*)

"Let them explain, and have explained, to the people the efficacy and use of the Sacraments, and also instil into the hearts of all both the Sacred Scriptures and salutary warnings, leaving aside questions which serve no useful purpose; and let them endeavour to instruct the people in the law of the Lord."

—(*Sess. xxiv de Reformat., c. vii.*)

And following the mind of the above-mentioned Council, the catechism of Pius V, called also the Council of Trent Catechism, has this to say:

"Greater care and diligence will have to be
shown so as to enable the faithful to know and
grasp the meaning of the ceremonies accompanying
the administration of each of the Sacraments."
—(*Part II*, 16.)

### III

This, then, is the sum of what I, as a priest, can and
ought to preach to the people from the pulpit, from the
altar, and from wherever else I exercise the ministry
of the Word: the Gospel, Catholic dogma, vices to
eschew, virtues to practise, the Mass and the Sacraments with their deep mysteries and attendant ceremonies. This is what is contained in the words *verbum
Dei*. And since the life histories of the Saints are but
a practical confirmation of these truths, there is also a
place for panegyrics; and the Fathers themselves, in the
panegyrics they preached, took occasion to explain some
point of faith or morals.

O Jesus, imprisoned in the Tabernacle of Thy
churches, surely it is a torment to Thee to listen to
those who call themselves *divini verbi praecones*, heralds
of the divine Word; to listen to doctrine which is so
different from, and perhaps even opposed to, Thine
own! Couldst Thou not say to the people, gathered together so eagerly very often, what the Prophet said in
his Lamentations?

> Thy prophets have seen false and foolish things
> for thee: and they have not laid open thy iniquity,
> to excite thee to penance: but they have seen for
> thee false revelations and banishments.—(*Lam. ii*,
> 14.)

Have I been one of those false prophets? Have I been

one of those who consider the Word of God not good enough for their flights of oratory, or of those who, while recognising its worth, wish to play to the gallery or win applause or line their pockets* by pandering to the fads and fashions of the hour, fearing otherwise to lose prestige?

## IV

*When must I preach?*—If piety were the very life of my life, and the salvation of souls my one ambition, I should have little difficulty in fulfilling St. Paul's stern command:

> " I adjure thee in the sight of God, and of Jesus Christ, who is to be the judge of living and dead, in the name of his coming and of his kingdom: preach the word, dwelling upon it continually, welcome or unwelcome; bring home wrong-doing, comfort the waverer, rebuke the sinner, with all the patience of a teacher."—(II *Timothy iv*, 1-2.)

" *Welcome or unwelcome* "—*opportune, importune*—an expression used nowhere else in Holy Writ, and a reminder that when it is a question of announcing the Word of God human expediency is not to govern us; it is always *in season*.

Would you say this was an exaggeration? If you have ever allowed politics, patriotism, or any other passionate cause, to grip you, you know what little you thought of " opportuneness " when it was a matter of communicating your ideas.

But there are certain times when the Church im-

---

* In English-speaking countries circumstances are usually different, (*Trans.*)

poses on Her priests the duty of preaching, a duty *sub gravi in se,* and *sub levi ex parvitate materiae*:

> *Canon* 1344, 1: "On Sundays and Holy Days of Obligation throughout the year it is the duty of the parish priest to preach to the people the Word of God in the customary homily, especially during the Holy Mass in which the attendance of the people is usually more numerous."

> *Canon* 1346: "Local Ordinaries shall attend to it that during the Lenten season, and also, if they judge it useful, during Advent, sermons are more frequently given in the Cathedral and parochial churches."

To which must be added the preaching of missions at least every ten years, and the Church's desire that there should be a brief explanation of the Gospel or some doctrinal point in all churches and public oratories where Mass is said on Sundays and Days of Obligation.

Have I by any chance incurred God's grievous Anger by omitting one or other of those official duties of mine during a considerable period? Have I sinned venially by omitting them occasionally without an adequate excuse? And even though neither office nor benefice obliged me, could I not have easily, and dozens of times, fallen in with the Church's motherly desire that during every Mass of Obligation the faithful hear the Gospel or Christian doctrine? Could I not at least have preached while another priest said the Mass? Why should the people, in their eagerness to hear the Word of God, have to run off to novenas and triduums where, very often, they get little more than sound and fury?

## V

*How must I preach?*—In the pulpit I can be elegant, most elegant, like an Augustine or a Chrysostom, so long as I adhere to the beautiful and terse rule given to preachers by Pius XI.

> " Don't reel things off from memory; don't read; don't declaim—speak!"

And when one speaks he tries, if he is in his sane mind, to make himself understood and to draw his listeners' attention.

Above all, I must strictly observe, when in front of a congregation, canon 1347-2; which is full of heavenly wisdom:

> "Preachers of the Word of God should abstain from profane arguments or arguments so deep as to exceed the common understanding of their hearers; and they should not exercise the evangelical ministry with skilled words of human wisdom, nor with a profane demonstration of vain and ambitious eloquence, but in the power and strength of the Spirit of God, not preaching themselves, but Christ crucified."

When God and men were expecting to hear eternal truths from my lips, and to see me taking the part of "herald" of the great King and announcer of Christ crucified, have I in the pulpit descended to the low category of a pander or a kind of spiritual procurer? If so, the curse uttered by Ezechiel would be most appropriate:

> Thus saith the Lord God: Woe to them that sew cushions under every elbow and make pillows for the heads of persons of every age to catch

souls: and when they caught the souls of my people, they gave life to their souls!—(*Ez. xiii,* 18.)

Sew cushions under every elbow with my soothing words of flattery! Soft pillows for every head! I would allow souls to slumber in their sins, cradled by my soft-caressing "eloquence"! I would cast a net round souls for their destruction, in order to nourish my own shadowy reputation of a popular preacher!

Dear Lord! Would it not be better to be struck dumb or to tear my tongue out?

### RESOLUTION

Besides observing in every point the above-quoted canons of the Code and of common-sense, I shall earnestly apply myself to the study of Religion exactly as I have to preach it to the people, until I have a thorough grasp of it, sorted out ideas, given them definite shape in my own mind, and have become competent in the art of concise, lively, and energetic exposition.

O Jesus, Model of sacred preachers! Add to my efforts what it is Thine alone to give, because only from Thy Heart does it flow: that divine quality which no secular orator ever knew, that evangelical unction deriving from the Unction for which Thou art named "The Christ," "The Anointed." *The Spirit of the Lord is upon me, wherefore He hath anointed me."* (*Luke iv,* 18.)

# CATECHETICAL INSTRUCTION

## FIRST MEDITATION

### *Divine Example and Precept*

#### I

It was Christ's delightful task in passing through this world *to evangelise the poor* (Luke iv, 18); therefore, to teach the rudiments of the Faith to children and to those who in this respect are also children, the ignorant, is a work of the ministry which is nothing less than divine. What need had our Divine Lord of exquisitely-couched and loftily-declaimed orations, or of intricate reasonings, or very abstruse arguments, when talking to poor ignorant people and to crowds uninitiated in the doctrines of the Redemption?

Apart from a few discourses to the doctors of the Law within the precincts of the Temple, His doctrine was usually imparted in the form of catechetical instruction: an instruction full of unction, of suggestion, and of astounding simplicity. The very places He chose to preach from, His gestures, His illustrations, His parables, even the questions and answers He welcomed from His listeners: they all breathed a sort of heavenly fragrance born of a charming familiarity, of a teaching that was homely and appealing to the hearts of little ones. It was the perfect catechetical instruction. No wonder He could say: *Learn of me, for I am meek and humble of heart.* (Matt. xi, 29.)

My Jesus, ever God, and yet, ever a Child and

273

humble with little ones: shall I disdain as beneath me what Thou didst so love and practise?

## II

And if Christ in His catechising had to accommodate Himself to the people and come down to the level of an illiterate audience, what of the Apostles? Our Lord, we must remember, spoke to Jewish believers who knew the primary truths and the preliminaries of our Faith —the existence of God, the immortality of the soul, creation, etc., etc.—but what did those countless multitudes know or believe whom St. Paul evangelised? What could his sermons be but the rudiments of our Faith expounded in conversational style by the wayside, in the street, in the forum, and within the home?

The same procedure had to be followed, and still is followed to-day, by that galaxy of apostolic men who by their lives of self-denial and by the spoken word have in every Christian age been instrumental in widening the boundaries of Christ's Kingdom so as to embrace barbarous and savage peoples. Of mighty little use would they find the embellishments of our pompous rhetoric when dealing with members of a stunted civilisation, with races that never knew civilisation, or which are in a state of profound decadence.

No, I shall not be ashamed to be a catechist; it is the catechists who have changed the world.

## III

The Gospels are abundantly clear on this matter. Jesus preaches to the poor; it is the hallmark of His

Divine Mission, the motto, so to speak, of His royal escutcheon. It is the poor, usually, who are the ignorant (particularly was this the case in our Lord's time) and Christ teaches them wherever He finds them: in the fields, on the mountainside, on the road, on the banks of the lake, in their homes, in their villages. (*Cfr. Matt. ix, 35.*)

He instructs them by using commonplace objects of comparison: the cornfields swaying within His view, the fig-trees that shaded the road; and He invents for the people's benefit examples and parables of unequalled loveliness, borrowing materials from occurrences of everyday life. He repeats His maxims time and time again, invites questions, and gives answers. In a word, He reveals Himself towards the poor as their great Catechist.

Shed Thy divine Catechist spirit, O Lord, upon every one of Thy priests, or at least upon a goodly number of them, and they will renew the face of the earth.

## RESOLUTION

If my stupid pride and a false idea of my dignity have prejudiced me until now against the teaching of the catechism, with shame for the past I shall henceforth esteem this work of the ministry at its full value; as a work which is truly evangelical and absolutely necessary for the spreading and preservation of the Faith, and without which every other style of preaching is little better than a mere exercise of vocalisation.

It is a positive fact that the Church, now and always, needs far more catechists than famed orators.

# CATECHETICAL INSTRUCTION

## *Importance and Efficacy*

### I

The Glory of God and the salvation of souls are the priest's exclusive aims when acting as a priest, and there is nothing like the catechetical instruction for achieving them. There is not much fear that pride will enter into our conversation with children and ignorant people when trying to speak to them so simply, so completely down to their level, that they understand us and listen with quiet eagerness. Such a method of conversing, however, will be to the eyes of the world, and even to otherwise sensible and talented people, something contemptible and unworthy of attention.

The great advantage of this is that the catechist priest will have only the Glory of God and the enlightenment of souls to concern him; he will be carrying out the command that Jesus uttered so tenderly: *Suffer the little children to come unto me. (Matt. xix, 14.)*

Lord, that is most consoling. When I am belittled in everyone's estimation because they see me stooping down for Thee to the little child, in reality I shall be ascending higher and higher in Thy esteem and love.

### II

How necessary and irreplaceable this humble ministerial duty is in the Church throughout every age! Who, if the interests of souls mean anything to him, can fail to see it? The primary evil, and the root of a great many other evils, is ignorance.

Those who never or very seldom approach the Sacraments—and they are legion—nor even go anywhere near a church, are mostly the victims of crass ignorance. And a very large proportion of those who hear Mass on Sundays and do their Easter duties, how imperfectly they understand what they are about!

Ignorance of things divine is a real epidemic these days. We are far indeed from witnessing the fulfilment of Isaias's promise:

> The earth is filled with the knowledge of the Lord, as the covering waters of the sea.—(*Is. xi*, 9.)

What overwhelms us, with the deafening roar and uncontrollable might of a tidal wave, is supercilious ignorance.

> For there is no truth . . . and there is no knowledge of God in the land.—(*Osee. iv*, 1.)

The multitudes, with their leaders at the head, seem to be shouting to their God and their Redeemer: *Depart from us. We desire not the knowledge of thy ways.* (*Job. xxi*, 14.)

What will be the fate of so many wretched Christians who are ignorant of the doctrines required—necessitate medii—for salvation? What will befall those who have not the slightest interest in performing the essential duties of a Christian, simply because they do not know what they are?

### III

But—you may say, or feel—I'm surely born for higher things. Look at my brilliant career, my talents, my power of imagery, my advanced and solid studies, my merits (and perhaps subconsciously) my desire for self-advancement and publicity: all this demands higher and wider scope for my energies.

Is there really scope for lofty enterprise in mealy-mouthed pimpering and pandering to frivolous mortals, in what the Code calls *lenocinium,* in the scattering of withered and stinking flowers of an empty and dated oratory? Are we to cater for a public

"quorum cibus nugae sunt" (*St. Augustine: Lib. de cat. c.* lv)

whose only taste is for puerilities? Or if we impart ideas, must those ideas be so flimsy and useless that they float away and vanish like pretty bubbles?

What nobler enterprise than to drill into the minds of the ignorant—ignorant but redeemed by the Precious Blood of Christ—ideas of the existence of the Supreme Being and His high Attributes, the divine origin of man and his ineffable, eternal destiny, and the treasures of Mercy locked up in the Heart of the Saviour?

Why, dear Jesus, oh, why do we Thy priests, after so many years of study and clerical training, after having pronounced solemnly on bended knees: *Dominus pars haereditatis meae et calicis mei;* why do we also have to pride ourselves on tinsel and empty vanity?

## IV

Experience proves that the only means of restoring the Christian life to many places where it has ceased to exist is the religious education of the children. When the little ones take to the catechism class it is only a matter of time for them to be given their First Communion—and how the Church longs to see, and positively commands, the union of Christ with souls at the first dawning of reason!—and afterwards to join in General Communions for children several times a year, to the accompaniment of festivities and ceremonies that children so love.

It is my duty to see that they learn appropriate hymns, to keep them in some sort of order, to announce the forthcoming event with a great flourish of trumpets, so to speak, getting the children themselves to do the trumpeting; and I should select a day when the whole parish can conveniently attend. It will not be long before I see the church crowded, either out of curiosity or from any other motive, and then I shall be able to speak to all and sundry, young and old.

Why should not we priests seize these golden opportunities of making contact with lapsed parents by winning over the children? Unless a priest gives himself ridiculous airs or repels by brusqueness or apathy, the child comes to him gladly and naturally. Therefore, can any one among us be justified in saying: "I can't do anything with these people," without a rebuff from God and from our own consciences: "The very thing you can do you won't, and you even despise it."

## RESOLUTIONS

1. I shall read and meditate over and over again, and with a firm determination to carry it out as far as my strength and office allow, chapter one of Section (Titulus) XX of the Code: "De catechetica institutione," canons 1329-1336.

2. With regard to the obligatory catechetical instruction to adults, mentioned in canon 1332, I shall over-

come its difficulties as well as I can. If the parishioners do not attend the Rosary in the evening, I shall have catechism for them during the Mass they frequent most, if there are several Masses in the same church; if only one, and I find no other way, I shall divide the homily into two parts: seven minutes for the explaining of the Gospel and another seven for some point of doctrine; and the latter I shall expound with orderliness and methodical sequence, even though the second part of my instruction may have no visible relationship with the first.

3. Although I may not have the charge of souls I shall offer my services most readily to the parish priest to help him in this work of the ministry, thus fulfilling canon 1333, 2nd par.; and besides this, I shall not miss an opportunity of teaching the essentials for salvation to anyone ignorant of them.

4. In the conviction that unless the child in school learns the doctrinal formulas by heart—formulas that no individual teacher can safely change—he will never know the catechism, I shall try to enlist the co-operation of school teachers in this matter. I shall take every prudent measure my zeal suggests and requires in order to win over the teacher, yielding, if necessary, my personal rights and points of dignity; and if he is not a good Christian I shall do my utmost to make him one; and I shall offer him my services in the teaching of Religion. The teacher and myself working together in harness would certainly do an immense good to souls and to the whole parish.

# THIRD PART

# VIRTUES AND VICES

## FAITH

### FIRST MEDITATION

*General Motives for Esteeming the Faith*

## I

It is a great boon to be a Christian. For, not least among the priceless treasures I possess in the Church is a complete science of salvation.

Any Christian with an ordinary knowledge of the Catholic Faith knows as much as is required to be known about matters of primary importance and necessity concerning human life: God, self, the immortality of the soul, the life to come.

He knows these capital truths with absolute certainty, infallibly, with greater assurance than if he perceived them with his bodily senses. It is not surprising; he is taught them by the only Person who has an essential and inalienable right to the title of Master: *one is your master, Christ.* (Matt. xxiii, 10.)

> "In old days, God spoke to our fathers in many ways, and by many means, through the prophets;

now at last in these times he has spoken to us, with
a Son to speak for him; a Son whom he has
appointed to inherit all things, just as it was
through him that he created this world of time;
a Son, who is the radiance of his Father's splendour, and the full expression of his being."—
(*Heb. i,* 1-3.)

And this knowledge, which is absolute, complete,
immune from error, and at the same time the most
human and divine; this knowledge, which, when perceived by the mind and embraced by the will and
relished in action, constitutes the only real wisdom—
spoken of in such lofty terms by Job and Baruch—is
arrived at by faith alone. (*Cfr. Job xxviii; Bar. iii.*)

## II

Our Divine Lord turned to His disciples and said to
them:

> Blessed are your eyes, because they see; and your
> ears, because they hear.
>
> For, amen, I say to you: many prophets and just
> men have desired to see the things that you see,
> and have not seen them; and to hear the things
> that you hear, and have not heard them.—(*Matt.
> xiii,* 16-17.)

This is the Beatitude obtained through faith, which
enables us to see Christ, listen to Him and believe in
Him.

I thank Thee, good Jesus, because by Thy mercy
alone Thou hast so readily given me access to a happiness more perfect than was ever the lot of Elias and
Isaias, of Abraham and David, through my more en-

lightened and deeper knowledge of Thee. Trusting in
Thy words, I have no desire to change places with the
prophets of old, or with the most glorious kings, nor
even with John the Baptist, because

> he that is the lesser in the kingdom of heaven is
> greater than he.—(*Matt. xi,* 11.)

Who am I, Lord, that Thou shouldst remember me
and raise me to such a dignity?

### III

> Because thou hast seen me, Thomas, thou hast
> believed: blessed are they that have not seen, and
> have believed.—(*John xx,* 29.)

Blessed those eyes that saw Christ in mortal flesh
along the roads and lanes, sitting down tired on the
stones by the wayside, evangelising the poor and the
little ones, like a father among his children; by His
words imparting health to the sick and sorrowful,
nourishment to hungering bodies and souls, new life
to the dead; and dying Himself for us all. More blessed
still, those eyes that beheld Him, those hands that
touched Him, after He arose immortal from the tomb.
Blessed were they, indeed. What should I not give to
have been among their number!

Yet, I should not envy them; it is they, rather, who
should envy *me;* because Christ has said: Blessed are
they that have *not* seen, and have *believed.*

Jesus, I believe; with every ounce of strength of every
atom of my being, I believe in Thee, even though I
have not seen or touched Thee; with Thomas, on
bended knees I confess to Thee:

> My Lord and my God.—(*John xx,* 28.)

## IV

Let Thy inspiration, O Lord, teach me the real meaning of that Beatitude of Thine. Where is it to be found? What does it consist in? The Apostle St. Paul gives me the answer:

> "What is faith? It is that which gives substance to our hopes, which convinces us of things we cannot see."—(*Heb. xi, 1.*)

St. Thomas Aquinas defines faith as

> "a habit of the mind whereby eternal life begins," *Habitus mentis quo inchoatur vita aeterna.*

By faith then, I carry in my soul a lamp of light that never fails, a day that knows no setting, perennial youth, eternal life. Of course, I know that the full effects of faith are not as yet diffused throughout my whole being; they have not yet steeped my senses and faculties in a rushing torrent of delight; but as long as I persevere in a living, active faith, death's gentle hand will one day open the flood-gates that keep the stream pent up in the summit of the soul, and the trimphant waves will leap in unrestrained cataracts unto life everlasting.

### RESOLUTION

Lord, I am determined to lose all rather than forfeit or whittle down one iota of my faith. Let every burning desire grow cold within me, every dream be shattered, rather than quench by a single sin the life that is radiant light in the lamp of my faith.

# FAITH

## SECOND MEDITATION

### Priestly Motives for Frequent Acts of Faith

#### I

Not every kind of Christian faith produces happiness, only that which is steeped in, and animated by, charity, and made fruitful in good works; " the faith that finds its expression in love." (Gal. v, 6.) And more especially, the faith that waxes resplendent, like the rising sun, until it reaches the zenith brightness of heavenly glory; the faith that goes from strength to strenth by dint of repeated and fervent acts.

If every Christian must needs live by faith in order to win God's blessings, much more so the priest, who must win blessings for himself and for others.

What a blessing it would be if our Lord could address to His priests, to every one of them, those admiring words He spoke to the woman of Canaan: *O woman, great is thy faith!* (Matt. xv, 28.)

#### II

The priest, more than anyone else, has to bear in himself and for the sake of others, the brunt of that fearful battle which St. Paul describes so sombrely:

> " It is not against flesh and blood that we enter the lists; we have to do with princedoms and powers, with those who have mastery of the world in these dark days, with malign influences in an order higher than ours."—(*Eph. vi,* 12.)

What priest has not often felt in his flesh and spirit

the crack of the whip from those mastering influences. What priestly heart has not been seared by the Enemy's " fire-tipped arrows "? Where is our refuge and defence? The Faith. No other weapons but those so vividly depicted by the Apostle:

> " Take up the shield of faith, with which you will be able to quench all the fire-tipped arrows of your wicked enemy."—(*Eph. vi,* 16.)

Dear Lord, if my flesh and spirit have been scorched so often and have quivered under the poisonous sting, is it not because I have kept the solid shield of faith thrown into one corner, like a rusty old heirloom, instead of burnishing it daily, forging and re-forging it in the furnace of Thy Sacred Heart, and studding it with the diamonds of Thy love?

### III

The Catholic priest, in his particular capacity as teacher and educator, has only one thing to justify his existence; faith. No Catholic priest should answer the description of a Protestant minister given by a certain wit: a gentleman dressed in black, who on Sundays ascends the pulpit to say sweet reasonable things. The commission from Christ is: *Teach all nations whatsoever I have commanded you.* (Matt. xxviii, 19.)

Our task is to teach and command what He taught and commanded, nothing else; and our teaching must rest on His divine Authority, not on our own fallible reasoning.

Christ, the Redeemer, is pledged to continue being the Light scattering the darkness of the nations from century to century through the medium of my words given life and shape in the living mould of the Faith.

Hence, the torch of faith must be ever burning bright, in my heart, on my lips, in my hands.

## IV

Very serious harm is done to the faithful if we give them the slightest justification for saying what they say only too often about an individual priest, and even about priests as a whole when illicitly indulging in generalisations: "They haven't any faith; they don't even believe it themselves!" What a dreadful calamity when that malicious remark seems to rest on solid proof, when there are facts to show that the priest does not possess the faith, the living faith! It is a Satanic call to surrender arms, to stage a general withdrawal, to desert from the army of Christ.

How many parishes and villages and towns there are which no longer acknowledge Christ as their God, have formally withdrawn their allegiance; for no reason at all except the evil life of one of Christ's ministers, a life that fails to square with his preaching, or even a life of unbelief and apostasy!

Such is the terrible power which I wield as a priest; a kind of omnipotence over men, even to the point, O Jesus, of stripping Thee in their minds of Thy Divinity, or of tearing It to shreds.

## V

In my ministerial duties, in my struggle against certain temptations, that is, as often as my priestly calling constrains me to undertake things beyond the reach of my human weakness, why not have recourse to faith? To the man of faith everything becomes a possibility. The difficulty lies, not so much in things themselves, as in maintaining my faith at its proper level. I can do all things only in Him who strengthens me, only when God places His own Power into my hands. Then, why not take Him at His word?

> "We have learned to recognise the love God has in our regard, to recognise it, and to make it our belief."—(*I John iv,* 16.)

If I have faith in God's love for me, why not have faith concerning things so much less astounding and stupendous? God, who does not refuse me His love, will not refuse me these lesser things, will refuse me nothing.

## RESOLUTIONS

1. To flee from vice, in particular, sensuality, on whose slippery gradient a priest would easily and very soon slide down to the depths of unbelief and even apostasy. I shall keep my conscience pure, because "*some, through refusing this duty, have made ship-wreck of the faith.*" (*Tim. i,* 19.)

2. To act by faith's impulse, to increase the number of acts, or at least to put more life or intensity into the acts I already make in the course of my ministerial duties.

3. To inform my whole life with the light and life of the Faith; my intellect, with thoughts of the Faith; my will, with longings born of the Faith; my words, with ideas and affections inspired by the Faith; my undertakings, under the guidance of the Faith. Let all who know me closely be obliged to think and say of me: "He's a man of faith."

4. To take real delight in teaching the ignorant and children the rudiments of the Faith.

# HOPE

## *The Foundations of Hope*

### I

The Holy Spirit intercedes for us, with groans beyond all utterance; He asks for us to be given eternal life; He petitions the Father from the inmost sanctuary of our hearts, where He dwells by His grace. (*Cfr. Rom. viii, 25-27.*)

And our Divine Redeemer Himself, how eagerly He exhorts us to lay up treasures for Heaven!

Are my ideas and aspirations in consonance with the pleadings of the Holy Spirit and with the Saviour's exhortation? To be honest with myself, are there not goods of this world which I desire with greater yearning and towards which I tend with stronger impulse and in whose attainment I spend more energy than for eternal life?

Why should I not expect to receive from my Father in Heaven what He so frequently and loyally promises, and so insistently begs me to take? But, have I imagined that He will give it me without even a thought on my part? without forcing myself to acquire it?

> "The kingdom of heaven has opened to force, and the forceful are even now making it their prize."—(*Matt. xi, 12.*)

289

K

## II

For God's part, we are so certain of heaven that, in the Gospel phrase, if we live in His grace we are already in possession of eternal life. Grace is the gift of the Holy Ghost, of the Spirit of God, of the Spirit of Christ, infused into our souls; it is a spirit of divine adoption, whereby God makes us His children and grants us full right to call Him *Abba*, Father. And, being children of God, we are also God's heirs, and co-heirs with Christ: heirs to God's estate, to Christ's kingdom, the kingdom of heaven. (*Cfr. Rom. viii,* 17.) Moreover, the spirit of adoption, grace, confers upon us not so much a lawful claim to inherit as the inheritance itself, eternal life:

> And I give them life everlasting: and they shall not perish for ever.—(*John x,* 28.)

At the small cost of obtaining forgiveness of my sins and of remaining in His friendship, I can, thanks to my heavenly Father, possess even here below His Life, life everlasting.

Do I enjoy the moral certainty that now, at this very moment, I am the holder of so rich a treasure? Do I esteem it higher than all worldly goods? Do I use every precaution to safeguard it?

## III

Another pledge of eternal life is given me, a pledge of still greater value: the Son of God Himself! O Father, Thy own divine Son, Thine only-Begotten Son, is given to the world to answer for the truth of Thy promises!

> For God so loved the world, as to give his only-begotten Son: that whosoever believeth in him may

not perish, but may have life everlasting.—(*John iii*, 16.)

Not content with delivering Him to us by the Incarnation, the Father did not spare the Son, but gave Him up to death for our ransom. As Origen says: "His own He gave up to strangers, His own Son, for the sake of sons of adoption." Jesus signs the Father's promise for us in His Blood on the Cross. He remains our Divine Hostage in the tabernacle of our Altars, the pledge of our eternal peace.

Father in Heaven, what will it cost Thee to communicate Thy happiness to us—Thy happiness which does not diminish or lose in the communicating—seeing that Thou gavest us the very Blood of Thy own Son, in Whom Thou hast all Thy delight?

Believing all this, as I do, am I still in doubt about God's promise? Do I still hesitate?

## IV

There is still another pledge and earnest of eternal life, the *pignus futurae gloriae,* as I call it using the Church's words: the sacred Banquet wherein Christ is received.

> "This is my body, given up for you; this cup is the new testament in my blood."

Certain people insist on drawing up their wills in their own handwriting, they do not entrust them to another's hand: a sign of the scrupulous and painstaking care they demand in the execution of their wills. But Thou, Lord, hast surpassed them all. Thou didst write Thy last will in Thy own Blood; or rather, it is Thy Blood Itself which constitutes Thy will on my behalf; not only Thy Blood on Mount Calvary, but, as it were, a fresh copy every day in the Sacrifice of the Mass. And this Blood of the New Covenant, this Will of Thine written in Thy Blood, is to be not merely handed over to me, but incorporated, by drinking, into my inmost being.

> Hic calix Novum Testamentum est in meo sanguine. . . .

A testament that stands, that is valid, unchangeable, eternal.

And what dost Thou leave me, O Lord, in Thy will?

> qui pro vobis et pro multis effundetur in remissionem peccatorum.

The remission of sin, and Thy grace; and therefore, as a consequence, Thy own glory.

Could I ask of Thee, or couldst Thou possibly give me, a better guarantee? Lord, I hope, I trust, I have confidence, in Thee!


## RESOLUTION

I will not put my trust in the wealth of this world, nor in mortal man—a staff that easily breaks and splinters the hand which leans too heavily upon it; nor in my own earthly life—a fleeting shadow, a wisp of cloud that the breeze evaporates; nor in my own personal worth, which is very meagre; but in God alone. Yes, even in the affairs of ordinary daily life; but much more so when it comes to obtaining the grace of avoiding sin or of rising up from sin and of persevering and finally winning eternal life.

# HOPE

## Priestly Motives

### I

Once ordained a priest, what is there for me to hope for, apart from eternal life? The good things of earth? At my ordination I deliberately placed them out of my reach. And even in my enjoyment of those which my priestly condition does not forbid me, it is my personal experience, or the experience of others I know, or both together, that no sooner have my itching fingers begun to clutch them, no sooner have my thirsting lips tried to suck their sweetness, than their hollowness and deceptiveness have stood revealed and they have been true only to the name written upon their inmost nature: *delusion, satiety!* Even if they were something solidly good, how shortlived, how ephemeral, how frail they are!

But, whatever their nature, I solemnly renounced them when at my ordination I claimed the Lord for my prize and inheritance:

> Dominus pars hereditatis meae et calicis mei, tu es qui restitues hereditatem meam mihi.—(*Ps. xv*, 5.)

With St. Augustine I said: "Let others make their choice of the good things of earth and of time for their enjoyment; the Lord is my lot. Let others drink of deadly pleasures; it is the Lord who fills my cup."

Am I going to retract that renouncement? Was it all a farce?

## II

We priests bear a heavier yoke than the laity, and in like measure our difficulties increase, our temptations gather fury, discouragements multiply; our souls are ships braving wilder storms, their frail sides are lashed more mercilessly. There is but one anchor to hold fast and firm: the anchor of which the Apostle speaks: the anchor of hope, which is sure and immovable, reaching that inner sanctuary beyond the veil, where Jesus Christ, our escort, has entered already. (*Heb. vi,* 18-20.)

How many times in my priestly life has my conscience made shipwreck through not casting this anchor of hope, but keeping it idle on deck like a piece of scrap iron?

## III

It is a tragic thing for the faithful when their priests and instructors in the Faith fail to live by the hope of eternal reward. What will their practice of religion be like? Either they will give up all practice of Christianity, because if there is nothing to hope for in another life the crucified Christ will appear an absurdity; or else, by-passing the pith and substance of every Christian act, hope of eternal life, they will debase practice to the level of empty, meaningless formula and vocal articulation, nothing more. Or again, by a certain inconsistency, as illogical as it is frequent, they will give honour and have recourse to Christ and the Saints with Christian prayer and belief, but in that same spirit with which the pagans of old invoked Mercury, the god of wealth and plunder, and Bacchus, the god of wine, and Venus, the goddess of lust; they will turn to Christ for precisely those same boons and favours which were expected from the false gods of old.

Just think of it; asking a crucified God solely or in the first place for honours, pleasures, and riches! I only hope that my own example has not led them to it!

## IV

Who is there who does not cherish the hope of something this world can give? What is our life but a texture of a thousand colours being woven by the loom of hope? A texture, however, which reality is all the time unravelling without mercy, breaking and scattering the strands in big handfuls along the roads and crossroads of our earthly existence. Hopes of the past were my day-dreams: *vigilantium somnia;* money, prosperity, pleasures, appointments, dignities, honours: these are my dreams of the morrow. To-morrow, that cruel god at whose shrine I have been slaughtering and sacrificing all my yesterdays; the god who, when he comes, brings instead of achievement a sneer and empty hands or hands full of bitter disappointment, and vanishes into thin air like the rest of my days.

It is God's command that we should keep on hoping. It is part and parcel of my inner nature that I should hope for something. Then why let this irrepressible energy run to waste? Why not divert my hope from possessions which shall never be mine, which are always ephemeral, and which even if they were permanently mine would still leave me hungering and empty as ever; and direct my longings, like a compass-needle, to the magnetic North of God and everlasting life? Hope is a force that was given me as a spur to goad me along the road which leads to eternal happiness.

## RESOLUTIONS

1.   I shall meditate more assiduously on the eternal life which awaits me, until I have pinned all my hopes upon it, like an anchor pinned to the bottom of the sea. My God, when wilt Thou grant me the grace to be able to say with all sincerity these words of the Psalmist: *Ps. xxvi*, 4:

> "One request I have ever made of the Lord, let me claim it still, to dwell in the Lord's house my whole life long."

2.   Not to be satisfied with a lifeless sort of hope, but ever to possess a hope vivified by charity; and therefore, to avoid grievous sin, which robs hope of its principle of life; even though it may not reject it altogether from my soul, it deprives it of supernatural energy.

3.   If I am a prey to vice, especially sensual vice, to combat despair, vice's poisonous fruit. The greatest temptation for any sensual person is always either to believe oneself irrevocably lost on account of the apparent impossibility of returning to the path of Christian chastity, or stupidly to assume that God will somehow manage to save one's soul without any great effort on one's part. Oh, the danger of soft sensuality! Greater than we imagine!

4.   To profess the tenderest love for Mary, the Mother of Mercy, our life, our sweetness, and our hope.

# CHARITY OR THE LOVE OF GOD

## General Motives

### I

What is charity? A supernatural habit of the mind whereby we love God above all things for His own sake, and ourselves and our neighbour for Him.

It is a theological virtue like the two previous ones, but higher than they, and the only eternal one of the three. Faith and hope will take us as far as the threshold of eternity, but when we actually enter it they will have fallen away. Only of charity St. Paul has said: charity never falleth away, never dies; it is eternal, like God Himself, like the Holy Spirit who pours it into our hearts; and of such surpassing excellence that only the Divine Spirit can infuse it; of a quality that no human force or even the strength of the seraphim, the spirits of love, can impart it to us.

It directs man's most rebellious faculty, his rational appetite, to his final goal. It elevates a man's free will above all desirable things of earth and beyond every creature visible and invisible of the universe, to fix it securely on God, the Supreme Good. It is the last word in human perfection, even now: *vinculum perfectionis*. (*Colos. iii*, 14.) It is, in a sense, the possession here below of the Sovereign Good, if not in the fulness of union as in heaven, intentionally and affectively, which is the only union possible to us while we are wayfarers.

O God, my only Good, do I possess this glorious supernatural endowment? Is my mind and my heart a temple, here and now, of Thy Spirit? Dost Thou at this moment keep my inconstant will bound fast to Thee by that perfect bond, that bond so gentle and delightful and strong?

## II

Even supposing—an impossible supposition, of course —that every virtue were enshrined in my soul, my whole existence a most fertile soil and limitless source of heroism, if I lack charity, *nihil mihi prodest, nihil sum:* it would avail me nothing, I should count for nothing. (*Cor. xiii,* 3.)

Charity is necessary—*necessitate medii*—for my justification and salvation. Who does not love God is in sin. So it is not to be thought a mere flash from a heart on fire when St. Paul exclaims:

> " If there is anyone who has no love for the Lord, let him be held accursed—anathema sit!"
>
> —(*I Cor. xvi,* 22.)

It is but God's irrevocable statement. Whoever does not love God remains apart and severed from God; whoever appears before the Judgement-seat of God without the cloth-of-gold garment of divine love will have his part and lot with the hypocrites in the unquenchable fire.

O God, let the solemn, imperative, and burning proclamation which accompanied the issuing of the great precept of love on Mount Sinai serve to impel my entry into the kingdom of those that love thee.

Thou shalt love the Lord thy God with thy

whole heart and with thy whole soul, and with thy
whole strength and with thy whole mind (*Deut. vi,
5*):

for this is the greatest and the first commandment
(*Matt. xxii, 37*).

Or, as St. Thomas of Villanova says:

"Love the Lord your God, at least because He
is yours. You love your field and your clothing,
because they belong to you, they are yours. Then,
why not love God who is also yours? Of all that is
yours, will God alone be unworthy of love?"

## III

The love of God is the royal road leading to God, the
shortest, the quickest, or rather, the only way of
approach to union with God. Thus St. Paul devotes a
long and beautiful chapter (*I Cor. xii*) to a consideration
of the various charismatic gifts and graces—gratiae gratis
datae—which attracted so many souls in those early
Christian centuries to the Fold of the Divine Redeemer:
prophecy, the gift of healing, of tongues, of mind-
reading, etc., but he concludes with these words:

"Prize the best gifts of heaven; meanwhile, I can
show you a way which is better than any other."
—(*I Cor. xii, 41.*)

and that better way is no other than charity, the soul of
every other virtue, the life and value of every good
work, to which he devotes the most beautiful of all his
writings, chapter thirteen of the same Epistle.

The act of least outward significance, for instance,
to give someone a drink of water, if done out of supernatural charity is of greater value in the sight of the

Supreme Judge than the tortures of a St. Laurence if endured without charity.

And I, poor blind soul, how often I have tormented myself hunting after elaborate ways and means of spiritual perfection, looking out for by-ways and unbeaten tracks, and meanwhile, perhaps, by-passing the shortest and easiest and most satisfying route: the love of God.

### IV

"Wilt thou not learn to love the Lord thy God, and obey him, and keep close to his side? Thou hast no life, no hope of long continuance, but in him."
—(*Deut. xxx,* 20.)

Even on earth, where the senses crave for satisfaction with drunken fury: even here, my happiness and my life is to love the Lord my God and to keep closely united to Him. Surely experience has given me a taste of this. And I know what befalls the reckless soul who separates from God expecting to find something better! As St. Augustine says in his *Confessions*:

"My soul lay down among creatures, seeking sweet repose; she tossed from one side to another . . . but found the bed hard and unbearable; because Thou alone, Lord, art rest. *Tu solus, Domine, requies.*"

"Repose and sweetness; because the day my soul loved Thee, remained in Thy Presence, and dwelt within Thee, she was like a bee in its honeycomb cell, seeing nought, touching nought, tasting nought but honey and peace and rest."
—(*Bk. VI, chap. xvi.*)

## RESOLUTIONS

1. Intimately convinced that the charity which unites me to God is far superior to mercy and any other virtue —because nothing is higher and more perfect than union with the Supreme Being, the Source of all that is—and that such close union with God is the exclusive outcome of true interior love, I resolve to train myself to make frequent and ardent acts of affective charity every day, rejoicing and finding delight in God's infinite Goodness, and thanking Him in terms such as those of the Gloria in excelsis Deo: *Gratias agimus tibi propter magnam gloriam tuam;* and fostering a keen desire that all intelligent and free-willed creatures should join with me in this same praise and thanksgiving for all eternity.

2. I shall, by God's mercy, remain always in the state of sanctifying grace, or I shall do my utmost to recover it as soon as I have lost it, so that God may have some regard for my desire and praise, which from sinful lips would not be a handsome tribute.


## CHARITY OR THE LOVE OF GOD

### SECOND MEDITATION

#### Priestly Motives

### I

Our innate weakness offers many an obstacle to the keeping of God's law, and our twisted inclinations and vicious habits provide many more. But greater still are the stumbling-blocks on the steep climb of priestly duty. We cannot but strain and stagger under this yoke with all its extra burdens, enough to tax the strength of an angel.

All the more reason why we should not forget that charity alone endows with superabundant energies, for " Charity sustains, believes, hopes, endures to the last " and, giving a little twist to our Lord's words: all things are possible to him that loveth.

The author of the *Imitation,* in an immortal passage worthy of Plato, has this to say:

> " Love does not feel the burden nor take account of hard work; it desires more than it can cope with; it does not complain if the impossible is commanded, being sure of accomplishing everything in God; and it brings many things to a successful issue where one who loves not would falter and fall."—(*Bk. III, ch.* vi.)

There is one label for all my cowardice and lack of courage, that chafes at any restraint and sees mountains in mole-hills: want of the love of God.

## II

Our Divine Lord, when making me His distinguished and privileged minister, might well have asked me: " Dost thou love me more than these?" (*John xxi,* 15).

Who should love Thee, Lord, if not I? Into these feeble hands of mine Thou didst deposit Thy doctrine, Thy Sacraments, Thy honour and glory, Thy own Person; a complete retractation, it would seem, of a former statement: *I will not give my glory to another* (*Is. xlii,* 8).

No one contemplates and actually touches the inexhaustible wealth of the Lord's Mercy so closely as I, and for all that, this tremendous Lover comes begging to me for a few crumbs of my love, of that paltry love which I have lavished so prodigally up to now on a host of vile creatures without receiving or even asking in return for so much as a disdainful " thank you "; and yet, of a love which is my heart's only treasure to dispose of freely.

I must confess with shame, O Lord, that when I did give Thee something of my love it was only after a lot of bargaining, only by driblets, as it were; and many a time I just answered thee with a round refusal, or else, I asked for, or snatched, it back after giving it, as though repentant of having deposited my sole treasure in such hands, or rather, in such a Heart, as Thine.

## III

And yet, I would love Thee! Yes, I would that my heart were a red-hot cinder in the brazier of Thy divine Charity! Because if love unites and transforms, what more desirable gain than to transform my heart into Thine? Ah, but I find it hard to accomplish. It is hard for the mind to ascend the rugged heights of faith to the Absolute Truth where God dwells in Light inaccessible (*I Tim. v*, 16); harder still for the human will to keep to the hilly road of love and the fulfilment of God's Will and reach the All-spiritual Sovereign Good, which is so remote and so estranged from the greater number of my tastes and pleasures. And I am so accustomed to, and glutted with, the clammy sweetness of tangible things—portrayed to me so fascinatingly amid the auroral splendours of desire—and I am so much at home with the love of what is human and with the human ways of love, that my soul refuses to face, rejects as an airy nothingness, as unsubstantial food, the love of what is purely Divine.

And precisely for this reason the Word of God became Man, became *flesh,* as St. John puts it, who also writes:

> " Our message concerns that Word, who is Life; what he was from the first, what we have heard about him, what our own eyes have seen of him; what it was that met our gaze, and the touch of our hands."—(*I John i,* 1.)

The result is, O Jesus, that now when I think of Thee, remember Thy actions, bring Thee before my imagination, sympathise with Thy griefs, ruminate Thy words, and love Thee in all things, I am entering into a mind like my own, cherishing a flesh like mine, loving a heart like mine; and at the same time, I am loving my God and keeping the greatest and first Commandment; because in seeing and loving Thee, one sees and loves Thy Father; for Thou and the Father are One (*John xiv,* 9; *x,* 30).

I thank Thee, dear Jesus, for having placed the precept of loving God within such easy reach of me. No, it will not be hard for me now, it will be something easy and smooth to love Thee; for Thy life I read and ponder over every day; Thy doctrine I teach; Thy flesh I eat, and Thy blood I drink.

St. Gregory no longer baffles me when he says that " the Saints learn by loving what they speak about when teaching ".

## IV

The precept to love God is very much like God Himself: unseen and unfelt, and yet it is in everything, sustaining and giving life to everything. So too, this commandment seems to impose no particular obligation, but it is the soul of the entire decalogue. I shall therefore derive motives for observing it from the fact of its being so gently-insinuating and easy to fulfil. Negatively, I shall observe this precept by a fixed determination never to offend God and to lose everything rather than God. And on the positive side, when the occasion arises of offending Him, I shall choose to forgo any other good, however great, rather than incur mortal sin; and when tempted and allured by the enemies of my soul to go astray, I shall sooner see them disappointed and myself stripped of everything than insult and forfeit God. Moreover, I shall thank the good God who in His loving-kindness has so condescended to my human condition and so adapted Himself to my natural manner that, without reproach, He allows me to love all created things, as many as I wish, on the sole condition that their place in my affections is not opposed to, and incompatible with, His; and even allows me to love them with stronger feeling and greater intensity than Himself, as long as I hold Him in higher esteem and appreciate His love more than that of all creatures.

### RESOLUTIONS

1. I shall school myself in the affective love of God by directing all my activities to His greater glory; that is, to a clearer and more adequate knowledge of God

and to loving Him and conforming to His divine Will in everything:

(a) Choosing whatever pleases Him best either in work or in suffering,

(b) Doing so in the mode and manner most acceptable to Him; and

(c) Simply and solely because it does please Him, with that purest intention alone.

2.    Putting it in a nutshell: I shall transfer the fourth commandment to the first, conducting myself towards God as to a true and only Lord and Father; caring for Him, revering Him, and obeying Him as such; for this is the Christian manner of divine worship. And thus my whole life, with all its yearnings and in all its dealings, will be but one long act of piety and filial fear and worship in spirit and truth towards my Father who is in heaven.

3.    In sum, I shall stake my all on loving in every way my Lord and Saviour Jesus Christ, God and Man; studying Him affectionately, meditating on His life and character, feasting my mind and senses on Him; preferring Him to all my friends, all my kith and kin, to father and mother, and to my own self; because he that loves father or mother more than Christ is not worthy of Christ (*Matt. x,* 37).

# FRATERNAL CHARITY

### OR

# THE LOVE FOR ONE'S NEIGHBOUR

#### FIRST MEDITATION

## *Nature of Fraternal Charity*

### I

How far should our love go—that love which enshrines everything contained in God's law? God has been pleased to give us the answer in a most striking manner. He, Whom no one has seen in this life, condescended to show Himself through the medium of manifold and awe-inspiring apparitions to His ancient People, as if to establish a tangible right to their whole-hearted allegiance; and at length revealed Himself in Person, became Man, and held converse with mortal man, so as to be able to say to us:

He that seeth me, seeth the Father also.

We are face to face with God when we look upon Christ, and anyone who says he believes in God and loves God but at the same time refuses to acknowledge and love Christ is to be accounted a liar.

Well now, according to the Apostle of Love, it is impossible to love God or Christ without having love for one's neighbour:

" If a man boasts of loving God, while he hates
his own brother, he is a liar."—(*I John iv*, 20.)

and the same Apostle adduces this apparently strange reason:

"He has seen his brother, and has no love for him; what love can he have for the God he has never seen?" (*id.*)

The love we have for our neighbour, therefore, is the hallmark and gauge of our love for God. And, on the contrary, without this love for our neighbour our love for God is false. There is falsehood and delusion and vain observance—*religio vana*—in that so-called love and worship of God, in those devotions and prayers of ours, if we lean on them and think to find in them support for despising and judging rashly and slandering or criticising with venom and mercilessly hurting our neighbour by crushing him in his weaknesses or ignoring him callously in his griefs and losses, no matter what his race, his nationality, his position, or even his morals and beliefs.

Has my supposed piety ever been a sort of buskin and toga like those of the old Roman Patrician, in which I felt authorised to strut about with a leering glance at my neighbour and to exclaim with Horace: "Odi profanum vulgus et arceo"—I loathe the common herd and I keep my distance? If so, my piety was a pietism execrated by God and by Christ.

## II

There is something mysterious and attractive about every man, about human nature, which would seem to captivate God Himself, enamouring Him, so to speak, in such a manner that it elicits from Him acts of the most generous loving-kindness; Self-belittlement, abasement, sacrifice, dedication in body, soul and Divinity to the lofty enterprise, the only enterprise worthy of God, of winning over at all costs the love of the human heart. *God so loved the world !—(John iii, 16.)*

Not a single human being exists who cannot exclaim with absolute truth, whatever his caste or condition:

" I know and I believe in the love God has for me " (*I John iv, 16*). It is a belief exclusively Catholic. Other cults and sects reject it, it offends them; their spirit of contradiction and denial rather prompts them to ask with the Psalmist:

> What is man, O God, that thou shouldst keep him in remembrance?

But how can I, who believe in the love God has for man, refuse to love whom God has loved so exceedingly? And why should I wonder, Lord, that Thou art so exacting in demanding of me, with threats of lightning Wrath, that I too love my fellow men out of regard for Thy incomprehensible love?

### III

In this precept God shows Himself exacting: *Thou shalt love thy neighbour as thyself* (*Matt. xix, 8*). Self-love is the standard and a high one it is. He could have chosen another standard, for instance the things a man is fondest of, his wife, his children, his mother. No, " as thyself ". In the human heart is lodged no affection more widespread, more profound, more unquenchable and ready to serve than the love of self. If we analyse our-selves carefully, if we take apart this complicated machinery of human nature, we shall find that our whole being, our whole life, with all its variety of phenomena and manifestations, with all its long list of appetites and tendencies, comes down to but one thing: that boundless, limitless love we have for ourselves. According to that model, then, I am commanded by My Lord and God to love others: thou shalt love thy neighbour as thyself.

And that there might be no mistake about it, God, in His ten commandments, has devoted seven of them to the various works of love towards my neighbour; three for Himself, seven for man. So jealous is He of the honour and welfare of the children of Adam that He does not leave a single human value without a wall of defence, without the shield and flashing sword of a divine precept: Thou shalt not kill; thou shalt not commit adultery; thou shalt not steal, etc., etc.

## RESOLUTIONS

I shall try to purify my love for my neighbour of all its dross and base metal. It is not a Christian love if its foundation is my selfishness or sensuality, no matter how fervent and self-denying it may appear on the surface. Nor is that honourable and noble human love, which rests merely on the wisdom or virtue or generous qualities of a fellow man, to be accounted Christian; it can be made Christian, but of itself it falls far short. The driving force behind true Christian charity towards all men—for it embraces everyone without any possible exception—is the supreme fact that they were created by God, endowed with an immortal soul, made into God's image and likeness, raised to the supernatural level, and are destined for eternal happiness through the redeeming Blood of Jesus Christ. Christian love is based on motives inspired by Christian faith, nothing less.

I shall, therefore, try to bring myself to love my

neighbour precisely for these motives, rejecting as worthless any other motive which cancels out the former, and subordinating those other human motives that are naturally honourable and good to the higher motives of faith.

## FRATERNAL CHARITY OR THE LOVE FOR ONE'S NEIGHBOUR

### SECOND MEDITATION

#### The New Commandment

### I

St. Paul's definition of a priest is simply: a man who is specially appointed to the task of loving God and his fellow men, a man chosen from among men to devote himself to a ministry on their behalf at every hour of the day.

This explains why the Divine Master reserved his most touching lessons of fraternal charity for His Apostles and for the very moment they were made priests:

> Little children . . . a new commandment I give unto you: that you love one another as I have loved you . . .
>
> By this shall all men know that you are my disciples, if you have love one for another.
>
> —(*John xiii*, 33-35.)

The distinctive feature, the hall-mark, the unmistakable sign of discipleship of Christ is going to be, not so much faith or miracles or even martyrdom for Christ, as their love for one another.

*Little children!* It is the second time Jesus calls His Apostles by this endearing title, and perhaps it was the last. Servants, friends, brothers, were terms frequently on His lips, but *filioli* only when speaking to them of mutual charity. This term of endearment was the honey-tipped point which made the precept of love penetrate like an arrow into our hearts, by nature so prone to hatred.

## II

In calm and silence let us ponder over the newness of this precept which our Saviour and Lawgiver entrusted to His first newly-ordained priests.

The precept is *new* by reason of the manner and author of its promulgation; not Jehova, at whose touch the mountain-tops burst into angry flame; but the Word, made flesh and blood for our sakes, who took upon Himself, as it were, our common touch, our own gentle mode of human speech. It is *new,* by reason of the place where the precept was given: not the wild rugged peaks of Sinai wrapped in lightning and thunder, but the familiar and heart-to-heart talk of a father among his children after supper; not Jaweh in glorious pomp and splendour, but Jesus of Nazareth, girded with a towel, like a slave, on His knees at Judas's feet, washing and kissing them. The command of love issues from under the feet of the man consumed with fiendish rancour! It was also *new* in the preamble introducing the command; not the solemn, awe-inspiring *I am the Lord thy God* (*Ex. xx,* 2), but that most tender: *Filioli mei!* my darling children!

## III

New also is the standard model of our love for our neighbour.

Formerly it was: Thou shalt love thy neighbour as thyself; now it is: love one another as I have loved you.

Love for myself, self-love, which is so liable to delusion and perversity, and which I must renounce if I am to become a true disciple of Christ—*if any will come after me, let him deny himself and take up his cross and follow me (Matt. xvi, 24)*—is not sufficient a model for other loves; I must take my standard from the incomparably wise, unconquerable, disinterested, infinite love which the Good Shepherd feels for His sheep.

Finally, this commandment is *new* in extension: "as I have loved you"—to the limits reached by our Lord, to the extremes to which His love has brought Him for our sakes: the Eucharist He had just given us, and the Cross that was awaiting Him.

> Greater love than this no man hath, that a man lay down his life for his friends.—(*John xv*, 13.)

> "It is hard enough to find anyone who will die on behalf of a just man. . . . but here, as if God meant to prove how well he loves us, it was while we were still sinners that Christ, in his own appointed time, died for us."—(*Rom. v*, 7-8.)

> ". . . the Son of God, who loved me, and gave himself for me.—(*Gal. ii*, 20.)

Any commentary on so many and such sublime "novelties" of the new precept would only unsettle the deep impression that takes hold of any human heart pondering over them carefully.

## RESOLUTIONS

Persuaded that I have to love my neighbour, and being anxious to see unmistakable signs of this love in me, I am going to examine myself and find out whether I possess or no this threefold love, because if I do not I am determined to struggle until it is firmly ensconced in my life:

1.  Love for souls, whose loss is my grief, and their salvation my one abiding interest;

2.  Love for my enemies, because God created them also, gave them an immortal soul, the same as mine, redeemed them in the Blood of the Lamb, and made them capable of eternal happiness;

3.  Love for the poor, with whom Christ identifies Himself and through whose hands He imparts eternal life:

> "Make use of your base wealth to win yourselves friends, who, when you leave it behind, will welcome you into eternal habitations."
>
> —(*Luke xvi,* 9.)

I shall have the poor sit at the banquet of my love, and I shall be delighted, O Jesus, that they cannot repay me even with their gratitude; because it is Thou who, according to Thy promise, wilt requite me when the just shall rise again.

Possessed of this threefold love, I shall, by Thy Mercy, O Lord, be able to boast that I observe Thy new precept of charity.

# ZEAL

## FIRST MEDITATION

### Aim and Scope of Priestly Zeal

#### I

What is zeal? In order to understand it let us study its three constituent elements.

The *cause* (causa efficiens) is no other than charity or love of God and our neighbour, the twofold object of zeal. But not every degree of charity or love fructifies in zeal; this divine plant brings forth the flower and fruit of zeal only when its life is vigorous and its sap is abundant; or, as St. Thomas says: " the cause of zeal is love's fervency "—Zelus sumitur causaliter pro ferventi dilectione.

Its *inner nature* (ratio formalis) is the sadness experienced by fervent love when the objects of that love, God or the neighbour, are seen to be deprived of the good which ought to be theirs;—Zelus formaliter sumitur pro tristitia deficientium sibi vel amicis. Hence, the soul of zeal is a great grief, increasing in the measure that our zeal increases, at the sight of the beloved one's lacking all the good and perfection, interior or exterior, which our love so vehemently desires him to have.

The *effect* of zeal, the product of sorrowing love, can be described as " a movement of the irascible appetite against anything and everything impeding the welfare of the beloved one ". It is a movement that resolves itself in a struggle to acquire for the beloved one the good we desire him and, as a consequence, a fight against all who impair or clash with the well-being and perfection of the beloved.

Every kind of love, if strong and vehement, produces its own type of zeal: love of concupiscence or carnal love produces jealousy, an unleashed fury that engages in deadly conflict anyone trying to take unlawful possession of a heart where one had found all one's pleasure and delight. Self-love, the love for one's personal excellence and prestige, brings forth another type of zeal: the viper that envenoms and gnaws the heart at the sight of another's triumph, the dismal grief which one experiences because another excels precisely in those qualities in which one is lacking and which one longs to possess. Even the noble love of benevolence and friendship has its zeal, a true zeal crowning it with a royal diadem, a generous regret that the friend is deprived of some advantage or prerogative eminently his by right or convenience. (*Cfr. Summa Theologica*, I-II, q. 28, art. 4.)

## II

The Love of God and our neighbour is not, when truly Christian, a movement of the sensible appetite towards its earthly object, useful or delectable; nor is it a mere tendency of the rational will towards the " honourable good " (bonum honestum) either of God or man; it must be pure love. In other words, Christian zeal is based on the love we have for God and man after a deliberate choice of the intellect, which sees in them objects of the highest esteem, both themselves personally and the good which we desire them to possess. So there is no question of wishing them mere temporal goods and fortune, things which of their nature are too low in the hierarchy of values for supernatural charity to stoop to their level, but divine good things and treasures, whose value is infinite and immense. God's intrinsic Perfections nobody can impair or plunder; therefore they do not strictly come within the scope of zeal; but the external good constituted by His being glorified and honoured by intelligent and free-willed creatures, and the accomplishment among them of His most holy Will, are certainly the primary objects of zeal, which perceives how greatly God is offended. And as regards man, zeal looks to that eternal life, that life of grace with all the gifts flowing from grace, and realises how men can be without this immense good, and how they can forfeit it after once enjoying its possession.

When the true Christian love for God and my neighbour really begins to burn in my heart the sight of their being deprived of all this good will produce in me the sadness of zeal, and even my irascible appetite and my whole being will be drawn into the fight to procure for them this immeasurable good. This will be my great endeavour, for this I will give, as trifles, time, energy, talents, labours, even blood and life. Such is the logical process of zeal. Have I been through it?

### III

Zeal in all its Christian manifestations has but one aim: to further God's glory among men through the fulfilment of His adorable Will and the leading of men to their final destiny.

A worthy employment, indeed, of man's frail existence. In vain will he look for a higher one: neither the scrutinising and spying and bringing to the light of the conscious mind or of public knowledge the secrets cherished under the lock and key of avaricious Nature's enigmatic phenomena—the noble aspiration of students and men of learning; nor the subjugating of the nations and the ruling of the masses by the might and clash of arms or the subtle sophistries of diplomacy—the ambition of conquerors and politicians; nor yet the fascinating of the human eye and imagination with dazzling portrayals of created beauty—the dream of artists, writers, and poets. Zeal is something greater than all this. To devote oneself to enterprises of Christian zeal is tantamount to giving triumphant factual existence to the divine ideals which Jesus Christ condensed in the brief but all-embracing formula of the *Our Father*:

> Hallowed be thy name, thy kingdom come, thy will be done on earth as it is in heaven. Forgive us our trespasses . . . lead us not into temptation . . .

Here we have zeal's plan of action. Is it not enough to absorb all the activities of the most ardent heart and richly-endowed mortal life?

## IV

In the practice of zeal the priest is not alone. The Son of God made Man had no other assignment, nor does He at present know of any other. This is the whole meaning of His human existence; this is the reason for the Name of Jesus which the Angel announced at His coming: *for he will save his people from their sins.* (*Matt. i, 21.*)

The Gospel does not record a single event, word,

gesture, or movement belonging to the Redeemer which is not directed to this goal. The infinite activities of the God-Man all bear upon and find expression in one thing: to save souls and further the kingdom and glory of His Eternal Father. And to-day seated at the Right Hand of the Most High, *He makes intercession for us* (*Rom. viii*, 34) for this same purpose; and He will abdicate only after He has put the enemies of God and of souls as the footstool to His feet.

Praise to Thee, O Lord, who so graciously permittest me to co-operate in Thy lofty enterprise. Thou art the sturdy father allowing his little son to help him with his insignificant and feeble contribution so as to train and strengthen him and make him a man.

## V

Ever since our adorable Redeemer came to the world, from among the countless legions of those souls that have believed in Him, embraced His doctrine, and followed His footsteps on the way to heaven, the purest, the most generous, the cream of mankind, have devoted themselves to the Redeemer's own task of saving souls and spreading the glory and kingdom of God. They form an immense galaxy of heroes, the only heroes truly worthy of the human race, of its praise and glory. All the most outstanding historical figures: those who stunned the earth with their clamorous achievements and at whose feet islands and continents fell prostrate and those who fill the annals of history with the lustre of their name are mostly, by comparison with the heroes of Christian zeal, either robbers or murderers on the grand scale, or wretched little glow-worms or frivolous jesters and the sport of their fellow-men.

What glorious company is mine! Let others with boastful pride display the coat-of-arms and ancient motto of their ancestors—and how eager they are: *Prius mori quam foedari*—*Satis ipse sibi*—etc.!—I, when I take up the task of saving souls, have the right and duty to wield the same weapons and display the same family mottoes that so many real heroes used:

> The good shepherd giveth his life for his sheep.
> —*(John x, 11.)*

> " I will gladly spend and be spent on your souls' behalf."—*(II Cor. xii, 15.)*

### RESOLUTION

Since the work of zeal is the spreading of God's glory and kingdom, and the salvation of souls, it is only common decency that I should begin with myself, glorifying God and submitting like a good subject to all the Sovereign's ordinances, never rebelling against my Lord and Father by offence or injury, and always keeping to the road that leads to eternal life. The zealous priest's very first conquest is himself. I resolve, therefore, to remain ever in His grace, and if at any time I should fall away, to rise from sin without delay by an act of perfect contrition and Confession at my earliest convenience.

Is it possible for a priest to exercise the ministry out of pure zeal while he himself is living in mortal sin? The very idea of it involves a paradox and poses a problem of strange inconsistency. If zeal is the flower and flame of charity, and I have not charity, what kind of zeal will be mine? If it so saddens me to see God offended that I wish to cancel out that offence in others, why not begin with my own offences? If so great a good I esteem the saving of souls, why not save my own? If I am in mortal sin and yet I appear to be zealous, either the motives for my zeal are not genuine, or there is something in me which defies my conscious mind and logical procedure.

# ZEAL

## SECOND MEDITATION

### *The Unzealous Priest*

#### I

Zeal for God's glory and the salvation of souls is the essential purpose of our priesthood, just as the purpose of the lawyer is the defence of legal justice, and that of the doctor to heal disease, and of the soldier to fight for his country. Without this eminently priestly virtue I should be a strange paradox, a mere cipher, wine without body, soldier without weapons, or, as St. Vincent de Paul expressed it—a "pasteboard priest"; because the essence and spirit of the priesthood would have evaporated, leaving me only a skeleton.

Thine eyes, O Lord, will never fail to detect in me the gift of Thy priesthood, but will they look in vain for priestly works? Hast Thou not been appealing to my conscience for years now and repeating the words spoken by Isaias to Sobna, the temple prefect:

> What dost thou here, or as if thou were some-
> body here? . . . the shame of the house of thy Lord
> —(*Is. xxii*, 16-17.)

Thou dwellest in my House (Thou canst say to me) and hast command as my steward, and yet thou wearest not my livery, the livery of charity which never fails to display the badge of zeal.

## II

The priest who devoted all his money and time to the service of the sick and poor would be held in veneration as a Saint; but surely spiritual misfortunes are not less harmful than those afflicting the body, and they are far more frequent. The spiritual Jobs are more numerous and more wretched. Their plight is incomparably worse, because their wounds are deeper and more festering and dangerous, penetrating as they do into the very principle of life, both temporal and eternal, the human soul. To heal the soul diseased and wounded by sin is therefore a work of greater merit than the relieving of temporal distress in all its shapes and forms.

Moreover, every Christian-minded person has the right to devote himself to corporal works of mercy; and in actual fact, many thousands of both sexes give their time, money, and personal attention to their neighbours' physical ailments; but when it comes to drawing souls away from sin, to announcing the eternal truths, to pardoning sin and infusing grace into their souls and strengthening them in grace through the administration of the Sacraments; in a word, to opening the gates of heaven to them; then it is the priest alone who has to act, for to him it was said:

> And to thee I will give the keys of the kingdom of heaven.

And God help me if, due to my indolence, I come under the curse spoken by Christ:

> Woe to you, lawyers. for you have taken away the key of knowledge. You yourselves have not entered in, and those that were entering in you have hindered.—(*Luke xi, 52.*)

Or this other curse:

> Woe to you, scribes and pharisees, hypocrites, because you shut the kingdom of heaven against men; for you yourselves do not enter in, and those that are going in you suffer not to enter.—(*Matt. xxiii, 13.*)

### III

St. Bernard says somewhere: "A beast of burden falls and all run to the rescue; a soul perishes, and nobody gives a thought." But the most shameful thing for an unzealous priest would be to confront his indifference and thoughtlessness, while souls around him perish, with the satanic determination of so many wicked men bent on their ruin, men who expend formidable energy, often quite disinterestedly, in the accomplishment of this dire enterprise; priests of Satan who serve their Master extremely well and nearly always for the sheer delight it affords them.

To this might be added another comparison equally humiliating to me if I am a priest without zeal; namely, the contrast between my idle, fruitless existence and the holy, tireless efforts of so many Catholic men and women in the world who are making use of every means at their disposal to lead the lost sheep lovingly back to the Fold of the Good Shepherd. And here am I, chosen by Christ Himself, made shepherd and swain by divine

right of office, squandering my trivial existence in counting and checking up the emoluments my office yields
me, complaining of my small dividends, and with my
back turned to the care of my flock, who are

> distressed and lying like sheep that have no shep-
> herd.—(*Matt. ix*, 36.)

And maybe I am also criticising and damning and
opposing with all my strength the labours of those good
lay people, who should be, not my model and confusion,
but simply my collaborators. At the Judgement-seat of
God they will be my judges.

### IV

The following words were spoken by a famous
political orator in Spain before the civil war:

> " A cloud of prosaic suffocation has been stifling
> modern society for a long time now. Ideals are taken
> as a joke; any aspiration rising a foot above the
> earth is considered a laughable chimera. We are
> being invaded by the bureaucratic spirit, we are
> suffering from what I might call a ' promotion and
> grub ' mentality, we have come to think that there
> are no undertakings of sufficient nobility to warrant
> exceptional energy; and thus we have seen this
> country of ours turned into an immense provisions
> store, where the body is given meagre contentment
> and where the soul has to fend for itself. The
> priest, the soldier, the university professor, the
> artist, seem to renounce all dream of conquest and
> settle down to while their time away as best they
> can, without considering or seeking or caring for
> anything beyond their own individuality."

O Jesus, Divine Craftsman of pure and high ideals, I shall never consent to such a lamentable state of affairs within the sphere of my own life; I do not renounce all dream of conquest, I do not wish to pitch my tent in a No-man's land; with all those legions of Thy heroes, I will encamp in the well-defined and glorious zone of Thy infinite love for the glory of Thy heavenly Father and the eternal salvation of souls. I wish to die and to live like Thee, like so many of Thy followers, furthering Thy Kingdom among those whom Thou hast redeemed by Thy Precious Blood.

## RESOLUTIONS

1. I shall scrupulously discharge the ministerial duties pertaining to my office. This is enough, if I am unable to do more, and God will be well pleased.

2. Although I may not be obliged to perform certain ministerial duties by reason of strict justice or equity, I shall nevertheless administer the Sacraments and preach out of charity, offering to help the parish priest, etc., if I haven't a church of my own.

3. My main concern, for the right practice of zeal, will be what the Church expressly demands of Her priests in virtue of their orders and respective functions; but I shall not refuse to open my mind or my heart or my hands to any other method of apostleship no matter how unusual or new it may seem, because every age brings with it its own peculiar needs; and I myself shall devise ways and means if the traditional ones fail to meet my requirements, on condition that I am not forbidden by lawful Authority. Flexibility is the most needful attribute of the Christian Apostle. I must be able to say:

"I have been everything by turns to everybody, to bring everybody salvation."—(*I Cor. ix, 22.*)

4.    The one thing I will not do, not even to save the whole world, is to offend God or to expose myself to the proximate danger of sinning; for I am never permitted to prefer any good, however secure, high-minded, or supernatural it may appear, to my own spiritual welfare necessary to save my own soul.

# CONTEMPT FOR THIS WORLD'S PLEASURES

## *Priestly Detachment*

### I

Contempt for the pleasures of the world is an imposition of the Church and of our own priestly status. It is a duty as imperative for us as for a soldier the readiness to give his life for his country.

If we go through Titulus III of the Code, *De obligationibus Clericorum,* we shall see that there is hardly a pleasure, honour, or good thing of this world that it does not forbid us. Priests are forbidden to marry. They must wear clerical attire. They must abstain from everything unbecoming their state. They must not engage in affairs improper to their state. They are not to indulge in gambling. They ought not to attend worldly shows, parties, displays, etc.

Neither riches nor pleasures of the flesh nor worldly honours; these three great gratifications of the world are forbidden us, the approach to them is closed against our entry, once and for all.

And the Church on this point has never changed Her mind.

### II

The faithful and even the world itself demand this of us. Our first duty is to bring the world to God, teaching it to esteem the things of eternity and to make little of the things of earth, bearing in mind and having on our lips at all times the words of St. Paul:

> " The fashion of this world is soon to pass away."—(*I Cor. viii,* 31.)

But these are truths and exhortations completely at variance with our human nature's perverted instincts, they are hard to believe and to take for our fixed standard of conduct; and if my personal life is in flat contradiction with my profession, how will the world receive them from my lips? St. John Chrysostom puts it well:

> " Our living example is more moving than miracles. If they hear us condemn avarice, lewdness, and straightway hear that we practise the opposite of what we teach, they will consider our exhortations sheer mockery, and our doctrine, just child's play.
>
> To speak fulsomely in praise of the highest morality is easy; many of the old philosophers did so. What they demand of us is good works. It isn't enough for us to point to the Saints of the past, they see only the present, and they insist on our meeting the challenge: ' Prove thy belief to us by thy good works '."

Only by our own example shall we convey to souls the lesson of detachment from things of earth which clears the way to eternal life.

### III

The practice of this detachment must begin by our cherishing it inwardly, and even then, how difficult it is to bring practice into line with the strength of one's convictions! Not even the greatest Saints succeeded completely in giving outward expression to their inmost thoughts and desires, and can I expect to progress very far in detachment from all things visible if my heart succumbs to them and builds an altar of worship to them?

What is my real assessment, O God, of the value of these frail and transitory things which I am obliged to hold in contempt? Are the Gospel utterances on the vanity of this world's pleasures just borrowed formulas which my lips alone do justice to? If I haven't begun by despising them inwardly, how shall I detach myself from them outwardly? How shall I observe the strict obligations laid down in Canon Law? And won't the discrepancy between my preaching and my example be a stumbling-block to the faithful?

## RESOLUTION

God does not forbid me to covet riches, honours and pleasures, but He does demand that they be in keeping with my personal dignity as a child of God; so I shall go in eager quest of the riches, honours and pleasures of eternal life. *Quae sursum sunt, quaerite.* (Col. iii, 1.)

I shall deposit my vested interests and my heavenly treasures in the only Bank that never suffers bankruptcy, the Hands of my Father in Heaven; and great will be my gain.


# CONTEMPT FOR THIS WORLD'S PLEASURES

### SECOND MEDITATION

*Divine Example and Precept*

### I

Let us hear what He has to say about this world's pleasures:

Blessed are the poor . . . the meek . . . those
that mourn . . . those that hunger and thirst after
justice . . . the clean of heart . . . the peace-makers
. . . those that suffer calumny and persecution. . . .

Woe to the rich . . . to those that have their
fill . . . woe to those that jeer and scoff . . . to
those who are blessed and honoured by men. . . .

What an amazing and enlightening chapter—but a
terrifying one to our softness—could be compiled from
just the very grave words spoken by our Divine Master
about these passing pleasures which so fascinate us!
How shattering His words are about those false idols
which, in one way or another, we all worship, before
whose shrine we have all at one time or another burnt
the incense of our heart's desire!

Do I really and truly acknowledge Thee, O Jesus, as
my Master and my life's Guide? Do I deserve to be
enrolled on Thy register? Even if I do, I must confess
that some of Thy lessons have remained unlearnt, and
that certain theories of Thine my heart would like to
dispute, if not my intellect.

O give me strength, Lord, to declare myself Thy
disciple with my whole being, without mental reser-
vations or dark corners unillumined by Thy Light!


## II

What arguments does the Son of God use to prove
His austere theory? In case His word should not suffice,
He adduces a proof that no one can reject, the example
of his entire mortal life.

There is not the slightest indication in His life that
He ever attached any importance to the things the world

esteems so highly and so recklessly pursues as the goal of happiness. He is born in poverty, lives in poverty, dies in destitution; He has no longing to receive anything from anybody, makes no demands for anything, except the human heart; He flees from worldly ostentation, renounces power, hates pleasures, amasses neither silver nor gold, and, if given to Him in alms, He hands it over to Judas's administration, to the only disciple who was covetous and grasping.

The life of Jesus, from stable to sepulchre, bears eloquent testimony to the fact that He, the Teacher of teachers, found nothing in this world's material values worthy of the human heart's ambition; and His was the most sensitive of human hearts.

Such were Thy inmost convictions, dear Jesus; I realise what they are and I shall not be so rash as to doubt their deep sincerity; with all my sinfulness I have not yet come to deny veracity and honesty to Thy words and Thy irreproachable life.

### III

Let me compare my convictions on this matter with the Divine Master's, if only for the sake of understanding that I, too, am included in the universal indictment spoken by David: *Omnis homo mendax*. (Ps. xcv, 2.)

What is my opinion of pleasures, not excluding the illicit ones? By God's mercy, or by some physical impossibility, I may live at a distance from them . . . but is there no faint feeling of regret? is there no secret envy of those who can indulge in them without undue risks?

How do I feel about worldly honours? Don't I strain

after them in desire, only to crash against a wall of restraint confining me within the narrow limits of my priestly office and personal limitations?

How do I regard wealth? I have not gone so far as to barter away my Lord and Master, like Judas—at least I don't think I have—but if I stop to think, perhaps I should not like to swear that money has played no part in my priestly zeal. Have I never thought and decided to study, preach, say Mass, or perform other ministerial duties for the sole or primary purpose of raking in a few odd shillings? Have my interests been vested in money rather than in souls and the glory of God?

There seem to be points of doctrine where Christ and myself are not of one and the same mind. How long will this estrangement last?

### IV

I am convinced that just as the might of a nation rests on its armies and armaments, so does the strength of a disciple of Christ, especially that of a priest, depend upon detachment from everything worldly and upon closest union with God. This is the meaning of the two comparisons adduced by St. Luke: of the man who has a mind to build a tower but does not sit down first and reckon whether or no he has sufficient money to finish the task; and that of the king setting out to join battle with another king and not studying beforehand whether he can cope with numerical superiority; and our Lord concludes:

> So likewise, every one of you that doth not renounce all that he possesseth cannot be my disciple—(*Luke xiv*, 28-33.)

How much more the clergy would accomplish, even if priests were less numerous, with greater detachment and self-denial! What a handicap our unruly affections are! How they bring us into disrepute!

## RESOLUTION

Contempt for this world's pleasures will in future be one of the lessons I shall learn, O Lord, from Thy Cross, on which Thou, in utter detachment and destitution, hast attracted the world.

# PRIESTLY CHASTITY

## FIRST MEDITATION

### *Motives*

### I

St. Thomas Aquinas tells us that the Church permits the chalice of the Blood of Christ only to priests, because, among other reasons, She considers them purer than the general body of the faithful: *ad habendum vas congruum hujus Sanguinis contentivum.* (Opusc. 58, c. xxix.)

As wine is served in cleaner and choicer vessels than those used for bread, so also the priest is granted the Precious Blood under the Species of wine because he is the vessel of the Lord consecrated to divine worship and bound to God by the vow of chastity, and burnished brighter than other men by the beauty and purity of a more virtuous life.

God grant that the Church may always find in me the fulfilment of Her intention and desire! A terrible contrast it would be if the purity and infinite wealth of the Blood of Christ—*vinum germinans virgines*—were poured into a heart made a sink, day by day, year after year, of lewd iniquity. So let me keep my ears open to St. Paul's grave admonition:

> "Each of you must learn to control his own body, as something holy and held in honour, not yielding to the promptings of passion."—(*Thess. xv,* 4.)

## II

It is well to stress this idea. I am a vessel consecrated to God; a temple, a tabernacle set apart for the sole purpose of containing God, by His grace, by the fulfilment of His law, and by my daily dealings with the Blessed Sacrament. On the frontispiece of this temple rather than on the fanes of ancient paganism should be sculptured the motto: *Deo sacrum*.

I am a monstrance and a chalice of the Holy Eucharist. Every day for a number of years, and, I hope, until the end of my life, I have been the Tabernacle of the Most Holy Body and Blood of my Lord Jesus Christ. Lips, tongue, hands, and my whole body are sanctified by contact with the Sacramental Species, more so than the corporals and the chalice: I am, so to speak, the earthly vesture now of the Word made flesh. Hence, to stain myself with the repulsive vice of impurity would be tantamount to assigning the sacred vessels, my body and soul, to profane and unworthy uses, in imitation of the sacrilegious King of Babylon; and so horrible a crime, I fear, would suffice to make God's Patience yield to His infinite Wrath, and once again would appear the writing on the wall above my sinful head: *Mane, Thekel, Phares*.

## III

If we have any esteem at all for the inheritance Christ has promised us, for the souls He treasured and redeemed at such a price, for the vineyard He planted with so much sweat and toil, let us priests be chaste. For it is one of the sad lessons of history in every age of the Church that the vice which has wrenched the greatest number of souls, communities, and nations from

Christ's Fold is the sensuality of His evil ministers. Of this particular vice we might say in the words of the Vulgate Psalter: *singularis ferus depastus est eam.* (Ps. lxxix, 14.) A terrible curse afflicts those individuals and nations who stand witness to the long-continued sexual laxity of the altar's ministers, of the dispensers of the divine word and mysteries. No morals, however pure; no faith, however deep-rooted, but will eventually succumb to the infernal force of such an evil example. Impiety and vice will build up a stronghold of impregnable defence from the sexual laxity of the clergy; this is Hell's infallible boast.

Am I, O Jesus, on the black list of those priests whom Thou, century after century, canst point to with a finger of scorn and flay with the devastating rebuke:

> Ignominia domus Domini!
> Abominatio desolationis in templo sancto!?

### RESOLUTION

I shall often repeat the meditations on the Holy Sacrifice and Blessed Sacrament and the Sacrilegious Mass contained in earlier pages of this book, as an incentive to keep myself chaste and pure, at least out of reverence for such sublime mysteries.


## PRIESTLY CHASTITY

### SECOND MEDITATION

### *The Mind of the Church*

#### I

Let us see the mind of the Church in this matter; it is not of recent date but of every age right down to the Apostles and to Jesus Christ Himself.

So pure and chaste was our Lord that, although accused of so many crimes by enemies who had no scruples when it came to putting into operation their perverse intrigues and giving expression to their malevolent designs, nowhere do we read in the Gospels, impartial and serene as they are, of the slightest hint or most veiled insinuation against the absolute purity of Christ; and that in spite of a number of opportunities which might possibly have given His enemies some shadow or glimpse of an excuse for accusing or suspecting Him. For example, on the occasion when Christ confronted them with that scathing reply about the woman caught in adultery: *He that is without sin among you, let him first cast a stone at her,* and clearly showed them that He knew they were as guilty in their obstinacy and hard-heartedness as ever the woman was guilty in her adultery, they could not take up the challenge; one after another (" being reproached by their own consciences " add some Greek codices), starting by the older men, they all slunk away covered with confusion. What a grand opportunity it would have been to throw a *tu quoque* into our Lord's face had He ever furnished them with the slenderest pretext! No, never were they given a chance to accuse Him of impurity.

O Jesus, that slinking away of Thy slanderers was the most eloquent panegyric of Thy immaculate purity; I endorse their testimony and confess Thee to be the all-pure Son of a Virgin Mother. Only once didst Thou defy all laws of nature, and that was in order to take flesh and blood from a Woman who out-dazzled the sun's rays in radiant purity, who was never defiled by any most fleeting shadow of lascivious touch or thought.

## II

The Fathers and Doctors of the Church are unanimous in their praise and practice of celibacy.

The Gospels gave them the first lead in those graphic words of the Saviour:

> There are eunuchs who have made themselves eunuchs for the kingdom of heaven; he that can take, let him take it.—(*Matt. xix*, 12);

they had from St. Paul those admirable lessons on total victory over sensual cravings, lessons which the Apostle prefaced and endorsed with his own example:

> "I wish you were all in the same state as myself. . . . To the unmarried, and to the widows, I would say that they will do well to remain in the same state as myself."—(*I Cor. xvv*, 7-9.)

And lest he should provide the least motive for suspecting his personal integrity, he renounces things quite lawful in themselves:

> "Have we not the right to travel about with a woman who is a sister, as the other apostles do, as the Lord's brethren do, and Cephas? . . . Yet I have not availed myself of any such right."—(*I Cor. ix*, 6 *and* 15.)

Moreover, St. Paul gives us to understand quite clearly what the practice was among the priests of that time; because, while telling us in detail the duties of priests towards others, including the priest's own children, if before his ordination he had had them in lawful wedlock, never does he make the slightest allusion to the conduct he should observe towards his wife, supposing she lived on after the priest's ordination; an evident sign that she had no further claim over her husband who, once a priest, lived in separation from her.

## III

That St. Paul demanded of the priest absolute abstention from marital intercourse follows from his teachings.

For the Apostle of the Gentiles—who with a touch of self-assertiveness declares, in proof of the truth of his teachings on the merit of virginity, " and I, too, claim to have the spirit of God "—the priest is essentially the " *homo Dei* " (I Tim. vi, 11), the man wholly consecrated to God's service. He is the soldier of Christ with no other possible task in life than to fight for Christ:

> " Thou art God's soldier; and the soldier on service, if he would please the captain who enlisted him, will refuse to be entangled in the business of daily life ".—(*II Tim. ii, 4.*)

A text which expresses the same line of thought, even if we omit the word " God " that is missing in some of the old codices; the idea that just as a soldier renounces all other worldly pursuits and business in order to be exclusively a soldier and to please and serve his enlisting captain, so also the priest, as a soldier of Christ, called to Christ's colours, must renounce every occupation and aspiration other than soldiering for Christ.

Here we have the supreme and unanswerable argument for ecclesiastical celibacy set forth in so many words by the same Apostle:

> " I would have you free from concern. He who is unmarried is concerned with God's claim, asking how he is to please God; whereas the married man is concerned with the world's claim, asking

how he is to please his wife; and thus he is at issue with himself."—(*I Cor. vii,* 32-33.)

How should the priest, the *miles Christi,* the *homo Dei,* who has renounced all other concern, be allowed to tie himself down to the rearing of a family? St. Paul does not think so, he considers this task precisely the source of this world's anxieties, worries and aspirations.

I may well observe the law of celibacy in its sexual meaning, but do I live solicitous for the affairs of God? Or do I squander the energies of my solitary celibate life for the sake of stupidly trying to raise the economic status of my parental home, of my nephews and nieces, or, sadder still, of strangers? Will not this misplaced concern of mine be one day my stunning reproach?

### RESOLUTION

With all that is truest and best in me, and notwithstanding the rebellion of my lower nature, I will cherish the privations of my celibate state of life, even when rendered really painful by the occasional impetus of passion. I will cherish continence such as was practised by Christ, my Master and High Priest, by the Apostles, who learnt the lesson from Him, and by the Church in every age.

But I wish to cherish it for the sole purpose for which the Church imposes it upon me; namely, in order to live with the one concern of pleasing God by my ministry and my life of piety. I am not going to be so foolish as to allow the immense energies, which the faithful preservation of this virtue demands, to be harnessed to the economic advancement of my family or of anyone else, instead of the interests of God's glory.

No, dear Lord, I have not bent my shoulders to the heavy yoke of celibacy for the sake of bettering my father's position in life or of giving a career to my nephews, or of enabling my nieces to marry "well"; I have taken the burden on for Thee, and for nothing but Thy glory and the salvation of souls.

## PRIESTLY CHASTITY

### THIRD MEDITATION

### *The Church's Ruling*

### I

Let us see in this meditation how the unchanging Mind and law of the Church is concretely expressed in current Canon Law:

*Canon* 132.—1. Clerics in major orders are, under pain of nullity, forbidden to marry, and they have the obligation of observing chastity, so that sins against this virtue are also a sacrilege.

2. Clerics in minor orders may indeed get married but, unless the marriage was invalid on account of their being forced to such a marriage by grave fear or violence, they cease to be clerics *ipso facto*.

3. A married man who, though in good faith, receives major orders without a dispensation from the Holy See is forbidden to exercise such orders.

I recognise the whole force of this obligation, Lord, because one of the articles of faith which I profess every day is: Credo in unam, sanctam, catholicam, et apostolicam Ecclesiam.

## II

From the day I received the sacred Sub-diaconate, the first of major orders, I became disqualified for life, by a diriment impediment, from contracting holy matrimony.

Since any sexual act, of those forbidden by the sixth and ninth commandments, both interior and exterior, by desire or by act, would be lawful only within the legitimate use of marriage; from the moment I received major orders I came under the law of absolute continence, exterior and interior; and I shall break the law only at the cost of grievously offending Almighty God.

Not only do I offend Him, like any other person sinning against the commandments; I become guilty of sacrilege, of profaning something holy, something offered to God and to His service. The law entails not only the obligation of observing the sixth and ninth commandment, it becomes a matter of the first commandment, that is, an act and duty of religion.

Chastity for me, therefore, is an obligation resulting from a vow. I live bound by the vow of chastity, the same as any man in religion; and every sin of mine against my vow would be no less grave than the transgression of a religious against his. On the other hand, the merit of my observing the vow is no less sublime.

Do I really accept my obligation in this sense, such as is expressed above, such as I understood it when it was enjoined on me, such as I then embraced it? And am I aware that the following words of St. Paul apply to me more than to anybody else?

"Do you not understand that you are God's

temple and that God's Spirit has his dwelling in you?"—(*I Cor. iii*, 16.)

"Surely you know that your bodies are the shrines of the Holy Spirit, who dwells in you."—(*I Cor. vi*, 19.)

"If anybody desecrates the temple of God, God will bring him to ruin."—(*I Cor. iii*, 17.)

## III

Let us listen to the voice of opposition, and answer it.

"A tyrannical imposition, this law of celibacy."—Yes, this has often been said, but there is nothing in the statement except a vile calumny. The Church has never imposed celibacy on anyone. She excommunicates with all the might of Her authority any person who has the audacity to do so. One example, among many, should be referred to:

> *Canon* 214. The cleric who received a major order out of grave fear may by the sentence of the ecclesiastical judge be reduced to the lay state, provided he can prove that he was ordained in fear and has not ratified the ordination afterwards, at least tacitly, by the exercise of the order with the intention of subjecting himself to the obligations of the major orders. He is then free from the obligation of celibacy and from the duty of saying the Divine Office. . . .

To the law of celibacy, however harsh it may seem, you submitted entirely of your own free will, and for ever.

"But I didn't understand properly what I was

doing."—What? At 23 years of age, at the youngest, when curiosity, the source of so many evil suggestions, is most irresistible; when the passions and the physiological life have reached their highest development; hadn't you felt a thousand times in your flesh and heart and brain the storms of sexual desire? Then, when are they going to be felt? At twenty-three, when the intelligence had matured and you had finished your studies, didn't you realise exactly what celibacy entailed?

"But I was forced into it."—A lie, and you know it is! Remember the ordaining Prelate's serious admonition to you just before you received the sub-diaconate:

> "You must attentively consider again and again that the burden you ask to assume to-day you ask for entirely of your own free will. Until this you are free . . . think over it while there is yet time. If you receive this order you will be obliged to observe chastity. Therefore, while there is yet time, take thought; and if you are ready to persevere in your holy endeavour, in the Lord's name, approach."

"Oh, there were other coercions: my parents, uncles and aunts, vested interests, etc."—And what has that got to do with the Church? Are you going to make the Church responsible for the blunders and even crimes of your family? And don't you blush for shame that at the age of twenty-three you hadn't the courage to withstand your family in a matter of such supreme importance? Didn't God and His Church warn you against approaching the altar for such disreputable aims as these?

Now, be honest with yourself, and if to-day you are weighed down under a law to which you freely and spontaneously—*ultro*—submitted, own up to the fact that what you need most is manliness. *Esto vir,* be a man who can stick to his word, to that sacred word the most solemn that ever came from your lips, to that word you spoke to the whole world, to the Church, to God Himself.

## RESOLUTIONS

I shall find out whether I am keeping to my word. I resolve most firmly to keep to it from now onwards, even if, as Christ commands, I have to cut off my right hand and foot and pluck my eye out from me and cast it away, to avoid its becoming a stumbling-block and an occasion of sin. I am resolved from this moment, if in the past I have not done so, to observe with scrupulosity canon 133:

1. The clergy shall take care not to have in their houses, nor to visit, women that may give reason for suspicion.

2. They are allowed to have in their houses only such women as those concerning whom there can be no suspicion, either on account of the natural bond as mother, sister, aunt, or from whom on account of their character and likewise their more advanced age all suspicion is removed.

Don't complain of the harshness of this law; it would be more than harsh, it would be cruel, if the Church did not lay down the law. Having bound me to continence, could the Church have left me free in the midst of the greatest dangers without being a cruel and bad Mother?

Experience clearly shows how easy it is, relatively

speaking, to keep this virtue if only we get away from the occasions which so readily excite and blind us and are the cause of over ninety-nine per cent. of our lapses. It is incomparably less painful to pluck out one's eyes and to cast them away, that is, to cut away from those people, however dear and necessary they may seem to us, if they afford us a proximate occasion of sin, than to remain in their midst and resist the brutal onslaughts of passion.

It is Thou, my God, who commandest me; do not therefore deny me Thy abundant and efficacious grace, that I may faithfully abide by Thy Will.

## PRIESTLY CHASTITY

### FOURTH MEDITATION

#### Evils Arising from Impurity

### I

With a view to understanding the purely supernatural Christian motives for being chaste, and in order to convince ourselves at the same time how useful we should find a deep and sustained study of the Holy Scriptures, let us meditate on eleven verses (9-20) of chapter six of St. Paul's first epistle to the Corinthians:

"Make no mistake about it,"

—or, as he repeats to the Ephesians (*v*, 6): "Do not allow anyone to cheat you with empty promises." There is no moral theme where more deceptive persuasiveness is brought to bear; there is no other commandment of God that has unleashed more storms of protest and seduction: voices from the world around us, whisperings of the Serpent, hymns intoned by every age to the goddess of lust, the countless specious errors pledged to the defence of sensual gratification's imperial sway, dressed up though they may be in scientific garb; and the still fiercer voices from within: apparent physiological necessity, the delirious fury of desire, the magic palette of our imagination prone to exhaust every resource in an effort to depict libidinous pleasure as the acme of delight; and, more powerful than all the rest, the thrust of bad habit, capable of sweeping away the most resolute determination.

To all this the Apostle opposes in Christ's name the grave warning: " Do not allow anyone to cheat you with empty promises "—with promises devoid of meaning, illogical statements. For the terrible and unanswerable truth is:

" it is not the debauched . . . nor the adulterous; it is not the effeminate, nor the sinners against nature . . . that will inherit the kingdom of God." —(9, 10.)

Add to these vile deeds the condemnation of all impure desire and complacency, about which our Divine Lord spoke:

The things which proceed out of the mouth come forth from the heart: and those things defile a man.

For from the heart come forth evil thoughts . . . adulteries, fornications . . . (Matt. xv, 18, 19.)

I say to you that whosoever shall look on a woman to lust after her hath already committed adultery with her in his heart.—(Matt. v, 28.)

Now, make no mistake about it, and let no one cheat

you with empty promises, none of these sinners will inherit the kingdom of God; or, as St. Paul writes to the Ephesians, none of them " can claim a share in Christ's kingdom, God's kingdom."

As Esau gambled his birthright for a dish of lentil broth, the lustful man, for the sake of mere lewd delectation, even imaginary, deliberately embraced by the free will, gambles away his divine sonship, scraps the title-deeds of his divine adoption, casts from his soul the Spirit of Christ, remains disinherited *in aeternum et ultra* of the royal estate and patrimony of his Heavenly Father. Is the vile impure pleasure worth it?

## II

" This is what some of you once were ". . .

It was public knowledge; many of those Christians recently converted from paganism had given themselves up body and soul to the worship of Venus, to all the abominations of Corinth, the most corrupt city in Greece for centuries. " Debauched, adulterers, effeminate, sinners against nature," that is what they were, it was no defamation of character to mention it in a public document, it was only too well known; but that was now a thing of the past, their penance and amendment was also the talk of the town. Which proves that, however deeply sunk into the mire, it is possible for a man to get out of it, and still more feasible for a man not to fall, if so far he has remained pure.

Chastity is, therefore, a definite possibility. In this matter, as in all others, God does not command the impossible. At the same time our own unaided efforts are not enough:

> I knew that I could not be continent except God
> gave it. . . (*Wisdom viii, 21.*)

On what conditions does God give us this grace?

> " That is what some of you once were; but now
> you have been washed clean, now you have been
> sanctified, now you have been justified in the name
> of the Lord Jesus, by the Spirit of the God we
> serve."—(11.)

This grace is given us in that Name which alone of
all names under heaven has been appointed to men as
the Name whereby we must needs be saved, and given
us by that Spirit whereby the love of God is poured
into our hearts, cleansing them of all defilement.

My own strength alone is not to be trusted.
Boundless as the energy of the human will is, the
primary force of visible creation, a force that routs
armies, assaults strongholds, makes thrones and sceptres
crumble to dust, leaps over mountains, bridles the
tempest waves of ocean; what it has never accomplished,
unaided, is the taming of its own fleshly passion, more
brutal than all the unleashed elements; only the vigour
of divine grace enables our will to rule victorious over
concupiscence.

### III

> " But your bodies are not meant for debauchery."
> —(13.)

The body's purpose in life is not, as so many most
erroneously maintain, sensual satisfaction. All men of
wisdom, both of antiquity and in modern times, are
agreed that the human body is the most wonderful
mechanism in existence. Now, if God has assigned to

the vilest little worm and to every part of the tiniest
insect a definite purpose, would not He, the Creator of
our bodies, assign also to our bodies, as a whole, some
purpose worthy of its perfections? No, not for fornication, says St. Paul, were these bodies of ours appointed;
their destiny is not sensual pleasure, in spite of their
lively and intense craving for pleasure;

> "they are meant for the Lord" (13),

and here the word "Lord", the same as in other
passages of the Apostle's writings, refers to Christ. So
our bodies have Christ for their goal; and, what is more
astonishing still, *et Dominus corpori,* the Lord has a
claim over our bodies, and, St. Paul seems to hint, there
is a sublime sense in which Christ is meant for our
bodies—a consequence of the Incarnation.

This is the final purpose of my body:

> "And God, just as he has raised our Lord from
> the dead by his great power, will raise us up too."

This body of ours, in appearance but a vessel of uncleanness and corruption, an unquenchable source of perverted appetites, is to be raised up, in the likeness, and
sharing the splendour, of the Risen body of Christ, as
Christ's escort; and in virtue of Christ's Headship of all
the elect, made glorious and immortal. This is my body's
destiny if, like Christ, I live a spotless life, mastering,
by His grace, the body's animal instincts.

## IV

> "Have you never been told that your bodies
> belong to the body of Christ?"—(15.)

Our bodies are as much Christ's property as His own
eyes or His own Heart; they belong to Him more than a

child belongs to its parent and home; we are not just members of Christ's Household, we are part and parcel of Himself. Such is the mind of St. Paul, and such is my belief. *Corpus Domino, et Dominus corpori.* Christ the Lord claims my body for Himself, claims it as much as He claims His own eyes and Heart. Will not my body, then, show every regard for those divine eyes, whose mere glance converted and melted the souls of men? Will not my body show respect for the Heart of Christ, where every divine Attribute and noblest human perfection were fused? Would my body, in the vehemence of passion, fling Christ into the mire? Would it see the Heart of Christ thrown on a refuse dump? The body is nothing less than one of Christ's members;

> " and am I to take what belongs to Christ and make it one with a harlot?"—(15.)

Would I give the eyes and Heart of Christ to a woman of the street, as a trophy of her conquest over mine? No, let there be no excuses—"I stain my body, but what is the body? *omnis caro foenum* "—because if I do not respect my own body as my own property, let me listen to St. Augustine: " Recognise Christ in thyself, spare Christ in thee." How much more profitable and noble it is to unite with the Lord than with flesh that is profaned, because

> " the man who unites himself to the Lord becomes one spirit with him."—(17.)

Through union with Christ my very flesh becomes spiritualised.

## RESOLUTIONS

1. Impure pleasure is not so worthy of esteem that we should sacrifice everything to it: our life, and perhaps the life of another, our honour as men and as priests, money, time, the honour of Christ and His Church, divine grace, heaven. The price is far too high; and since it cannot be bought for less, from now onward and for ever I renounce such a costly luxury. It is not for me, never. The clamourings of my unruly appetite will ever remain unheeded, its impulses will be shackled with ironlike fetters; I prefer death itself, the total disintegration of the flesh, to its sinful gratification.

2. The struggle I have to keep on waging, whether as victor or as vanquished, is a struggle that never abates; and the more I yield the fiercer the struggle becomes. Therefore, even though I may not feel I can brace myself up to real austerities, such as fasting, scourging, stinted sleep, very heavy work, etc.—and would to God I were given some of the strength He gives to His more faithful servants!—at least I shall adhere to the minimum: sobriety, regular work that keeps me sufficiently and properly occupied, sleep in moderation, no excess in food, temperance and sobriety in drink especially; no fussiness or softness; entertainments few and for a worthy purpose. Moreover, I shall keep vigilant watch over dangers, sighting them at a distance before they come too near and entangle me; and there shall always be a priestly composure in my bearing, never familiarities with women, much less in the exercise of my ministry. In short, I shall carry out in practice the order issued by the Apostle St. Peter:

" Be sober, and watch well."—(*I Peter v*, 8.)

# PRIESTLY CHASTITY

*Further Evils of Impurity*

## I

It is not enough to withdraw from the impure vice. St. Paul says *fugite fornicationem*, scuttle away from it, as from a monster whose very breath poisons, whose mere glance is deadly. If in itself this is not the sin of greatest objective malice, it is certainly the sin that digs its claws deepest into the depths of human nature.

> "Any other sin a man commits, leaves the body untouched."—(*I Cor. vi,* 18.)

Any other crime, even the most hideous imaginable, is by comparison only on the surface of human nature; because, while deciding, for example, to steal or while actually stealing, while blaspheming or even getting drunk, there still remain certain faculties free, both interior and exterior, which one can apply to objects outside the scope of the crime being committed: *Extra corpus est.* Not every sin enlists our whole being; that is the direful sovereignty reserved to lust. When surrendered to lust, the plain fact is that we are incapable of imagining, thinking of, remembering, desiring, employing the smallest part of ourselves in, any other object. So St. Paul continues:

> "but the fornicator is committing a crime against his own body";

he is staining body and soul, he is making over to

353

M

lust's absolute, tyrannical mastery every faculty, organism, driving force, and particle of his being.

Not an atom in me is immune to the filth and poison of impurity. As long as my surrender lasts I have become wholly flesh, complete corruption, not only in my flesh but also in my spiritual faculties, God's living image in me; and even my intellect, with its power of uplift shattered, is reduced to the condition of an unclean animal rooting among the fetid swamps of lust.

Have I lost all self-respect? Am I so little worthy of esteem?

## II

Such a total profanation of my being should inspire me with profoundest horror, because

> " surely, you know that your bodies are the shrines of the Holy Spirit, who dwells in you ".

Beautiful masonry does not make the church, nor do sumptuous ornament, graceful clustered columns, airy vaults, or gilded retables. A building becomes a church when it is consecrated to the worship of God, when God dwells in it in a special manner, for example, in the Blessed Sacrament; even though it may consist of mud and straw like a swallow's nest.

Through Baptism and all the other Sacraments I have received, my body was consecrated to God; in Communion I became Christ's Tabernacle and Monstrance, a living one; by Holy Orders I became God's possession, in a still more particular way, for the purpose of dedication to the worship of God. In fine, I am a shrine where the Spirit of God dwells, the treasury containing God's richest gift to me, the gift of His Spirit. " *He is God's gift to you.*"—(19.)

We venerate shrines of stone and marble, tabernacles of carved wood, sacred vessels of gold and other precious metals; but our own bodies are deserving of far greater veneration; they are the living shrines of the Spirit of God. And when we surrender to impurity we are profaning and desecrating, as it were, everything in the shrine: vaults, columns, floor, walls, altars, retables; even into the tabernacle we pour the filth of lewd desire. . . .

Such is the treatment we give to the Spirit of God when we are impure; such is our appreciation of God's best Gift, of God's best Self, so to speak, when enshrined in our impure bodies. No wonder St. Paul fulminates against this type of profanation:

> " If anybody desecrates the temple of God, God will bring him to ruin."—(*I Cor. iii*, 17.)

### III

The deepest reason for self-respect and the most persuasive one is very simply summed up in the words:

> "You are no longer your own masters."—(19.)

At no time was I my own property, but God's; especially since the price of my Redemption was paid for me. I am, therefore, the property of the Purchaser, my Redeemer. Even had I cost Him but a trifle, even were I a mere trinket or toy bought for a song, I would still be His. But no:

> "A great price was paid to ransom you."—(20.)

Do I want to see the bill? I have only to look at Christ crucified; I have only to contemplate His brow, shattered and streaming with blood; His face, livid with blows; His hair and beard ignominiously tousled and dishevelled; His body torn to shreds by the scourging; His feet pierced by the nails; His Heart open. I have but to listen to the sad voices of lament spoken by each wound and sorrow: "we are the price of thy ransom; this was the price named, and it was given without bargaining."

Christ is a generous purchaser: He is asked for sorrows, and He gives an ocean of them; He is asked for wounds and insults and blood, He gives them willingly; and as though all this were not enough, He empties His purse over the seller's counter: from His wide-open Heart He pours every last drop of blood and of love.

"Glorify God by making your bodies the shrines of his presence."—(20.)

## RESOLUTIONS

1. Since the chastity demanded of me is a divine ideal surpassing human strength, even the most exuberant, I shall have recourse to supernatural strength, which God offers me gratuitously.

2. The best and only efficacious means, provided the other means are not lacking, to preserve chastity is to go to Confession very often; each week, if possible. So many lay people do this, and their lives bear witness to the efficacy of this Sacrament in matters of chastity. Once I have fully made up my mind to overcome all difficulties impeding the practice of weekly confession, they almost dissolve into thin air; and should they still subsist, I shall conquer them and offer the price up to my crucified God as some small token in order to obtain the gift of continence. If needs be, I shall go to Confession even more frequently, rather than desecrate the Body and Blood of Christ in the Holy Mass.

3. Besides keeping a careful watch over my senses, faculties, and, above all, my heart, I shall gather strength from frequent prayer, especially when I feel myself the object of the Enemy's attacks in any of his many forms and disguises.

4. To Mary Immaculate I shall profess a most tender and childlike love. So terrifying to the devil is her very Name, that through invoking it whole armies, of men and women, boys and girls, and little children come through life victorious in the struggle against impurity. Mary is truly "terrible as an army in battle array".— (*C. of C. vi*, 3.)

# MORTIFICATION

## FIRST MEDITATION

### General Motives

#### I

Our destiny in this life and the next is union with God; in the next life, by a real, everlasting union and conscious possession of the Divine Essence; in this life, by what St. Thomas calls " intentional union " through charity. Now, this charity is the effect of grace operating through prayer and meditation on supernatural realities, right intention in our works, and the accomplishment of the Will of God in all our free activities. It is union with God through faith, hope, and charity.

O God, my Creator, such is the high destiny which Thy sovereign Will has marked out for me; only for the sake of reaching this destiny dost Thou suffer me on earth; this is the sole purpose behind Thy command to love Thee with my whole heart and my whole soul and with all my strength.

#### II

Union with God! To become one with God, as Christ is One with the Father! It all seems so remote. The course seems to lie through so many rocks and reefs! How different my human condition is from God's Being! There is need of a constant process of self-adjustment and adaptation if I am to conform to God; there must be an entire transformation, a paring down, a remodelling of my inmost being before I can live with God and make myself at home with my heavenly Father.

And what about the rebelliousness of so much in me against these radical changes: the anguish and fierce protests of each sense and faculty when asked to unite with God instead of its own immediate objects, usually so different from, and even opposed to, God, so insubstantial or so deep in the mire? Added to which are the siren lures of the world and the subtle suggestions of the spirit of darkness.

Lord, Thou art the fixed pole-star of my voyaging soul; show me the course by which to arrive at the beckoning shores without sinking or being stranded on the rocks.

### III

Evil inducements and fallacious charms and all instigations to rebellion go by the general name of temptation, or of the primary personal source of temptation, of whom St. Peter speaks as

" a roaring lion seeking whom he may devour "—
(*I Peter v*, 8);

a hungry lion seeking to feed on me as long as I live on earth. This means continual warfare on my part, as Job declares; a life beset with temptation and snares, all so many obstacles on the road to my union with God, which must be struggled against at every hour. It means that this relentless struggle, which bears the frightening name of " mortification ", is not something which is left only to generous hearts anxious to go beyond the strict terms of the law, it is not something we can freely choose to take or leave, it is a virtue that nobody who submits to God's Will and commands can afford to do without, a virtue without which no one can cross the threshold of everlasting life.

## RESOLUTION

In order to keep my spiritual life within the narrow gauge of mortification, I resolve to read and absorb the first eight chapters of the Epistle to the Romans, where the theory of Christian mortification, usually so little understood, is expounded with logical precision. I shall do this until I am forced by inner conviction to accept as a rule of conduct the conclusion arrived at by the Apostle when he says:

" If you live a life of nature, you are marked out for death; if you mortify the ways of nature through the power of the Spirit, you will have life.

" Those who follow the leading of God's Spirit are all God's sons."—(*Rom. viii*, 13-14.)

## MORTIFICATION

### SECOND MEDITATION

*Priestly Motives*

#### I

My priestly state imperiously demands mortification. It is a collar-harness strapped round my neck by God's Hand from the moment He imprinted on me the Character of my priesthood. My enemies will assault me; they have already done so with greater rage and unexpectedness than other mortals. The world, with its traps and snares, with its scorn and jeering; Satan, with the full force of his wily seductions, so consciously aware of what he stands to gain by my downfall; the very delicate tasks entrusted to me, so exceedingly sublime, so numerous; my own priestly state, so holy in itself; all these are sources of conflict.

However well-balanced I may be, however vigorous my free will, I am necessarily, by the very nature of things, up against a host of difficulties lashing me in wave after wave and seeking to undermine my courage and my peace of mind. Mine must be a heart of diamond strength not to succumb ignominiously, but to confront and confound them all.

And the struggle and resistance demanded of me is no other than the " self-denial " of the Gospel, the " mortifying of the ways of nature through the power of the Spirit " of St. Paul's Epistle to the Romans.

## II

" The time will surely come, when men will grow tired of sound doctrine, always itching to hear something fresh; and so they will provide themselves with a continuous succession of new teachers, as the whim takes them. . . ."—(*II Tim. iv*, 3.)

Does this apply to me? Am I deceiving the faithful with soft words and booming periods or gentle harmonies, just catering for that " itch " to hear something fresh, instead of giving them the staple food of sound doctrine? The nerves of Christian living are not the poetry and magnificence of public ritual, nor what we add to it of what is flattering to the senses; the soul of all Christian endeavour, modelled on Christ crucified, is contained in these words of St. James the Apostle:

> "If he is to offer service pure and unblemished in the sight of God, who is our Father, he must take care of orphans and widows in their need, and keep himself untained by the world."—(*James i*, 27.)

Which means that we must offer resistance to our perverse inclinations so as to reduce them to reason, and in all our good works we must pursue the good and the pure, a costly feat, and bring our inmost being in harmony with the purity and serene holiness of God.

People will listen respectfully when I preach the austere lesson only if the most short-sighted in the congregation see it unmistakably exemplified, through mortification, in my personal conduct; otherwise it might be better not to mention the subject, or not to preach at all.

### III

There are two basic principles of Christian and priestly mortification, which we should do well to enumerate before specifying individual practices; they are as follows:—

1. To forbid myself, for all time and without the slenderest hope of turning back, every type of gratification, pleasure, pastime, and possession which I cannot reach out to without straying from the path or going beyond the circle of restrictions and prohibitions marked out for the man, the Christian, and the priest.

2. Resolutely to embrace, as part of the cross which Christ, the God of the Cross, has laid upon my

shoulders, all the unpleasantness, bitterness, contra-
dictions, and privations entailed by the exact performance of my duties.

3. These are the two basic principles of justice; they
cannot be transgressed or undermined without my
incurring what is sinful and without my being included
among the ranks of those souls whom Christ rejects with
the terrible curse:

> Depart from me, all ye workers of iniquity; I
> know not whence ye are.—(*Luke xiii*, 27.)

I am, therefore, going to be generous with God, who
so generously died for me. I am going to pluck up
courage to embrace even mortifications of supererogation: such and such an austerity, maceration, or fast.
And I will bend my back to the ministerial duties that
are positively painful; for example, hearing confessions,
visiting the sick, teaching the catechism, etc.; doing it
purely to please God, even though no one or no rule
may oblige me to take them up.

## Resolutions

1. Jesus Christ, who in former times was often called
" Captain-in-command " and the " Lord of hosts ", has,
besides the general line of battle, certain strategic positions scattered here and there which must be defended in
a special manner. One of these positions is my heart,
under heavy attack and entrusted to my courage and
loyalty. And the struggle, with its various incidents,
centring round this position is called spiritual
mortification.

But what about those traditional practices of bodily
punishment: hair-shirt, discipline, black fast, short

sleep, etc.? "Oh, that's not my line," you may say, "those weird things give me the creeps." Yes, and like a child whistling in the dark, you mask your lack of courage by laughing them to scorn; "Things of the past; dead and gone; gross exaggerations. . . ." Cowardly, effeminate soul, why not try one of them occasionally? Why such tender love for sinful flesh? Why not do something to be able to say with the Apostle: " I buffet my own body, and make it my slave "?—(*I Cor. ix*, 27.)

2. If, after examining my life before God, I discover something redundant, superfluous, effeminate and out of keeping with priestly simplicity and austerity, either in my clothing, bed, food, furniture, or in my reactions to whatever is unpleasant, I shall resolve to root it out unmercifully.

3. I am determined to be a man of hard work; work that is becoming, useful and constant. Every living particle of my being must be linked together by a solid occupation; only at the cost of this apparent slavery shall I purchase true freedom of the spirit, the independence of a child of God, and self-mastery.

# ALMSGIVING

## FIRST MEDITATION

### *The Works of Mercy*

#### I

We here understand the term *almsgiving* not so much in its specific and popular meaning—"Money or anything given to the poor to relieve their corporal needs" (*Summa II-II, q. 32*)—as signifying the practice of conferring corporal or spiritual benefits upon the needy of body or soul, the exercise of all the works of mercy.

The great gain accruing to any kind of almoner is stressed by Christ when He insistently promises a hundredfold in return. A hundred per cent. profit! What mercantile or industrial enterprise, however well insured; what bank, even the most flourishing, would make such an offer and dole out such high dividends? A hundred for one! What a rush there would be to invest our savings in a business concern which promised and could guarantee such a return! Our Lord announces His terms so often that the four Gospel writers set it down in the four best public documents:

> You shall receive a hundredfold and shall possess eternal life.

Lord, Thou didst well underline Thy promise, but, in spite of the quadruplicated and authorised copy of it, I still wonder whether I can really trust it without running undue risks of being disappointed. Isn't there a snag somewhere, a hook hidden at the end of the line? . . .

## II

A mere running commentary on the many passages of the Old and New Testaments extolling the good effects of almsgiving would furnish material for several very beautiful meditations. The Sacred Scriptures are old receipts, authenticated by God's Truthfulness and the Church's infallibility, expressing God's promise to pay the hundredfold for works of mercy done in His Name. Why not trust them? Would we not give credence to any ordinary human document properly drafted and signed, even by the hand of a usurer? Lord, help Thou my unbelief.

Daniel the prophet speaks to Nabuchodonosor, who is threatened with God's avenging Justice:

> Let my counsel be acceptable to thee, and redeem thou thy sins with alms and thy iniquities with works of mercy to the poor; and perhaps he will forgive thy offences.—(*Dan. iv, 24.*)

After rebuking the Pharisees for their avarice and wickedness, our Lord tells them of the cleansing effects of almsgiving:

> " You should give alms out of the store you have, and at once all that is yours becomes clean."
> —(*Lk. ix, 41.*)

My works of mercy will constitute, therefore, the surest pledge of pardon for my sins. So why do I not make a bid for it, seeing all the motives I have to regret my past life of sinfulness?

## III

My works of mercy will stand me in good stead at each critical moment of my existence.

At the moment of death or grave illness: "Blessed is the man," sings the Psalmist, "who takes thought for the poor and the destitute; the Lord will keep him safe in time of trouble; he will sustain him when he lies bedridden, turn all to health in his sickness"—

> Beatus qui intellegit super egenum et pauperem, in die mala liberabit eum Dominus.

> Dominus opem ferat illi super lectum doloris ejus; universum stratum ejus versasti in infirmitate ejus.

Or, as the new version of the Psalter says:

> totam infirmitatem ejus auferet in morbo ejus.
> —(*Ps. xl.*)

On the Day of Judgement and for all eternity my works of mercy will be a shield of protection:

> Alms shall be a great confidence before the most High God to all them that gave it.—(*Tobias iv,* 12.)

> Alms deliver from all sin and from death, and will not suffer the soul to go into darkness.—(*ib.* 11.)

But what greater gain than to hear from Christ's own lips this tenderest of loving invitations:

> Come, ye blessed of my Father . . . for I was hungry, and you gave me to eat."—(*Matt. xxv,* 34.)

Wholeheartedly I believe, O God, in the magnificent offers, made by Thy prophets and ratified by Thy Son, to the practice of works of mercy. Then why do I take them so coldly? Do they mean so little to me?

## RESOLUTIONS

1. There is no need to beat about the bush with God, so let us ask and answer a straightforward question: Has the priest a duty of religion (it is not a matter of strict justice) to employ in works of mercy the surplus of his priestly income? In theory, yes. In actual practice, the question is whether he has any surplus after providing for his decent maintenance. Beneficiary goods alone, according to Canon Law (*cfr. cc.* 1,473 and 1,410), are subject to this ruling, not stole fees and the offerings of the faithful.

2. A grave obligation in charity to give alms is incumbent upon the priest who has abundant means, the same as any other Christian, but in the vast majority of cases we priests are not among the opulent, and for many their penury is such, perhaps, as to entail not a single case of grave obligation in a life-time.

3. In matters of strict justice and religion I shall be scrupulously fair, administering properly the funds belonging to the Church or the poor or pious foundations (Christ's property, as they were called), even when I am not obliged to render a statement of accounts to anyone, even though it may prove impossible to take legal action against me for embezzlement of funds; because though I may escape the scrutiny of men I cannot hide from God. Have I a clean conscience and clean hands in the sight of God? Is there nothing demanding restitution on my part?

4. I shall observe Canon 1235, par. 2: " The poor shall be given decent funeral services and burial free of charge, according to the laws of liturgy and the diocesan

statutes." And I shall not acquire a habit of under-estimating another's poverty.

I shall also abide by Canon 463, par. 4: "He must not refuse to serve gratuitously those who are not able to pay for the services."

If I have to intervene in anything relating to cases of canonical procedure, I shall adhere faithfully to what the Code in chapter II of Book IV prescribes about lending my services to the poor free of charge.

O Jesus, Father of the poor, I prefer, even for my own sake, when dealing with the poor, Thy favourites, to err on the side of excessive indulgence. What they fail to pay me, Lord, I shall in future pass over to Thy account; and to be sure, I shall not do badly!

5. In all my ministerial duties I shall be at the disposal of the poor with the same thoroughness, kindliness, and courtesy as for the well-to-do, without any discrimination. Or, if there are to be exceptions, it will be the poor. The rich have ordinarily more than enough of everything, even in the Church of God: Sacraments, confessors, preachers, etc. If they want for anything it will not be for any shortage of supply; whereas the poor are often allowed to go without.

## ALMSGIVING

### SECOND MEDITATION

*The Priest's Love for the Poor*

### I

Jesus Christ was poor in this world's goods, so how can we love Him if we do not also love the poor, His own image and likeness?

"You do not need to be reminded how gracious our Lord Jesus Christ was; how he impoverished himself for your sakes . . . when he was so rich. . . ."—(*II Cor. viii,* 9.)

He showed His preference for poverty in the choice He made of a Mother and a home. He wished to be known as a carpenter's son and, as St. Jerome says, as the child of a poor seamstress. He was born not in a home, which, however lowly, could at least be called His own; but in a hillside cave, the property of another, borrowing from animals of the field their manger, and straw for His cradle and mattress. He was ever the Poor Man, even when, on account of His teaching and miracles, He was in the public eye.

The foxes have lairs, and the birds of the air, nests; but the Son of man hath not where to lay his head.—(*Matt. viii,* 20.)

His poverty became utter destitution at the hour of death, with a gallows for a bed, His nakedness clothed in streams of His own blood for bed-clothes, the rough executioners' hands the only hands that nursed Him; and from His torments He is constrained, like Dives in hell, to beg for a sip of water: *I thirst!* only to be refreshed with bitter gall and vinegar.

O Jesus, so impoverished for our sake; a Beggar in the midst of Thy creatures whom Thou didst fill with the abundant store of Thy Providence! O Jesus, poor Thyself and Father of the poor, how can I possibly love and serve Thee if I do not love and serve the poor, or if I even despise and hate the poor, Thy little brothers and sisters?

## II

So tenderly did Christ love the poor that we might call them His life's great love, His predominant passion.

In His preaching and teaching, destined to be perpetuated on the lips of His Church, how He exalts the poor!

> Blessed are the poor in spirit, for theirs is the kingdom of heaven.—(*Matt. v, 3.*)

In His earthly wanderings He seems incapable of choosing any company other than that of the poor: disciples, listeners, places. When performing miracles, His omnipotence, usually concealed beneath the thick veil of His mortality and obscured by all the physical weaknesses of human nature, surges up triumphant and unfettered in order to be at the service of the poor, healing their diseases, satisfying their hunger, consoling them, soothing their afflictions, and sympathising with them with words that never before had issued from a human heart.

It is to the poor that we are indebted for a large portion of the Gospel, for most of the loveliest words and actions of the Divine Redeemer, which gushed like fountain sprays from the loving Heart of Christ in touch with human wretchedness. Such was the tenderness aroused in Him by the poor, that He was contented with nothing less than identifying Himself with them personally until the end of the world. Sitting in judgment over the world, He will say:

> I was hungry, and you gave me to eat; I was thirsty, and you gave me to drink; I was a stranger, and you took me in. . . .

Amen, I say to you, as long as you did it to one of these my least brethren, you did it to me.
—(*Matt. xxv*, 35, 40.)

### III

His love for the poor was the first sign given to the people to convince them that He was the Messiah and the Son of God:

He sent me to preach the Gospel to the poor.
—(*Is. xxxv*, 5.)

The blind see, the lame walk, the lepers are cleansed . . . the poor have the gospel preached to them.—(*Matt. xi*, 5.)

It seems a strange sort of "title" for Christ's Priesthood, but it was well understood by the people, who knew that the poor were one day to have a Preacher of the "Good News" sent to them by God, a Master and Physician, the Messiah, the Divine "Envoy".

All the documents signed and sealed by the ordaining Bishop, all our faculties and faculty examinations, will be of little avail to persuade the people, Catholic and non-Catholic, to welcome us as God's envoys and the heralds of Christ as compared with our profound affection and practical love for the poor and the disinherited of this world.

If so many of my labours and endeavours, to all appearances quite brilliant and much publicised, have not been made good use of and have not produced the results desired of them, is it not because of my harsh and disdainful attitude towards the poor and humble? Is it not, O Jesus, because in my words, in my actions, and in my life there is wanting that outward mark or seal of my supernatural mission in the world, love for the poor for the sake of Thee?

## IV

It is sometimes stated—let us hope to God it is sheer calumny; it would be an intolerable shame to us if it were the truth!—that any work on behalf of the poor, such as public subscriptions for the relief of some misfortune, charitable associations, etc., etc., break down or lead a languid, anæmic kind of life, or even die of wretched suffocation, in the parish due to the indifference, opposition, or deficient administration on the part of the priest. The priest is said to regard the poor as dangerous rivals, as though the alms given to them were so much money snatched from the hands of the minister of the altar, who seems to think that whatever is used on food and clothing for the benefit of the poor might be put to other purposes, such as Masses and solemn, well-remunerated acts of worship.

This is, perhaps, sheer calumny; but there is a fact that should make us bow our priestly heads in shame, the fact that there exist so many works of charity completely " secularised," works in whose functioning the clergy had no say at all, and were regarded as more of a hindrance than a help. It is no small ignominy for us priests that we were not initially responsible for those works of charity whose roots are to be found in the teachings and spirit of the Gospel.

This, more than all the depredations suffered by the Church at different times in nearly every European country, should be our shame and confusion; because the Church is thereby deprived of Her rightful patrimony, the poor, whom She was sent to minister to and administer for. The poor are the pride of the Church, and if iniquitous political Powers have despoiled Her of them, it has not been for love of the poor; it has been because these Powers coveted the goods belonging to the poor administered by the hands of the Church—like Judas or the Roman Prefect who tortured St. Laurence.

It is sad to think that there are charitable souls who, victims of calumniating prejudice, want to have nothing to do with us, thinking that we priests are without love for the poor.

### V

But am I so desperately poor that I can never spare an alms? Experience teaches that the most habitual and generous almsgivers are not always to be sought among the very well-to-do, they are too remote from the poor to know them and understand their needs; and hence the great accomplishment of the Divine Word in descending to our lowly human habitation from the Mansions of His heavenly Father. The people who sympathise with and serve the poor the best are the average middle-class people or the poor themselves.

In conclusion, let us heed the kindly and time-honoured counsel:

> "According to thy ability be merciful. If thou have much, give abundantly; if thou have little, take care even so to bestow willingly a little."—(*Tobias iv*, 8-9.)

> "It is the cheerful giver God loves."—(*II Cor. ix*, 7.)

## Resolutions

1. I shall often exhort the faithful to practise works of mercy, indicating to them some concrete example where help is required; such and such a family or needy person. To aid me in this, I shall read what the Roman Ritual ordains in Titulus V, chapter four, paragraph five.

2. I shall be the first to undertake works of mercy, and shall not allow any lay person to outdo me in the knowledge of the temporal distress afflicting the people confided to my care, and in devising solid Christian ways and means of ministering to their relief. In this manner I shall become like many other good priests, past and present, who immediately and in every case were looked upon, and reckoned with, as the rightful representatives of Christ's compassion whenever there was a question of aiding the poor. And that explains how so many priests have been instrumental in distributing abundant alms; not that they were rich themselves, far from it, but they were detached from wealth, and great lovers of the poor.

3. Instead of looking askance at modern welfare institutions, I shall do all I can to help them, because they bestow the best kind of relief by placing the poor in a position to earn their own living by their own work without being a burden to others; such modern institutions as syndicates, social welfare schemes, savings banks, etc. The most lasting and dignified alms are forthcoming through these social security agencies.

# MODERATION IN EATING AND DRINKING

## FIRST MEDITATION

### *Nature and Importance of Moderation*

#### I

Abstinence and sobriety, as against gluttony and drunkenness, are two subjective species of the virtue of temperance, taking the latter in its general philosophical sense.

Not all appetite for eating and drinking incurs the reproach of gluttony and drunkenness. An appetite in itself is necessary for the preservation of life and, as such, is a good thing. It is sinful only when indulged in to excess, in a manner offensive to right reason.

St. Thomas teaches that everything delectable which is of service to human needs has these needs for its goal, and therefore, we should make use of pleasurable things in so far as they are required by necessity or the lawful usages of life. Now, the vice of gluttony or drunkenness consists in gratifying the appetites of eating or drinking without reference to what is a guiding principle of human life, right reason. If excesses are due, not to ill-regulated desire, but to a misjudgement as to what is necessary for life and health, then there is not a sin of intemperance but mere lack of practical wisdom and knowledge that does not come within the province of morality or immorality. To eat and drink for the exclusive purpose of gratifying an appetite for pleasure and to go beyond the bounds of moderation in doing so would definitely be a sin. The natural need of food, which comes under the principle of the "vegetative" life in man, does not enter the orbit of virtue or vice; it is the sensitive pleasure which should be subordinated to reason, and the insubordination of which constitutes vice, in this case gluttony or drunkenness. This is the excess which we are going to meditate upon here, so that, by God's favour, we may keep our appetites under restraint.

## II

Abstinence and sobriety are the two specific applications of the virtue of temperance which bridle and moderate the appetite for eating and drinking in accordance with the dictates of reason. Reason demands that, since these two animal functions have health and life as their sole aim, there must be no gratification either in quantity, quality, manner, or other circumstances except in so far as they contribute to the life and well-being of the body entrusted to our administration by God, the Author of our being.

Thus it is that these two manifestations of the virtue of temperance raise the lowliest freely-willed acts of our composite human nature, acts of themselves wholly on the animal level, to the lofty sphere of reasonable and spiritual acts, to the sphere of human acts, wherewith, if done in the state of God's sanctifying grace, heaven itself is purchased.

What a pity, what a shame, I have so often behaved like a mere animal, like a being without rule or reason, perhaps stooping even lower than the brutes, which are never entirely ungoverned by law, the law of instinct and natural need! In my intemperance I come under the indictment of the psalmist: " Short is man's enjoyment of earthly goods; match him with the brute beasts, and he is no better than they."

> Homo cum in honore esset non intellexit; comparatus est jumentis insipientibus et similis factus est illis.—(*Ps. xlviii*, 13.)

### III

In speaking of moral beauty, St. Thomas points out that " Decorum est convenientia, et honestum dicitur quod nihil habet turpitudinis, nam honestas dicitur quasi honoris status." Where there is balance of proportion and harmony under the guidance of a higher principle there is that " honestas," that " becomingness " which belongs to the essence of moral beauty. And since temperance is the virtue which establishes due proportion and appropriateness, and moreover diffuses the light of the intelligence, among our animal acts of eating and drinking, it is a principle of moral beauty, its absence brings ugliness into morals and manners, debasing man to the brute level, to the extent of extinguishing the light of reason and plunging us into the darkness and quagmire of matter.

Haven't I dishonoured myself sometimes with this hideous vice? Haven't I chosen to shut out the light of reason, as something of a hindrance, in order to wallow—*more pecudum*—in the low-down pleasures of eating and drinking, as if God had created me only to gratify my palate and my belly? *Agnosce, Christiane, dignitatem tuam.*

## IV

My priesthood imposes on me an additional obligation of repressing these vicious instincts. With so many privations inescapably ours as priests, the appetite for those pleasures permitted to us and necessary for self-preservation is perhaps all the sharper in us; or, as it is put sometimes rather too bluntly: "It's the only enjoyment left to us." But, the stronger the craving and the greater its aptitude for disguise, the more need there is for the bridling force of temperance to deliver us from its slavery.

My age, ministry, state, the integrity and alertness of mind and senses required for teaching others, the devout attentiveness with which I should assist and preside at divine worship, the wisdom and discretion I need to govern my flock well; all this bids me live absolutely untrammelled by the base fetters of intemperance, which so weaken, obstruct, and upset, the right use of reason.

In solemn acts of worship I, as a priest, am on a higher plane than the laity, I am in a leading position; but in my ordinary life in spirit and in flesh, do I rise above my senses and their short-term satisfaction? Has my mind descended so low to earth that its flight is arrested by the bird-lime of pleasures of the palate?

### RESOLUTIONS

1.   Intemperance is one of the capital sins because it is the source and root of many others. It is a mortal sin, however, only when it involves a grave transgression of the law of God or of the Church; for example, failing to observe the fasts through the pleasures of eating or drinking; deliberately forfeiting by drink the use of one's

faculties to the point of being unable rightly to distinguish between good and evil and thus to expose oneself, without adequate reason, to the grave, voluntary, and immediate danger of committing a mortally sinful act, at least *gravis in causa*. So I resolve to keep a careful watch over myself lest I incur this vice; and I shall be on my guard against minor offences, which, being such a slippery slope, would soon bring out the truth of the utterance: " Little things despise, and little by little thou shalt fall." (*Ecclesiasticus xviii*, 1.)

2. I shall diligently avoid the following defects at table, defects, moreover, which are thoroughly bad manners and unworthy of my priestly state, and destined only to make me repulsive to others: namely, to eat " *praepropere, laute, nimis, ardenter, and studiose*"; *praepropere* before the appointed time, like a greedy and ill-bred child; *laute,* sumptuously and splendidly, at variance with priestly modesty and simplicity; *nimis,* in excessive or huge quantities, more proper of animals being fattened for the kill; *ardenter,* with great zest, as if there was no soul inhabiting the body and possessed of noble faculties, as if every atom of my being was just a voice clamouring for the satisfaction of its base appetite; and *studiose,* with elaborate presenting and flavouring of dishes, which might be all right for a royal banquet but not for the table of a servant of Christ, the Father of the poor.

Grant, Lord, that neither my table nor my spirit be sullied by such base practices.

# MODERATION IN EATING AND DRINKING

*Evils of Intemperance*

## I

A word about the physical evils of lack of moderation in eating and drinking. How many lives it shortens! How much distress is caused to the poor human organism by unreasonable overloading with food! We tax our bodies, most of us, with a burden that often breaks them down or drags them along thorny and unclean ways.

Our existence would be more cheerful and vigorous, and perhaps even longer, if we always kept the animal senses tempered by the demands of physical well-being, not to mention those of faith and right reason.

How shall we calculate all the misfortunes which the spirit, housed in its tenement of clay, has to suffer from excessive eating and drinking? There is a debasing of the mind, drowsed and darkened by the coarse vapours of over-feeding; that *hebetudo sensus* of which St. Thomas speaks, that blunting and impairing of the senses; the expansion or contraction of the heart with meaningless cheer or depressing sadness; immoderation in speech; the propensity to indulge in buffoonery, the atmosphere of every piled-up table; and the awakening of sexual appetite due to the plethora of heat and blood.

It may have occurred to me to put the blame for all these misfortunes on constitutional derangements or on God Himself, as Adam and Eve put the blame for their guilt on the Serpent or on the divine Plan; as if God and Nature, which God created, did not agree in condemning excess; and as if they were responsible for voluntary deviations of mine from the law of moderation!

## II

Numerous are the texts in Old and New Testaments condemning drunkenness:

> "A reckless counsellor is wine, strong drink a riotous friend."—(*Prov. xx,* 1.)
>
> "Do not besot yourselves with wine; that leads to ruin."—(*Eph. v,* 18.)

But the chief evil of immoderation is, according to our Lord, the danger of sudden death:

> And take heed to yourselves, lest perhaps your hearts be overcharged with surfeiting and drunkenness and the cares of this life, and that day come upon you suddenly.—(*Luke xxi,* 34.)

Christ reckons that surfeiting and drunkenness and the worries consequent upon these vices are the greatest obstacle to watching and praying and continual preparation of the soul—virtues culminating in the supreme gift of a good death. What greater misfortune could there be?

Lord, if until now these unworthy pleasures absorbed a heart made to seek and rest in Thee alone, I trust, by Thy fatherly mercy, to do battle with my degraded instincts, to master them and make them slaves to my free will.

> "Lord, that gavest my life and guidest it . . .
> let the itch of gluttony pass me by . . . do not leave

me at the mercy of a shameless, an unprofitable mind!"—(*Ecclus. xxiii*, 4 and 6.)

## III

Holy Scripture, the Fathers, the Doctors of the Church, all the guides of the spiritual life, and the Church Herself, in the laws and the liturgy, praise and ponder most highly not only sobriety but also fasting and the severe curbing of the flesh.

> "O Holy Lord, Father Almighty and everlasting God, who by the fasting of the body dost curb our vices, elevate our minds and bestow virtue and reward. . . ." (*Lenten preface.*)

The mere narrative of the terrible macerations and abstinential practices of so many of the Saints surprises, terrorises, and well-nigh scandalises us amid the softness of the modern world; but the facts are there, they cannot be denied; nor is the Church, acting by the Spirit of Christ, tired of holding up to our admiration those noble souls who so perfectly mastered the wild impulses of an appetite connatural to man.

I shall not make a mockery of these achievements of the Saints. If I haven't the courage or the desire to scale such heights, I shall own up to my cowardice; and in future I shall hold these virtues in the same high esteem as the Church does, and try to walk in the footsteps of so many valiant souls, at least by leading a reasonably sober and temperate life.

### RESOLUTIONS

1. I shall bear in mind and strictly observe Canon 138, which mentions some of the things and places that

clerics should abstain from as unbecoming to their state: clerics "should not enter public houses and other similar places, except out of necessity or for some other just cause approved by the local Ordinary." I shall also be chary of big dinners in the company of lay people, on account of the dangers that are always inherent in them.

2. I shall not drink wines and spirits outside meal times, unless I am justified in doing so by some social need or convenience. (And why not do better still? Why not imitate so many good priests and lay people, who abstain completely from all alcoholic drink? If I have shown the slightest weakness for drink in the past, surely I should forestall a tragedy by cutting out drink altogether.—Trans.)

3. I shall not think or talk needlessly about eating and drinking. The chief danger in every kind of intemperance is, according to St. Thomas, thinking about the specific or particular object which gives pleasure.

4. I shall raise my meals to the rank of acts of piety and religion, blessing the table according to the formula of the Breviary, if I am alone or with other priests, or saying grace before and after meals, if with lay people. If possible, I shall do some spiritual reading during meals, in order to take my mind off food. I shall keep to all the rules of good manners while at table.

5. I shall fast, at least when the Church commands it. And if one day I have the pluck to fast out of devotion and to deprive myself occasionally even of what is convenient, in order to atone for my frequent lack of moderation in the past, I shall be a happier man for it.

# THE LOVE OF HARD WORK

## FIRST MEDITATION

### *The Priest must be a Hard Worker*

#### I

Church history testifies that the grave laxity which overcame the clergy during certain periods of decadence and which paved the way for tremendous catastrophes, such as Protestantism, was rooted primarily in the forced idleness consequent upon considerable wealth combined with frequent lack of worthy occupation. And, speaking of the general history of the nations, it is indolence which breeds degradation and decline, especially in sex morality; and this same indolence is corroding certain classes of society in modern times. Very short hours of very easy work mean long hours of corruption. Only work has the power to stem the continual flow of ideas and desires that come bubbling up from our unruly instincts. With indolence and idleness come evil thoughts and worse desires, " *donec navis cordis succumbens in peccato periclitetur* " says St. Bernard, until the vessel of the heart founders and becomes stranded on the rocks of sin.

Does this account for many of my lapses?

#### II

The priest, to-day more than ever before, has to be a man of ability; through his personal good qualities he has to regain for Religion the respect which unbelief

385

N

otherwise refuses to pay it. If a bad priest is a black stain on Christ's brow, the good priest is Christ's earthly crown of glory:

> And thou shalt be a crown of glory in the hand of the Lord, and a royal diadem in the hand of thy God.—(*Is. lxii,* 3.)

Will a priest who thrives on perpetual idleness be anyone's crown of glory? Only hard work will raise him above the average. And how will a lazy priest deliver St. Paul's stirring words to the faithful?

> "We charge you in the name of our Lord Jesus Christ to have nothing to do with any brother who lives a vagabond life, contrary to the tradition which we handed on. . . .
>
> The charge we gave you on our visit was that a man who refuses to work must be left to starve. . . .
>
> We charge all such, we appeal to them in the Lord Jesus Christ, to earn their bread by going on calmly with their work."—(*II Thess. iii,* 6, 10, 12.)

In obedience to these commands, the faithful ought instinctively to shun me if I spend my life in idleness, without earning my daily bread, being a parasite living by the fruits of others; and, for my part, giving ample cause for the taunts of the Church's enemies when they dub Her ministers loafers and regard them as "socially unproductive."

### III

Even supposing that there is no likelihood of this, that the people's respect for the clergy is well established, and that you personally are indebted to God for a balanced temperament which knows how to control energies and tame unruly desires; you must remember that those active powers of yours, if left unexercised, will constitute so much frozen capital; whereas God's contract is to remunerate a hundredfold only those supernatural assets which are in active circulation, especially those of His ministers.

How many bad habits would have been rooted out from people's hearts, how many lives regenerated, how many souls conducted to their heavenly destiny, how many errors deleted from their minds, if only I had made a slightly better use of my time during all the perhaps long years of my priesthood! All that store of good, which God had a right to expect from me and which my wretched laziness refused to supply, will it not oblige Him to curse my fruitless existence with the words:

> Cut it down therefore; why cumbereth it the ground?—(*Luke xiii,* 7.)?

## RESOLUTIONS

1. By the strength of God's grace I resolve to be a man of hard work, as though St. Paul had written to me personally:

> "Aim first at winning God's approval, as a workman who does not need to be ashamed of his work."—(*II Tim. ii,* 15.)

By dint of constant hard work I shall gradually equip myself for the proper discharge of my ministerial duties, including a well-prepared announcing of the word of God. But for this I shall need to make profitable use of every day and every hour.

2.   In order to accomplish this, I propose to bring a methodical approach to my occupations, seeking the most convenient time for each one, and drawing up a well thought-out time-table or schedule for each day, week, month, and year, making no alterations in it without necessity or some considerable advantage. The Apostle's warning not to roam about in a discreditable and restless fashion, minding other people's business but not their own, and his recommendation of silent hard work, were and still are the secret of the Saints. Thus, in the hands of the Saints, each day seemed of double length, like Josue's; there is no other explanation for those countless marvellous works and foundations which they brought to a successful issue; achievements that, to our reckoning, would be enough to fill and overcrowd the lives of several ordinary men.

3.   Lord, I acknowledge that the lack of method and order in my affairs, allowing them to be governed by caprice instead of a definite rule, has been the reason that my work has yielded so little and my priestly years have been both in appearance and in reality a barren wilderness, without fruits of salvation either for myself or for others.

## THE LOVE OF HARD WORK

### SECOND MEDITATION

*Models of Hard Work*

### I

Solomon advises us to go to school with the ant and learn from this little creature the ways of diligence and hard work (Prov. vi, 6). But we priests have only to look around us: into factories of modern industrialism, into iron foundries and blast furnaces where such heavy and dangerous work is being done night and day; and in the countryside itself, only by sheer hard work can farmers manage to earn their daily bread honestly for themselves and their families; hard work that spans the long daylight hours of a summer's day from the first glimmerings of dawn until evening dusk; and even then, the day is all too short, and the struggle for existence is unceasing. If I, a priest, need a spur to hard work, I have not far to look for it; perhaps my own hard-working parents set me the earliest example.

And what about those thousands upon thousands of saintly people who have been the salt of the earth, from whose sweated toil the world has always drunk in abundance? Is it possible to imagine a lazy Saint? These are my masters and models in keeping with my priestly state. But there are certain models of supreme significance and value to me; let us take some of them: St. Paul, the Blessed Mother of Jesus, and finally, Jesus Christ Himself, the God-Man who had a better right than any other child of Adam to say: *in laboribus a juventute mea.*

## II

*Saint Paul.*—When, as we saw in our last meditation, the Apostle administered such severe warnings to the faithful about hard work, he was well authorised to do so; he was the first to give the lead.

> " You do not need to be reminded how, on our visit, we set you an example to be imitated; we were no vagabonds ourselves.

We would not even be indebted to you for our daily bread, we earned it in weariness and toil, working with our hands, night and day, so as not to be a burden to any of you."—(*II Thess, iii,* 7.8.)

Every word of this beautiful chapter should be the subject of meditation. And I should do well to ponder over these moving words which St. Paul addressed to the early Christians of Ephesus on his departure from the city:

" You yourselves can testify how I have lived among you since the first day when I set foot on Asia serving the Lord in all humility, not without tears over the trials which beset me through the plots of the Jews:

And how I have never failed you when there was any need of preaching to you, or teaching you, whether publicly or house by house.

I have proclaimed both to Jew and to Greek repentance before God and faith in our Lord Jesus Christ."—(*Acts xx,* 18-21.)

" Be on the watch, then; do not forget the three years I spent, instructing every one of you continually, and with tears."—(*xx,* 31.)

For three years, uninterruptedly, day and night, in public and in each individual household; all the while ambushed by Jews and Gentiles, and ill-treated by them: that would seem crushing enough. But without rest, without consolation, through cities, by the wayside, by land and sea, in failing health, battered and assaulted; and yet, building up so many Christian communities, covering so many parts of Asia Minor, so

many parts of Europe. Surely he has well earned his
daily bread! Surely he should receive at least the means
of self-support! No. Those labours are free of charge.
That is his boast, and he says:

> "I would rather die than have this boast taken
> from me."—(*I Cor. ix,* 15.)

No wonder, when he came to leave those vast territories and populous centres through which he had passed
establishing the kingdom of God, he could, with legitimate pride, say to his converts:

> "I have never asked for silver or gold or cloth-
> ing from any man; you will bear me out, that these
> hands of mine have sufficed for all that I and my
> companions needed."—(*Acts xx,* 33-34.)

And no doubt, in saying this, he extended those hands
and showed them to the people; hands that had so often
stretched out before the multitudes in gestures of irresistible persuasiveness from the preacher of the Gospel
and the pacifier of agitated masses, hands that had
touched the dead to raise them to life again, and had
been laid on the sick to heal them. He shows them those
hands of his grown callous from constant use of the
hemp and bodkin with which he sewed the canvas
cloths together for the making of tents, the lowly manual
labour which earned him his meagre pittance. A great
man, indeed, is Paul when he perorates in the Areo-
pagus, but his stature is not diminished when he rests
from his consuming apostolic labours to sew canvas
sheets throughout the night, lest he die of starvation, and
to provide for those that help him in the task of evangelisation.

### III

*The Mother of Jesus.*—It is very little the Gospels
tell us about her, and even that little reveals her inner
life rather than her outward activities. But what was
the need? Was your own mother poor? Or, at least,
don't you know some good woman, the mother of a
Christian family, with a very small share of this world's
goods? Consider her occupations, her life of unremitting
toil. Such was Mary's life, Mary the Mother of the
humble home of Nazareth. Call to mind the picture of
the Strong Woman, the " vigorous wife," as contained
in the Book of Proverbs; those were the household cares
of *the* Strong Woman and Vigorous Wife, Mary of
Nazareth. To rise at first light of dawn, tidy the house,
sweep, scrub, wash the dishes, sew or mend; and to be
the last to go to bed at night. Those blessed hands,
which now emit heavenly rays of beauty, and which
dispense to us all the great stream of graces won by
Christ, are hands that once were chapped and roughened
with the cleansing of pots and pans, the scrubbing of
floors, the plying of the needle, the carrying of the
pitcher to the well.

If you ask Christ, the Judge of living and dead, the
Rewarder of every virtue: " Lord, what are those
precious stones in Thy Mother's crown of glory which
shine more refulgent than the stars of the heavens?" His
answer will be: " No, not ostentatious deeds, not lofty
preachments, not the conversion of whole nations, not
martyrdoms or consuming flames or agonising crosses;
they are the humble household tasks of my Mother, the
worries and cares of a very humble home which, in
passing through my Mother's hands, or rather, through
her Heart ablaze with divine love more burning than

that of all the Seraphim, were fashioned into that crown of glory, heaven's most lustrous adornment."

O God, however much the world may despise hard work, *I* will not despise it; and seeing the transformations it undergoes when suffused by Thy love, I shall *love* it, too.

## IV

*Jesus Christ.*—" In laboribus a juventute mea " are words that sum up, if we exclude physical ailments, the life of our Lord.

Carpenter, craftsman, the artisan's son, are the terms used by fellow-citizens and countrymen when speaking of Jesus; terms spoken in a tone of derision when refusing to accept the wisdom that flowed from His lips.

> How came this man by all these things? What wisdom is this that is given to him, and such mighty works as are wrought by his hands?—(*Mark vi, 2.*)

From the age of twelve to thirty, His whole life, which St. Luke compresses into the words "He was subject to them," was a life of obedience to Mary, His hard-working Mother, and to Joseph, the carpenter. With Joseph He cuts, saws, planes, and nails, wood; He makes or repairs window-frames, doors, ploughs; earning His bread with the sweat of His brow and the toil of His hands. Dispossessed, as it were, of His God-head's crown, which He had seemed to leave behind Him among the bright angelic choirs, on earth He wears two crowns: during the last hours of His laborious existence, the crown of thorns, studded with the rubies and gems of His precious blood; during His whole life, the crown of hard work, studded with the drops of sweat when wielding the tools of His carpenter's trade day after day.

And how often, during the years of His public ministry, while proving to the world His Mastery, He would go back in thought and yearning to those peaceful hours spent at the workshop of Nazareth! Is there anything more exhausting to a man than to be constantly dealing with vast throngs of people? There He is: the Word of God, surrendering to their demands, hemmed in by them, crushed, carried along by them through the hilly tracks and dusty roads of Judea and Galilee and over the shores of Tiberias. His lodging-place is besieged by the crowds from dawn to dusk; He has not even time for a meal; He instructs them, listens to them, heals the sick, suffers the thousand-and-one impertinences of friends, the suspicions and captious questionings of shrewd enemies; and over the heads of those same crowds, within reach of their sarcasm, overwhelmed by the cataract of His own torments, He finally utters from the cross the triumphant cry of liberation: *Consummatum est.* It was liberation from crushing toil, an end to all those years of unspeakable labour in which every muscle, every sense, and every faculty and fibre of His being had been consumed by hard work.

That is one more lesson from the Cross; the lesson to every priest on the meaning of hard work.

O Lord, do I, Thy minister; do I, *alter Christus,* propose to squat down under the sheltering shadow of the Cross and spend my life in idleness, adducing my very priesthood as a reason for taking things easy?

## RESOLUTIONS

This will be my work programme:

1. Not to omit a single one of my priestly acts of piety: mental prayer, Mass, Divine Office, spiritual reading, visit to the Blessed Sacrament, the Rosary; and to give to each act all the time, space, quiet, and serious attention which my dealings with God require, performing them in places conducive to recollection, and considering them my noblest occupation and exercises of the day.

2. To prepare for preaching: sermons, homilies, catechetical instructions, and whatever entails the announcing of God's word. To devote to this preparation all the time and labour that my audience and my ability demand, because otherwise I should be profaning the word of God taught us so reverently by its first Herald, the Word of God in Person.

3. To discharge my ministerial duties towards my neighbour, not only those due in strict justice, but also those of equity, charity, or simply out of devotion, with that fixed attention and calm repose which everything divine demands, not allowing any human interest to abbreviate or hurry them unduly.

4. Not to despise any form of zeal, however new and unusual it may appear to me, so long as the Church does not disapprove of it and it seems to be effective; and even to make use of these new manifestations of zeal in so far as prudence and timely circumstances call for them: schools, lectures, works of charity, social or quasi-social institutions.

O God, as Thou didst pour the new wine of the Gospel into new wine-skins, notwithstanding the persecution by fire and sword on the part of the keepers of the old wine-skins, I also shall try the new as well as the old, so as to be able to sum up my life in the words of Thy Apostle:

"I have been everything by turns to everybody to bring everybody salvation."—(*I Cor. ix,* 22.)

## THE LOVE OF HARD WORK

### THIRD MEDITATION

*Excuses for not Working Hard*

### I

Many plausible excuses will occur to me for not getting down to hard work. Here are some of them:

"There's nothing for me to do." Is that possible? What privileged domain has the Church or your lucky star assigned to you where there is nothing to do? In the Kingdom Christ established by His blood and toil, can there be any such place? Perhaps you have the cure of souls, you are a parish priest, an administrator, a curate, a chaplain to nuns or to some other religious institute?

"Yes, I have some sort of a job like that, but my predecessor left nothing for me to do."

That baffles me. You seem to me to imply only one of two things: either everything remains to be done and created anew: confraternities, associations, the visiting of the sick, the teaching of catechism, preaching, frequenting of the Sacraments, going in search of the sheep that have strayed, a serious effort to increase the Fold with converts, a re-calling and re-shepherding of those that have fled; in other words: nothing is being done and everything needs doing. Or else, everything *has* been done: your predecessors were men of zeal who established Christian institutions and transmitted them to you in a condition of perfect life and vigour, leaving your catechism classes well organised, ample opportunities for preaching, sick people accustomed to seeing the priest at their bedside and with them at the hour of death, a confessional always ready to receive penitents, altar-rails crowded every day. If this is happily your case, woe betide you if you do not get down to real hard work, otherwise all the solicitude of your predecessors will gradually be robbed of all its fruits, everything will cool down, and eventually will die altogether. Can you think of anything that imposes more hard work than the cultivation of a fervent parish?

" In my case, I haven't a pastoral office of any kind; I just say Mass, and perhaps not every day."

I can only say that if you're not an old priest on the sick list or in retirement after many a long year and noble striving, you move me to tears; I seem to hear Christ say to you the words spoken by Isaias to Sobna, prefect of the Temple: *What dost thou here? . . . the shame of the house of thy Lord!* (Is. xxii, 16.) You mean to tell me you are in constant idleness while there are still so many unbelievers to whom the Gospel has not yet been preached? so many penitents without priests to hear them? so many dying without the last Sacraments? so many parishes without catechetical instruction? If the Lord's vineyard is nearly choked with thistles and thorns, it is not for scarcity of workers, but because there are hundreds like you whose wretched lives God will condense, at the last Day, in that bitter remonstration of the owner of the vineyard:

> Why stand you here all the day idle?—(*Matt. xx,* 6.)

## II

"My case is different. My lot, for my sins, is work on a very stony patch of the Lord's vineyard, not a decent cluster ever grows there: souls so obdurate, so estranged from God, that no human strength, and I was going to say, divine Power as well, will bring them to their duties. A reprobate lot of straying sheep on whom the shepherd's callings are lost, as in a wilderness, however zealous the shepherd."

That is a possibility; but do you think the nations evangelised by St. Paul were any better disposed to receive the Gospel? And coming nearer to our own age, do you think those savage and most degraded American tribes in the sixteenth century were a more promising field? And yet, in little more than a century, there were priests who converted them in their millions.

But let us suppose that all your best efforts crash against the stone wall of indifference, that after years and years of labour the field remains as sterile as ever; discouraging and depressing it certainly is, but don't forget that St. James, for example, the Apostle of Spain, was in the same plight, and yet the time came when the seed brought forth fruits of benediction so plentiful that even to-day the "Son of thunder" from his high place in heaven rejoices to see his field as one of the most beautiful and richest fields in the Church of God. But, whatever there may be in store for you, console yourself in your distress by thinking that God will reward you not for the number of souls converted but for the efforts you have made by His grace with the sole purpose of pleasing and serving Him.

### III

"But I'm a sick man, I can't take up a lot of work; I've enough to do looking after my wretched health."

Yes, a poor specimen you are, indeed, if you have to devote your pitiful existence to the sole task of spinning it out a little longer, living just for the sake of living, with no wider prospects and no ulterior purpose; a lamp that feeds on its own light and sheds light on nobody. But, come to think of it, is your illness so severe that you can't do a stroke of work? Surely you can pray for souls and offer to God your aches and pains for their benefit; by your example you can stimulate those around you to do good.

But this sort of excuse is not usually heard in cases of totally disabling sickness. Examine yourself impartially, and see whether there isn't an element of exaggeration, egoism, inborn indolence, self-deception and squeamishness in your complaint: there is frequently so much of this in the ailments of the clergy! To dig, to do hard manual labour, no, perhaps your health isn't strong enough for that, and your vocation doesn't require it; but look at all those farm and factory workers who in spite of severe bouts of sickness keep on with their jobs, until their health and very life break down in the process. . . .

A glance at Church history in every age, including our own, will give you the shock you need: the priests who carried out the most strenuous achievements were usually men of indifferent health, and sometimes very sick men: St. Paul, St. Basil, St. Vincent de Paul, the Curé d'Ars, Cardinal Newman, Father Faber, etc. Far less bitter your life would be if, instead of keeping your mental and physical energies pent up for twenty-four hours a day within the narrow preoccupation of your aches and pains and their hypothetical remedy, you opened the flood-gates and launched out to do what good you can for your fellow men.

## IV

"I can't say I work terribly hard, but my remuneration is a mere pittance."

That may be quite true. The casual labourer, the road-mender, the porter, any unskilled mechanic, is often better paid than the priest, who, with his pittance, is nevertheless looked upon as rolling in money. His supposed wealth is sometimes a charge against him; he is represented as the prototype of spivs and drones—one of the hardest insults we priests have to bear. If this is your case; if injuries and meanness of this kind come your way and you have to live almost continually a beggarly existence; I ask you to lift your eyes to God, and in your desolation remember the blessing announced to us by the Prince of the Apostles:

"If, after all, you should have to suffer in the cause of right, yours is a blessed lot. . . .

"It may be God's will that we should suffer for doing right; better that, than for doing wrong."
—(*I Peter iii,* 14 and 17.)

Besides, the work of a priest is not a commodity that can be priced, like the work of a road-mender; all the millions in the world cannot purchase a single act of supernatural zeal. So never tolerate the question: "How much do I owe you?" You have a right to a decent maintenance; it's only just that "he who serveth at the altar should live by the altar". But you are not like the doctor or any other professional man, your priestly work does not come under the category of "do ut des", it must remain for ever intact and unremunerated, here on earth. Only God can reward you in terms of strict justice. Are you going to debase the value of your priestly ministry to the level of any chattel at an auction sale?

Rich or poor, stipends large or small, I shall keep on toiling for Thee, O God, with the eternal reward ever in my sight. I would not have Thee, at the end of my working day, utter those words: "*Believe me, you have received your reward already.*"

## V

"If I attempt anything out of the ordinary, my fellow priests will bring me to heel, they'll spy on me like a dangerous criminal, they'll give a twist to my best intentions, they'll point a finger of scorn at me and make me a laughing-stock."

Sadly enough, such may be the case . . . oh, there are so many cases! . . . Don't do a thing; neglect your most sacred and obvious duties; don't preach or teach catechism; leave your sick to die like dogs; let your whole life glide softly away in peevish inactivity; allow your vineyard to clutter up with weeds and thistles and even become infested with poisonous reptiles. . . . Worse still, surrender to vice, let your conduct be a by-word in the neighbourhood and the ignominy of priestly circles . . . you may yet be allowed to live in peace. And if ecclesiastical justice is bent on providing a remedy for your misdeeds, its hands will be tied, there will be no witnesses to inform against you; your fellow priests, although among themselves and in the privacy of their own little gatherings they may lament your straying, when called upon to give evidence to your ecclesiastical Superiors about you, they will stand up for you and almost canonise you. . . . There has been more than one case of this!

On the other hand, if you make up your mind to be really zealous, to spend talent and energy on the work of God, to attain distinction in preaching and in constant vigilance for the salvation of souls; and should God show His Good-Pleasure by showering His blessing upon your watchful efforts, making the fear of God and Christian works flourish all round you through your zeal . . . ah, get ready! they'll fix a scrutinising pair of eyes on you; you'll be the target of scorching criticism; you'll be accounted a hypocrite and a pest; they may even try to find chapter and verse in the Code for your indictment, and then, " in a spirit of humility and charity ", they will denounce you to the Prelate.

Grossly exaggerated as this may appear, it *has* happened; the saintly Curé d'Ars is a case in point; and there have been others, if not so resonant, no less unfortunate.

This is all very heart-rending, but, far from forcing you to throw in the sponge, it should goad and spur you to greater things still. You have the hallmark, the identity seal, that God imprints on the works most pleasing to Him. Rejoice, your works are the works of God; they are indelibly marked with the divine approval.

Blessed are ye when they shall revile and persecute you and speak all that is evil against you, untruly, for my sake:

Be glad and rejoice, for your reward is very great in heaven; for so they persecuted the prophets that were before you.—(*Matt. v,* 11-12.)

## RESOLUTIONS

1. There is a type of work which no priest can ever afford to omit: study, books. Without study, without books, I shall not be long in falling back to my native uncouthness. The intellect is not a fountain-head of ideas, it is a reservoir; and if these ideas are not renewed frequently, they will leak through the cracks and crevices of the forgetful mind; and thus, I shall come to be an empty barrel: words without ideas, phrases bereft of judgement and discrimination, formulas stripped of affections, platitudes stale and stodgy. The priest without his books will never rise to great heights; but he can, due to his aversion to study, sink to the depths; more than one such priest has ended up a poor clod-hopper or thrown up everything to become an industrialist-on-the-make or a peddler of common wares.

2. I shall devote an hour or so each day to the following studies: Holy Scripture, devoutly read and meditated upon, especially the New Testament; Moral and Dogmatic theology, in its catechetical form rather than its Scholastic presentation, which seeks an understanding, and as far as possible a clear and definite grasp, of the truths of our holy Faith and of the commandments of God and the Church in their vital and practical import, even though I omit a host of controversies among theologians, of little practical benefit either to myself or to my people of the parish.

3. I shall not disdain to revise Christian philosophy, Theology's pedestal, nor the study of the Humanities, so necessary to the priest who needs to know how to use the spoken and written word efficiently. The Humanities most needed by the priest are, according to Leo XIII, the Greek and Latin classics and the good writers in the priest's native tongue.

4. I shall try to keep on a level with those people who are in the front ranks of general culture; because if I lag behind in these matters I shall be out of touch with good society and shall be dismissed as an ignorant bumpkin.

## THE LOVE OF HARD WORK

### FOURTH MEDITATION

*What should and should not be done*

### I

To do nothing at all is the first degree of idleness. To say Mass and recite the Divine Office hurriedly, just to get it done with, and then to kill time (as though time was some sort of harmful and poisonous creature!) talking for hours on end, reading the newspaper (if I have sufficient energy to do so)—a parasite of a priest, a fruitless tree sucking the sap of other trees, marked out for those words of burning scorn and concentrated wrath from Christ's own lips:

"Why cumbereth it the ground?"

—(*Luke xiii*, 7.)

A miserable, aimless, dishonest existence!

Haven't I spent days, months, years with my talents, many or few,—five, three, or one—buried in the barren sands of a somnolent survival? Am I not to be numbered among those whom the Master of the vineyard greets in the evening with the sad reproof: "*What do ye here all the day idle?*"

## II

Perhaps mere lack of activity is not in your line; on the contrary, you are naturally active, and neither your youth nor your impulsive imagination will allow a life of idleness; you feel the need to move around, to be always on the go, to keep your mind constantly nourished. Yes, but hasn't your mind up to now been a furnace feeding on fuel as quick-burning as it is useless—occupations that estrange you from yourself, that entertain, divert, and distract you? Aren't you like a traveller who is bored while the train swallows up mile after mile, and takes to smoking, reading a novel, looking out of the window, for no other purpose than to deaden the sensation of forced inactivity imposed by the long journey?

Distraction, diversion, entertainment, are all ways and means of escaping from the realities of the hour and from one's own personality. Is that the formula for the life of a priest? If it is, our Lord would certainly have to revise the schedule of the priestly vocation contained in these words:

> I have chosen you, and have appointed you, that you should go and should bring forth fruit, and your fruit should remain.—(*John xv*, 16.)

### III

Perhaps my case is different again. I consider it improper for any steady person to fritter his life away in aimless activity; that might be all right for children or people in the green of youth, but not for mature age, and much less for a priest—presbyter: an old man. At the moment of my ordination, in the full vigour of my twenty-four years, I said good-bye to my youth and I cannot go back to it without forfeiting the glorious title of priest.

Nevertheless, in preference to priestly duties and clerical activities, which seemed to clash with my worldly outlook, I may have chosen other occupations apparently more glamorous, remunerative, and honourable, almost to the point of cancelling out the former.

Have I unreservedly obeyed the injunction of the Apostle:

"Like a good soldier of Christ Jesus, take thy share of hardship.

"Thou art God's soldier, and the soldier on service, if he would please the captain who enlisted him, will refuse to be entangled in the business of daily life."—(*II Tim. ii*, 3-4)?

Can I swear to God and to my own conscience that I have observed the ruling of the Church—a ruling that has never changed from the beginning—about keeping away from certain secular employments?

### RESOLUTIONS

1. I shall positively keep away from any occupation which is at variance with, or less conformable to, Canon Law, if only because experience teaches that the priest

comes to grief therein every time. Moreover, I resolve not to attach more importance to any work, however pleasant and useful it may seem, than to my ministerial duties.

2. If I cannot conveniently forgo all relaxation, while keeping within the narrowest limits of what is permissible, I shall prefer those forms of recreation that have an educational value for me or which enable me to develop my priestly capabilities; such as travel or sight-seeing suitable to my state.

3. While I do not propose to deprive myself till the end of my days of games in every shape and form, I shall most definitely refrain from games of chance, a pitfall and a snare that has been the ruin of many a good priest; and so I shall say good-bye for ever to gambling-houses, casinos, etc.

4. Since card games can so easily captivate one and arouse one even to frenzy, if I do not decide to renounce them entirely, at least I promise to hold myself in check and to take them as a mere diversion; and, if I begin to find myself tied down to the card table because of an eager desire for monetary gain, or to revenge my piqued or wounded feelings, or for the sake of mere pleasure, I shall give up card games immediately.

I shall never allow the faithful to witness the degrading spectacle of, for instance, my spending the whole night at a game of cards; a thing so unworthy of the priest who has so much else to do, and who in the morning has to offer to God the Holy Sacrifice of the Body and Blood of Jesus Christ.

# AVARICE

## Evils of Avarice in the Priest

### I

St. Paul speaks of avarice as a kind of idolatry—
"*that love of money which makes a man an idolater.*"
(Eph. v, 5.)

Just as the idolater surrenders to a creature, adoring it
as his God, the avaricious person surrenders and sacrifices himself to riches, with an all-absorbing desire to
possess them.

Once covetousness dominates over me, I shall regard
and assign the amassing and worship and service of the
ephemeral goods of earth, in the form of coin, chattels,
or paper money, as the whole of life's purpose. My
spiritual faculties will live a life of dedication to the
worship of my idol. This will be the pursuit of my
probing mind day and night. This will be my love
above all other loves. My heart, created for the God of
heaven, will be full of the craving for wealth—*auri
sacra fames*—and this will be my despicable god, whom
I shall love with my whole heart, with my whole soul,
with my whole mind, and with all my strength.

Even in the holiest works of my ministry: in preaching, administering the Sacraments, in the Sacrifice of
the Mass, and in the very Person of Christ sacrificed,
I shall seek no other value beyond their emolument
value in cash. To this idol I shall sacrifice not only my
own soul with its understanding, will, and affections, but

408

the Word of God as well; yes, the very Person of the
Word, if avarice becomes my ruling passion.

Have not these abominations the stench of sacrilege
and apostasy about them? Should I not richly deserve,
if I stooped so low, the bitter reproach conveyed
through the prophet Isaias:

> Thou hast made me to serve with thy sins
> (*Is. xliii*, 24),

or that uttered by Ezechiel:

> " For a handful of meal, or a crust of bread, they
> will put me to shame before my own people."
> —(*Ez. xiii*, 19.)

## II

There is a semblance of perfect happiness in the
possession of riches: we can procure with them most of
the good things of this life, and their sovereignty in this
world is practically undisputed. Hence, the unruly desire
to possess and retain, which is avarice, becomes by its
force and widespread action the origin of other keen
desires equally irregular and vicious; in other words,
avarice is a capital sin. From this poisoned source flows
in an unquenchable and continual stream insensitive-
ness and callousness of heart at the sight of our neighbours' sorrows and miseries—the hard-heartedness of
the rich glutton towards Lazarus—and also a tormenting
solicitude to increase our store.

Money alone does not satisfy the covetous man; in
order to acquire and retain his ill-gotten goods he resorts
to violence, extortion, deceit, perjury, fraud, treachery,
and every species of injustice. And in the case of a
covetous or avaricious priest, these injustices would find

expression in his imposing taxes and stole-fees in accordance with his craving for quick gains, not with the rulings of Canon Law and common honesty; he will be led, in imitation of Judas, to maladminister the sacred property of the poor, of the Church, of Christ, and to fleece the devout or simple people under the pretext of piety.

You may think this an exaggeration, but, if the priest is avaricious, what other line of business or source of income can he exploit for quick gains outside the sphere of the altar and public worship and whatever pertains thereto?

### III

To the above-mentioned evils of priestly avarice must be added another no less serious. Zeal for the salvation of souls is diametrically opposed to, and absolutely incompatible with, greed for gain and hoarding; therefore, those works of zeal which do not yield ready cash, which bring no increase to his emoluments, will be a hindrance to him, a hateful task, an irreparable loss of time; because to him "time is money." He will not exercise these "non-productive" duties of the ministry, or, if he cannot evade them entirely, he will spare as little time for them as possible, and will never put his whole heart and mind into them. They will be, for a priestly victim of avarice, nothing more than matters of form and tiresome courtesies. And what are those *unproductive* priestly duties? Catechetical instruction, the preaching that goes with his appointment, the confessional, attending the sick and poor; all these will be the target of his hatred and contempt, as being the enemies of his happiness.

Not all these dark stains defile my conscience; that, I can well and piously believe; but am I sure of not being contaminated by a few drops, so to speak, of this deadly poison in a diluted form? Even diluted they can gradually blacken my soul, obscure my ways of thought and action; they can imperceptibly cast me almost unawares at the feet of the golden calf.

## QUERIES

Instead of *resolutions*, to-day I'm going to put myself some queries on a number of points, with full determination to correct, if necessary, anything crooked or not quite straight and honest, anything unfair or frankly dishonest, that may emerge from this self-examination.

1. Money being the common denominator for all external goods, avarice usually takes the form of avid desire for money—*aeris aviditas;* so, do I experience that immoderate craving for money? has it become a sort of kink in my mind? has it become a minting-machine for converting all my activities of body and soul into money?

2. Is your desire to acquire and hold on to things a desire that goes unrestrained? The principle that should govern this desire is as follows:

> All exterior goods and possessions interchangeable among themselves or exchangeable for money —such is the general meaning of "riches"—are in the nature of useful means to an end; therefore, these goods must necessarily be adjusted to a certain order or measure in keeping with what is necessary or useful for the maintenance of man's life according to his particular state and condition, and in harmony with his eternal interests.

It follows, then, that the practical consideration in matters of desiring, seeking and possessing material goods is simply: "Are they necessary or convenient in order to live?"

3.   The sin of avarice comes in when this practical consideration is set aside, when acquiring and retaining go beyond the limits approved by right reason, for the mere delight of possessing, of continually increasing one's store, or for the purpose of employing possessions in ways that are sinful. The essence of avarice is the immoderate craving to have things. How often have I been unrestrained in my desires? How often have I trespassed, in my desire for gain? How often have I, as a priest, yielded to avarice? Have I struggled with myself in order to acquire the noble virtue of generosity, which moderates according to reason this affection and craving for possession?

4.   Avarice is a twofold disorder:

(a) In acquiring and retaining, it goes beyond what is proper and just, either taking by force what belongs to another or keeping it against the owner's reasonable will; this is avarice in its crudest form of injustice, the avarice of thieves, extortioners, forgers, dishonest administrators, etc. Surely, such ignoble company is not mine! But it is not altogether impossible!

(b) In the affections of the heart towards riches, avarice entails inordinate pleasure and disorder: a too ardent desire or fondness for them, excessive delight and complacency in them, even though there may be no question of wanting to appropriate another's belongings unjustly. This type of avarice, less blameworthy than the former type, is still something base and vile; it is in clean opposition to the virtue of generosity, and, if nurtured, can develop into the first type. Could I swear that I am not a prey to this form of covetousness? If I were, I should sooner or later warrant the terrible words of St. John Chrysostom: "tenebrae animae est pecuniarum cupido"—the craving for money is darkness to the soul.

5. All avarice is a sin, but not all of the same gravity. The first type of avarice we have mentioned is grave sin (*per se, ex genere suo*) with the gravity attaching to theft and robbery; but it could be venial sin through lack of perfect knowledge and wilfulness (*ex imperfectione actus*); or when the quantities concerned are small—*ex parvitate materiae*. If I have committed sins of avarice of this type, have they been grievous sins? If they have, there is a name for me: *thief*.

As regards the second type of avarice: disorderly craving will amount to mortal sin only if I gloat on worldly possessions to the extent of preferring them to charity; that is, if for love of worldly goods I am ready to offend the love of God and the neighbour by breaking some serious precept of the divine law. If I am disposed to forfeit riches rather than offend God in this way, my avarice does not exceed venial sin.

What is my position? Where do I stand as regards my affections for the perishable things of earth? How far do these affections go? Where do I draw the line?

6. In conclusion, have I stooped so far as to convert the corruptible treasures of earth into objects of a spiritual love? Avarice is a spiritual disorder, because what takes delight in the possessing and counting of riches and in gloating over them is not the body but the soul, the soul created to find its delight in God.

That is why St. John calls this vice *concupiscentia oculorum* (I John ii, 16), covetousness of the eyes, that is, of the intelligence. And this is a serious aberration and debasement.

## AVARICE

### SECOND MEDITATION

### *Further Evils of Avarice in the Priest*

#### I

The avaricious priest becomes a stumbling-block to the faithful. According to Church historians, the most balanced and conscientious, one of the sparks that produced the conflagration of Protestantism and caused the explosion of the combustible material piled up by so many abuses and laxity of both people and clergy was the ecclesiastical demand for money, sometimes unjust, sometimes immoderate.

The constant spectacle of a shepherd of souls attached to money soon persuades the people that religion is just another money-making business or concern, a means of livelihood for a person who is either unwilling to earn or incapable of earning a living in any other way.

Eternal and spiritual values are not believed in or are despised, because the master and dispenser of them lives as though for him they did not exist, or as if his only hope was linked up with the tangible good things of earth. If he preaches about spiritual goods, it is taken as a joke, as a hackneyed pulpit theme that nobody believes, least of all the preacher himself; and thus, under the impact of the priest's example, souls will cling more and more firmly to pleasures, honours, and wealth; and religion, if any trace of it should remain, becomes a mixture of Christian formulas and mercenary —not to say ungodly—spirit.

And there are so many instances of this soul-destroying and corroding avarice!

## II

There is a further consideration: this particular vice, with all its ruinous effects on the avaricious person, especially the priest, turns out to be absolutely of no use; it has not the slightest compensation by way of pleasure in his life.

Lord, there is many a time when Thou couldst have asked Thy priests who had enslaved themselves to the cruel demon of covetousness:

> Thou fool! . . . And whose shall those things be which thou hast provided?—(*Luke xii*, 20.)

Upon the wrinkled and frowning brow of the avaricious cleric might well be stamped, in stigmatisation of his foolishness, these sarcastic remarks from the Book of Ecclesiastes:

> "And there was another kind of frustration I marked, here under the sun.
> Here is one that works alone, partner nor son nor brother to aid him, yet still works on, never content with his bright hoard, never asking, as he toils and stints himself, who shall gain by it.
> Frustration and lost labour, here, too."—(*Eccl. iv*, 7-8.)

Brother priest, who is going to inherit from you here

on earth? Who is going to survive you? Who is going to eat and drink the "pretium sanguinis" of your parishioners and of Christ, the fruit of your sordid life, unworthy of God's minister? Who is going to make merry and do himself well on the strength of what your covetous niggardliness kept in hiding and seclusion, like the dragon of the fable? Who is so closely related to you, so deeply loved by you, so near to your heart and so grateful to you for your sacrifices and stintings, that for the sake of leaving him well endowed you even profane your priesthood, make purchaseable products out of your priesthood's sublimest functions, extinguish the flickering flame of conscience, spend your days in sordidness, harrowed by worry, in order to make your little pile? Who ever loved you so much that, with a view to bettering his worldly condition, you do not hesitate to fling your good name to the gossiping public, and your soul to the unquenchable fire?

### III

St. Thomas teaches (*S.T. II-II q.* 118, *a.* 5) that there are graver sins, in themselves, than avarice; most sins are, in fact: those directly affronting and injuring God, those that violate human rights; for the simple reason that avarice has for its object exterior goods, goods very inferior to the Glory of God and the welfare of souls. Avarice, we may say, has to do with goods of the lowest grade. But there is no sin more hideous and indecorous for human dignity than that of enslaving the human will to riches, to things of such paltry value, inferior by far to the things which constitute the object of spiritual vices, lower even than the mire of fleshly wallowing. The basest, the lewdest, the most hideous thing on earth is to identify the soul and its yearnings with these empty shadows of good; because the soul is what it loves: heaven, if in love with heaven; if mud, mud.

And if this applies to every avaricious person, even to the man aspiring after fabulous wealth, what degradation, what sordidness this vice will take on in the priest, who perhaps has to live a beggarly existence in order to save up in shillings and pence!

Avarice is also the most dangerous of vices. Those of the spirit, pride, for example, are cured or relieved by disillusionment; those of the flesh, with all their powerful sting, are mitigated or neutralised by the winter of one's declining years; whereas avarice of its own nature tends to increase with age. The older one gets, the more helpless and needy one becomes and the less one is able to fend for oneself, and therefore, the more avid one is to possess and to hoard, as the only remedy for one's indigence and the only support for one's weakness. Hasn't experience taught a lesson or two in demonstration of this sad fact? How many old people, fast approaching death, already on the threshold of eternity, on those frontiers that allow no earthly chattel to pass through, seem to have no hands or eyes or memory or desire except for the service of their god—money!

## QUERIES

1. Could I swear that I have never committed real injustice: larceny, theft, or fraud, with the goods of my parishioners, of the Church, or of the charitable works, that I administer? The diocesan Authorities may not perhaps be able to convict me, but what about my inmost conscience and God's justice?

2. Have I been scrupulously honest in giving an account of all my administrative acts to the person who, according to Canon Law, has a right and a duty to receive it from me? It would be the best guarantee of my straightforwardness and honesty.

3. Have I ever taken advantage of the faithful's ignorance and demanded more than what is permitted by diocesan regulations or lawful custom in matters pertaining to burials, weddings, and church functions? At the hour of death, will my conscience disturb me on this issue?

4. And while supposing that I have proceeded in everything with absolute justice—the world demands as much of any decent person—do I not demand my rights with excessive haste and harshness, like a tax-gatherer or a moneylender?

5. Apart from everything else, am I not mean in aiding the poor? What alms do I give? What sympathy do I show towards the poor? What do people think of me in this matter, those who know me well? However biassed or distorted their opinion may be, I should do well to find out what it is, not in order to reproach them or to revenge myself, but to arrive at an objective knowledge of myself, to gather clues for passing on myself a correct judgement.

# UNPRIESTLY CONCERN FOR KITH AND KIN

## FIRST MEDITATION

### *Motives for Avoiding it*

### I

We read a significant example of it in the Gospel.
The two brothers, John and James, and their mother
were following our Lord. They had just heard Him
announce His Passion and Death with all harrowing
detail:

> Behold, we go up to Jerusalem, and the Son of
> man shall be betrayed to the chief priests and the
> scribes: and they shall condemn him to death, and
> shall deliver him to the Gentiles to be mocked and
> scourged and crucified.—(*Matt. xx*, 18-19.)

And *then* (says the Gospel), at that very moment
when the forecast of those impending events was steeping the Heart of Christ in bitterness of grief, the im-
petuous mother of the two Apostles goes up to Jesus,
and with much bowing she begins asking Him for something. Womanly shrewdness, but untimely. What is she
going to ask Him for in those circumstances when He
is rather to be consoled than asked to bestow favours
upon others?

> Say that these my two sons may sit, the one on
> thy right hand, and the other on thy left, in thy
> kingdom.

No lack of asking in the dear mother! As the Eternal
Father says to the Son: *Sit on my right hand;* as Pharao

said to Joseph: *Only in the kingly throne will I be above thee;* so the two sons of Zebedee the fisherman should be appointed, thinks their ambitious mother, to the first places in Christ's kingdom.

The other Apostles did not welcome the request, and the Redeemer Himself, while refusing to comply with the untimely and worldly dreams of the mother—and of the sons as well, who seem to have prompted her to ask for them—not only reproaches them for their childish ignorance—*you know not what you ask*—but promises them a place and a dignity very much at variance with the petition:

> Can you drink the chalice that I shall drink? My chalice indeed you shall drink.—(*Matt. xx,* 22-23.)

That is the result of the imprudent mother's hasty request: an infallible announcement of, from a worldly point of view, the tragic fate of her two sons. From that moment, no doubt, the poor mother would keep these words in her heart: not the fulfilment of her dreams, but shafts of burning grief.

> For my thoughts are not your thoughts, nor your ways my ways.—(*Is. lv,* 8.)

Lord, O Lord, make us deaf to the voice of flesh and blood so as to listen intently to Thy call, even though Thou shouldst promise us only painful sharing in Thy Cross and sips of gall from Thy chalice.

## II

Let us take next the example of Jesus Christ, an example that baffles our weak understanding and even seems to cut across the tender love we have for His Blessed Mother.

After three days of anguish, Mary has just found her adolescent Boy, the flower of all grace and beauty; and, in the rush of her motherly affection, she gently chides Him:

> Son, why hast thou done so to us? (*Luke ii*, 48).

The only explanation and consolation He gives is to answer with the words:

> How is it that you sought me? Did you not know that I must be about my Father's business?

That is the standard which should govern our dealings with our kith and kin, not excluding our parents. We owe a primary allegiance to the interests and concerns of our Heavenly Father; parents come after.

Another day, while preaching to His disciples and to the crowds, He is interrupted to be told:

> Behold, thy mother and thy brethren stand without, seeking thee.—(*Matt. xii*, 47.)

Our Lord takes occasion from this to expound His lesson still further:

> Whoever shall do the will of my Father that is in heaven, he is my brother, and sister, and mother.

There was something dearer and more precious to Him than Mary's divine Motherhood: the nobility of souls who are docile to His precepts, as Mary was herself.

At the very moment of dying He reserved for His Mother, who stood at the foot of the Cross—her heart pierced by the sword, as Simeon prophesied, and her whole being drenched in bitter sorrow—only a few words: *Woman, behold thy son* (John xix, 25); whereas from His bloodless and parched lips issued cries of pardon for His executioners and magnificent promises for the repentant thief.

*Durus est hic sermo,* flesh and blood will exclaim; but I do not know, and I doubt whether there can be, a holier and more perfect testimony to the value of our immortal souls.

### III

The priesthood has its demands, and very heavy demands, the same as those of the doctor and the soldier.

The priest is the man of God appointed to look after the interests of God and of souls. He was raised to his high dignity in order to devote himself exclusively to the things of God, as St. Paul teaches with Christ's example before Him : *I must be about my Father's business.* The sole reason for ecclesiastical celibacy, with all its inherent difficulties, is precisely that the priest, in the words of the Apostle, may be " *concerned with the Lord's claim, intent on holiness, bodily and spiritual* " (I Cor. vii, 34), that is to say, free from the thousand and one cares and worries arising from married life in order to devote himself single-mindedly and unfettered to the service of God and the welfare of souls.

If, in spite of my celibacy, my life is constantly tied up with the temporal and selfish aspirations of my relations and the rearing of children not my own, what do I gain by remaining celibate? My sacrifice will be to their advantage, but no one else's. I sacrificed having a wife and children to attend to, I freed myself from the burden of having to please a wife; and yet I am foolishly allowing myself to be yoked to the service of a woman and children who do not belong to me, who perhaps even despise my meaningless celibacy, and are out merely to exploit my celibate condition for their own selfish interests. A sorry sort of celibacy mine is! Sterile for God and the Church! Impotent to prevent my heart from being divided among the multiple vexatious cares of a family and family possessions! What a wretched fate for the most beautiful, radiant, and difficult virtue of the priestly state!

This must not be! O Lord, I choose rather to abide by the Apostle's exhortation:

> "I appeal to you by God's mercies to offer up your bodies as a living sacrifice, consecrated to God and worthy of his acceptance; this is the worship due from you as rational creatures."—(*Rom. xii,* 1.)

Lord, I will keep my chastity and keep it whole and entire for Thee; no, not to increase the material well-being of my father on earth or of my father's children.

## RESOLUTIONS

1. In thought and action I shall be the master of my own house and property, never allowing anyone, not even my own close relations, to administer it independently of me or to treat me as if I were never to be more than a child; and this holds for my parents and brothers and sisters, although I shall not, of course, be mean towards any of them, especially if I am permitted to have them live with me.

2. Apart from my parents or immediate blood relations, whoever serves me will enter into my consideration and treatment as a person hired for services, to whom just wages must be given at the proper times, for instance, each week or once a month. I shall not allow years and years to elapse and wages to accumulate without knowing how much I owe them and without giving them their due; otherwise, besides the countless dangers

of a serious moral nature to which I thus expose myself, I enslave myself to a servant who will soon come to think herself the owner of my belongings—and not without some semblance of truth!—with the result that I shall be unable to dismiss her when the need arises or prevent her appropriating what she likes, with or without my knowledge.

Lord, I do not want to merit the reproach administered by St. Paul when he says:

> "If a man has not learned how to manage his own household, will he know how to govern God's church?"—(*I Tim. iii, 5.*)

## UNPRIESTLY CONCERN FOR KITH AND KIN

### SECOND MEDITATION

*Evils Inherent in this Inordinate Concern*

### I

*Harm to the Church.*—Is the Church suffering to-day from the ill-regulated desire of priests to promote the material welfare of their kith and kin? It is hard to say. But that the Church *has* suffered and suffered grievously in the past, for instance in the sixteenth century, is common knowledge. The sacred Council of Trent assures us with all solemnity that such was the case:

> "The sacred Council, with all the severity at Its command, warns bishops to put aside completely all that merely human concern for brothers and sisters, nephews, and blood relations, which has become a hot-bed of many evils within the Church. And what is said to bishops is decreed not only

for its observance by those obtaining possession of any ecclesiastical benefice, both regular and secular, each in his own sphere, but equally for the Cardinals of the Holy Roman Church."—(*Session xxv, I de Reformat.*)

A "hot-bed of many evils within the Church"—why did not the Council enumerate them? They were there for everyone to see! . . .

Hence that contempt and hatred of the Church, of a Church reduced, in the eyes of Her enemies, to a mere political faction bent on robbing the nation and rifling the national Treasury for Her own selfish interests and those of Her "hangers-on"; hence that vilification of the clergy, when the latter appear desirous of sordid gain even amid the divinest works of the priestly ministry; hence that mistrust of a priest's intentions and even of his faith, and the wholesale squandering of a priest's time and possessions which belong exclusively to God, to the poor, and to souls.

O Jesus, Master of my heart, couldst Thou not whisper to my inmost conscience, like an annoying but true refrain of a song, that complaint which the Council of Trent so sorrowfully voiced to the whole Church:

"Multorum malorum seminarium exstat in hoc tuo humano affectu erga propinquos tuos"?

If this unruly craving is buried in my heart, tear it out, O Lord, tear it out, even if my heart should break under the strain!

## II

*Harm to one's own relatives.*—Experience has taught us time and again that the wealth inherited or received as a gift from clerics does far more harm than good to its possessors. It is put to as little profit as, and even less than, big sums from a national sweepstake. Some how or other it seems to be riddled with the curse of God and brings only misfortune. No wonder there is the old Irish saying: " The priest's money is never lucky " —economic disaster and moral harm in such cases have coined the phrase.

Many souls have become estranged from God on account of the moneys they received from a priest relation. Many a family has abandoned the Church and the way of salvation. There are nephews and nieces and other relations who indulge in an easy-going and idle life, even in a life of vicious habits, on the score that their priest brother or uncle is stinting himself on their behalf and scraping together every penny for love of them. What does it matter if he is nearly killing himself in the process? What concern is it of theirs that he is depriving himself of a decent maintenance? Their path is clear: the money is rolling in, and they're going to spend it, as long as it lasts, on what they like.

But for the subsidies of that poor, anxious cleric they would have to earn their daily bread like any other honest man, and theirs would be that virtue and noble peace which flows from hard-won self-support. But why go to all the trouble if it is their good fortune to have a priest bread-winner to slave for them? Why not drink from the ever-flowing fountain?

Now, has any priest the duty to sacrifice himself so stupidly for kith and kin? Does my conscience reproach me before God?

## III

*Harm to the priest himself.*—Untold harm will come to myself. I shall discharge my ministerial duties badly, because all my energies will be undermined or frittered away or crushed out of me through endless worrying about my people's temporal affairs.

I shall expose myself defenceless to the temptation of wanting to be wealthy—with all the trail of dangers and ruinous consequences that follow from this desire.

> " Those who would be rich fall into temptation, the devil's trap for them ";
> " all those useless and dangerous appetites which sink men into ruin here and perdition hereafter."
> —(I *Tim. vi,* 9.)

And the Apostle adds:

> " The love of money is a root from which every kind of evil springs, and there are those who have wandered away from the faith by making it their ambition, involving themselves in a world of sorrows."—(10.)

Once this desire for wealth takes hold of a priest, Church possessions are not safe in his hands: he will not administer them efficiently, he will even squander them; he will offend against common justice by demanding dues dictated by his own insatiable greed instead of lawful custom and diocesan regulations; with the result that both the priest and his heirs will incur the obligation of making restitution for ill-gotten goods. What a legacy for a priest to leave behind!

And yet the priest should, above all other men, be deeply conscious of St. Paul's bald philosophical statement:

> "Empty-handed we came into the world, and empty-handed, beyond question, we must leave it; why then, if we have food and clothing to last us out, let us be content with that."—(*I Tim. vi*, 7-8.)

The priest cannot argue that he is saving up to leave something for others to inherit: that argument would be valid coming from the father of a family, not from the priest. Since God has been pleased to spare us priests that anxiety, why be so foolish as to go looking for it?

## IV

If we priests burden ourselves with excessive concern for the temporal advancement of relatives and friends we come under the reproach voiced by the Scriptures:

> "Here is one that works alone, partner nor son nor brother to aid him, yet still works on, never content with his bright hoard, never asking, as he toils and stints himself, who shall gain by it. Frustration and lost labour, here too."—(*Eccles. iv*, 8.)

If we haven't the courage to practise absolute renunciation of this world's goods, at least let us have the sense to live at ease, enjoying the emoluments of our labours, free from useless cares. While God may never allow your dreams of leaving your relatives well-endowed, of pushing them into a social position above them, or of pulling them out of tight corners, to materialise, He will not refuse you the little you need for your honest keep.

And if all this doesn't convince you, let us learn from the misfortunes which have overwhelmed so many unwary priests in the past. There are cases of priests who were literally besieged and ransacked by the exorbitant demands of relatives, who thought they had a right to everything when it came to a priest of their own kith and kin; and with implacable cruelty they left him almost penniless. There are instances where decrepit old parish priests had to go to their bishops and ask them on bended knees to remove them from the parish and give them some out-of-the-way chaplaincy to a convent or institution, so as to be free of their relatives' extortionate demands. The poor old priest has perhaps been saving up money year after year, has deposited it in his nephew's name, and is then treated like a beggar by the very people he stinted himself for. Or take the case of a priest who boasted of having been cute enough to keep his last illness a secret from his sister and niece so that at least he might be allowed to die in peace. What he feared to witness actually came about immediately after his death: they sacked the presbytery like a pair of highway robbers.

By what priestly title should I be obliged to undergo such tortures?

## RESOLUTIONS

In my dealings with my relations I shall govern myself by the following rules based on justice and the Canon Law:

1. For the sake of their souls, I will love my relations as Christ would have me love them, taking care to keep them in the holy fear of God and sound morals. What a scandal it is when the priest's own relations are not even good-living Christians, especially if they live with him! In more than one parish, the priest's niece, and even his parents, have been the chief stumbling-block to Christian faith and morals.

2. As regards temporal goods there are three points to consider: (a) what the priest ought not to do; (b) what he is not obliged to do; and (c) what he is lawfully permitted to do.

(a) *What the priest ought not to do*: He ought not to give to his relations the funds belonging to the Church or to pious foundations, or sell to them the immovable goods of the Church. See Canon 1540. He should not hand over to them any "surplus" income from benefice goods, taking the latter in the strict sense; a breach of this kind would not be an injustice (*cfr.* Canon 1473), but it would be against the virtue of religion.

I shall bear in mind the very serious warning of the Council of Trent:

> "The Council absolutely forbids clerics to attempt to enrich their blood-relations and the members of their household with Church revenues, or to make them a gift of ecclesiastical belongings, whose Owner is God; but if their blood-relations and household members be poor, they should be helped like other poor people out of those same goods; these goods should not on their account be made available indiscriminately."—(*Sess. xxv, cap. I, de Reformat.*)

(b) *What the priest is not obliged to do.*—Apart from my parents—whom I must venerate and help by the same titles of justice as any other son—to whom I, as a priest, should attend and for whom I should care, if anything, better than other children, with the knowledge that God, far from holding it against me, will reward me for this greater care; apart from my parents, I have, as a general rule, no obligation to look after the temporal welfare of other members of my family, neither brothers and sisters nor (still less) nieces and nephews; just as a married man has no obligation, usually, towards the temporal welfare of his brothers and sisters, though they be poorer than he. Why should more be required of me because I am a priest? Is it because my studies cost more? In order to become a priest, did I get more than my share of the family budget, at the expense of my brothers and sisters? If needs be, I shall repay in cash what I owe to them, as far as I can; and I shall be quit of further obligations.

(c) *What the priest is lawfully permitted to do.*—I am permitted, by right of justice, to dispose of my non-benefice income in favour of my relations or anyone else I please, whether this income falls to me as the portion of my inheritance or I earn it myself, even by my priestly work; for instance, preaching, stole fees, etc.; on condition that they do not constitute benefice goods in the strict sense of the word. But while keeping within the limits of what I can dispose of lawfully, I shall not forget that I am a priest and that my first household is the Church, my chief relations, the poor.

# HUMILITY

*The Priest's Need of Humility*

## I

Humility consists in a very true knowledge of oneself and self-contempt based upon that knowledge: *sui ipsius verissima cognitio et despectio*. But self-contempt of the right type, not the kind that, if carried too far, would lead to a moral breakdown. For, as Lactantius says when reproaching the old pagans with this false humility: *Ne se tam opere despiciant, neve se infirmos et supervacuos et nihili et frustra omnino natos putent; quae opinio plerosque ad vitia compellit*—let them not despise themselves so utterly, or think themselves so weak and useless and devoid of purpose in life, because that idea of theirs drives many of them to vice.

No; man is something great; the world and all its wonders were devised for him alone, to provide him with a habitation; he was created to know God, his Father and the Creator of the universe; and as a Father man worships Him, serves, loves, and reveres Him; thus meriting to enter into His Father's inheritance, into everlasting Life, into the Kingdom of God. This is the great mystery of man: of man who in outward appearance would seem as lowly as the creatures that do not survive the dust of earth.

The human being is of infinite worth: the very Son of God became Man, and for mankind He shed His Blood, and raised man to a level where he might share in the Nature of God Himself: *Divinae consortes Naturae.*

And I, as a priest, over and above all other titles to respect, have that participation in Christ's Eternal Priesthood, that ineffable power to change the substances of bread and wine into His Body and Blood, and that equally unspeakable power to reach right down to the centre of the human soul in order to cleanse it from the leprosy of sin.

O God, I have no right to despise myself; like the humble Virgin of Nazareth, I have the right and duty to sing:

> Magnificat anima mea Dominum. . . .
>
> Quia fecit mihi magna qui potens est.—(*Luke i*, 46.)

Great wonders, O God, Thou hast wrought in me; wonders that would be dismissed as incredible, were it not for the lamp of Christian Faith which enlightens them and me.

From now on, Lord, I shall esteem myself as Thy child, as a vessel of clay, no doubt, but a vessel brimming over from the torrents of Thy gracious Bounty.

## II

The tragedy is that these great wonders and mercies are not usually the things which fascinate me and sweep me off my feet, they are not the things that fill me with pride. No, the sin of pride, says St. Chrysostom, belongs to small-minded people. I take pride in the supposed riches of my intellect: I'm clever, wise, and have a keen sense of justice; I'm not like the other fellow—as the puffed-up pharisee would say.

For the sake of argument let me just suppose that, really, I am outstanding in talent and good qualities: I shone in my class as a student, I put my fellow-students in the shade; and now the praises of my priestly virtue and ability are being sung for miles around. Moreover, let me suppose that this opinion of myself is not the outcome of stupid vanity; I'm not blinded by vanity, like so many others of my acquaintance who entertain the very same opinion of themselves; no—for argument's sake—it is an unchallengeable fact—which is saying a lot!—and everybody else feels about me the same as I do, or even better than I do. Now, without comparing myself with others, what "riches" does my privileged intellect enshrine? What knowledge do I possess? What truths have I discovered for myself? What chasm depths have I penetrated and scrutinised? Yes, I have a few shallow notions stored up in my memory, the fruit of random reading; but could I reduce them to any semblance of order? Do I venture to call wisdom and knowledge a certain facility for stringing a few words together and giving a bit of polish to an odd phrase or two? Am I to go down in history as a man of learning, as an intellectual star of the first or tenth magnitude? The plain truth is that I know very little, and what little I do know I know very imperfectly, and I know it because I've taken it from a book. My boast of cleverness and learning is something very hollow, ridiculous, puerile.

And what about the pride I take in my moral goodness? Could I call myself good when face to face with the Crucifix or my own conscience? Have I forgotten all my disloyalties? Have the unruly cravings of the flesh left no trace in my memory or in my flesh of shameful condescensions? And even if, by God's special mercy, I am gradually and reluctantly gaining the upperhand over them, can't I see clearly that, but for this

Mercy, and left to my own devices, those same cravings would soon turn my heart into a cesspool, and would tear to rags and tatters the precious vesture of my nobility of soul and my priestly dignity?

O Jesus, Scrutiniser of hearts and souls, I confess in Thy sight that each time I boasted of my learning I was a fool; each time I gloried in my personal goodness, I was a whited sepulchre.

### III

And if pride has made me ambitious; if I have aspired to the limelight; if I have sought to have my own way and thought myself worthy of the highest preferences, complaining within myself unashamedly when those preferences were not held out to me, ascribing it to malicious intent on the part of my superiors, and not for a moment to my personal short-comings intellectual and moral. . . . And if, by devious ways and means, my search for the high places was crowned with success, I arrived at the titles of *Lord* and *Master*, was reverenced in the market place and in Church assemblies; I now confess before Thee, O God crucified and sacramentally abased in the Tabernacle, I confess that I have not understood the lesson Thou taughtest at the Last Supper:

> It shall not be so among you: but whosoever will be the greater among you, let him be your minister.
>
> And he that will be first among you shall be your servant.
>
> Even as the Son of man is not come to be ministered unto, but to minister and to give his life a redemption for many.—(*Matt. xx,* 26-28.)

And if, after reaching the (more or less) high dignities of the Church—whatever the approach may have been: by the front door or *aliunde,* as our Lord would say—and safely ensconced therein, I began to think myself superior to the rest of men, even above my peers in hierarchical dignity—the " other priests "—and swelled with pride, taking the richly embroidered vestments and precious ornaments and extrinsic titles befitting my rank as signs and symbols of my own personal worth, as though I were no longer a fellow-servant of my brethren, even the lowliest; as though no one should dare call me my mother's son; if I have stuck my nose into the air and drawn myself up and raised my eyebrows and demanded the courtesy given to God; if to those who humbled themselves before me, perhaps because their daily bread depends on me, I have replied —if indeed any reply has been forthcoming—with disdain and arrogance; if I have made myself unapproachable to others, except through the valley of fear and dread; to others who, to say the least, are also children of God the same as myself . . . ah, then, besides exposing to hatred and contempt an ecclesiastical authority which is but a participation of the Fatherly Authority of God and of the merciful Dominion of Christ over souls purchased by His love and blood, how can I evade the curse fulminated by Holy Scripture?

He that exalteth himself shall be humbled.— (*Luke xviii,* 14.)

A most severe judgement shall be for them that bear rule.—(*Wisdom vi,* 6.)

## Resolutions

1. By God's grace, I shall overcome that smallmindedness which sometimes proceeds from pride, at

other times from mere cowardice, but invariably issues from effeminacy and laziness; I shall re-act strongly against it, considering that any priest, however untalented, can do an immense good, both by administering the Sacraments assiduously—where the divine effects are produced partly *ex opere operato*—and by zealously instructing, exhorting, going in search of, souls; all of which requires mainly will-power and a burning love for God and souls, rather than a mind teeming with lofty thoughts.

2. I renew a resolution I took before: not to aspire after ecclesiastical dignities along any but the most lawful channels; and if I do not get them, instead of murmuring against human injustices, I shall silently adhere to the Will of God, without Whose permission not a leaf stirs upon a tree; and I shall establish myself in the conviction that God's Will is for the best, and perhaps my being denied such and such a dignity is one of God's greatest mercies towards me. Surely I have seen how, for some, their elevation to high office was the beginning and the occasion of their own undoing both spiritual and temporal.

3. If, in God's inscrutable Designs, I should come to be burdened with those high dignities, I shall struggle against all self-elation; I shall retain my sense of proportion, of my own lowliness in the eyes of God and those of my own conscience, knowing as I do that there is much in me of base and vile; and I shall treat my equals, and especially those subordinate to me, with all kindness and courtesy, after the manner of Christ

> " Whose nature is, from the first, Divine, and yet he did not see, in the rank of Godhead, a prize to be coveted."

No, He did not imperiously demand that at every moment men should be in fear and trembling in His Presence, as in the awe-inspiring Presence of God; He waived aside, as it were, all preferential treatment,

> "he dispossessed himself, and took the nature of a slave, fashioned in the likeness of men, and presenting himself to us in human form; and then he lowered his own dignity, accepted an obedience which brought him to death, death on a cross." (*Philip. ii, 5-8.*)

Jesus, no, I do not want to stoop so low as to act the part of the heathen; I do not wish to make myself a little tin-god with those ecclesiastical dignities instituted by Thee and Thy holy Church, not for the sake of creating repulsion, but in order to attract souls to their Redeemer.

# MEEKNESS

## FIRST MEDITATION

### Christian Motives

#### I

Let Christ's example spur us on to acquire the virtue of meekness. Not content with staking a claim to meekness—*Learn of me, for I am meek and humble of heart (Matt. xi, 29)*—He proved His possession of it by countless acts of perfect Self-mastery. How obvious it is, from the Gospel, that not once did the eruptions of anger obfuscate the august serenity of His wonderfully clear mind and powerful will! Neither the tirades bespattered with insults, nor the vile calumnies which no one could prove, nor ignominious buffetings, scourgings, blows, and spittle. At every hour, in the most trying circumstances, the words of Isaias apply to Him most aptly :

> "Lamb that stands dumb while it is shorn; no word from him."—(*Is. liii,* 7.)

No wonder St. Paul, in summing up the character of the Messiah, tells us

> "Then the kindness of God, our Saviour, dawned on us, his great love for man."
>
> —(*Titus iii,* 4);

and the Baptist, when setting eyes on Jesus, sums up the divine graciousness of everything about Him in the lovely expression :

> Behold the lamb of God!

439

And that loving-kindness is symbolised even by the
Holy Spirit—Whom Moses called a " devouring Fire "
—by appearing in the form of a dove. And the Church,
Christ's Bride, glories in the title " Holy Mother
Church "—a title given Her by the same Divine Spirit.
Kind and loving She is, because holy; kinder and more
loving still, because She is a Mother. *Holy Mother* is
applied analogically to the mightiest Empire the world
has ever seen, the most widespread and most deeply
revered Authority on earth; but greater Power has Her
Founder, and He affirms categorically of Himself: " I
am meek and humble of heart."

## II

The words " humanity " and " humaneness " signify
meekness and mercifulness. By nature, man possesses
no other weapons with which to win over the hearts of
other men. If other weapons there are, to turn the world
upside-down and sow the seeds of terror and death, it
is men themselves who have deliberately fashioned them.
Such weapons of force were given by God to animals.
To me God gave for my only defence wisdom and
gentle persuasion: so often a source of strength
unmatched by swords and cannon.

If this does not convince me, let me convince myself
that there is nothing more fruitful for good than love,
nothing more sterile than hatred. What good does
history record ever came from hatred? Hatred is as
fruitless as fire and death; hatred dissolves, sterilises,
and kills every living germ of goodness.

Happy the priest who, disarmed of all hatred even in
persecution the most iniquitous, even when anger would
seem the heart's natural flowering of strength and

wounded dignity's inevitable redress, can quench the flame and say with St. Ambrose: "My prayers and my tears are the only weapons I wield"—*Preces et lacrymae meae mea arma sunt.* If they do not always succeed in leading souls to goodness and to God, they will never lead to evil and to Hell.

### III

Forbearance and gentleness, you'll say perhaps, is beyond you; your temperament doesn't allow you to be meek; and, after all, who can subjugate the wild impulses of the heart?

That you can't give copious alms, because you haven't the means; yes, I understand that; but meekness and kindly dealing with others is not from the pocket, it issues from the heart:

> "A good man utters good words from his store of goodness."—(*Matt. xii*, 35.)

Or is it that you haven't got a heart? Or is there nothing in your heart but bitter gall? Are you as bad as all that?

The least you can do is to abide by what the Gospel commands:

> Do unto others as you would have them do unto you.

What is it that rankles in your mind, that has been the cause of bitterness, that you find the hardest to forget and forgive? Perhaps the bad treatment or raw deal you thought you received from those in charge. How often and how bitterly you have resented it! But haven't other people, however lowly their station, feelings as well? Haven't they the same rights to consideration as you?

Continuing in self-defence, you will allege that you are harsh by nature, of an austere type of temperament. Well then, if you are not ready to soften down a little, keep on with your harshness and austerity, but turn them on yourself alone. "Be austere towards yourself," says St. Augustine, "towards others be kindly; let people hear you giving few orders and accomplishing great things."

### RESOLUTION

I shall be obliging in everything and towards every one, great and small, so long as I can be so without infringing the demands of duty, the rights of God and my neighbour; limits which no kindness may ever transgress.

## MEEKNESS

### SECOND MEDITATION

#### Priestly Motives

#### I

If in the course of our priestly ministry we are to do any good to souls we need respect, but unless we curb our anger we run the risk of placing ourselves in situations that ill befit our priestly condition and make us appear contemptible. People will not fear us because of our anger; fits of bad temper convict us of weakness and invite ridicule. And let us remember this: apart from a few places, where respect for the priest is very solidly established and where the priest enjoys a particularly high social status, the Catholic priest, no matter what his rank within the Church's Hierarchy, means very little, as a priest, to society at large. People are absolutely at liberty to approach us, if they will; if not, we shall be left to kick our heels in the most appalling loneliness. So why get upset? Why shout and let off steam in outbursts of impotent rage, the effect of which would be merely to repel people?

On the other hand, what great respect and love and esteem is given to the priest who knows how to be gentle and forbearing! How the priest, who by the grace of God and by his own sustained efforts has mastered his angry impulses, attracts and captivates!

Having learned first to wield absolute sovereignty over the domains of his own soul, having checked the brutal thrust of his own passions with the bridle of grace and reason, he has mastery over others. Like a keeper who has tamed wild beasts, he has other souls at his command.

This, in many priests, is the source of the great good they do and of the obedience so willingly rendered to them; not their learning, which is nothing extraordinary; not their wealth, which they do not possess; not the influence of friends or of politicians, a hindrance rather than a help to them; no, it is their kindness and gentleness that suffice; they make themselves all to all men; they maintain their self-control; and thus, by their quiet manner and gracious words, they are able to witness even in this life the fulfilment of the Beatitude:

> Blessed are the meek, for they shall possess the land.

## II

Unfortunately, among the clergy, in every rank, there are to be found unpleasant characters, embittered souls, as high-voltaged, it would seem, as electric storm clouds. A sad fact which does us very little honour, being so much at variance with the spirit of Christ, who came not to destroy or to terrorise. No man more self-adapting, more gracious and better-mannered, than the Virgin's Son.

Brusqueness of manner does not square with our task of winning souls over by our speech; the words that enthrall and conquer are not tempestuous words. Anger is not in keeping with our position as gentlemen of good breeding and manners. If genuine good manners are simply the spontaneous expression of inward goodness made manifest in words and actions, of whom more than of the priest can this inward goodness be expected? The priest, above all men, is called upon to bear out the words of Christ:

"A good man utters good words from his store of goodness."

He is not expected to bring from his heart a store of vinegar and gall, fire and fury, nettles and thorns.

If the world, so trained in the art of apparent good manners, detects a streak of inhumanity in you, it will form its own conclusions; namely, you are uncouth because you are unfamiliar with your social medium, and the intolerance you show is to be attributed to the fact that you were suddenly and without due preparation "jumped up" socially; you were lifted out of an inferior social stratum and made to live among educated people; and therefore, in your proud conceit and miscalculation you thought that by arching or knitting your eyebrows, by blowing alternately hot and cold of temper, you would succeed in convincing others of your immense superiority over them, and would display your

*Savoir faire* in the craft of bringing your subjects to heel.

O God, however eminent the dignity of Thy priests, do not withhold from them that courtesy and good manners which even among many souls who are entirely estranged from Thee have a captivating and irresistible power.

## III

This " benignitas " is for St. Paul something more than good manners, it is the flower of all virtue, the proof that charity abides in us: the charity which surpasses the gifts of tongues and prophecy, almsgiving, even martyrdom itself. When St. Paul comes to analyse the essence of charity, he does not enter into lofty theological disquisitions, he makes this sovereign virtue consist in something that is eminently practical, homely, and of everyday life:

" Charity is patient, is kind; charity feels no envy;

" Charity is never perverse or proud, never insolent;

" Does not claim its rights, cannot be provoked, does not brood over an injury;

" Takes no pleasure in wrongdoing, but rejoices at the victory of truth;

" Sustains, believes, hopes, endures, to the last."
—(*I Cor. xiii,* 4-7.)

Endow a soul with that rich store of qualities, and you will have a paragon of kindness, thoughtfulness, courtesy, meekness. Such a soul will be fashioned after the likeness of Christ, the great Model, who in His dealings with men was full of exquisite graciousness; he will be like St. Paul, whose letters, besides being treatises of Christian belief and its adaptation to human speech, may well be taken as a handbook of social propriety and dignified courtesy.

Dear Lord, that is my ambition. May the warmth of Thy grace dry up in my embittered heart every source of rudeness, harshness, and arrogant pride.

### RESOLUTION

To the best of my ability I shall avoid the occasions that provoke me to anger, because I realise that with this particular passion, as with lust, it is flight that makes for conquest; and the most dangerous occasion of exceeding the bounds of moderation is to indulge in arguing. How few succeed in remaining calm and composed amid the tumult of an argument! I shall follow the advice given by the Apostle:

"A servant of the Lord has no business with quarrelling; he must be kindly towards all men, persuasive and tolerant,

"With a gentle hand for correcting those who are obstinate in their errors."—(*II Tim. ii*, 24-25.)

If the Apostle demands gentleness and affability in the defence of the truth already known, what should we expect him to demand when the argument deals with mere opinions?

"There must be no wordy disputes, such as can only unsettle the minds of those who are listening."
—(*II Tim. ii*, 14.)

Such is the effect of mere controversy, according to the Apostle of the Gentiles; instead of clarity, darkness, doubt, anger, and an unsettled mind. These are the bitter and poisonous fruits we have tasted ourselves whenever we have argued for argument's sake; therefore, I shall never allow myself to be drawn into a heated discussion; and if I am requested to take part, I shall know what answer to give:

"And if anyone is prepared to argue the matter, he must know that no such custom is found among us, or in any of God's churches."—(*I Cor. xi*, 16.)

# MODERATION IN SPEECH

*Motives*

## I

Let us by-pass the great defects: blasphemy, cursing, perjury, obscenity . . . we are dealing in terms of Christian and priestly perfection. All the while, however, let us be alive to the possibility of our easily stooping to calumny or of becoming an accomplice and thorough-going purveyor of calumny. Of this possibility there is observable, even in pious people, in religious, in priests, a symptom that is unmistakable: the tendency to disbelieve or give little adherence to the good that is reported of our neighbour. We want substantial evidence, we fear an exaggeration; and even when a thorough investigation establishes the fact, we begin to query our neighbour's good intentions; or else we forget the good report, as being of trivial importance. The evil we hear, on the other hand, would seem to commend itself to our ready acceptance; we are inclined to take it almost as an article of faith at the first intimation; one witness is enough, no matter how little trustworthy; or rather, we have no need of witnesses, we don't want them; the slightest rumour commands our assent without our going to the trouble of asking from what low-down haunts the pestilential breath of gossip arose. Why should this be? Belief belongs to a great extent to the will—*motus voluntatis*—so we believe what we wish to believe; and thus we believe the evil about our neigh-

448

bour because it gives us a sort of joy and satisfaction, whereas we reject belief in the good because in some way it pains us to see our neighbour possessed of something good, it clashes with our own self-interests; therefore we are more pleased to hear evil of our neighbour than good. Such are the *pious* instincts we harbour in our hearts, however much we try to camouflage them with the holiest of appearances.

If this analysis corresponds to facts, would it not be enough to make any right-minded person reject off-hand all imputation of blame against his neighbour? At least, in the words of Fr. Avila, until he had given to the accused or calumniated thirty days in which to defend himself? Even the greatest criminal is not denied this right by the law of the land.

## II

The tongue is one of the bodily members subject to the sovereign jurisdiction of the will, its acts are commanded by the will—*actus imperati*—like those of the hands and the feet; and more so than the acts of eyes, ears, and imagination. The tongue is in bondage to the free will.

But the free will in all its operations, elicited and commanded, should be governed by the dictates of right reason and moral principle; and the tongue is no exception. Consequently, every word that strays from this simple and obvious rule is to be considered morally defective, a sin; more or less grievous according to the speaker's intentions, the gravity of the matter, and other circumstances.

In the light of this plain reasoning, how clearly I see the distance I have to travel before I acquire mastery

P

over the tongue's domain! A domain of insignificant dimensions, it would appear, but a domain vast enough for the tongue to run amok as a slave, not to reason or faith, but to caprice, to a riotous imagination, or to the basest appetites of lust, envy, and anger!

### III

Many advantages accrue from the right use of the tongue. Prudence, for example.

> "Where least is said, most prudence is."
> —(*Prov. x*, 19.)

And prudence is the standard measure for all human life; without prudence the good becomes weakness and turns into evil.

Peace of mind is another advantage:

> "Guard lips and tongue, as thou wouldst guard thy life from peril."—(*Prov. xxi*, 23.)

Peace of mind is imperilled, countless griefs gnaw the heart, when the tongue goes unchecked. Which of us has never known the torture of an untimely or imprudent word, that could not be taken back?

And which of us would have suspected that Christian perfection, that high estate to which our Divine Lord so eagerly invites us, could be purchased at the small price of keeping the tongue under control? Yet that is the mind of the Apostle St. James:

> "A man who is not betrayed into any faults of the tongue must be a man perfect at every point."
> —(*James iii*, 2.)

## IV

Let us follow up the thoughts of St. James concerning the tongue's tremendous power for evil, as he sets them down in the lively third chapter of his Canonical Epistle. The unrestrained tongue produces evils beyond computation, but this is what he says: to curb the tongue is to curb the whole body, just as by putting a curb in their mouths we can make horses obey us and we can turn their whole bodies this way and that; just as with a tiny rudder a huge ship, driven along by boisterous winds, is steered by the ship's pilot in the direction he wills; just as a small spark is enough to set fire to a vast forest. And this, precisely, is what the tongue is: a raging fire, fire caught from hell itself, a fire that devastates the whole course of our lives. Everything that is harmful seems to find its natural abode in the ungoverned tongue. It defies all mere human effort to tame it down. It is a pest that is never allayed, all deadly poison, a source of infection to the whole body. Why should this be? asks the Apostle. Why should we use it to bless God our Father, and at the same time use it to curse our fellow men, who were made in God's image? Blessing and cursing from the same mouth!

> " My brethren, there is no reason in this. Does the fountain gush out fresh and salt water from the same outlet? . . . can a fig-tree yield olives, or a vine figs? No more easily will brackish water yield fresh."—(*Cfr. James iii*, 1-12.)

If these terrible truths remained only on paper! But is it not truer to say that they are engraved on my life with the corrosive ink of the many ravages that immoderation in speech has inflicted upon me?

With subtle discernment the same Apostle singles out

the good or evil use of the tongue as the mark of true or false piety:

> "If anyone deludes himself by thinking he is serving God, when he has not learned to control his tongue, the service he gives is vain."
>
> —(*James* i, 26.)

### RESOLUTIONS

1. I shall attach far greater importance to short-comings of the tongue, examining them more seriously and frequently at night, taking them as subject-matter for my weekly confession, and, if needs be, making my daily particular examen before my midday and evening meals on this particular weakness of mine if I find it hard to cure.

2. Seeing that, according to St. James, "no human being has ever found out how to tame the tongue", I shall ask God for this mercy, knowing that "it is the part of man to prepare the soul, and of the Lord to govern the tongue". (*Prov. xvi*, 1.) I shall beg God to hold my tongue in check, and not to permit the monstrosity of its being used at one and same time to bless Him and to curse man, who is made to His image and likeness. When any special danger looms ahead I shall try to forestall lapses of the tongue by reciting the words of the psalm:

> Pone, Domine, custodiam ori meo, et ostium circumstantiae labiis meis; non declines cor meum in verba malitiae ad excusandas excusationes in peccatis.—(*Ps. cxl*, 3-4.)

"Lord, set a guard on my mouth, post a sentry before my lips; do not turn my heart towards thoughts of evil, that point the way to wrong-doing."

# MODERATION IN SPEECH

## *Means*

### I

I shall carry out the excellent advice given by St. James the Apostle when he says, in words that might worthily take rank among the sentences of the Book of Proverbs:

> "It is for us men to be ready listeners, slow to speak our minds, slow to take offence."
>
> —(*James i*, 19.)

If only I possessed that lovable characteristic, that quality so precious, because so rare, of knowing how to listen; how to listen to my neighbour intently, with lively interest, with joy, without ill-humoured and disdainful haste; I should run less risks than in speaking, and I should learn a vast amount of good I am now ignorant of, or which I know but very indifferently; and I should gain the good will of my neighbour into the bargain. How flattered we all are when people listen to us, though our speech should dwell on mere trivialities! I must confess that people are never more congenial to me, however well-spoken they may be, than when they give me a good hearing, and, by their kind attentiveness, take stock of my views without interrupting and, much less, contradicting me.

But we should also be "slow to speak our minds", more especially when anger or any other passion gets hold of us. When in a passionate mood, it is preferable to refrain even from saying what in itself is good. And that goes also for the word of God, because in the pulpit we must be aware that

> " Man's anger does not bear the fruit that is acceptable to God."—(*James i*, 20.)

I shall bring passion into my service, but only as a helpmate under the wise discretion of the mind, to whom it belongs to give orders as to how and when passion should communicate colour and movement and life and persuasive, emotional force to my words. Never should passion become tyrannical mistress of my speech.

## II

I shall banish from my lips, as being unworthy of a man, of a gentleman, and of a priest, all manner of lying; so that it may be said of me with all sincerity and justification:

> One that is a priest . . . he will not deceive us.
> —(*I Machab. vii*, 14.)

All deception, fraud, and simulation are a disgrace to our cloth. Trivial as a lie may appear, it will always be, in the sight of the divine Scrutiniser of hearts, an evil infinitely greater than the evils I may wish to avoid by lying.

From my lips not a word, from my hands not a deed, redolent of flattery. Flattery is always a lie, a low-down lie because of the unconfessable aims it usually pursues; a lie that is detrimental both to the person indulging in it and to the one who is simple or vain enough to accept it.

Towards my own hierarchical Superiors I shall be

deferential, respectful, perhaps even very friendly; but servile and fawning, never. No smoke of incense has blinded more eyes and caused more tears to flow than the incense of flattery.

And what about the itch to argue and to contradict just for argument's and contradiction's sake? I shall loathe it as something stupid, unmannerly, insufferable. Tolerance for all shades of opinion, as long as they are opinions not at variance with dogmatic truth, defined morals, or another's rights, ranks high among the loveliest virtues that adorn the human soul. It is more important to live in peace than to see my views prevail.

Excessive jocularity, when habitual, easily degenerates into buffoonery, insults, impudence; it stoops to coarse scurrility. Very few have the enviable gift of a restrained and delightful sense of humour, the cream of human talent.

And, in due measure, I shall love and practise silence, so useful to the religious man and priest. If I whittle my life away in garrulous nonsense, when or where shall I find time and leisure for my devotional exercises and for serious reflections on the eternal truths? When shall I devote myself to study, which is absolutely indispensable to me if I am not to forfeit my standing as a man of education, and render myself incapable of rising to the high demands of my life's calling?

Woe betide me if I am unable to control myself in the matter of speaking or remaining silent when my conscience bids! How many very grave indiscretions and sacrileges and crimes my talkativeness could expose me to! The priest has to be a closed and sealed coffer— such is the nature and quality of the secrets confided to his keeping; secrets natural, professional, sacramental or quasi-sacramental, which he has to guard with impenetrable reserve; secrets that no human force or power of persuasion or threats and torments or death itself should avail to rifle and wrench from him.

Do I measure up to these lofty standards? Or do I bring my priestly ministry into disrepute through my womanish indiscretions of the tongue?

# ENVY

*Its Malice and Destructiveness*

## I

" Peace of mind is health of body; more than all else, envy wastes the frame."—(*Prov. xiv,* 30.)

There is nothing like envy for spreading sickness of mind and heart throughout the whole body, until it eats into the very marrow of the bones. Envious people, we may say, adapting a quotation from Shakespeare,

... like serpents are, who though they feed
On sweetest flowers, yet they poison breed.

Let us see how this is.

We know, from that very human and consoling Dogma of the Communion of the Saints, that Christian charity, in rejoicing over another's well-being, makes it part of one's own possession. You do a good work, and I, through the medium of my sympathetic rejoicing, convert its supernatural substance into something which belongs to me as well; I appropriate to myself something of its satisfactory and impetratory value, and, in a certain sense, even its personal merit, on account of my noble attitude towards your well-being. You see? It is the bee sucking honey from sweetest flowers; it is health of body from a sound heart and a peaceful mind.

On the other hand, if I envy you for the good you have done, my envy not only misses the opportunity of making that good my own, it is fain to destroy whatever good you possess. Envy would rather your good did not exist, did not give glory to God or service to the neighbour; it begrudges you the merit of climbing a step higher up the path of moral goodness and perfection. And yet everyone else rejoices at the good you have done: God, His holy angels, the just, the sound of mind and the upright of heart. Only two beings are sad, only two people fret and consume with anguish—the devil and envious me! What blindness! To perish by what brings health to others! To waste away on the strength of what imparts life and joy! What a dreadful calamity: another's gain, my loss; the good tidings of others, my sentence of doom!

Envy is certainly the dark secret of those

> "who though they feed on sweetest flowers, yet
> poison breed."

The miserable process continues. Because you did well, I am filled with grief; therefore, how I should rejoice if you did wrong, if you were incompetent and wicked and a stumbling-block to others! I rejoice at your misfortune. My joy feeds on what the Vulgate calls *putredo ossium,* rotten bones; your own undoing.

How very low envy can thrust me! How envy can befoul the heart of man, the heart created to fill with God and to say with Him:

> Well done! thou good and faithful servant; enter
> into the joy of thy Lord!

## II

Envy is a fire devouring and destroying every germ of life. Envy, by its very nature, is death and deals death, being born of Satan, who *was a murderer from the beginning.* (*John viii,* 44.) It was envy that instigated him to bring about the fall of our first parents, and *by*

*the envy of the devil death came into the world.*
(*Wisdom ii, 24.*) Envy was the evil genius which inspired
the first human murderer to assassinate his own brother,
on the noble score that this brother of his was a better
man than he. It is envy that has put weapons into the
hands of man, and so blinded man as to make him
commit the foulest crimes that have ever stained the
face of this earth. It was envy which challenged God
Himself, persecuted Him, calumniated Him, nailed Him
to the wood of the Cross—

> For he (Pilate) knew that for envy they had
> delivered him.—(*Matt xxvii,* 13.)

No other passion could go to such an extreme; only
in envy does there remain not a trace of common
humanity. Our Lord's enemies saw that He preached
better than they, though they were supposedly the sole
custodians of the Law; they saw that the people admired
and revered Him more highly than them; they could not
hope to reproduce, much less surpass, the wonders He
wrought, the admirable holiness of life that was His, His
greatness of mind; and so they found but one expedient:
to kill Him. Had it been in their power to reduce Him
to His lowly station in life as a carpenter, perhaps they
would not have thought of crucifying Him.

O the Satanic love of self, self above all else, what
power it can command! In order to defend its own
interests, envy would sweep everything away, would
annihilate even God Himself. No wonder the serpent
of envy is loth to come out in its true colours, but seeks
every possible device of camouflage, and hides itself in
the grass among the flowers! Thus, for example, the
Pharisees donned the mask of zeal for the Law of Moses
and the common good of the nation:

This man is not of God who keepeth not the sabbath.—(*John ix*, 16.)

The Romans will come, and take away our place and nation.—(*John xi*, 48.)

If with courage and determination I probe the inner recesses of my own conscience and tear away every mask, I may well discover twisted round many of my ambitions and my bitter disappointments the serpent coils of envy.

### III

Envy, as a passion, is a specific form of zeal. To be "jealous" is closely akin to being "zealous", the difference being that jealousy is brought about by vehement self-love, or the love of someone whom I identify with my self-love; whereas zeal is born of my intense love for a fellow-creature or for God. We are envious or jealous, essentially, because we wrongly feel that the prestige or wealth or welfare which might be ours is enjoyed by another. The effect of envy is an impulse and an endeavour proceeding from the irascible appetite against any person whose possession of something we should like for ourselves seems unjustly to deprive us of it; in short, the effect of envy is an instinctive snatching from another for ourselves, or at least for the satisfaction of seeing the other person without the thing we begrudge him.

If I am envious of another priest, I shall be saddened at his enjoyment of prestige and power: the prestige that comes to him for working harder than myself, for winning more souls to God than I do, for establishing pious and social Associations, for being respected as a holy, humble, and learned priest. All this becomes for me a source of bitter regret; and, in consequence, my irascible appetite becomes irritated, devises ways and means of bringing all those good things to nought. And if I should succeed in my aims, I shall take a vile complacency in seeing my rival priest less virtuous and less highly esteemed; I shall stand by and gloat on the spectacle when that priest's works come crashing down and his power over souls diminishes. My grief will turn to delight—the delight experienced by Satan at the sight of Adam and Eve become enemies of God, the satisfaction that puffed up the perverse heart of Cain when he saw his brother Abel, the preferred of God, dead and bathed in his blood.

And all these horrors, the natural outcome of envy, arise when I am not guided by the prinicples of faith, when I care not a straw for God's glory and the welfare of souls; that is, when I foster but one love, self-love; the cruel idol at whose altar I have slaughtered every other love.

A very sombre picture, but a very true one, of the envious priest; even though he himself may fail to recognise his own resemblance, even though he may cast about for specious motives, religious motives perhaps, in order to disguise his grovelling passion.

## IV

Let us probe still deeper. How many works of zeal have miscarried because of envy! How many excellent priests have been scared to undertake these works for fear of dire persecution which envy had plotted against them, or have called off the good begun in view of the fury excited thereby in envious hearts or because of the unjust denunciations—all, of course, under the mask of zeal for the House of the Lord!—in which vile emulation had involved them!

In every age—and there is no reason to exempt our own—envy has proved itself to be a diabolic steriliser of the holiest of priestly endeavours. Satan knows this well, he is the father of envy, and his triumph is secured once he has found a collaborator among our own priestly ranks. It is enough to poison a priest's heart with his own envy, and the corrosive will be a death-blow to the most glorious works of Christ's most saintly ministers.

Can I solemnly swear to Thee, O Jesus, that in the whole course of my ministerial life I have never been chosen by the infernal monster to collaborate in any of his evil designs?

### RESOLUTIONS

1.  The hardest resolve is that of owning up to the fact that we *are* envious and jealous. We may readily confess to being proud, overbearing, sensual, etc., but who acknowledges himself to be envious? Who is ready to admit that he has been tarred with the black brush of envy? No vice more intent on disguise. How difficult and rare it is to say: " Father, I'm jealous, the good qualities of another fill me with envy; in such-and-such circumstances I criticised him out of pure jealousy; I bore him ill-will because I envied him."

Lord, I promise Thee that I shall open my heart wide in order to detect any hatred or antipathy that may be nestling inside it, and in order to know exactly which and how many of these sentiments are nothing but the products of envy.

2. I will not speak ill of those against whom this passion blinds me.

3. With my own hands I shall suffocate the first promptings of envy, and, under the guidance of faith-inspired motives, I shall not withhold my approval and even my active support, if I can be of help, from any priest who is working fruitfully in the Lord's vineyard.

# AMBITION

*Christ's Example and Precept*

## I

Christ is our Model, and He was not ambitious. As St. Paul says:

> " His nature is, from the first, divine, and yet he did not see, in the rank of Godhead, a prize to be coveted."

He did not wish to make His divine dignity overwhelmingly conspicuous at every hour to the minds of the men with whom He conversed. He was not like those kings of old, of whom it was said: They took their crown and sceptre with them when they retired for the night's rest. On the contrary:

> " He dispossessed himself, and took the nature of a slave, fashioned in the likeness of men, and presenting himself to us in human form."—(*Philip ii*, 6-7.)

The Archangel Gabriel had foretold that He would be great, with all the greatness of the Son of the Most High God; that to Him would be given the throne of David, His ancestor in the flesh, and that He would reign in the House of Jacob for ever. And yet, knowing that the people were looking for Him on a certain occasion in order to snatch Him away and make Him King, He mysteriously slipped out of their hands. When sum-

464

moned before Pilate He did not indeed deny His King-
ship, but He took pains to explain that His Kingdom
was quite different from the kingdoms of this world;
it was not based on physical force, pomp and circum-
stance. (*Cfr. John xviii*, 36.)

We might be tempted to say that, in becoming man,
Christ forgot to bring the crown of His Godhead with
Him, and left it behind in Heaven!

What a contrast! God fashioned in the likeness of a
slave, and man's ambition to be treated like God!

## II

And what were Christ's ideas and teaching on the
subject of commanding and bearing rule? On several
occasions, particularly at His solemn farewell during the
Last Supper, He allows His disciples to bring up the
thorny question of precedence, after they had quar-
relled among themselves about which of them was to
take the first place (*Luke xxii*, 24); and this is the solution He gave:

> "The kings of the Gentiles lord it over them,
> and those who bear rule over them win the name
> of benefactors.
>
> With you it is not to be so; no difference is to
> be made, among you, between the greatest and the
> youngest of all, between him who commands and
> him who serves."—(25-26.)

Eve thought she was going to be like God; and we,
her children, so often cherish in our hearts and even
bring to our lips the claim to preferential treatment,
that, lest this new doctrine, so opposed to common
practice at the time, should sound unduly strange and

harsh to His disciples, Christ appeals to His own example:

> "Tell me (*He continues*) which is greater, the man who sits at table, or the man who serves him? Surely the man who sits at table; yet I am here among you as your servant."—(27.)

Jesus had just got up from washing His disciples' feet; His cheeks were still flushed from the strain and the fatigue.

### III

Let me now spend a few moments taking stock of my inmost convictions on this subject:

What do I think of that anxious longing for honour and rank, which St. John lists as one of the three *concupiscences,* one of those three types of gratification which, in their totality and admixture, build up what Christ calls *the world,* His great enemy; and what the beloved Disciple calls the *pride of life,* the "empty pomp of living"? (*I John ii,* 16.)

Do I not consider them very fortunate, those that have obtained and enjoy high honour and dignity? Even though my lips may not betray me, do I not, in my heart, envy them?

Haven't I fostered in my heart the same ambitions, but, as it were, in the disguise of strange "dreamforms," like a snake hiding in the grass? Don't I often feel pangs of grief and sadness when I see how my dreams of office and advancement elude my grasp, like a youngster chasing in vain after butterflies?

And to think that twenty centuries of Christianity have elapsed, during which the ideas of the God-Man have filtered down through so many layers of civilisation, and I, who am not only His disciple but also His priest and imitator by profession, am still so backward that I continue in the worship of those vain idols of power and prestige, as though I were just another of Nero's pretorian guards or centurions!

## RESOLUTIONS

1. If so far I haven't succeeded in occupying the dignity or place of my ambitions, and if at the same time I see clearly that they are beyond my reach, I shall struggle with my pride until I have come by that peace of mind which follows from a true spirit of resignation; so that I can say with Job, and say with all sincerity: *in nidulo meo moriar*: this is my little nest, and here I'm going to end my days, if God so wills.

And when all is said and done, what do the highest ranks in the Church and the richest of flowing robes mean to the vast unbelieving modern world?

2. If, due to my merits or another's good offices, I happen to have been raised to some degree of hierarchial dignity and have many people at my beck and call, I shall not forget that I am my mother's son, flesh and blood like any other of my subordinates, and that I, the same as they, am among those whom Christ calls *servants*—" to whom his master will entrust the care of the household, to give them their food at the appointed time." (*Matt. xxiv*, 45.) And so, instead of being excessively concerned about my dignity in the things which depend upon others: due honour and respect, perhaps to the point of expecting them to cringe before me, as to an infallible and superior sort of being, etc., etc., I

shall concentrate on the things that come under my control: the exact discharging of my duties and functions, kindly dealings with everyone, trying to dissimulate any disregard for my personal convenience; because this, too, is included in the command: *forgive, and you shall be forgiven.* (Luke vi, 37.)

## AMBITION

### SECOND MEDITATION

### *Inordinate Desire for High Office*

#### I

By ambition is understood an unruly craving for honours and dignities.

This craving may well be the last ditch where the evil spirit takes his stand.

You may have tamed the coarse tendencies of the flesh, dismissed wealth as unworthy of consideration; you may be admired for your austere and pious priestly life; and yet you may still qualify for the indictment worded by St. Cyprian:

"In the bosom of pious priests ambition slumbers; there in the shade it cuddles up, there it artfully hides, as in a nuptial bed "—

and, to be sure, the gentlest stir in the air is enough to awaken it!

While obedient to the hissing of the wily serpent, you will all the time swear to God and to man that your only aim is the salvation of souls, and that only the glory of God could induce you to shoulder such a burden. Or you will argue that justice is fulfilled. Without suspecting the existence of a capital vice, and borne along, as it were, by the gentle-blowing breeze of your sense of justice, you will eventually find yourself caught up in the tempestuous whirlwind of ambition.

## II

Keep a careful watch: *latet anguis sub herba,* the snake is hiding in the grass. From its place of hiding it watches and waits, that fallen angel of ambition, who one day said: *I will ascend into heaven; I will exalt my throne above the stars of God. . . . I will be like the Most High.* (Is. xiv, 13-14.) Knowing, like St. Paul (*cfr. II Cor. ii,* 11), how resourceful this evil spirit is, you also must be on the alert to forestall his tricks and to allow him no advantage over you.

At least have the sense to mind your step and to take a shuddering glance at the abyss of evil to which ambition will thrust you even in this life:

> "all those useless and dangerous appetites which sink men into ruin here and perdition hereafter."
> —(*Tim. vi,* 9.)

Like the love of money, ambition " is a root from which every kind of evil springs," causing the ambitious to involve themselves in a world of sorrows.

What anguish of mind, contempt, humiliation, hatred, shame, difficulties, blind alleys, there are concealed under the empty pomp of rank and honour! Honours are the harlequin of Italian comedy: boisterous mirth smeared with brightest vermilion, but inwardly a terrible void and the gnawing of relentless pain. How many, like King Saul, would be happier, now and eternally, if they had remained a few rungs lower!

And if to the above we add that the "grace of state" is not forthcoming to the ambitious, because God is not obliged to give it to anyone who has intruded into an office against His Will, it is greatly to be feared that the ministerial duties attached to the office and dignity will be badly performed, and the office-holder will prove more of a hindrance than a help. Is not this the explanation of so many high posts unworthily sought and unworthily held?

### III

"It is for thee, servant of God, to shun all this."
—(*I Tim. vi,* 11.)

And God grant that fear of the Judgement-to-come may lend wings to your flight! The more you are given, the more you shall be asked for. What, then, will be demanded of the man who *proprio marte,* by his own devices, worked his way up to positions of eminence to which God had not called him, to heights where he was not endowed by God with sufficient balance to keep him from suffering vertigo?

"Do not be too eager, brethren, to impart instruction to others; be sure that, if we do, we shall be called to account all the more strictly."
—(*James iii,* 1.)

What account will you render of those heavy burdens if you are bent on assuming and carrying them on your own shoulders without the aid of God's supporting Hand? Yours is a yoke imposed by presumptuous ambition, not Christ's yoke; a crushing burden, not Christ's; *for my yoke*—says Christ—*is easy, and my burden is light.* (Matt. xi, 30.)

On the Last Day the ambitious priest may well have to fear lest the Finger of God should write on his conscience in burning characters:

> Thou art weighed in the balance and art found wanting.—(*Dan. v, 27*.)

Therefore, as a preliminary resolution, I shall read slowly chapter six of the Book of Wisdom, which contains the following:

> "Listen well, all you that have multitudes at your command. . . . Swift and terrible shall be his coming; strictly his doom falls where heads rise high. . . . For the meanest, there may be pardon; for greatness, greater torment is reserved. . . .

Such is God's schedule—a schedule He adheres to inexorably.

## RESOLUTIONS

The road to ecclesiastical dignities is not absolutely blocked. After all, I am a priest, and, as such, a potential candidate for Church dignities; and in some places, the Church encourages lawful aspiration by the fact of holding competitive examinations, etc., for the promoting of candidates to higher office. Besides, ambition is an ungoverned and disorderly craving; a well-regulated desire is a worthy type of ambition, perhaps one that I should do well to possess and to foster, so long as I observe these three conditions:

1. Never to aspire after any office except for the sole, or at least the principal, purpose for which the office was instituted; e.g., the office of parish priest, for the sake of instructing the faithful, administering the Sacraments, doing conversion work, etc.; in short, to

bring souls to God. Is there any dignity in the Church of Jesus Christ, the Redeemer of souls, with any other assigned purpose? Would Christ have died in order to provide me with a *sinecure* and keep me in comfortable idleness here below?

2. Not to entertain the thought of possessing any ecclesiastical dignity whatsoever unless I am personally and properly convinced, or better still, unless others in a position to know me thoroughly are convinced, that I have the moral and intellectual qualities which such a dignity requires. Were a doctor to aspire after a medical post for which he knew himself to be unequipped, his ambition would be criminal. And are souls of less account than bodies?

3. In spite of all human injustices and lack of appreciation that I may come up against, I will not enter upon any office except through the proper canonical channels, not *aliunde*—through the back-stage door of wire-pulling, simony, or pharisaic pretensions. Far better to remain a beggar on the door-step of the Lord's House!

# OBEDIENCE

## Esteem for Obedience

### I

The most pernicious temptation against obedience is *contempt,* sizing it up as something mean and unworthy of a human being, or at least as indecorous for cultured and noble minds.

Submission to obedience, according to this view, requires a servile type of mind—*anima dimidiata,* as Homer would say, if translated into Latin, a "reduced personality."

The reluctance experienced by Satan in submitting to God, which made him cry out *I will not serve !*; the self-elation which drove our first parents to gamble away their own and all their posterity's inheritance by an act of rebellion against their Father and Creator; that inward struggle which takes place within the soul of every one of us when it comes to surrendering our will to the will of another; these things are not trivialities; and therefore obedience is not something to be brushed aside with a sneer; because obedience is given only at a very high price, at the cost of breaking in our natural appetites, and going through death-like agony in the process. Call obedience what you will, but deem it not contemptible. It is not a contemptible thing to refrain the human personality from running wild through the fantastic regions of caprice and savage independence.

To obey wholeheartedly is noble, most noble; if only because no other virtue taxes us so sorely: neither the repressing of anger, nor the stern bridling of sensuality. Noble, most noble, is that which one obtains only by dint of absolute self-denial and high-mindedness; namely, to deposit into another's keeping not merely external acts of submission—any slave or beast of burden at the crack of the master's whip will do that—but also the reins of our internal desire, sacrificing our own wishes for the sake of some great good which surpasses human fickleness and even human reasoning. Say what you will, then, about obedience, but do not hold it in contempt.

## II

Do not despise obedience; obedience is all-powerful, and such power may well be feared and hated, but despised, never.

Where lies the strength of a home, a city, a nation, an army? In their being *one*. Scattered forces spell weakness, dissolution, corruption, death; union is strength—a phrase elevated to the rank of universal dictum. And what is union? Not the singular, but the plural, the multiple made one. What is it, finally, that makes the multiple one in human affairs? A uniform and unified leadership: one aim, identical means, unity of plan and execution; in other words: the submission of all to the direction of one, obedience to the person in charge.

No power exists, human or divine, without a definite plan, without order, direction, obedience. Take away from the army its discipline—another name for obedience—and however powerful and well-equipped with weapons and men, its striking power is lost.

If you do not love obedience, at least refrain from incurring the insincerity of despising and belittling it; obedience has always been the mother of everything great in the world.

## III

Do not despise obedience, obedience is divine, and the divine is not despicable. Divine, not only because, as St. Paul says, "Authority comes from God only" (*Rom. xiii*, 1), but also because of Christ's example.

The God Who became Man, possessing the human faculties of the mind and the will, was by His very Nature our only Sovereign—*This title is written on his cloak, over his thigh: the King of kings, and the Lord of lords* (Apoc. xix, 16); He had the eternal and inalienable right to present Himself to the High Priest in the Holy of Holies and say: "Deliver unto Me the attributes of the High-Priesthood, I am the Eternal Priest"; He could have stood before the all-powerful Roman Emperor and said to him: "Yield me that throne, it is Mine, *through Me kings reign*"; He had a perfect right to exercise dominion over every household in the Name of His Father "from Whom all fatherhood in heaven and on earth takes its title" (*Eph. iii*, 15); He was God, God's Equal; and yet, He forwent the privileges due to His Godhead; He hid them away, as though they did not belong to Him; He lived as a man, appeared in most of His manifestations just as a man; He lived as a slave:

> "He dispossessed himself, accepted an obedience which brought him to death,
> death on a cross."—(*Philip i, ii*, 6-8.)

That is the meaning of the Cross of Christ! There

we have the great lesson of the Crucifix! So before you despise obedience, despise your crucifix, if you dare; tear it from the altar; tear it from your own heart!

My God, crucified through obedience: Thou knowest well how hard it is for me to obey; I instinctively loathe humble submission; but one thing I will never do: I will never say that obedience is something low and mean. Thou wert not low and mean, and Thou wast the great Model of all who obey.

### Resolutions

1.   Notwithstanding ideas or examples to the contrary, whatever their source, from to-day I shall never allow in my facial expression the slightest hint of contempt for obedience to lawful Authority; and, should the need arise, I undertake to defend with knight-errant chivalry that great virtue in whose arms my Redeemer gave Himself up to the death of the Cross.

2.   This is the lesson I shall preach by word and example to the faithful under my care, in an effort to quell the upsurge of those barbaric forces of insubordination which seem to echo the Biblical cry: *"Let us break away from their bondage, let us throw off their yoke!"* (Ps. ii, 3.)

## OBEDIENCE

### SECOND MEDITATION

### *Practice of Obedience*

### I

The exercise of this costly virtue must be ennobled and transformed into the virtue of religion; it must become as much an exercise of religion and piety as any act of worship.

To obey because you hope thereby to reap some personal profit, or because you will thus win the sympathy of the Prelate for the furtherance of your own selfish interests, would be vile adulation. To obey because of the courtesy and kindly manner with which you are given orders, because you have taken a liking to the Superior, or on account of the rectitude and prudence you recognise in him, are so many titles for serving only the Superior. And this will enable you to live a life of submission and earn the reputation of being easy to handle; you will bring to a successful issue works of considerable renown and self-sacrifice; but when you come to ask your Divine Lord to reward you, He will say: "You worked for your Superior, it is for him to pay you." And meanwhile you will have lived in subjection to a man like yourself, to a man with no other claims to your submission (as far as you are concerned) than those human and fallible claims which you yourself have endowed him with; he is a man you hope to get something from, he is pleasant and courteous, he is superior to you in knowledge and prudence.

Slavery would seem your birthright; you are no better off than any slave of an old Roman patrician.

## II

There is no creature, human or angelic, who deserves that I should dedicate to him the humblest act of my free will. My "commanded" or "elicited" acts, when informed by God's grace and a right intention, no matter how insignificant they may appear, such as eating, sleeping, etc., are worthy of eternal life; this alone is their adequate recompense. Am I going to forfeit so great a reward for the sake of some temporal advantage or convenience?

But for an act of obedience to yield its perfect fruit, God must be its " ratio formalis ": God's Authority delegated to my Superior. You see now how an act of submission can be transformed into something religious and devotional?

There is no other means of ennobling our subjection to man.

Has your obedience ever reached that perfection? Have you instructed the faithful in this truth of our holy religion, which would so ennoble and lighten the yoke of obedience in those who obey, and render the exercise of authority so considerate in those who command?

If you accord to the person-in-charge, not only external submission, but also inward honour and respect, to which he is entitled, you will soon experience for yourself obedience's ennobling influence: " Pay every man his due . . . respect and honour. . . ." (*Rom. xiii,* 7.)

How reluctantly and how badly one obeys when the person in authority has become an object of contempt! And perhaps nothing lowers him more in the eyes of his subjects than a continual criticism of his actions: it poisons good will, alienates affection; and those under him, when obliged to obey, are like a wheel that creaks through lack of lubricating oil. And while supposing that calumny and detraction play no part, what do we stand to gain by our carping criticism, except to lower the whole tone of the moral body of which we are members, which in this case is the Church Herself?

That there are stains on those of us who are, so to speak, the Church's feet and the hem of Her garment, is bad enough; but it certainly does us no honour to be constantly harping upon and pointing out those stains when they mar the Church's very countenance. Oh, what great scorn has been poured upon the ministers of the altar by those murmurings and malicious, gossiping tongues! How often these have caused many of the faithful to waver and weaken in their Catholic belief!

## RESOLUTIONS

1. I shall obey all my Superiors as I would God Himself, readily, joyfully, without discussing their orders.

2. On every occasion, in their presence or otherwise, I shall not refuse them the tribute of respect and veneration to which they are entitled as representatives of Jesus Christ; and if they have their faults I shall not allow these to prejudice me, but shall do my best to draw a veil over them.

3. From now on I forbid myself all murmuring against them; and when others indulge in it in my hearing and I cannot suitably stand up for their defence, I shall observe a discreet silence, not showing any sign of assent.

These standards required of me are all the more reasonable the more strongly I myself insist, and always will insist, on their observance by my own subjects in their relations towards me.

# PURITY OF INTENTION

## Its Importance

### I

Good works, by themselves, are valueless in the eyes of God. What imparts real value to them, supernatural value, is our right intention informed by divine grace. Therefore, the soul of every virtue is the intention. The divinest act with a perfect intention will be most pure; with an indifferent intention, indifferent; with a wicked intention, abominable.

For example, a kiss imprinted on Christ's brow. When the lips were those of His Mother Mary, burning with motherly and divine love, it was the sublimest act of religion and devotion, the blending and fusing of all the highests acts of human love into the adoration of the Son of God; when the kiss came from the lips of some woman in the Nazareth neighbourhood who, not knowing who Jesus was, kissed Him simply because He was a comely and winsome child, the act was morally an indifferent one; from the lips of Judas in the Garden, it was the most monstrous crime that ever defiled the race of Adam.

Yet in all three kisses only one thing changed: the intention.

This doctrine is applicable to every free-willed act of my life. Scrutinising my deepest intention, God judges me accordingly.

## II

Let us meditate on the profound utterance of our Lord when He compares our inward intention to our bodily eyesight:

"Thy body has the eye for its lamp; and if thy eye is clear, the whole of thy body will be lit up; when it is diseased, the whole of thy body will be in darkness."

"Take good care, then, that this principle of light which is in thee is light, not darkness; then, if thy whole body is in the light, with no part of it darkness, it will all be lit up as if by a bright lamp enlightening thee."—(*Luke xi*, 34-36.)

The lamp which lights up your good works, rendering them visible and either acceptable or displeasing to God, is your intention; so, if your intention is resplendent with clarity, rectitude, and holiness, all your works bask in splendour; if your intention is crooked, obscure, and evil, your works are darkness itself, because the very principle of light, your good intention, is extinguished.

## III

By my priestly office I am obliged to perform, during the greater part of my life, works that are not merely good but eminently holy and divine; and yet, have I not miserably forfeited the merit attaching to most of them because they lacked that very simple and practical quality, right intention? Either I try to please people for the sake of pleasing them, or I perform my duties for the stipend, just to avoid comment, to satisfy my own vanity, or simply to indulge my natural impulse for an active occupation. How often, dear Lord, have I ful-

Q

filled my duties for Thee alone? How often to win eternal life myself and to save the souls of others?

What a tremendous pity! After death, when I shall have left everything behind me, including the idols before whose altar I sacrificed so many of my illustrious actions, I shall be taken before that inexorable Court of Justice from which there is no appeal; I shall have no other credit or defence than the good works which were holy in appearance but which, when lit up by Jesus Christ in the light of eternity, will stand revealed in all their hollowness, like artificial fruit models; or else they will exhibit an inner core of corruption: white sepulchres concealing the carrion flesh of puny abortive creatures that were delivered stillborn within the pantheon of my heart.

## RESOLUTIONS

The natural products of my actions: human prestige, emoluments, and so forth, are not the fruit, specifically, of any intention or thought of mine; in other words, I shall get the same stipend for a sermon or a Mass whether I think of the stipend or not. On the other hand, there is another kind of fruit, the most valuable kind; namely, grace and eternal life; and this I obtain only through my purity of intention. Therefore, I am not going to be so stupid as to worry about what comes to me independently of any intention of mine, and at the same time pay little or no heed to the one thing that demands it.

I shall henceforth purify my intention, offering all my works to God each morning; and I shall ratify my intention every time I am prompted to seek in my actions interests that are unworthy of a priest or fall short of priestly perfection.

# PURITY OF INTENTION

## SECOND MEDITATION

### *Its Necessity in Works of Zeal*

#### I

There is no truly human work that cannot become worthy of God and which God cannot claim for Himself, provided it keeps within the limits imposed by the divine commandments; even eating, drinking and sleeping.

> "In eating, in drinking, in all that you do, do everything as for God's glory."—(*I Cor. x,* 31.)

If such is the injunction concerning any human action, even those on the level of animal life, what will God not expect from me concerning the divine actions of my priesthood: the celebrating of Mass, administering the Sacraments, preaching, worshipping God in spirit and in truth, saving souls redeemed by His Blood?

So, one of two things: either God is kind and benevolent, to the point of weakness, towards everything human, like a father towards the lispings of his tender child; or else God sees something mysteriously precious in our free wills, which gives immense value to the slightest act issuing from them. The mysterious tree of the knowledge of good and evil!

#### II

To eat or drink from a motive that is not virtuous, is unreasonable, or which does not enter into the supernatural order, would be something unworthy of the Christian. Yes, even in matters like these, which pertain to the animal and inferior part of our being.

To practise the smallest work of virtue just because we take the notion, without any reference to God, would be unpleasing to Him and of no value.

> Why have we fasted, and thou hast not regarded? humbled our souls, and thou hast not taken notice? —Behold, in the day of your fast your own will is found. . . .—(Is. lviii, 3.)

But what if we announce the word of God merely for the stipend or human applause? What if we consecrate the Body and Blood of Christ exclusively for the sake of the five or ten shilling offering? What if I do anything in the line of priestly functions because it may figure on my record sheet and tell in my favour when there is the possibility of some paltry promotion? Puny heart! Wretched little mind! For so little would you barter away your God and your glorious, eternal destiny?

### III

With the light of faith and reason I shall enter resolutely into the murky chasms of my intentions, and I shall try to discover at least the measure and quality of these intentions as they inform each one of my priestly actions. No doubt I shall find, with no small shock to my pride, that there has been such a swarm of vile little passions and worldly interests, each clamouring for and obtaining with no great difficulty its own particular share of satisfaction, in all my ministerial duties, that God, the only rightful Claimant, has been left empty-handed

or with only a meagre portion, and a portion certainly
not the most presentable.

If this be so, I shall have to confess I have wasted
my time, and that I can hope for no further reward.
*Amen dico vobis, recepistis mercedem vestram.* (Matt.
vi, 16.)

## RESOLUTION

If my wretchedness and unspiritual frame of mind is
such that I do not succeed in making entirely Thine the
fruits of my priesthood by means of an all-pure intention, I resolve in future, Lord, at least not to carry out
any priestly work wherein Thou hast not the primary
and principal share.

# SOME MEANS OF PERSEVERANCE

## PERSEVERANCE

*Meaning and Characteristics of Perseverance*

### I

Every pious exercise, in particular that intensive series known as a retreat or the " spiritual exercises " has a purpose which goes beyond mere performance for the sake of adhering to a point of daily routine or of carrying out the Church's wishes or command; its primary purpose is to unite us ever more closely to God and to amend our lives; or, as the ascetical phrase runs, to advance in perfection. To *advance*—that is the great Christian word. To advance *continually*—because no one with any understanding of the Gospel spirit will ever boast of having reached the goal, no matter how many years of progressing he may count to his credit, no matter how swift his flight towards the summits of the Christian life.

> " Not that I have already won the prize, already reached fulfilment. I only press on, in hope of winning the mastery."—(*Philip iii*, 12.)

And the same Apostle, whose life was coming to an end, continues:

> " No, brethren, I do not claim to have the

mastery already, but this at least I do: forgetting what I have left behind, intent on what lies before me, I press on with the goal in view, eager for the prize, God's heavenly summons in Christ Jesus." —(*id.* 13-14.)

Christ Himself expressed the height of our supreme calling in life when He said: *Be perfect as your heavenly Father is perfect*. We shall never reach up to that infinite Model however much we may have run.

If, therefore, after any exercise of perfection, such as a retreat, I remain where I was before, as backward and lukewarm and sinful as before, it means that the exercise I was supposed to perform proved useless to me, or even harmful. *Verbum meum non revertetur ad me vacuum.* The grace of God is never ineffectual either one way or the other, for better or for worse. It either brings us nearer to God, if we correspond to it; or, if we reject it, we become inexcusable in God's sight.

> If I had not come and spoken to them, they would not have sin; but now they have no excuse for their sin.—(*John* xv, 22.)

## II

The two great hallmarks of perseverance and continual progress in the good begun are, first, an unshakable determination—burned into my deepest soul by the fire of the Holy Spirit—not to sin, and to avoid the occasions of sin, especially the *proximate voluntary* occasions; and, second, to repent without delay for any relapse.

In carrying out the good resolutions of a retreat or any other pious exercise, I must avoid two extremes.

I must not make the mistake of imagining that from

now onwards, thanks to the light and ardent desires enkindled in me by a life of solid piety or a fervent retreat, I am immune to the possibility of offending God or of relapsing into former sins.

No, I cannot afford to rest on my laurels; it would be a most dangerous illusion. Satan is not going to relax —his onslaughts may well increase until he has got us back to our old habits of sin. Our passions have not died at the hands of grace and enlightenment during the retreat—a temporary respite, perhaps, in order to bide their time and return to the charge at a more favourable opportunity; a dozing off for a while, and then the old incentives both from within and from the outer world will re-appear: the blood will boil up again, my imagination will conjure up fresh allurements, I shall experience anew the fascination of things and people, and my wild appetites will shake off their drowsiness and leap to the clamorous pursuit of pleasure.

These strong, treacherous enemies of mine are only lying in ambush, so I shall be always on the alert, with God's grace for my shield of protection, and armed with my resolve not to sin and to flee from the occasions of sin.

## III

Another pitfall would be to exaggerate unreasonably the difficulties and obstacles which beset the path of my perseverance and progress. If, as is not unlikely, I have the misfortune to fall again into sin, I must beware of considering the resolutions I now make the utopian and imprudent dreams of a passing fervour. I must not stray from the charted course because of unforeseen circumstances or past experience. To adopt the attitude that such and such a line of conduct is not for me to follow, having failed to follow it before, is a fatal illusion that causes the loss of many and drives them into the depths of despair, or very near. Because I have fallen once or twice or a hundred times I am tempted to jump to the conclusion that I simply cannot keep to the right path and that all my efforts will be of no avail. But what would happen if we adopted this despairing attitude in human affairs? What should we say of a sick man who after a second, third, or hundredth relapse gave it all up as a bad job, neglected himself, refused all doctors and medical aid? Don't we see people going year after year to drink and bathe in the same medicinal spring-waters? And what do they say? " Oh, if I'm not entirely cured, at least I get some relief, and I'm able to carry on."

Likewise in the ailments of the spirit. The reasonable thing to do, as soon as you feel you are down again, is to rise up, and to rise up as often as you fall, be it twice or a thousand times; to rise up, first, by an act of perfect contrition elicited immediately after you realise you have fallen, while the natural and healthy reaction is still upon you; and, secondly, to go to confession at the earliest opportunity. There is far greater harm and danger in allowing one single sin to take root undisturbed than in frequent relapse coupled with frequent and immediate repentance where the sins are not given time to seep into your inmost soul and poison you. This undelayed repentance is the second essential practical means of perseverance.

## IV

As a safeguard and outer wall of defence, make use of the following practices:

1. Weekly confession, whatever the cost, and preferably with the same confessor or spiritual director. Confession as often as required in order to celebrate Mass worthily. This is not an impossibility, far from it; you will find it easier than is commonly supposed; a strong, inflexible will is all that is needed. And if this practice of weekly or even more frequent confession is adhered to faithfully, it will suffice to keep you on the path of virtue.

2. On rising, to say your morning prayers and make your meditation.

3. To prepare properly for the Holy Mass, at least by making your daily meditation; and to say Mass always in the state of grace, never, never in mortal sin. If you have fallen into this wretched condition, never approach the altar without first having gone to confession, no matter what amount of trouble this may put you to.

4. To recite the Divine Office, giving to each Hour ample time, and choosing a place conducive to recollection.

5. A protracted visit to the Blessed Sacrament in the afternoon. This practice, besides being an act of faith and piety, and good example to the faithful, will ensure the observance of the Church's law to keep open for a few hours each day every place of worship where the Blessed Sacrament is reserved.

6. To bear in a penitential spirit the griefs and afflictions which accompany my priestly state and office.

7. To live united with my Lord Jesus Christ, taking refuge within the sacred sanctuary of His Divine Heart, safely ensconced away from my own weakness and from the seductions and ingratitude of the world.

# PRIESTLY PIETY

## *Its Nature and Source*

### I

What is piety? According to Cicero's definition,
adopted by St. Thomas and afterwards by all the
Scholastics:

> Pietas est per quam a sanguine junctis patriaeque
> benevolis officium et diligens tribuitur cultus.
> —(*I Rhet., lib. ii.*)

And St. Laurence Justinian emphasises piety's interior
dispositions and exterior manifestation:

> per quam a conjunctis sanguine et benevolentia
> *affectus* et diligens tribuitur *cultus.*

Piety therefore regards immediately and principally
one's own parents, with whom one is primarily con-
nected by the ties of blood and benevolence; and the
term " pious " applies in its first acceptation to the man
who loves, respects, reverences, obeys and serves his
parents. That is why St. Monica on her deathbed could
call her son *pious*, notwithstanding his dissipated life.
And St. Augustine himself tells us:

> " It was a joy to me to have this one testimony
> from her: when her illness was close to its end,
> meeting with expressions of endearment such ser-
> vices as I rendered, she called me a dutiful, loving
> son, and said in the great affection of her love that
> she had never heard from my mouth any harsh or

reproachful word addressed to herself. But what possible comparison was there, O my God who made us, between the honour I showed her and the service she rendered me?"—(*Confessions, Bk. ix, chap. xii.—Trans. Sheed.*)

*Obsequium, honor, servitus.* Obedience, honour, service: these three things, when rendered to our parents, constitute natural piety. But since God is

" the Father from whom all fatherhood in heaven and on earth takes its title "—(*Eph. iv,* 15);

since God is the Supreme being, excelling all others, their Source and Origin; since God created us to His own image and likeness, and communicated to us, by grace, His own divine Spirit whereby we cry out to God: Abba—Father! (*Rom. viii,* 15)—in short, because God is our Father first and foremost, before any earthly parents, the term " pious " belongs primarily to the person who renders filial obedience, honour and service to God our Father in Heaven. We may say that piety is the keeping of the fourth commandment fused with the first; it is the Father and the child living together in the same home, the child never leaving it, never running away either in thought or desire or deed. Piety is being, living, willing at one with God our Father.

## II

Piety means living by the Faith; not merely possessing the Faith, carrying it silently in the depths of the soul like a jewel in its casket or in the vaults of a bank. Piety means that the capital truths of our Faith have sunk into our minds, like a gentle dew from the heavens, taking up the leadership, becoming the very soul and centre, of all other knowledge and truth. Piety means that our wills are continually being drawn towards, and unceasingly aspire after, the everlasting good as revealed by the dogmas of the Faith, with a longing that surpasses all other longing. Piety means that our exterior acts are all informed and conditioned by the divine teachings and precepts; that in all our trials and difficulties we turn to God, our Father, to Whom we confide our hopes and our joys. Piety enables us to put into practice the words of the psalmist:

> "Familiaris est Dominus timentibus eum, et foedus suum manifestat eis."—(*Ps. xxiv,* 14, *revised.*)

"No man ever feared the Lord, but found graciousness in Him, and revelation in His covenant." It enables us to sing perpetually:

> "Benedictus Deus, qui non amovit orationem meam, et misericordiam suam a me."—(*Ps. lxv,* 20.)

"Blessed be God, who does not reject my prayer, does not withhold His mercy from me." It brings us to that happy state described by the Apostle St. Paul in Chapter vii of his Epistle to the Romans: a state which may be summed up in the following words: we are liberated in Jesus Christ by virtue of a spiritual principle of life from the principle of sin and death; set free, we think the thoughts of the spirit, the wisdom that brings life and peace; our spirit is no longer one of slavery, to govern us by fear; it is a spirit of adoption, which makes us cry out to God as a child cries to its father; it is the Spirit of God Himself making us His children, His heirs, giving us a share of Christ's inheritance after we have partaken of Christ's sufferings.

So Piety is something very intimate; it issues from

the Heart of God into the heart of man, and thence it flows into outward acts, which are its fruit and necessary manifestation. Piety is the worship of the Father in spirit and in truth; it is the virtue of religion spread over the whole man and raised to filial heights, making us exclaim at every elevation of our spirit to God: "Our Father who art in heaven."

## III

*The Word was God. The Word was made flesh and dwelt amongst us.* And that same divine Word told us:

> He that seeth me, seeth the Father also.—(*John xiv, 9.*)

And to love the Son is to love also the Father.

All our piety towards God, then, should be directed through Christ, who, being the God-Man, has come within our easy reach. There is nothing like St. Matthew's eleventh chapter for showing us how we should be pious towards our Divine Lord Jesus Christ. Let us transcribe the evangelist's recording of Christ's words, and let these words sink deeply into our minds and hearts:

> "I confess to Thee, O Father, Lord of heaven and earth, because Thou hast hid these things from the wise and prudent and hast revealed them to little ones."

So great is God our Father—*Tu solus Altissimus*—that in order to become good children of God we must ever remain as little ones.

> "Yea, Father: for so hath it seemed good in Thy sight."

> "All things are delivered to me by my Father."

All belongs to Christ, and as an indication of Christ's greatness He would have us understand that:

> "No one knoweth the Son, but the Father,"

neither men of learning nor prophets nor cherubim, but only the Father, whose understanding is infinite. And

> "neither doth any one know the Father, but the Son"—

not all our deepest lucubrations on the Nature of the Godhead can adequately teach us Who the Father is; only the Son, infinite like the Father, can impart this knowledge:

> "and he to whom it shall please the Son to reveal Him."

Hence, all knowledge of God that strays from the doctrine given by the Son is falsehood; there is no true knowledge of God except in the teachings of Christ, who, therefore, says to us:

> "Come to me, all ye that labour and are heavily burdened."

"All who are burdened by life's cares, or by the heavy duties of the priestly ministry, or by sin, come to Me and I shall give you relief and rest; I shall encourage and give you consolation; take My yoke upon you and learn of Me; take Me for your Master, making yourselves My constant disciples; take Me as the universal Teacher of your lives, because I am meek and gentle and of kindly dispositions. Notwithstanding My personal greatness I know how to make Myself a little child towards those who submit to My teaching; I am humble of heart, like a mother stooping to instruct her little one, lisping in a language that the child understands. Come to Me, because only by following My system of teaching, only by relishing My teaching in actual practice, becoming wise through the knowledge I impart with a wisdom that combines goodness and truth, only by learning My words and moulding your conduct entirely upon them will you find rest for your souls, that source of true happiness about which men so copiously and so unavailingly discuss and argue. Come to Me, because the yoke I lay upon you is sweet, the burden I impose is light; and My hand, with its infinite strength helps you to bear them; and My Spirit will buoy you up and make them easy to bear."

O Jesus, keep me very small and make me sit down in the classroom with Thy pupils, where do Thou infuse into my inmost soul the law of Faith and of the Spirit, that wisdom which we call piety, wherewith the Father of Lights is venerated and worshipped, the Father from Whom descends every good and perfect gift!

## RESOLUTIONS

Since every living being produces acts in conformity with its specific nature, I wish my piety to be a living thing, manifesting itself spontaneously in acts of piety. Therefore:

1. I am resolved to animate my entire priestly ministry with a spirit of piety, saying Mass and the Divine Office, exposing the Blessed Sacrament, reciting the rosary or Novena prayers, preaching and teaching catechism, all under the impulse and guidance of the selfsame spirit of piety.

2. Not satisfied with the above, I shall imbue all my liturgical acts with this spirit of piety, considering that each one yields a very special fruit which belongs exclusively to the officiating priest; for example, in dis-

tributing the Sacraments, in blessings and consecrations.

When administering the Holy Viaticum, let us say, what great profit for my soul, in terms of devotion and piety, if I had stopped to reflect that this particular task was essentially mine to perform, holier, more pleasing to God and more profitable to my soul, than any mere meditation! Alas! Haven't I turned the whole liturgical system into something mechanical, cold and fruitless, as though it were instituted only for the benefit of others? How holy a priest would become if he once began to take the liturgical acts as his own proud personal possession!

3. And since the perfect worship of God consists in loving God, revering Him, and rendering Him service by obeying His commands; from now onwards I wish to consider the observance of every divine precept or evangelical counsel, and the works of zeal and of mercy as so many acts of piety and religion; so that one day God may be able to say for my benefit:

> I will be to him a Father, and he shall be to Me a son.—(*II Kings vii*, 14.)

## PRIESTLY PIETY

### SECOND MEDITATION

### *The Need for Priestly Piety*

#### I

The priest is the man of God, appointed by his fellow-men their ambassador before God. When man must appear before God in order to obtain mercy or the remission of sin or supernatural grace and strength

or temporal and eternal gifts, he fears for his own little-
ness or unworthiness, he is afraid lest he be not admitted
to the Divine Presence, his petitions be left unheeded;
because he knows he is not pleasing to the Lord's
scrutinising gaze. He, therefore, instinctively goes to the
priest, as to a person who enjoys God's familiar friendship; and in the priest's hands he lays his confidence
and his requests. He knows that the priest of Christ, like
Christ Himself, will be given audience at the Throne of
the Eternal God; he knows that the priest has free
access, for he is the King's close friend and privy coun-
cillor. Such is the idea of the priest in the minds of
Christians; and, in its main outline, such is the idea of
every priest from the day the world began.

But what if the priest is actually God's enemy? What
if the priest has not practice in conversing with God
but rather flees from the divine Countenance as from a
source of annoyance? What if the man of God is hateful
to God? How will he put before God the petitions of
the people whom he represents? Will he appease God,
or will he provoke God to anger? Here we have,
perhaps, the clue to the doctrine taught by so many
holy and hard-thinking men, the doctrine that one bad
priest is the ruin of a whole town or nation, and is
responsible for the greater part of public calamities.

It is obvious, O God, that if I am to acquit myself
properly of my office as the world's ambassador and
mediator, in imitation of Christ, I must render myself
acceptable to Thee, must be a friend of Thine, a member
of Thy Household, a true pleader at Thy Court; in a
word: pious.

## II

As a means of bringing souls to God, riches are of no avail, nor learning, nor eloquence, nor worldly pomp and power. How many surprises time springs upon the educators of candidates for the priesthood! We have all witnessed it: young men who seemed to be the cream of talent while in the seminary, when raised to the priesthood and given the cure of souls they proved to be very mediocre or even failures. On the other hand, young men who were almost thrown out by their professors, soon after ordination began to do wonders for the conversion and renewal of souls throughout the district. What hidden talent came to light in the latter, that was missing in the former? The Spirit of Christ, Who wielded mastery over their hearts, Who guided them in their holy endeavours.

When it comes to returning to God in all sincerity, to being converted, to following the inspirations of divine grace, the human heart obeys only one deep impulse: God's personal invitation; it obeys only one attraction: the pure light of the Faith; one thing alone fascinates and captures: *the life-giving perfume of Christ*. (II Cor. ii, 15.) And priests who are full of the Spirit of God, not merely good and honest men like any soldier or father of a family but solidly pious, have become this life-giving perfume of Christ, and souls run to them, and in their voice they hear the voice of the Good Shepherd.

Thy Church, O Lord, has need of learned ministers, men steeped in the sciences of things human and divine; grant them unto Her. Thy Church needs priests without blemish in the eyes of a prying world; refuse them not to Her, O Lord. But little will the Church accomplish without pious priests, Her best treasure, fishers of men for Thee. Lord, never refuse Thy Church these priests of piety; increase their number; let them be the salt of the earth, to free the earth from its so great corruption; let them be the light of the world, to scatter the world's darkness!

## III

God help me if I am not pious! An ordinary Christian, a farmer or a family man, will perhaps manage to observe all the commandments, will go for months and years without a single serious breach of the divine law, merely on the strength of Sunday Mass, Easter duties, and a few popular practices of devotion; that is, without being particularly pious. But shall I, a priest, be as good and as honest without real, solid piety? I wish to God it would bear contradiction, but no, the fact is that if a priest is not solidly pious he will not even reach the standards of ordinary decency and honesty, in the elastic meaning given by the world to these terms. The fundamental and unassailable truth is that a priest who is not pious will very soon degenerate into a perverse Christian, into a man without a moral conscience, into a rake, a blackguard, a public scandal. . . .

The duties incumbent upon me are so very heavy! Take, for example, the duty of observing absolute and perpetual chastity of body and soul. Am I going to break that vow freely entered into before God and the world? If I do not keep it, if my soul burns with impure desire, if my body seeks to wallow in lustful pleasure, how is it possible for me to give rein to my appetites and not sustain the loss of moral integrity and common decency? How can I indulge my passions without plunging into the direst depths of infamy and abomination? No, it is quite clear, I cannot. Therefore, an unchaste priest is a perverse and abominable man.

Now then, am I, or anyone else for that matter, capable of such absolute purity by my own unaided efforts?

> " To be master of myself was a thing I could not hope to come by except of God's Bounty; I was wise enough already to know whence the gift came. So to the Lord I turned, and made my request of him, praying with all my heart. . . ."—(*Wisdom viii*, 21.)

No merely human interest or consideration was ever, of itself, sufficient a bridle to fleshly concupiscence: neither the desire for health, nor the dread of disgrace, nor the natural esteem of purity, nor nature's noblest aspirations. Has not my own experience taught me the lesson? Only a longing for the rewards of everlasting life, the fear of eternal punishment, a respectful regard for God's constant and all-seeing Presence, a contempt for degrading satisfactions, a sober life united to Jesus Christ, the laborious steering clear of sinful allurements; all this, together with divine grace, is the only force which adequately refrains and harnesses to reason and to God our most violent appetite of the flesh. And all this is called *piety*.

## IV

Priestly piety encounters, to be sure, powerful and formidable opposition. One type of adversary proceeds—who would believe it?—from the ranks of some of your own fellow priests. Experience, unfortunately, bears witness to this. When certain priests get together for their little parties and gossiping parlours, perhaps your name crops up in the course of conversation. " We know him well enough; not what he makes himself out to be. What does he mean by going around with the face of a mystic, mumbling his prayers at every hour of the day —the old wheedling humbug!" They may even throw it into your face and make social contact almost an impossibility for you among your colleagues. You'll be the target of numberless unfair and scathing remarks. Take stock of it, but meanwhile, *esto vir,* be a man; don't let it daunt you. If God and your own temperament have endowed you with calmness of manner and strong convictions, choose an opportunity, when there are a number of witnesses, to face up to your accusers, and serenely, without losing your nerve or your temper, take the ring-leader to task along the following line of thought, if not in so many words:

" Let me be frank with you. Yes, I *am* trying to be pious, I *am* trying to keep in close touch with our Lord; and for very serious reasons. Experience has shown me how weak I am and how I am bound to yield to passion and break my most solemn promises, if I am left to my own devices. I don't want to take back every word I gave to God and the Church; loyalty is no more than common decency, like that of the military man not to run away from the firing-line; but I'm convinced that my own unaided efforts are not enough to ward off defeat; so I'm determined to gather strength to remain loyal. That strength has its source in God and in Christ, nowhere else; and it is piety that opens up that source of strength to me.

So now you know why I am trying to lead a life of piety."

## RESOLUTIONS

1.   From this very day I shall conform not only to the standards of liturgical piety and those of self-sacrificing obedience and service, as outlined in the last meditation, but also to the following prescriptions of Canon Law:

> *Canon 124 :* Both the interior life and the exterior behaviour of the clergy must be superior to that of the laity, and must excel them by the example of virtue and good deeds.

> *Canon 125 :* The Ordinary must take care (1) that the clergy frequently go to confession; (2) that they make each day a meditation of some duration, visit the Blessed Sacrament, say the rosary, and examine their consciences.

> *Canon 126 :* All secular priests must at least once in three years make a retreat for a length of time to be specified by the Ordinary, in a religious house or other place designated by the bishop. No one shall be exempted from the retreat, except in a particular case, for a just reason, and with the explicit permission of the Ordinary.

2.   Besides my ministerial duties and liturgical functions, my daily time-table of piety will include the devotional exercises prescribed by the above Canons; and I shall not omit any pious exercise except for serious reasons, giving preference to the above-mentioned over

any others, however holy, commendable, and enriched with indulgences, the latter may be.

This programme, besides being meritorious in itself and in the sight of Jesus Christ, who was obedient unto death, death on the Cross; besides consisting of acts which are essentially good and efficaciously sanctifying, will have the great merit of obedience to the divinest Authority on earth, our Holy Mother Church.

# DEVOTION TO OUR LADY

### FIRST MEDITATION

*General Motives*

### I

If we reflect, even superficially, on what the Gospels tell us about Mary—and what is written down is all too little to satisfy our filial piety—we shall find sufficient motives to live perpetually and tenderly enamoured of that Holy Woman. Her admirable virtues shine through the Gospel's simple, unadorned style: such delicate acts of sovereign purity, such glorious intimacies of soul; ineffable poise, absolute self-mastery, august serenity. Blessed is the hand which bequeathed us the lines from verse 26 to 56 of the first chapter of the Gospel according to St. Luke! The mere reading and knowledge of these lines would suffice, O Sovereign Mother of Christ, even if I knew nothing more about thee, to revere and love thee with my whole heart and soul for all eternity!

If heroicity of virtue, immaculate purity of soul, inexhaustible goodness of heart; if loftiness of aspiration, elevated dignity, and benefits showered like gentle morning dew upon mankind, are all potent to fill us with ardent devotion towards the Saints, where, O Mother of Jesus and my own dear Mother, shall I find these things so truly and so radiantly enshrined as in thee?

In venerating and loving and praising thee, I make willing obeisance to the flower of creation, to the crown of God's ineffable works and wonders. Were I to refuse thee the tribute of my love and piety, I should have to refuse it to every being that was not God, to the very heart of the woman who bore me in her womb.

## II

How can I fail to greet and, both inwardly and outwardly, express my love for her to whom one of the loftiest angelic spirits, one of the Seven in attendance at the Throne of God, the Archangel Gabriel, rendered, even before she was vested with the almost infinite dignity of Mother of God, such astounding tokens of veneration in the name of the Almighty Himself?

> Hail, full of grace, the Lord is with thee; blessed art thou among women. . . .

> Fear not, Mary, thou hast found grace with God.

> The Holy Ghost will come upon thee and the Power of the Most High will overshadow thee.
> —(*Luke i*, 28-31.)

Has the Catholic Church or any of her most distinguished children, however enthusiastic, fervent, and eloquent, ever gone further in Mary's praise?

All the flowers of poetry, love, art, liturgy, and all the flowers betokening imitation of thee, strewn at thy feet by twenty enamoured centuries; what are they as compared to this unfading, ever white and fragrant lily which the Archangel offered thee, O Mary, in the Lord's Name?

Hypocrites those who, boasting of the Christian name, reject the veneration which Catholicism of every age has rendered thee; a veneration which is but a pale reflection of that homage which thou didst receive from God's own

Messenger! Will it not be lawful for the children of men to do what God Himself commanded to be done by the Hierarchy of Heaven?

### III

> I have given you an example, that as I have done to you, so you do also.—(*John xiii, 15.*)

If our lives are worth living only in so far as they reproduce the likeness of Christ, let us take Christ as our model of devotion towards Mary, His Mother.

For thirty years the Word Incarnate had no other manifest occupation than that of obeying with absolute unreserve His Blessed Mother. Now, there is no form of devotion, veneration, and love, no manifestation of piety, more deep and true than the loving submission of a child or a youth to his mother. And that, precisely, is the devotion and piety chosen by Jesus for the space of thirty years.

Will my piety, with all its inventive genius, ever attain the measure of that total self-surrender of Him Who bears the world in the palm of His hand, at Whose summons the stars of the firmament tremblingly reply: *Adsumus?*

My Jesus, I thank Thee for bidding me share with Thee the filial love Thou hast for the Woman whom Thou callest " Mother ".

### RESOLUTIONS

First of all, can I honestly say that until now I have been truly devoted to Mary? Have I not allowed myself to be influenced by a certain type of impartial unconcern, regarding this attitude as the characteristic of men who rise above the devotional craze of the common people? Have I denied or disbelieved popular convictions about our Lady? Have I held aloof from the traditional practices of Marian devotion? In preaching about Mary, what has been my stimulus: personal conviction, or merely the law of supply and demand?

Therefore, I resolve to express my devotion towards Mary by the following:

1.  To meditate about her more, doing with regard to her what she did to her Divine Son: "*Mary treasured up all these sayings, and reflected on them in her heart.*" —(*Luke ii,* 19.)

2.  To have recourse to her every day by the recitation of the Rosary, the most popular of all prayers, and, after the liturgy, the nearest to the heart of the Church.

3.  To try to imitate her, for imitation is the hallmark of sincere love and devotion; and to imitate her particularly in those virtues which are essentially hers and which ought to be specifically the priest's—humility, purity of body and soul, love for Christ.

## DEVOTION TO OUR LADY

### SECOND MEDITATION

#### *Priestly Motives*

##### I

The Church in every age, and now more than ever, has professed such devotion to Mary that Protestants rabidly accuse her of *Mariolatry,* as though we Catholics venerated the Blessed Mother of Jesus as God. It is gross calumny; for in this, as in everything pertaining to piety, we know that the Holy Spirit comes to the aid of Christ's Bride, safeguarding her from all error.

How enthusiastically the faithful, saints and sinners, acclaim the Virgin of Nazareth! With what assured confidence they prostrate before her shrines! The face of the earth is decked with countless wonderful monuments to Mary: no name in history has them more numerous and more beautiful. O Mary, thy own prophetic utterance is ever being fulfilled with brilliant accuracy:

> Behold, from henceforth all generations shall call me blessed!

But who is called upon to guide, to consolidate, and to extend this veneration, so vital to the Church of God, if not the priest, by his fervent word and the holy inspiration of his daily example? A priest without devotion to our Blessed Lady would indeed be a strange and baffling phenomenon for the Catholic laity.

## II

We priests belong so closely to Jesus Christ, that, within His Scheme of Redemption, we must consider ourselves His necessary complement. It is only through our lips that He teaches the world His heavenly doctrine: *Going therefore, teach ye all nations.—* (*Matt. xxviii,* 19.) It is through our ministry that He incorporates members into His Mystical Body, pardons and purifies them: *Whose sins you shall forgive, they are forgiven them.—*(*John xx,* 23.) The keys of the Kingdom, both in its transitory phase here below and in its everlasting triumph, are completely under our control. Which means that, in authority, in word, and in office, I continue the saving life of Christ: *alter Christus.*

Who, then, dear Virgin Mother, can claim by so many titles as I the right to occupy in thy motherly affections the same place as thy Divine Son? Whose place will it be if not mine, seeing that, for thee, I am like another Christ?

But, in return, O Mother, it is my bounden duty to reserve in my soul for thee the throne whence thou didst reign in the Heart of Jesus.

No wonder the first to receive Mary for his Mother from the hands of the dying Saviour was a priest, John the Evangelist!

And from that hour, the disciple took her to his own.

To his own! To his heart and home. So, from to-day, dear Mother, I shall follow his example; I receive and welcome thee into the home of my heart, as someone inseparably mine, as my most cherished treasure.

### III

The Divine Word surrenders Himself into my hands every day, belittles, conceals, abases Himself to greater feebleness and silence than in the early years of His infancy; He surrenders to me as He did to Mary when He came into the world, as He did to His heavenly Father, when leaving the world: *Into thy hands, O Lord, I commend my spirit.*

In this wonderful office of mine, as tutor, master, and father and mother of Thy Sacramental Being, O divine Saviour, where shall I turn for lessons in reverence, tenderness, and chaste and loving dealings towards Thee, but to Thy own Mother? Only she ministered thus unto Thee during Thy life on earth. That I, wretched and stained, should inherit from her these sacred tasks seems unbelievable. How is it possible that I have lived a single day of my priestly life without having recourse to Mary, asking her on bended knees to teach me how to treat the Son of her womb in the Sacrament of our altars? To treat Him with that deep love and reverence with which she wrapped Him up in swaddling clothes, and served and kissed Him in the stable of Bethlehem, along the desert roads of Egypt, in the silent home of Nazareth?

## IV

*Auxilium Christianorum* is one of Mary's titles. Strength in our weakness, help in our struggles, guide in our darkness, support in our wavering: this is the firmest foundation of every popular devotion to Mary. The fallen, the attacked, the weak, will always seek refuge in Mary, by God's command. Every prayer voiced by the Church on earth throbs with all these human longings for protection: Mother of God, pray for us sinners now and at the hour of our death; Mother of mercy . . . turn thine eyes of mercy towards us. . . .

And I, a priest, am only too conscious of my weakness; in the midst of powerful enemies, who perhaps time and time again have worn me down and taken me captive, I definitely feel weak, the same as any other mortal man, and, I suspect, even weaker sometimes than they. All the powers of hell are up in arms against me and give me no respite; under the weight of so many and such heavy obligations my weak shoulders tremble.

Unto the merciful eyes of Mary, Help of Christians, therefore, I shall turn my own afflicted gaze; within the shelter of her protecting mantle, which gathers and keeps from harm her little children, as the hen gathers her chickens under her wing, I shall hide myself in life and in death.

## RESOLUTIONS

1. To attach the greatest importance to Mary's Feasts in my dealings with the faithful, announcing them in good time, bringing great numbers of souls to Confession and Communion in her honour, carrying out the liturgical Offices with pomp and splendour; and last, but by no means least, going to Confession myself on the eve of the Feasts.

It is an established fact that the above is very often the final and most effective means of bringing souls back to God and to the practice of religion, in cases of rebellion or of forgetful carelessness.

2. To start and build up one or more of those Marian Associations—Legion of Mary, Children of Mary, Miraculous Medal Association, etc.—which have proved their worth by the holy examples and actions with which they have become an inspiration to the whole Christian world.

3. To preach about Mary, about her life, her virtues, her prerogatives, not disdaining to mention well-authenticated miraculous occurrences deriving from her intercession. Let the faithful know and love her well, not merely by instinct or tradition, but with insight and depth of knowledge.

R

# THE PRIEST'S SPIRITUAL RETREAT

*Motives for making it*

## I

Let us begin by the lowest rung of the ladder: the case of the poor priest who unhappily has trampled underfoot and profaned the Sacraments by receiving and administering them in mortal sin; has celebrated Mass unworthily, making himself " guilty of the Body and Blood of the Lord "; has broken the most sacred vows of the priesthood. How will he rise up from such a state? How will he be spiritually regenerated? His ordinary exercises of piety, if any still remain, are ineffectual; his routine Confession, if he still confesses, makes little impression; nor is he impressed by the familiar sight and remembrance of the objects and things of our Religion which he handles so closely. Moreover, he knows from experience, perhaps over a number of years, that nothing serves to bring him back to the path of salvation and to amend his life. What is to be done? Will there be no remedy? Must he lose all hope? One hope remains, perhaps the one final remedy: a spiritual retreat well made.

A well-made retreat is the most efficacious means of awakening a slumbering soul; it stings the soul out of its drowsiness; it is a hot poultice for the soul frozen in sin.

For a priest in such a lamentable state, a retreat is

God's great gift, God's command, the last echoes of His grace, after which only a miracle can bring about his conversion: a miracle like that which was wrought in St. Paul but is not a common occurrence, and will surely be denied to the disloyal priest.

It is obvious that in these circumstances a spiritual retreat may well mean a priest's eternal salvation. Should he deliberately refuse or despise it, the Son of God will agonisingly say to him what He once said amid tears over Jerusalem:

> If thou also hadst known, and that in this thy day, the things that are to thy peace.
>
> —(*Luke xix*, 42.)

## II

We shall suppose that you have not fallen so low; but at the same time, you are sinking into tepidity, your pious exercises are performed grudgingly, or quite ungrudgingly you omit them or rush through them for mere formality's sake, without relish, without sustained attention of the mind, your heart far away from the mechanical motions of your lips. . . . And, granting that you have not plunged headlong into grievous sin, you are nevertheless skirting the edge of the precipice, you view temptation without dread, almost regretting your lack of courage to go the whole hog. . . . Or else, though mortal sin has not taken a firm hold on you, you at least consent to it frequently, rise up again half-heartedly, and just go limping along the path of harsh duty. In short, you live in the penumbra of lukewarmness, and God is repeating to you that mournful admonition:

"I would thou wert either hot or cold; being what thou art, lukewarm, neither hot nor cold, thou wilt make me vomit thee out of my mouth."

—(*Apoc. iii*, 15-16.)

To wrench yourself out of this most perilous condition, so near to total ruin, perhaps the only recourse left to you is a fervent retreat.


### III

If yours is the happiness not only to preserve the state of grace but also to be firmly grounded in piety, there will be no need to persuade you of the necessity of a spiritual retreat: your own conscience demands it, as a haven of peace and calm away from the tumult of external occupations, as an invitation from the Good Shepherd to withdraw a while and rest with Him:

And the Apostles coming together unto Jesus, related to him all things that they had done and taught.

And he said to them: Come apart into a desert place and rest a little.—(*Mark vi*, 30-31.)

You have learnt from a constant reading of your conscience how many resistances there are on the part of your natural inclinations, how faults can add to faults and bring your spiritual warmth right down to the freezing-point of mortal sin, how nauseating to God is lukewarmness, how numerous the obstacles which Satan and his allies put in the way of your salvation, and how difficult it is to overcome or foresee them. And you know, or at least you suspect, you have certain failings which are become part and parcel of your personality and character; and you realise that, although they constitute a hindrance in your dealings with others for the purpose of leading them to Christ or a handicap to your own spiritual advancement, you are nevertheless reluctant to face them squarely, and still more reluctant to correct them.

In this case, there is need of a thorough diagnosis and a strong antidote or a courageous amputation: drastic remedies which only a fervent retreat will provide.

## IV

Your personal honour is at stake.

> Both in their interior life and their exterior behaviour the clergy must be superior to the laity and excel them by the example of virtue and good works.—(*Canon* 124.)

You must surpass, or at least be the equal of, any lay person in moral qualities, for you are leader and guide, and without these qualities you forfeit the essential element of your leadership.

Now, if statistics were compiled of all the lay people from every class and walk of life—workers, artisans, farmers, men of letters, doctors, magistrates, military men, business people, merchants, journalists, etc.—who out of devotion only and with no other stimulant than that of their personal piety and desire for spiritual advancement make an annual retreat with all fervour and thoroughness, perhaps a glance at these statistics might make you feel ashamed of your reluctance to withdraw for a week or so every twelve months or every two or three years in order to meditate on the one thing necessary. If only we priests, I do not say excelled, but vied with, and followed after, all those good Christians in the world who, after all, have not the same pressing duty as priests have of steeping their lives in the truths of our Faith!

O Lord, do not permit among Thy ministers—the salt of the earth, the light of the world, the shepherds and guardians of Thy flock—the ignominy of their despising this triumphant means of sanctification, which so many of Thy little ones, at the promptings of Thy love, seek and apply to themselves so eagerly.

And do not look round for vain excuses. However numerous and urgent your occupations—and I take it for granted that they are occupations that have the salvation of souls for their purpose—do not merit the reproach spoken by our Lord to Martha, and bear in mind that tremendous sentence:

> What doth it profit a man if he gain the whole world and suffer the loss of his own soul?

Your works of zeal will gain considerably when you interrupt them, at the wish of the Church and of God Himself, in order to replenish your soul with the Spirit of Christ, dissipate discouragement, and purify your intentions. For Christ had you also in mind when He said: *without me you can do nothing.*

The fear of having to rough it during the retreat, because you won't get just the type of food and care you are used to, should be overcome if you take to heart our Lord's words:

> But this kind (of evil spirit) is not cast out but by prayer and fasting.—(*Matt. xvii,* 20.)

A retreat centre is not expected to turn into a first-class hotel for plutocrats and tourists; so, if necessary, put up with a little discomfort, which for many millions of poor mortals would be luxury itself. And remember, the evil spirit spoken of by Christ is still at large in the world to-day.

## RESOLUTIONS

1. For the sake of my salvation and to fulfil the express Will of God, I resolve to carry out faithfully, despite all difficulties, the instructions laid down by Canon Law and by my Ordinary concerning the spiritual retreat for the clergy.

2. If an annual retreat is not already commanded by my diocesan or religious regulations, I propose to make it voluntarily, unless I am impeded by some insurmountable obstacle. Thus I shall not be outdone by so many good layfolk.

O God, refuse me not the strength to adhere faithfully to this resolution. May I find accomplished in me each year the words of the Prophet:

> "It is but love's stratagem, thus to lead her out into the wilderness; once there, it shall be all words of comfort."—(*Osee ii*, 14.)

# THE PRIEST'S SPIRITUAL RETREAT

## SECOND MEDITATION

### *How to Make it*

#### I

I wish to make it well, with a real desire to profit by it, with deep recollection, in absolute silence.

There would be very little to commend me if through

dissipation and levity of spirit, which ill becomes a priest, i.e., an "old man" in office and profession, I squandered an opportunity entailing so many sacrifices, mine and other people's, so much expenditure of time and money, and thus disappointed the hopes of the Church and the faithful, who expected me to reap a harvest of spiritual fruit both for their own benefit and for the amendment of my life.

And according to the moralists, I should with difficulty escape the imputation of serious sin if, having entered into retreat by order of my Prelate and in fulfilment of Canon Law, I were to idle my time away, not meditating, not listening to the instructions and readings, not preparing for confession; all of which is an essential complement to the exterior observance rightly imposed by ecclesiastical law.

If the Ordinary bids me take part in a collective retreat, I shall willingly obey. If the arrangements are left to me personally, I shall always prefer to make it in company with my brother priests; for the simple reason that if I am not fervent and pious I shall have the good example of others better than myself to make me so: and if I have the good fortune to lead a devout life, I shall contribute to the spiritual welfare of those around me; and in any case, I shall share in the fulfilment of the Lord's promise:

> Where two or three are gathered together in my Name, there am I in the midst of them.
> —(*Matt. xviii.* 20.)

## II

I shall observe strict silence, ignoring every enticement and commitment to the contrary inspired by a type of companionship or "camaraderie" which, in the present circumstances, is completely out of place.

There is no gainsaying the fact that a retreat where there is talking, gossiping, back-stair buffoonery, and hole-and-corner murmuring is a retreat run to waste, barren, and harmful. On emerging from such turmoil I should be in a worse condition than on entering; far better suppress retreats altogether than have them conducted in this manner. Why impose a burden whose final upshot is an offence against God and the lowering of standards and prestige among the clergy? But where a retreat is conducted in jealously-guarded silence, it may possibly bear no fruit in an individual case, yet the general rule holds good: a silent retreat is a fruitful one.

Experience is witness: however low a priest may seem to have fallen he always preserves deep down in his soul some vestige of the divine, and in solitude God will speak to him; his smouldering faith will burst into flame; he will glimpse the darkness of the abyss whither his wanderings might plunge him, and he will draw back aghast, striking his breast with a repentance unequalled by that of any other contrite sinner. And if he has not fallen so low, he will find his soul lit up by the loveliest of supernatural lights; he will charge his spirit with new energy, a renewed determination to forge ahead along the ways of virtue.

Empty chatter being the ruin of such high hopes, and silence the pledge secure of so much good, am I going to risk the loss of all the benefits of a well-made retreat just because my thoughtlessness and childish whim demand the pleasure of blurting out some hackneyed joke, or because I cannot disappoint one or other of my light-headed old pals?

### III

To look for a quiet opportunity of stealing into a companion's room in order to while the time away in mere pleasantries; to evade supervision—if there is such a thing; far more in keeping with the clerical state not to have supervision and not to need it!—in order to play the same little pranks we left behind in the seminary; secret confabs and general criticisms; these and similar achievements may provide good cheer around the clerical dinner-table on the occasion of some big festivity; they might fit in well with the daily routine of a lay boarding-school; but surely we must agree that this kind of nonsense is not exactly a credit to a priest's retreat; it is not calculated to convey a very lofty idea of the good manners and culture (not to mention piety) of the priest, whose very name *Presbyter* implies that he is professionally mature, a man of years, destined to educate others, and who, as rector of a district or parish, would scarcely refrain from an outburst of temper if he saw youngsters acting in a similar fashion in church during the Rosary. It would be a sad day for the reputation of the clergy in any particular diocese if two or three or more of its priests had to be branded, on account of their misbehaviour during the retreat, as mischievous play-boys, incapable of taking seriously the only religious exercise where they find themselves alone; and to be put down, in the last resort, as churls unversed in the rudimentary forms of good Christian breeding, which demands at least that no one should unduly bore and harass another.

It is with profound grief and depression that one sometimes hears priests declaring they will not make another retreat at such and such a place, because their companions, by their notorious inattentiveness and ill-timed chatter, deprived them of that peace and tranquillity which those days of holy and urgent endeavour demanded.

Lord, grant me grace and strength never to be numbered among those thoughtless ministers of Thine.

## RESOLUTIONS

1. Let friends and acquaintances do and say what they will; let my natural craving to communicate with old pals protest as it likes; let those who seem to have no use for the retreat look at me askance and leeringly; I am determined to observe strict silence during the retreat, even at the cost of giving offence; for of greater value to me are the interests of my eternal salvation and respectful consideration for holy things than all the boon companionships in the world; therefore, if it is courage I need, I shall often recall the words of my Divine Master:

> For he that shall be ashamed of me and my words, of him the Son of man shall be ashamed, when he shall come in his Majesty and that of his Father and of the holy angels.—(*Luke ix*, 26.)

2. I shall refrain from proffering or countenancing the slightest criticism of what is said in the lectures, examinations of conscience, readings, etc., in the persuasion that adverse criticisms of this nature, especially when coupled with ridicule (whether just or unjust is beside the point), only serve to dry up and destroy in many cases all the fruit of the retreat, and can even give rise to incredible scandals.

# CONFESSION FOR THE PRIEST

## *The Need of Frequent Confession*

### I

All praise to Thee, dear Lord, Author of the Sacraments, for having bestowed on me, Thy most unworthy servant, so many graces and favours through the Sacrament of Penance!

*Ego te absolvo a peccatis tuis.* How sweet and tender Thy words of pardon ring in my ears: pardon for my hideous sins, a pardon so often and so abundantly flowing from Thy divine lips!

Thanks to this pardon I can face my own conscience without nightmarish fears, without a sense of unbearable loathing for the blackness and filth of the vile offences I have committed against Thee, and without having my heart torn to shreds by the thorns of remorse. Thanks to this Sacrament, I have learnt to know myself a little, having been constrained to probe so frequently into the tortuous, obscure, labyrinthine ways of my own mind; and thus I have succeeded in determining the substance, shape, and form of my duties in life. Sacramental confession has become for me the chief spur goading me along the path of virtue without deviating to the right or left; it has been, humanly speaking, a divine and human bridle, wrought of divine faith and lawful human respect, drawing me back with shame from life's miry swamps, reminding me that I should have to confess the evil which I was about to perpetrate.

Thou well knowest, O God, and I know too, that when in the vertigo of passions carrying me to the edge of the precipice, without this leash I would have thrown myself headlong into the abyss, never perhaps to rise again; this Thou knowest, and I know it, too.

And is it possible, dear Lord, for Christians, let alone Thy priests, to consider this Sacrament of Divine Pity something tyrannical and unworthy of our human dignity? Could the Goodness of God invent anything more concise, less arduous, more ennobling to the heart of man, and within easier reach of all, whereby man must lift himself up, spontaneously regenerate himself, so to speak, without the application of exterior forces?

Heaven and earth bless the Lord, for He is the Father of all mercies!

## II

These two concluding meditations are the most important in the whole book. For if they really convince me and make me determined to show practical devotion to the Sacrament of Penance they will profit me as much as all the other meditations combined.

I have to confess my sins very often. Why say, I *have* to? I certainly have the right, the supreme privilege, of confessing frequently, every week or oftener still; approaching the arms and feet of my heavenly Father, like a poor prodigal. And my Father wishes me to do this, He requires it of me:

Canon 906: Each and every one of the faithful of either sex has the obligation, from the time he attains the use of reason, to confess all his sins truthfully at least once a year, that is to say, all his mortal sins which have not yet been properly confessed and directly remitted by absolution.

What shame and sorrow for the Church, and what ignominy for the priest, if the latter should even fail to confess his sins once a year! Is it possible to visualise such a terrible case?

> *Canon* 125: The Ordinary must take care that the clergy go frequently to Confession.

What does " frequently " mean? Would you call three-monthly or even monthly confession frequent? Any Christian in the world would say no. Confession is frequent when made once a week or at least once a fortnight.

And remember your obligation *sub gravi* to administer the Sacraments in the state of grace, and the admonition given in the Missal under the heading *Ritus servandus in celebratione Missae*. In a prefatory paragraph it says:

> " The priest about to say Mass having, if necessary, made his sacramental confession . . ."

And Canon Law defines this obligation more explicitly:

> *Canon* 807: The priest who should find himself in mortal sin shall not dare to say Holy Mass without previous sacramental confession, no matter how contrite he may be over his sins.

You see? In order not to fall into grievous sin, or in order to rise again after having fallen, you must go to confession frequently, even twice a week or oftener, if needs be, so as not to sink into the deepest and most terrible profanations.

## III

There are obstacles in the way of frequent confession, occasionally obstacles that would seem insurmountable: either physical, such as the isolation of your parish, the rough roads and long distances to reach the neighbouring parish, your age and state of health; or moral obstacles, which are no less painful: the lack of a good confessor, a man of virtue and sound commonsense, in whom you can have confidence. There is no denying that such obstacles do exist, and Thou, Lord, who knowest and weighest these obstacles at their true value, art moved to pity for those poor priests who for Thy sake and in order to obey their Prelates deprive themselves of facilities which the laity themselves enjoy in abundant measure, the facilities to receive Thy forgiveness in the sacred Tribunal. Therefore in this, as in many other matters, we might apply the literal interpretation of the psalm as contained in the Vulgate:

Propter verba labiorum tuorum ego custodivi vias duras. . . .

But I must not exaggerate the difficulties and obstacles. If a medical doctor told me to go to him once a week or even more frequently, and promised me a definite cure on condition that I followed his orders, would bad roads or long journeys or any amount of expense and trouble stop me from going to him? Then, for the sake of spiritual healing, Lord, I shall overcome just as great difficulties; because life has taught me that the only treatment which cures or arrests the course of moral disease is the Sacrament of Penance; and if, unfortunately, I do not dispose of a prudent, understanding and virtuous confessor, I shall kneel before any priest, however unworthy and incompetent I may feel him to be. A loving trust in Thee, dear Lord, will enable me to do this. But besides, the efficacy of this spiritual treatment does not depend on the good or bad qualities of the minister of the Sacrament; it is Thou, Lord, who bestowest forgiveness through him.

## IV

Will-power is not enough to make me approach the confessor every week or as often as I need him. It is to be feared that my confessions are ineffective through lack of serious preparation. The day I go to confession I shall devote my morning meditation to preparing for it.

Here are the three main points I shall consider:

*First: Examination of conscience.*—I shall delve courageously into my conscience, not sparing its most rugged or boggy patches, asking God for strength and light to arrive at a clear-cut knowledge of the quality, kind, and number of my mortal sins, or, if I have no mortal sins, to discover three or four venial sins which expose me to the greatest dangers.

*Second: Contrition.*—In order to excite myself to sincere sorrow for having offended God my Redeemer, for having repaid Him with so much ingratitude, and transgressed His precepts, I shall dwell upon the most persuasive and impressive motives of faith, and I shall detest my wrong-doing wholeheartedly.

*Third: Purpose of amendment.*—I shall resolve, no matter what the cost, to correct all my seriously sinful lapses, and, if I have only venial sins, at least that which does me the most damage, and to promise their amendment specifically until my next confession.

If only I had taken my shortcomings one by one and combated each one with resoluteness and energy after each confession, how many of them would have been rooted out by now!

Above all and however much trouble it may entail, I shall resolve to cut out the *voluntary proximate* occasions of sin. If the occasion is not voluntary, if it is inevitable (and I shall not allow myself to be deceived easily on this point), I shall make it a remote occasion. This I shall resolve to do even if it should be as painful to me as cutting off my right hand or foot, or plucking out an eye. And I shall put my resolution into practice as soon as I have got up from confession, if I had not already done so before confession—which would be the best thing to do—or if a prudent confessor does not oblige me to take these measures before returning for absolution.

Dear Lord and God, I really do wish to save my soul, I do want to walk the road to heaven, even if I have to go all alone or eyeless or without hands and feet.

## RESOLUTIONS

1. As often as I confess my sins I shall do so making an effort to reap all the fruits of the Sacrament, considering my preparation for confession the most serious and profoundest act of my religious and moral life. I can make a good Communion without much reflexion, but I cannot confess properly without a complete renewal of my innermost mind:

> Cor mundum crea in me Deus, et spiritum rectum innova in visceribus meis.

2. I shall go to confession invariably once a week—or oftener if the need arises—with a fixed and well-chosen confessor, or, if I have no choice, with anyone available. God, Who sees my good will, is pledged to make up for the shortcomings of His minister. All my other acts of piety and self-denial must give place to this great and fundamental act of frequent confession.

Convinced that in the fulfilment of these two resolutions lies the surest sign of my predestination, I trust, O God and Father of the predestined, that Thou wilt not refuse me the strength of will required to carry them out faithfully.

## CONFESSION FOR THE PRIEST

### SECOND MEDITATION

*Evils Arising from the Priest's Neglect of Confession*

### I

If there is ever a priest who goes for weeks and months and possibly years without confessing his sins, without purifying his soul from stain in the Blood of the Lamb shed unto the remission of sin, how can this priest hope to escape the indictment of being a man devoid of piety or moral rectitude, of being downright wicked, dishonest, and dissolute?

Having fled from the Sacrament of Penance, how many weeks, how many months would he go through without profaning with detestable sacrilege not only as many Sacraments as he administers but the very Body and Blood of the Eternal Word in the Sacrifice of the Mass? How long could he hope by his own unaided efforts to remain free of grave sin?

When a priest reaches the stage of venturing with supreme audacity to eat and drink unworthily of Christ's Body and Blood by celebrating Mass sacrilegiously, when a priest tramples on the very Person of Christ, what else is there for him to respect? Christ's commands? Are they of greater value than Christ in Person? One may gather *a priori* that such a priest will contemn and walk over with equal audacity as many commandments (and they will be more than one) as come in the way of his unleashed passions; abandoned by God, he will treat God's laws with at least as little respect as he treated the Divine Person, the God of God. What qualms of conscience will refrain him from brushing aside the laws of justice when it comes to administering or exacting goods that do not belong to him? How lightly he will tear to tatters those bonds wherewith the fear of God and his own solemn priestly promise sought to curb the wild lustings of the flesh! Once the hope of eternal reward begins to evaporate, or nearly so, due to his habitual state of mortal sin, what depths of crime will he not plunge into?

## II

And each time farther and farther away from confession, he will perhaps begin to hate this last remedy like a bad dream; he will turn away indefinitely from all examination of his own interior; he will become estranged to himself, and by dint of refusing to listen to the appeals of his conscience, by sheer deliberate distraction in order to silence its importunate warnings, his conscience—the echo of God's Voice—will gradually lose pitch, will muffle and extinguish its jarring inflexions, and making common cause with the inadvertence and the crass ignorance of an intelligence which allowed years to elapse without revising its distasteful obligations, his conscience will finally drop off to sleep, losing all sensitiveness and delicate awareness in order to sink lower and lower into the most abominable excesses without noticing them and with such a hardness of heart that the most terrible admonitions of Divine Justice will be powerless to soften; and then will be fulfilled in that priest the fearful words of Isaias, transcribed by the four Evangelists:

"Go then . . . and give a message to this people of mine: Listen as you will, but ever without understanding: watch all, and nothing perceive!

Thy office is to dull the hearts of this people of mine, deaden their ears, dazzle their eyes, so that they cannot see with those eyes, hear with those ears, understand with that heart, and turn back to me, and win healing."—(*Is. vi*, 9-10.)

This is the foreshadowing of the just judgements of God against those who have spent their life's energies fighting and resisting the Holy Spirit.

Would to God such fearful lines were written only in the pages of Sacred Scripture! Would to God they were not engraved indelibly in more than one priestly heart lost beyond recovery and sealed with the death of the sinner! This, in the last resort, is the fate of the priest who fled from Sacramental Confession; this is the history of the impenitence of weeks and months and years issuing with relentless logic into an impenitence final and everlasting.

## III

A priest of the type described above, being insensitive to his own sad condition, will show a much greater indifference towards the spiritual evils of his neighbour, even of those souls whom he is bound by duty of justice to lead to salvation. He will obstinately refuse to sit down and hear confessions—he does not go to confession himself; and well may the Church appeal to him and command him in every pitch and key to draw souls to the Sacraments, he just turns a deaf ear: all her admonitions and precepts are dismissed as a piece of play-acting, as narrow-minded fads and pietistic extravagances.

That, O God, *that* is the reason for those Catholic churches and chapels where the confessional is a mere ornament gathering dust and cob-webs and mouldering away, where the Tabernacle is well-nigh superfluous and the altar-rails remain unused by the parishioners, who take it as the natural thing to go from one year's end to the other without receiving the Bread of Life, except during the period of Easter duties. And when that day arrives the indolent pastor will condescend, with no little reluctance and hurriedness, to sit down and hear his peoples' confessions with all the rush and fury of a hurricane, and without having gone to the trouble of preparing or instructing them in advance; and once the hurricane of confessions and the tornado of communions have blown over, again the Tabernacle doors are closed and the confessional is relegated to oblivion until the following year, to the great relief and rejoicing of both shepherd and flock. . . .

And God forbid that the only person in the parish

who has not fulfilled the Paschal precept be the priest, the confessor himself!

O Jesus, let there not be a single case of this; let this dark picture exist only in the writer's imagination, the outlet of his irrational pessimism and of his ill-founded fears; no, never, never an appalling reality!

## RESOLUTIONS

1. My first resolution is to confess my sins every week, as so many other people do who are not priests, and to confess as often as I need to in order to celebrate Mass worthily and administer the Sacraments in the state of grace. And this resolution is based on the following convictions: a proper and frequent reception of the Sacrament of Penance is sufficient to preserve a priest within the terms of honourableness and virtue befitting his priestly state, or to recall him if he has fallen away; not a few of the abuses and weaknesses and scandals among the clergy are directly the outcome of their neglecting this efficacious Sacrament; in spite of my inherent frailties, I know that frequent and fervent confession will keep me in the state of grace; my own experience has borne out the experience of others, namely, that nearly every virtue of Christian souls is rooted in them through this Sacrament. Therefore, to keep my resolution of frequent confession I shall crash my way through all difficulties.

2. Out of gratitude for the ineffable benefits God has bestowed and will continue to bestow upon me, in His loving Mercy, through this Divine Sacrament of Penance, I am resolved to hold this ministerial duty of mine in the highest esteem, as being my noblest occu-

pation and the task most profitable to my neighbour; and in spite of fatigue and annoyances that accompany the hearing of confessions I shall devote myself to it with all my heart and as often as I am permitted to do so; in order that God's other children may not be deprived of what I, unworthy sinner, can obtain for myself with such great ease and comfort to my soul.

# APPENDIX

## FROM THE LETTER OF BL. PIUS X
## TO CATHOLIC PRIESTS[1]

*Prayer is the chief means of holiness.*

Since sanctity of life, as everyone knows, is the
fruit of the will helped by divine grace, God has
provided abundantly for us that grace may never
be wanting to anyone who desires it. It is chiefly
obtained by assiduity in prayer, and there is this
inevitable connection between prayers and holiness:
that the latter cannot exist without the former.

This is a truth which St. Chrysostom wholly
endorses, saying: " I consider it evident to all that
it is simply impossible to continue in virtue without
the protection of prayer "; and St. Augustine says
pointedly: " He in truth knows how to live rightly
who knows how to pray rightly " (*Hom. IV. ex.* 50).

Christ Himself persuades us of the fact by His
frequent exhortations and still more by His own
example. He was wont to retire to the desert to
pray, or to go alone into the mountains, and even to
spend whole nights in prayer. He frequently went to
the Temple, and often, when surrounded by the

[1] This letter was sent on the 50th anniversary of the
Pope's priestly ordination. This extract is from the translation published by Burns Oates and Washbourne, 4th.
edition, 1944, pages 15-27. The sub-titles have been in-
serted by the translator of this book.

multitudes, He prayed publicly with eyes raised to Heaven. Lastly, upon the Cross, in the pangs of death, He besought His Father with a strong cry and tears.

### *The priest must be a man of prayer.*

Let us hold it as a fundamental truth, that if a priest wishes to live up to the standard required by his position and his calling, he must give himself with intense earnestness to prayer. It is much to be deplored that prayer is too often made rather out of routine than with fervour of spirit; the Psalms for the appointed Hours are recited listlessly, a few invocations are added, and no other time is set apart daily to commune with God with the piety which lifts the heart heavenwards. Yet the precept of Christ, "that we ought always to pray," should be obeyed by priests more than by others. St. Paul, faithful to its teaching, counsels us most earnestly: " Be instant in prayer, watching in it in thanksgiving " (*Col.* IV. 2); " Pray without ceasing " (*I Thess.* V. 17). How often does the soul which is eager for its own sanctification and that of others find opportunities of uniting itself to God during the day! Anguish of soul, strong and tenacious temptation, the need of virtue, slackness and failure in work, oft-repeated falls and negligences, and lastly, the fear of God's judgements, all these constrain us to cry out to God in prayer; and besides obtaining the help we need, we can easily enrich ourselves by good works. Nor must our prayers be confined to our own needs, for in the fearful deluge

of crime which overflows on all sides we must
earnestly implore and beseech the Divine mercy,
praying with insistence to Christ, Who is prodigal
of grace in the Adorable Sacrament of the Altar:
" Spare, O Lord, spare Thy people."

## Daily meditation

It is of capital importance with regard to prayer,
that a certain time should be set aside every day
to meditate on things eternal. No priest can omit
this without being guilty of great carelessness and
without grave loss to his soul. St. Bernard, Abbot,
writing to his former pupil, Eugenius III, then
Pope, frankly and earnestly cautioned him against
neglecting daily meditation and allowing the many
and great cares of his office to be an excuse for
remissness. With consummate prudence he proceeded to enumerate the advantages of this
exercise:

> " Meditation purifies the source from which
> it springs—that is, the mind; it disciplines the
> affections, directs action, restrains excess,
> regulates morals, ennobles and orders the
> whole life. In short, it gives the knowledge of
> Divine as well as of human things. It estab-
> lishes order where confusion reigned, it binds
> that which was loosened, gathers that which
> was scattered, penetrates hidden things, seeks
> out the truth, distinguishing it from false
> appearances, bringing to light falsehood and
> deceit. In meditating we foresee what has to
> be done, review what has been accomplished,

and thus leave no defect in the soul which needs correction. In prosperity it anticipates adversity, in adversity it seems not to suffer, showing in the latter case fortitude and in the former, prudence." *(De Consideratione.)*

This summary of the effects of meditation teaches us that it is not only most salutary, but that it is very necessary.

### Weariness of soul without prayer

Although all the functions of priesthood are sacred and worthy of veneration, it happens that through routine those engaged in them do not always appreciate them as befits religious things. In consequence the heart grows cold imperceptibly, tepidity easily follows, and weariness of things sacred ensues.

Furthermore, the priest's daily work is necessarily carried on, as it were, " among a perverse people," so that often in exercising charity towards his flock he has to beware of the insidious snares of the devil. What, then, if it be so easy for religious souls to be tarnished by contact with the world? It is clear how urgently necessary it is to contemplate eternal truth daily, in order to renew the mind and will and to strengthen them against temptation. Moreover, a certain heavenly-mindedness befits the priest, as being one who must himself know, speak of, and breathe into others the love of heavenly things; it behoves him, then, so to order his whole life that, with a lofty independence of human considerations, he may fulfil his sacred duties under the guidance of faith and according to the mind of God.

## *Meditation nourishes fervour*

That daily meditation helps more than anything else to produce and sustain this habit of mind, this almost natural union with God, is so obvious to the thinking mind that We need insist no further upon it. A sad proof of this necessity is found in the lives of those priests who despise and make light of this practice. They are men in whom that priceless blessing, *sensus Christi,* has grown feeble; they give themselves wholly to vain and earthly things, fufilling their sacred obligations negligently, coldly, and perhaps unworthily.

When the grace of Ordination was still fresh upon them they prepared their souls diligently for the prayer of praise, lest they should be as those who tempt God. Seeking times and places free from disturbance and striving to listen to and understand the Voice of God, in union with the Psalmist they poured forth their souls in praise, in sighs, and in rejoicings. But what a change has come to them! Hardly anything remains of that ardent piety with which the Divine Mysteries once inspired them. How beloved were those Tabernacles of old when they yearned not only to approach the table of the Lord themselves, but to invite and to bring others with them! What purity of heart and fervent desire in their preparation for the Holy Sacrifice! In its august ceremonies, what reverence and perfect decorum, what outpourings of gratitude followed while the blessed odour of Christ was diffused happily among the people! " Call to mind," We beseech you, beloved sons, " call to mind the former days" when the soul was fervent, nourished on holy meditation.

### Spiritual atrophy without mental prayer

Among those who fail to " consider in the heart" or who look upon mental prayer as a burden, there are some who, though aware of the consequent spiritual atrophy, excuse themselves on the plea that it is manifestly to the advantages of others that they should be wholly taken up with the distractions and cares of the ministry.

They make a sad mistake, for, not being accustomed to commune with God, when they speak to others of Him, or try to instruct them in the truths of Christianity, the divine Spirit breathes not through them, and the Gospel, in their hands, seems almost without life. Their voice, however striking, prudent, and eloquent it may be, is not the voice of the Good Shepherd, to which the sheep hearken unto their salvation; it is but empty noise and passing vanity, often bearing fruit only in pernicious example, to the discredit of religion and the scandal of the good.

So also it is with the whole life of such a man; it produces no solid fruit, or at least only a short-lived one, since there lacks that heavenly shower which " the prayer of him that humbleth himself " calls down in great abundance.

We can only grieve bitterly over those who, carried away by dangerous novelties, do not fail to hold opposite doctrines, and consider as lost, time spent on meditation and prayer. What terrible blindness! Would that, examining the matter seriously for themselves, they might realise whither this neglect and contempt of prayer leads. From it springs pride and obstinacy with the most bitter fruits, evils which Our fatherly affection dreads to mention and desires to check.

## The paramount importance of meditation

May Our exhortation, then, beloved sons, sink deep into their hearts and yours, for it is also Christ's: "Take ye heed, watch and pray." Let each one labour assiduously in holy meditation, trustfully asking at the same time, "Lord, teach us to pray." Nor ought we to think little of the reason which urges us to meditate—namely, the greatness of the counsel and the virtue which comes from it and which is so useful in that most difficult of all works, the cure of souls.

St. Charles Borromeo's words on this subject are to the point and worthy to be remembered: "Brethren, understand that nothing is so necessary to those in the Ecclesiastical state as mental prayer; it should precede, accompany, and follow all our actions. 'I will sing,' says the prophet, 'and I will understand.' If, brother, you administer the Sacraments, meditate on what you do; if you celebrate Mass, think upon what you offer; if you recite the Psalms, reflect on what you say and to Whom you speak; if you direct souls, ponder on the Blood by which they have been washed."

It is not without good reason, therefore, that the Church bids us frequently repeat after the Psalmist: "Blessed is the man who meditates on the law of the

Lord; his will remaineth day and night; all whatsoever he shall do shall ever prosper." Let, then, one noble motive take the place of all others; if the priest is called and is " another Christ " by sharing in His power, ought he not also to be " another Christ " by imitation? " Let it, then, be our chief study to meditate on the life of Jesus Christ." (*Imitation of Christ*, i. 11.)

### Spiritual reading as an aid to mental prayer

It is very important that to this daily meditation on holy things the priest should take care to add the reading of spiritual books, especially those divinely inspired. So did St. Paul direct Timothy: " Attend unto reading." (1 *Tim.* iv. 13.) So also St. Jerome, in instructing Nepotian on the sacerdotal life: " Let a spiritual book be ever in your hands," adding the reason: " Learn that which you will teach, acquire that which is according to truth, that your doctrine may be sound and that you may be able to convince the unbeliever." Great progress is made by priests who persevere in this habit of reading; they preach Christ with unction; instead of enervating and distracting the minds and hearts of their hearers, they lead them to better things, lifting up their souls with heavenly desires. . . .

Who does not know the very great influence exercised on the mind by a friend who advises freely, who counsels, rebukes, encourages, and preserves us from error? " Blessed is he that findeth a true friend" (*Ecclus.* xxv. 12). Now spiritual books may

be accounted as true and faithful friends. They
remind us forcibly of the precepts laid down by
authority concerning true discipline, awaken in us
the still small voices of Heaven, reprehend all falling away from resolutions, disturb deceitful calm,
expose less worthy affections and self-deception,
and reveal the many dangers that lie in the path of
the unwary.

This they do with such unobtrusive kindness that
they prove themselves to be, not only friends, but
the very best of friends. They are beside us whenever we please, ever ready to minister to our secret
needs, their voice is never harsh, their counsel
never biassed, their utterance never deceitful or
fainthearted.

### Spiritual reading consolidates belief

Many remarkable examples show the advantage
of reading spiritual books, notably St. Augustine,
who thus began his glorious service of the Church:

> " Take up and read; take up and read." . . .
> " I took up (the Epistles of the Apostle St.
> Paul), I opened and read in silence. . . . As if
> the light of certainty had been poured in upon
> my heart, the shades of all hesitation fled."
> (*Confessions*, Bk. viii. c. 12).

On the other hand, alas! it too often happens in
our days that some among the clergy are overcome
by the shadows of doubt and follow after the things
of this world because, instead of reading spiritual
works and the Scripture, they give the preference

to quite other matters and to the crowds of periodicals full of immorality and insidious errors.

Beware, beloved sons; trust not to age or to maturity, be not deluded by the false hope that by thus reading you can better serve the common weal. Keep to the fixed limits, those appointed by the Church, and those which prudence and charity dictate in your own case: for if poison be taken the victim rarely escapes without damage.

### Examination of conscience for the priest

The advantages derived from spiritual reading and meditation on heavenly things will be still more abundant if the priest tests himself as to how far his reading and meditation enter into his daily life.

On this point St. Chrysostom's words are specially applicable to priests. Every night before going to sleep " appeal to the judgment of your conscience; demand its account; examine, analyse the evil doings of the day, and inflict some penance."

The soundest advice and exhortations of most prudent spiritual directors prove how salutary this custom is, and how much it conduces to the practice of Christian virtue. For instance, St. Bernard teaches:

> " Sift thine own virtue diligently, by a daily revision of thy deeds. Observe carefully the advance made or count thy backslidings. . . . Seek to know thyself. . . . Set thy transgressions before thine eyes. Place thyself in thine own presence, as if thou wert another, and then bewail thy misdeeds."

What a matter for regret it will be if those words of Our Lord should be fulfilled in you: " The children of this world are wiser than the children of light " (*Luke* xvi. 8)! We know how carefully they look after their affairs, how they balance receipts and expenditure, auditing their accounts regularly and most accurately; they grieve over losses, and spare no energy to make them good. And we, if our minds are bent on attaining to honour, on acquiring property, or on gaining the glory of a public reputation for learning, we behave with indifference and contempt in that most important and most difficult matter: the attainment of sanctity . . . .

## The priest's need of the Sacrament of Penance

Nor does experience assert less authoritatively the loss and detriment that follow when a man turns from that tribunal where justice sits in judgment and conscience is both the accuser and the accused. In such a one you will not find that prudent behaviour so desirable in a Christian, which prompts him to avoid even venial sin, and that modesty so becoming to a priest which shudders at the slightest offence against God. Worse still, his indifference and negligence sometimes reaches such a pitch that he ceases to have recourse to the Sacrament of Penance, that most efficacious and ever-present help left to us by Christ, as a most liberal provision against our weakness and a most signal proof of His mercy. For unfortunately it is undeniable and most deplorable, though it not infrequently happens, that he who by thunderbolts of eloquence keeps others from sin has no fears about himself and is callous as to his own faults. While urging and exhorting others to hasten to purify their souls by confession, he himself acts slothfully and even delays for months; he who pours healing oil and wine into the wounds of others falls stricken by the wayside and foolishly fails to seek for himself the help of his brother near at hand.

The results of such carelessness spread far and wide, and are to-day a disgrace in the eyes of God and His Church, a scandal to Christian peoples, and a degradation to the priestly order.

### Woe to the priest who neglects his own soul

In considering these things, as We, in conscience, are bound to do, Our soul, beloved sons, is filled with grief, and We break forth into lamentations: Woe to the priest who is not loyal to his vocation and who, by his infidelity, dishonours the holy Name of God, to Whom he is consecrated in holiness! The falling away of those in honour is most disgraceful.

> "Great is the dignity of priests, but great is their ruin if they sin. Let us rejoice in their elevation, but tremble at their fall, for the joy at having held the heights is not comparable to the sorrow of being flung down from the summits" (*St. Jerome in Ezechiel*, Lib. XIII, c. 44, v. 30).

Woe, then, to the priest who, heedless of himself, gives up the practice of earnest prayer, who neglects spiritual reading, who never recollects himself in the examination of conscience. Neither the festering wounds of his soul, nor the tears of his Mother the Church will move him before he is smitten with the terrible denunciation:

> " Bind the heart of this people, and make their ears heavy, and shut their eyes, lest they see with their eyes, and hear with their ears, and understand with their heart, and be converted and I heal them" (*Isa.* vi. 10).

May God, Who is rich in mercy, deliver you all from such an unhappy fate, beloved sons. He Who reads our inmost heart sees there no bitterness, but the love of a pastor and of a father.

" For what is our hope, our joy, our crown of glory? Are not you, in the the presence of Our Lord Jesus Christ?" (1 *Thess.* ii. 19).

# PREPARATION FOR MASS

Lord, do not remember our sins, or those of our fathers, nor punish us for our misdeeds. (*Alleluia.*)

*Psalm 83*

Lord of hosts, how I love thy dwelling-place!

For the courts of the Lord's house, my soul faints with longing.

The living God! at his name my heart, my whole being thrills with joy.

Where else should the sparrow find a home, the dove a nest for her brood, but at thy altar, Lord of hosts, my King and my God?

How blessed, Lord, are those who dwell in thy house! They will be ever praising thee.

How blessed is the man who finds his strength in thee!

He sets his heart on an upward journey, that leads through a valley of weeping, but to his goal.

Strong in their Master's blessing, the pilgrims go on from height to height, till they meet him in Sion, the God of all gods.

Lord God of hosts, listen to my prayer; God of Israel, grant me audience!

God, ever our protector, do not disregard us now; look favourably upon him whom thou hast anointed.

Willingly would I give a thousand of my days for one spent in thy courts!

Willingly lie there forgotten, in the house of my God, so I might dwell no more in the abode of sinners!

God loves mercy and faithfulness; all favour, all honour, come of the Lord's gift.

To innocent lives he will never refuse his bounty;

Lord of hosts, blessed is the man who puts his confidence in thee.

Glory be to the Father.

## Psalm 84

What blessings, Lord, thou has granted to this land of thine, restoring Israel from captivity.

Pardoning thy people's guilt, burying away the record of their sins,

All thy anger calmed, thy fierce displeasure forgotten!

And now, God of our deliverance, do thou restore us; no longer let us see thy frown.

Wouldst thou always be indignant with us? Must thy resentment smoulder on, age after age?

Nay, thou wilt relent, O God, and give

fresh life, to rejoice the spirits of thy people.

Show us thy mercy, Lord; grant us thy deliverance!

Let me listen, now, to the voice of the Lord God within me; it is a message of peace he sends to his people;

To his loyal servants, that come back, now, to take counsel of their hearts.

For us, his worshippers, deliverance is close at hand; in this land of ours, the divine glory is to find a home.

See, where mercy and faithfulness meet in one; how justice and peace are united in one embrace!

Faithfulness grows up out of the earth, and from heaven, justice looks down.

The Lord, now, will grant us his blessing, to make our land yield its harvest;

Justice will go on before him to make the way ready for his progress.

Glory be to the Father.

## Psalm 85

Turn thy ear, Lord, and listen to me in my helplessness and my need.

Protect a life dedicated to thyself; rescue a servant of thine, my God, that puts his trust in thee.

Have mercy, O Lord; for mercy I plead continually; comfort thy servant's heart, this heart that aspires, Lord, to thee.

Who is so kind and forgiving, Lord, as thou art; who so rich in mercy to all who invoke thee?

Give a hearing then, Lord, to my prayer; listen to my plea when I cry out to thee in a time of sore distress, counting on thy audience.

There is none like thee, Lord, among the gods; none can do as thou doest.

Lord, all the nations thou hast made must needs come and worship thee, honouring thy name;

So great thou art, so marvellous in thy doings, thou who alone art God.

Guide me, Lord, in thy own way, protected by thy own faithful care; make this heart thrill with reverence for thy name.

O Lord my God, with all my heart I will give thee thanks, eternally hold thy name in honour.

For the greatness of the mercy thou hast shown me, in rescuing me thus from the lowest depths of hell.

And now, O God, see how the despisers of thy law have set upon me,

How their dread conspiracy threatens my life, with no thought of thee to restrain it!

But thou, Lord, art a God of mercy and pity, patient, compassionate, true to thy promise.

Look upon me and be merciful to me;

rescue, with thy sovereign aid, one whose mother bore him to thy service!

Show me some token of thy favour; let my enemies see, abashed, how thou, Lord, dost help me,

How thou, Lord, dost comfort me.

Glory be to the Father.

### Psalm. 115

I trusted, and trusting found words to utter in my abasement;

Bewildered, I said, Man's faith is false; but thy mercies, Lord, have never failed me;

What return shall I make to thee?

I will take the cup that is pledge of my deliverance, and invoke the name of the Lord upon it;

I will pay the Lord my vows in the presence of all his people.

Dear in the Lord's sight is the death of those who love him;

And am not I, Lord, thy servant, born of thy own handmaid?

Thou hast broken the chains that bound me; I will sacrifice in thy honour, and call on the name of the Lord.

Before a throng of worshippers I will pay the Lord my vows, here in the courts of the Lord's house, here, Jerusalem, in thy heart.

Glory be to the Father.

## *Psalm* 129

Out of the depths I cry to thee, O Lord,
Master, listen to my voice;

Let but thy ears be attentive to the voice
that calls on thee for pardon.

If thou, Lord, take heed of our iniquities,
Master, who has strength to bear it?

Ah, but with thee there is forgiveness; I will
wait for thee, Lord, as thou commandest.

My soul relies on his promise, my soul waits
patiently for the Lord.

From the morning watch till night has
fallen, let Israel trust in the Lord;

The Lord with whom there is mercy, the
Lord with whom there is power to ransom.

He it is that will ransom Israel from all his
iniquities.

Glory be to the Father.


### (*Then is repeated*)

*Ant.* Lord, do not remember our sins, or
those of our fathers, nor punish us for
our misdeeds. (*Alleluia.*)

Lord, have mercy,

Christ, have mercy,

Lord, have mercy.

Our Father.

V/.   And lead us not into temptation.

R/.   But deliver us from evil.

V/.   I said : Lord have mercy on me.

R/.   Heal my soul, thou against whom I have sinned.

V/.   Give but a glance, Lord.

R/.   And have pity on thy servants.

V/.   Be merciful to us, Lord,

R/.   As our hope is in thee.

V/.   Let thy priests be clad in righteousness.

R/.   Thy holy ones rejoice in thee.

V/.   Lord, cleanse me from my hidden sins.

R/.   And keep thy servant from all wilful wrongdoing.

V/.   Lord, heed my prayer.

R/.   And let my cry be heard by thee.

V/.   The Lord be with you.

R/.   And with *you*.

Let us pray.

Incline thy merciful ear to our prayers, all-gentle God, and enlighten our heart with the grace of the Holy Spirit, so that we may become worthy ministers of thy sacraments and love thee with undying love.

O God, to whom all hearts are open, all desires known, and from whom no secrets are hid, cleanse the thoughts of our hearts by the inpouring of thy Holy Spirit, giving us grace to love thee perfectly and praise thee worthily.

Refine our hearts and affections, Lord, in the fire of the Holy Spirit, so that our bodies may be chaste and our hearts clean to serve thee according to thy pleasure.

May the Comforter who proceeds from thee bring light into our minds, we pray thee, Lord, and guide us to all truth, as thy Son promised.

May the power of the Holy Spirit be with us, we pray thee, Lord; may it gently cleanse our hearts and guard us from all harm.

God, who didst teach the faithful by sending the light of the Holy Spirit into their hearts, grant that, by the gift of that Spirit, right judgment may be ours, and that we may ever find joy in his comfort.

Visit our consciences, we beg thee, Lord, and purify them, so that our Lord Jesus Christ, thy Son, may at his coming find in us a dwelling-place prepared for him; who is God, living and reigning with thee, in the unity of the Holy Spirit, for ever and ever. Amen.

## PRAYER
### (Attributed to St. Ambrose)

### SUNDAY

Thou, greatest of priests, true pontiff, Jesus Christ, who for the sake of us wretched sinners didst offer thyself, a pure and unblemished victim, to God the Father upon the altar of the cross; who didst give us thy flesh to eat and thy blood to drink; establishing this eucharist in the power of thy Holy Spirit, and saying: *Whenever you shall do these things, you shall do them in memory of me;* I pray thee, by that same blood of thine, the costly ransom paid for our salvation, by that wondrous and transcendent charity which moved thee so to love us wretched and unworthy beings that thou didst wash away our sins in thy blood: teach me, thy unworthy servant whom it has pleased thee, among thy other gifts, to call to the priestly office, not for any merits of mine, but only because of thy merciful kindness; teach me by thy Holy Spirit to approach this great sacrifice with that reverent worship and devout awe which is due and fitting. By thy grace give me such constant faith and understanding, so firm a grasp of its meaning, that whatever I think or say concerning this great sacramental rite may please thee and advance the welfare of my soul.

Let thy good Spirit enter my heart, there to utter its silent music, its wordless declaration of all truth. For here are deep mysteries, over which a sacred veil is drawn.

In thy great loving-kindness enable me to come with heart and mind unsoiled to the celebration of this Mass. Free my heart from those unholy, idle, and hurtful thoughts which defile it. Let the power of thy blessed angels give me tender and true protection, guarding me so stoutly that the enemies of all good shall retire abashed. By virtue of this great sacrament, and by the hand of thy holy angel, drive away from me and from all thy servants the hard and stubborn spirit of pride, vainglory, envy, blasphemy, fornication, uncleanness, doubt, and mistrust. Let those who persecute us be confounded; let those bent on our undoing be themselves undone.

## MONDAY

With the heavenly dew of thy blessing, King of virgins and Lover of stainless chastity, quench the wildfire of lust in my body, leaving all of me, body and soul, steadfast in purity. Deaden within me the stings of desire and all lustful excitements. Give me true and abiding chastity, and therewith all those other gifts of thine in which thou truly delightest, enabling me to offer sacrifice in praise of thee with a chaste body and clean heart. With what heartfelt contrition, what flowing tears and devout awe, what chastity of spirit and flesh ought I to offer up this heavenly, God-given sacrifice, in which thy body is truly eaten, thy blood is truly drunk: this marriage of heaven and earth, of heights and depths, in the presence of thy holy angels, wherein by a wonder past all telling thou art thyself both priest and sacrifice!

## TUESDAY

Almighty God, who shall be worthy to offer up this sacrifice unless thou make him so? I know, Lord, I know too well, and confess in thy merciful ear, that my grievous sins and countless omissions unfit me for approaching this great sacrament. But I know too, and truly believe with my whole heart, and with my lips proclaim, that thou canst make me worthy, thou who alone hast power to make the offspring of uncleanness clean, the sinner good and holy. By that almighty power of thine, my God, I pray thee grant that, sinner as I am, I may offer up this sacrifice in fear and trembling, in purity of heart, with flowing tears, and yet with heavenly triumph and spiritual gladness. Let my soul feel thy blessed presence, and have joy of it; let me feel that all around me thy holy angels are keeping watch and ward.

## WEDNESDAY

Remembering thy worshipful Passion, Lord, I, sinner that I am, approach thy altar to offer thee the sacrifice thou hast ordained, the sacrifice thou hast bidden us offer for our soul's health in remembrance of thee. Accept it, most high God, I beseech thee, for thy holy Church and for the people thou didst purchase with thy blood. And since it is thy pleasure that my sinful self should stand between thee and this people of thine, although thou findest in me no evidence of well-doing do not reject the service of my stewardship, nor suffer the ransom thou didst pay for man's salvation with thy own blood to be lost through my unworthiness.

Deign to look with compassion, Lord, upon these other offerings I lay before thee: the struggles of the poor, the perils of nations, the groans of captives, the desolation of orphans, the hardships of travellers, the helplessness of cripples, the anguish of the incurably sick, the failing strength of the aged, young men's sighs, the yearning of maidens, the grief of widows. For thou, Lord, art full of pity for all mankind, and hatest nothing which thou hast made.

## THURSDAY

Remember the clay of which we are wrought. Since thou art our Father and our God, do not be angry with us beyond measure, or close thy merciful heart against us. We prostrate ourselves in prayer before thee, relying not upon any merits of ours but upon thy countless mercies. Blot out our misdeeds, and graciously kindle in us the fire of the Holy

Spirit. Take from us our hearts of stone, and give us hearts of flesh, to love thee and long for thee and delight in thee; hearts that in following thee shall find the consummation of all joy.

We beg of thy great mercy, Lord, that thou wilt look with favour upon thy household, now preparing to do homage to thy holy Name. Under thy inspiration let our prayers be welcome to thee and such as thou delightest to hear and answer, so that no one's hope shall be in vain, no one's petition void.

## FRIDAY

Holy Father and Lord, we also entreat thee for the souls of the faithful departed, praying that this great sacrament, this pledge of thy loving-kindness, may bring them health and safety, joy and cool repose. My God and Lord, living Bread that camest down from heaven and givest life to all mankind, unblemished Lamb that takest away the sins of the world, call those departed souls to thy great feast this day, and let them have their fill of thee, of that holy and blessed flesh of thine that was conceived of the Holy Ghost and taken from the hallowed, glorious womb of the blessed Virgin Mary. Let them drink of that fountain of mercy that welled from thy sacred body when the soldier pierced thy side with his lance. Thereby refreshed and feasted, comforted and cooled, let them lift up their triumphant song in praise of thee.

In thy loving mercy, Lord, grant my petition that the fulness of thy blessing, the consecrating touch of thy Godhead, may be laid upon the bread we are offering up to thee, and that the unseen, all-embracing majesty of thy Holy Spirit may descend upon it, as it descended of old upon the sacrifices of the patriarchs, turning these offerings of ours into thy body and blood, and teaching me, thy unworthy priest, to handle this great sacrament in purity of heart, with tears of devotion and reverent awe. Gently and graciously accept the sacrifice at my hands for the salvation of all mankind, both living and dead.

## SATURDAY

Lord, by this same holy sacrament of thy body and blood which is our daily food and drink, our cleansing and sanctification whereby in the unity of thy Church we are made partners of the one sovereign Godhead, I entreat thee to grant me thy holy gifts in all their fulness, so that I may approach thy altar with a good conscience and find in this heavenly sacrament both life and health. Didst thou not say, with thy own blessed and holy lips: *The bread which I shall give is my flesh, given for the life of the world. I myself am the living bread that has come down from heaven. If any one eats of this bread, he shall live for ever?* Most delectable Bread, cure the sick palate of my soul, and let me taste the sweetness of thy love. Cure its numbness entirely, so that I may delight in no other food but thee. Purest Bread, thou who art all goodness to the taste, who while feeding us daily art never diminished, be thou the food of my heart; let thy sweet savour fill the inmost depths of my being. The angels eat their fill of thee: let pilgrim man in his own small measure do the same, and have thee as food for his journey, lest he faint by the wayside. Holy Bread, living and undefiled, who camest down from heaven and givest life to the world, enter into my heart and cleanse me from all defilement of flesh and spirit. Come, and dwell in my soul; heal and cleanse me within and without. Protect me and give me abiding health in all my being. Drive off the enemies that lie in wait for me; come in thy strength and put them to flight. Safeguard me, body and soul, and bring me by the straight road to thy kingdom, where we shall see thee, not veiled as now in sacraments and symbols, but face to face. Then wilt thou have given the kingdom up to God the Father, being thyself God, the All in all. Then will there be no hunger or thirst for evermore, but thou wilt feast us with marvels beyond all telling, and fill us with thyself, who livest and reignest with God the Father and God the Holy Ghost for ever. Amen.

## ANOTHER PRAYER OF ST. AMBROSE

My kind Lord Jesus Christ, I, sinner that I am, approach the delights of thy banquet in fear and trembling, not presuming on my own merits but relying upon thy merciful goodness. Many a sin defiles me, body and soul; I am guilty of many an unguarded thought and word. O gracious Deity, dread Majesty, I take refuge under thy protection; I fly to thee to be healed; I, a wretch caught in the toils, appeal to thee who art the very source of pity. I long for thy coming, my Saviour; but if thou comest as Judge I cannot face thee. To thee, Lord, I uncover my wounds; to thee I lay bare my shame. My sins, I know, are many and grievous; they fill me with fear, but my hope is in thy countless mercies. Lord Jesus Christ, eternal King, God-Man crucified for man, turn thy merciful gaze upon me and heed my prayer, for in thee I put my trust. Have mercy upon me! I am all misery and sin, but thou art an inexhaustible well of compassion. Hail, saving Victim, offered up for me and for all mankind upon the gibbet of the cross! Hail, noble and precious blood, flowing from the wounds of my crucified Lord Jesus Christ and washing away the sins of the whole world! Remember, Lord, thy creature whom thou hast ransomed with thy blood. I am sorry for my sins, and long to make amends. All-merciful Father, take away from me all my sins and iniquities, make me clean in soul and body, and give me grace to partake worthily of thy Holy of holies. Grant that this holy sacrifice of thy body and blood, which I am preparing to offer up, and of which, though unworthy, I mean to partake, may accomplish the remission of my sins, wash my guilt away entirely, banish evil thoughts, revive my better impulses, incite me to perform works pleasing to thee for my own good, and prove the strongest of defences, keeping me safe in body and soul from the wiles of my enemies. Amen.

## PRAYER OF ST. THOMAS AQUINAS

Almighty, everlasting God, behold, I approach the sacrament of thy only-begotten Son, our Lord Jesus Christ. I come to it as a sick man to the physician who will save his life, as a man unclean to the fountain of mercy, a blind man to the radiance of eternal light, one poor and needy to the Lord of heaven and earth; praying that in thy boundless generosity thou wilt deign to cure my sickness, wash my defilement away, enlighten my blindness, enrich my poverty, and clothe my nakedness.

May the Bread of angels, the King of kings and Lord of lords, be received by me with such humble reverence and devout contrition, such faith and purity, and such good resolutions as may help the salvation of my soul. Grant me grace, I beseech thee, to receive not only the sacrament of our Lord's body and blood, but also its inward power and effect. All-gentle God, grant that my receiving of that body, taken from the Virgin Mary's womb by thy only-begotten Son, our Lord Jesus Christ, may fit me to become part of his mystical body and to be reckoned one of its members. Most loving Father, grant that thy beloved Son, whom I, an earthly wayfarer, am now to receive in his sacramental guise, may one day give me sight of his face and let me gaze upon him for all eternity: who is God, living and reigning with thee in the unity of the Holy Spirit for ever and ever. Amen.

## PRAYER TO OUR LADY

O Mother of pity and loving kindness, most blessed Virgin Mary, I, a worthless and wretched sinner, fly to thee in heartfelt love and confidence, entreating thy compassion. Thou who didst stand by thy dear Son when he hung upon the cross, have pity and deign to stand by me too, wretched sinner that I am, and by all the priests who are offering Mass this day, here and elsewhere throughout holy Church. By the help of thy favour enable us to offer a sacrifice that shall be worthy and acceptable in the sight of the most high and undivided Trinity. Amen.

## PRAYER TO ST. JOSEPH ·

O blessed Joseph, happy man whose privilege it was, not only to see and hear that God whom many a king has longed to see, yet saw not, longed to hear, yet heard not: but also to carry him in thy arms and kiss him, to clothe him and watch over him!

V/.　Pray for us, blessed Joseph.

R/.　That we may be made worthy of the promises of Christ.

Let us pray.

God, who hast conferred upon us a royal priesthood, we pray thee give us grace to minister at thy holy altars with hearts as clean and lives as blameless as that blessed Joseph who was found worthy to hold in his arms and with all reverence to carry thy only-begotten Son, born of the Virgin Mary. Enable us this day to receive worthily the sacred body and blood of thy Son, and fit us to win an everlasting reward in the world to come: through the same Christ our Lord. Amen.

## PRAYER TO ALL THE ANGELS AND SAINTS

Angels, Archangels, Thrones, Dominations, Principalities, Powers, celestial Virtues, Cherubim and Seraphim; all Saints of God, holy men and women, and you especially, my patrons: deign to plead for me that I may have grace to offer worthily this sacrifice to almighty God, to the praise and glory of his Name, for my own welfare also and that of all his holy Church. Amen.

## PRAYER TO THE SAINT IN WHOSE HONOUR MASS IS TO BE CELEBRATED

O holy ............ lo, I, a wretched sinner, relying on thy merits, now offer up to thy honour and glory the most holy sacrament of the body and blood of our Lord Jesus Christ. In all devout humility I beg that thou wilt deign to intercede for me this day, and to plead that I may have grace to offer this great sacrifice in worthy and acceptable fashion, and be enabled to sing his praises with thee and with all his elect, eternally reigning with him who lives and reigns for ever and ever. Amen.

## THE PRIEST'S DECLARATION OF PURPOSE BEFORE MASS

My purpose is to celebrate Mass and to make the body and blood of our Lord Jesus Christ according to the rite of the holy Roman Church, to the praise of almighty God and of the whole Church triumphant in heaven, for my own welfare and that of the whole Church militant on earth, for all who in general and in particular have commended themselves to my prayers, and for the well-being of the holy Roman Church. Amen.

May joy and peace, amendment of life, room for true penitence, the grace and comfort of the Holy Spirit, and steadfastness in good works be granted us by the almighty and merciful Lord. Amen.

# THANKSGIVING AFTER MASS

*Ant.* Let us sing the hymn of the three young men, which those holy ones sang in the flaming furnace, praising the Lord. (*Alleluia.*)

*Canticle. Dan., iii, 57-88, 56.*

Bless the Lord, all things the Lord has made, praise and extol his Name for ever.

Bless the Lord, you, the Lord's angels; bless the Lord, you heavens.

Bless the Lord, waters above the heavens; bless the Lord, you, the Lord's armies.

Bless the Lord, sun and moon, bless the Lord, stars of heaven.

Bless the Lord, each drop of rain and moisture; bless the Lord, all you winds.

Bless the Lord, fire and heat; bless the Lord, cold and winter.

Bless the Lord, dew and rain; bless the Lord, frost and cold air.

Bless the Lord, rime and snow; bless the Lord, day-time and night-time.

Bless the Lord, light and darkness; bless the Lord, lightnings and storm-clouds.

Let the earth too bless the Lord, praise him and extol his Name for ever.

Bless the Lord, mountains and hills; bless the Lord, every growing thing that earth yields.

Bless the Lord, flowing fountains; bless the Lord, seas and rivers.

Bless the Lord, sea-monsters and all life that is bred in the waters; bless the Lord, all you birds that fly in heaven.

Bless the Lord, wild beasts and tame; bless the Lord, you sons of men;

And most let Israel bless the Lord; praise him and extol his Name for ever.

Bless the Lord, you, the Lord's priests; bless the Lord, you, the Lord's servants.

Bless the Lord, spirits and souls of all faithful men; bless the Lord, dedicated and humble hearts.

Well may Ananias, Azarias, and Misael bless the Lord, praise him and extol his Name for ever.

Let us bless Father, Son, and Holy Ghost, praising and extolling his Name for ever.

Blessed art thou, Lord, in the vault of heaven, praised, and renowned, and extolled for ever.

## Psalm 150.

Praise God in his sanctuary, praise him on his sovereign throne.

Praise him for his noble acts, praise him for his surpassing greatness.

Praise him with the bray of the trumpet, praise him with harp and zither.

Praise him with the tambour and the dance, praise him with the music of string and of reed.

Praise him with the clear note of the cymbals, praise him with the cymbals that tell of gladness.

Let everything that breathes praise the Lord.

Glory be to the Father.

*Ant.* Let us sing the hymn of the three young men, which those holy ones sang in the flaming furnace, praising the Lord. (*Alleluia.*)

Lord, have mercy.

Christ, have mercy.

Lord, have mercy.

Our Father.

V/.    And lead us not into temptation.

R/.    But deliver us from evil.

V/.    Let all thy works, Lord, acknowledge
thee.

R/.    And thy saints bless thee.

V/.    In triumph will thy faithful servants
rejoice.

R/.    Rejoice and take their rest.

V/.    Not to us, Lord, not to us.

R/.    But to thy Name give glory.

V/.    Lord, heed my prayer.

R/.    And let my cry be heard by thee.

V/.    The Lord be with you.

R/.    And with *you.*

Let us pray.

God, who didst allay the flames of the
furnace for the three young men, in thy mercy

grant that we, thy servants, may not be consumed by the flame of sin.

Lord, we pray thee let our doings be prompted by thy inspiration and furthered by thy help, so that every prayer and work of ours may begin from thee, and be through thee accomplished.

God, who gavest blessed Laurence strength to overcome his fiery torment, we pray thee grant us grace to extinguish in ourselves the flames of sin: through Christ our Lord.

R/. Amen.


## PRAYER OF ST. THOMAS AQUINAS

I thank thee, holy Lord, almighty Father, eternal God, who hast deigned to feast me, thy sinful and unworthy servant with the precious body and blood of thy Son, Jesus Christ our Lord, not for any merit of mine, but only because of thy merciful goodness. And I pray that this holy communion, far from condemning me to punishment, may bring about my pardon and salvation, encompassing me with the armour of faith and the shield of a good will. By it let my vices be done away, all lustful desires extinguished. May it advance me in charity, patience, humility, obedience, and every other virtue. Let it be my strong defence against the wiles of all my enemies, visible and invisible, allaying for me every disturbance of flesh and spirit, binding me firmly to thee, the one true God, and bringing my last hour to a happy close. I pray, too, that it may be thy pleasure to call my sinful self one day to that banquet, wonderful past all telling, where thou, with thy Son and the Holy Spirit, dost feast thy saints with the vision of thyself, who art true light, the fulfilment of all desires, the joy that knows no ending, gladness unalloyed, and perfect bliss: through the same Christ, our Lord. Amen.

## PRAYER OF ST. BONAVENTURE.

Dearest Lord Jesus, pierce the inmost depths of my being with the sweet and wholesome pang of thy love, with true and tranquil and most holy apostolic charity, so that from sheer melting love and desire of thee my soul may ever faint with longing, yearning for thee and for thy dwelling-place, asking only to be released from the flesh and to be with thee. Grant that my soul may hunger for thee, who art the bread of angels, the food of holy souls, our daily, supernatural bread, all sweetness and delight to the taste. Let my heart ever hunger for thee and feed upon thee, whom the angels yearn to look upon, and let the depths of my being be filled with thy sweet savour; let me ever thirst for thee, who art the source of life, source of wisdom and knowledge, source of eternal light, floodtide of pleasure, God's own treasure-house. Let me ever desire thee; seek thee and find thee; have thee for my goal and my achievement; think and speak of thee only, doing all that I do for the honour and glory of thy Name, humbly and prudently, with love and delight, with ready goodwill, and with perseverance to the end. Be thou ever, thou only, my hope and all my trust, my treasure and pleasure, my joy and delight, my rest, peace and quiet, my sweet and delicious fragrance, my food and support, my refuge and help, my wisdom, my heritage of wealth, my very own. Let my heart and soul be set on thee firmly and immovably rooted in thee for ever. Amen.

## ADORO TE DEVOTE

Adoro te devote, latens Deitas,
Quae sub his figuris vere latitas:
    Tibi se cor meum totum subjicit,
    Quia, te contemplans, totum deficit.

Visus, tactus, gustus in te fallitur,
Sed auditu solo tuto creditur:
   Credo quidquid dixit Dei Filius,
   Nil hoc verbo Veritatis verius.

In cruce latebat sola Deitas,
At hic latet simul et humanitas;
   Ambo tamen credens atque confitens,
   Peto quod petivit latro poenitens.

Plagus, sicut Thomas, non intueor
Deum tamen meum te confiteor:
   Fac me tibi semper magis credere,
   In te spem habere, te diligere.

O memoriale mortis Domini,
Panis vivus, vitam praestans homini,
   Praesta meae menti de te vivere
   Et te illi semper dulce sapere.

Pie pelicane, Jesu Domine,
Me immundum munda tuo sanguine,
   Cujus una stilla salvum facere
   Totum mundum quit ab omni scelere.

Jesu, quem velatum nunc aspicio,
Oro, fiat illud quod tam sitio;
  Ut, te revelata cernens facie,
  Visu sim beatus tuae gloriae. Amen.


## PETITIONS OF ST. IGNATIUS TO OUR HOLY REDEEMER

Soul of Christ, make me holy.

Body of Christ, be my salvation.

Blood of Christ, let me drink thy potent wine.

Water flowing from the side of Christ, wash
    me clean.

Passion of Christ, give me strength.

O kindest Jesus, hear my prayer.

Hide me within thy wounds.

And let me never be parted from thee.

Defend me from the villainous foe.

Call me at the hour of my death,

And summon me into thy presence,

There to praise thee with thy saints

For ever. Amen.

## SELF-DEDICATION

Take all my freedom, Lord; accept the
whole of my memory, understanding, and will.
Whatever I have or hold comes to me from thy
bounty. I give it all back to thee, surrender it
all to the guidance of thy will. Thy grace and
the love of thee are wealth enough: give me
but that, and I ask for nothing more

## PRAYER TO OUR LORD

Dearest Lord Jesus Christ, I entreat thee
to let me find in thy Passion a strong defence,
protection, and safeguard. Let thy wounds be
my food and drink to nourish and make me
drunk with delight. Let the shedding of thy
blood wash all my offences away: thy death
bring me the life that knows no ending: thy
cross be my everlasting glory. In them let my
heart find renewal, gladness, health, and
delight: thou who livest and reignest for ever
and ever. Amen.

# BEFORE A
# REPRESENTATION
# OF CHRIST
# CRUCIFIED

My good and dearest Jesus, lo, I kneel before thee, beseeching and praying thee with all the ardour of my soul to engrave deep and vivid impressions of faith, hope, and charity upon my heart, with true repentance for my sins, and a very firm resolve to make amends. Meanwhile I ponder thy five wounds, dwelling upon them with deep compassion and grief, and recalling the words that the prophet David long ago put into thy mouth, good Jesus, concerning thyself: They have pierced my hands and my feet: they have counted all my bones!

## A PRAYER TO OUR LADY

O Mary, most holy Virgin-Mother, lo, I have received thy well-beloved Son, whom thou didst conceive in thy stainless womb, didst bring forth and suckle, and enfold in thy sweet embraces. See, humbly and lovingly I give back to thee the Son whom it was all rapture and delight for thee to look upon; I offer him to be clasped in thy arms, to be loved with all thy heart, and to be offered up to the Holy Trinity in the supreme homage of adoration, for thy honour and glory, and for my needs and those of all mankind. Most loving Mother, I beg thee to obtain for me forgiveness of all my sins, grace in abundance to serve him more faithfully from now onwards, and lastly, final perseverance, so that I may praise him with thee for ever and ever. Amen.

## A PRAYER TO ST. JOSEPH

Saint Joseph, father and guardian of virgins, to whose faithful keeping Christ Jesus, innocence itself, and Mary, the Virgin of virgins, were entrusted, I pray and beseech thee by that twofold and most precious charge, by Jesus and Mary, to save me from all uncleanness, to keep my mind untainted, my heart pure, and my body chaste; and to help me always to serve Jesus and Mary in perfect chastity. Amen.

## PRAYER TO THE SAINT IN WHOSE HONOUR MASS WAS CELEBRATED

Holy ............, in whose honour I have offered up the bloodless sacrifice of the body and blood of Christ, cause me, through thy powerful intercession before God, to gain by the use of this sacrament the merits Christ our Saviour won by his Passion and death, and each time I partake of it to be led nearer to my salvation. Amen.